GREEN THEOLOGY

An eco-feminist and ecumenical perspective

TREES VAN MONTFOORT

DARTON · LONGMAN + TODD

In loving memory of my mother
Thea Kruythof († 2020)
and my mother-in-law
Gerry Reedijk-O'Hara († 2021)
– courageous women

First published in 2022 by
Darton, Longman and Todd Ltd
1 Spencer Court
140 – 142 Wandsworth High Street
London SW18 4JJ

Translation from the Dutch by Wim Reedijk

ISBN: 978-1-913657-28-4

A catalogue record for this book is available from the British Library.

Designed and produced by Judy Linard

Printed and bound by Scandbook AB, Sweden

'The Saxon saint Benno of Meissen (d. 1106) was disturbed in his contemplation by the loud croaking of a frog, and so he commanded it to be silent. But he then remembered the words of the Benedicite, which, among its exhortations to all creatures to worship God, includes: "bless the Lord you whales and all that swim in the waters" (Daniel 3:79). Reflecting that God might prefer the singing of the frogs to his own prayer, he commanded the frogs to continue praising God in their own way.'[1]

CONTENTS

CONTENTS

PREFACE

During the five years I was working on this book, I came across my subject in the most unexpected places. Whilst on holiday in Edinburgh, I spotted a poster next to the bus stop bearing the words 'How can studying theology combat climate change?' Many people passing by might have asked the same thing. How could theology and climate change be of importance to one another? For a long time, I myself thought that environmental problems were of no special interest to theologians.

At the age of 16, I got involved in both theology and sustainability, but the two were unconnected. As a student and later professionally as a theologian I took sustainability seriously, both privately and politically. I acquired a thorough grounding in Catholic and Protestant theology, worked as a radio journalist, served as a vicar, and was head of a communications department of the Protestant Church in the Netherlands. Privately, I rode my bicycle whenever possible and, for longer distances, made use of public transport. At home, I reduced my gas and electricity use, invested my savings in a sustainable bank, and my diet became more and more organic and vegetarian. For me, nature meant a place to find peace and quiet; the city was, and remains, my habitat.

THE HISTORY OF THIS BOOK

It has only been in the last ten years that ecological questions have started to impinge upon my theology, and vice versa. Connecting theology and sustainability, ecology and belief, was for me a real eye-opener. All of a sudden, I began to read in the Bible things that I had always overlooked. Theology became relevant to fields that beforehand seemingly had nothing to do with it. This was true the other way round. I started to undertake a serious study of ecological theology. It took me a year and a half to write a research proposal. I was convinced that eco-theology should be a vital component of theology and that I could make a contribution in this direction. However, after completing the proposal, I decided not to continue along this path, because I realised that writing a PhD thesis was not what I wished for after all. I wanted to write a book that would not only be aimed at scholars but that would reach a wider audience, both people engaged in sustainability practices in the churches and people who – inspired by their belief – are actively involved in environmental movements and politics. I decided to broaden my initial draft and to return to a more journalistic way of writing, at the same time retaining the precise and thorough basis of a scholarly study. This is the reason why in this book there are a lot of endnotes and why I am so grateful to all the knowledgeable people who were willing to read parts of the work in progress. The names of all involved whom I want to thank for their support, help and encouragement during the writing and translation process are listed in the acknowledgements.

Reception

The reception of this book in the Netherlands and Flanders has been beyond all expectations. Liberal Christians reacted with as much approval as did evangelicals, orthodox Protestants and Catholics. Many were vicars, pastors and scholars.

Green Theology even won the award of 'Best Theological Book of the Year' (2019). The jury called it 'a hyper-urgent and necessary book' that 'challenges a far-reaching Christian theological reflection on the relationship between God, creation, nature and man. This book engages with a timely revelation dawning for many, that ecology really concerns theology, that "who God is" has something to do with "how this world works." [The author] does this in a way that shows that theology matters in the public debate. *Green Theology* shows that theology has to do with everything and not just with ethics.'

Translation

Before I'd even finished the book, a university lecturer asked me if there was an English text available. Due to the international student body in Dutch theological universities, a considerable number of lectures are in English. The same question arose at the official presentation of the Dutch edition when I was asked to give a keynote lecture to a collective of Catholic European women's organisations. Whilst presenting a paper at the biennial conference of ESWTR (European Society of Women in Theological Research), I was again asked if the book had been translated into English.

The main reason for bringing out an English translation is that a publication like this, as far as I am aware, does not yet exist. It brings three differing eco-theologians together in a shared dialogue and offers a new and unique way of reading the Bible ecologically. This book may also be of use to international readers eager to know what happens beyond their cultural and linguistic territories. The dominance of North American culture is, although challenged, still formidable – a lot of eco-theology stems from the USA. Acquaintance with eco-theologians from Africa, Asia and Latin America is frequently channelled via American publications. In Europe, however, after the closing of the Conciliar Process of the World Council of Churches (WCC), a silence gradually set in around theology, ecology and sustainability. I would like to invite *Green Theology*'s readers, each from their own local and historical backgrounds, and their own religious backgrounds, to start a dialogue with the contents of this book.

In this new edition, I have deleted some passages and adjusted others to suit an international reading audience. If English translations of the non-English secondary literature exist, these are added accordingly, as far as possible.

INTRODUCTION

Sustainability has become a hot topic among Christians. Diaconal work and other forms of church support are not only enhancing social awareness within their communities but are also becoming more and more involved in ecological issues. Church administrators and church boards take a more sustainable line in the upkeep of their buildings. Collections are organised, for instance, for climate-friendly cooking equipment for India, and the coffee is Fairtrade. During Lent, churches serve frugal meals and develop all sorts of activities to promote a sustainable way of life. Some churches pay attention to World Day of Prayer for the Care of Creation, or they single out another church service for 'sustainability'; sometimes ecological awareness gives harvest festival services new substance.

The term 'sustainability' became well known as defined by the Brundtland Report of 1987: 'Sustainable development is the kind of development that meets the needs of the present without compromising the ability of future generations to meet their own needs.' One drawback is that it all too easily becomes an umbrella term that encompasses everything but gives offence to nobody. In this book, I'll use sustainability in the narrow sense of *ecological* sustainability, and in a wider sense by extending it to not just meeting the needs of human beings and their future, but letting in the future of the whole earth.

13

Although many good things do happen in churches when it comes to sustainability, these often do not seem to go further than activities involving diaconal work and church building improvements. Many communities tend to overlook the fact that what sustainability *really* means should also affect the way we think and believe. 'Creation' is for most believers nothing more than religious jargon for nature, in the same way as 'stewardship' has become a church term for ecological awareness. Whilst meekly following the general opinion, Christians miss the chance to make their own contribution to the public debate. Green theology and eco-theology are not just there to strengthen and stimulate a hesitant operating church practice, but to make theology less one-sided and to contribute from a Christian perspective to the wellbeing of the earth and all her – human and non-human – denizens. Theology is not important only for church usage; it can also draw from its own sources something to convey to the general public.

There is so much more to say from a Christian point of view about sustainability than just 'stewardship' and 'caring for creation'. In order to come to a sound ecological theology, one has to start reading the Bible much better. The *Green Bible* points out many relevant texts that outnumber by far the few creation stories at the beginning of Genesis.

Some take – not without some justification – Christianity as one of the causes of our ecological problems. Christians put men on a pedestal and see nature as nothing more than a tool to be freely and unconditionally exploited.[2] Is it really enough to counter this simply with 'Yes, certainly we may rule, as long as we do it caringly'? Does this not still leave men on top and above the earth? Eco-theology challenges the modern worldview with its belief in human prowess and progress, in which people are no longer part of the bigger picture of creation – they transcend it. One even finds support in Psalm 8 to substantiate this claim: 'You have given them dominion over the works of your hands; you have put all things under their feet …' (NRSV). But the Bible does not speak solely about God and people; it talks about God in relation to everything that exists – people, animals, plants, stones and so on. God also establishes a covenant with animals (Genesis 9), God feeds the wild animals and, above all, God is the Creator of heaven and earth, thus, of everything that is. But if God is not just a God of people, what place do human beings then have in the whole of creation? And can one rightly speak in general terms of human beings? A small farmer in Africa and a woman living in a slum in Latin America suffer more from ecological crisis than the wealthy westerner, and they have not even caused it.

Over the last decade, eco-theology has come to prominence everywhere, which is partly due to the workings of the WCC. In 1961, the Lutheran theologian Joseph Sittler pleaded in an assembly of the WCC for a theology that could rightly qualify as ecological. God is concerned with the *whole* earth, he said, and in God's salvation through Christ the whole world is involved, not just humanity. His conclusion was that care for the earth is a central concern of the Christian religion. His plea encountered much indifference. Strong resistance was voiced by those who took all links between God and nature as equalling Nazi theology.[3] In the 1980s, the WCC was taken up with the Conciliar Process for Justice, Peace and the Integrity of Creation. In 2015 it was Pope Francis who with *Laudato Si'* heralded a new phase in the proliferation of ecological insights. This encyclical condemned a belief in technical solutions and economic growth as these lay a heavy burden on the earth and the poor and counters by insisting on more frugality and humility. Feminists have also made important contributions to the field of eco-theology; eco-feminist theologians point out the similarities between the subduing of the earth and of women.

This book is also aimed at the general public, to whom I want to open up the field of thinking about belief and ecology, and invite readers to change their practices. It is also a quest for a belief that does justice to God, the earth and the people, especially to those who suffer most from environmental problems, that is, the poor and women.

This book is more than a collection of thoughts already found in other publications. It takes a stand and challenges the reader to take part in the discussion. That my inspiration is drawn from the Christian tradition does not disqualify other ways of seeing the world. Christianity happens to be the tradition in which I consider myself knowledgeable, the tradition that often unfortunately also legitimised the exploitation of the earth, but also a tradition that in its very depth and breadth has so much to offer in terms of ecological wisdom.

The first chapter, **Theology and sustainability**, deals with the role of theology in the current ecological crisis. This crisis goes deeper than just practical problems that ask for practical solutions. The modern worldview plays a significant part in its genesis. In our modern culture, we make the mistake of putting people at the centre of everything (anthropocentrism); we also expect too much from our technical abilities and economic growth (the technocratic–economic paradigm). Our current image of the world is interwoven with Christianity and therefore, according to some, Christianity is rightly blamed for the ecological crisis. It doesn't help that theology, as belief-based knowledge, has limited itself in modernity to thinking through the relation between God and human beings. Theology will become more relevant if it dares to speak out again for the whole world.

The common thread of the second chapter, **The different worldview of the Bible**, is a search for worldviews in texts. To gain a better understanding of the implicit worldview of Bible texts, I asked two questions in particular: what is the relation between God, people and world; and what is the relation between human and non-human creation? Some common strands can be detected that also encroach upon the image of God.

I will give much thought to texts that always appear in the discussions and to texts that should receive more attention. They are bundled in texts about creation, about animals and about saving the earth, taken from both the Old and the New Testaments. I will show that these texts are far less anthropocentric and dualistic in perspective than our modern worldview. The Bible counterbalances the narrowing of theology in modernity and uncovers a worldview that is extremely relevant in current ecological discussions because of its inclusiveness. Its interest lies not exclusively in people. The whole of reality is connected with God, and where this is done most explicitly, I find that the Bible generally uses inclusive images of God.

Chapter three, **Issues in eco-theology**, deals with the rise of eco-theology and the resistance against it, taking developments in the Low Countries as an example of what happens more or less everywhere in the West. The ecological perspective of the Bible is unwittingly filtered out from much Bible exposition, and many liturgical texts and sermons. What are the forces that are resisting this perspective? I analyse the persistent resistance against any positive assessment of nature in some Protestant circles, and I investigate the domineering anthropocentric strand in both Catholic and liberal theology. The expressions 'stewardship' and 'care of creation' are scrutinised and critically assessed. The encyclical *Laudato Si'* and an older document from the Dutch Reformed Church are analysed in depth, and a light is thrown on three recent publications that touch on eco-theological themes (two of them accessible in English). At the end, I sum up the main issues and start taking a stand on the themes of nature, creation, earth, people and God.

In chapter four, **Insights from eco-feminist theology worldwide,** some important examples of eco-feminist theology are presented. I start with a brief introduction to Sallie McFague's theology, as she is one of the founding mothers of eco-feminist theology. The approach and insights of Ivone Gebara (Roman Catholic and Latin American), Catherine Keller (Protestant and North American) and Elizabeth Theokritoff (Greek Orthodox and European) can give new impulses to eco-theology. I try to explain their ways of thinking and compare their contexts with the (western) European context. This brings us some critical and essential insights that should counterbalance the far-too-dominant terms 'stewardship' and 'caring for creation'. I complete this chapter by arranging an imaginary dialogue between Gebara, Keller and Theokritoff.

Chapter five, **The harvest**, takes stock of all that has been discussed and moves subsequently towards the question of the relationship between God and the world and the place of people within, focusing on what is central to Christian theology: Christ. If the ecological crisis is of importance to theology, then it must have serious consequences for the way we have to understand who Jesus is. I finish this book with an example of ecological spirituality and ethics taken from my own practical pastoral work.

Although this book has been carefully thought through and juxtaposed as a whole, one should be able to read the chapters separately and randomly. Those who want to start with the main conclusions may begin at the end. Those interested in what I say about the Bible may directly move on to chapter two. Readers preferring a systematic theological exposition of this subject should start with chapters three and four. If anyone still wonders if ecological sustainability is a subject that should be handled by theology, and, if so, how that should be tackled, they can continue reading on the next page.

CHAPTER ONE
Theology and sustainability

That sustainability is essential to theology does not go without saying. Sustainability is often dealt with in a practical frame of mind whereas a sound theological reflection is really needed to de-marginalise sustainable activities in the churches and, more importantly, to make theology less one sided. A fair amount of (mostly Anglophone) eco-theology is already available, furnished with a diversity of links between theology and sustainability depending on the choice of theological field of knowledge. Ethics brings up the question of what we should do, and, more fundamentally, what our norms and values entail when it comes to sustainability, as well as how these developed.[4] In diaconal work, one will focus on care and justice. I will approach sustainability from a systematic theological angle with biblical exegesis as an important source to draw from. Questions that will likely come up are: What does the Bible contribute if read in the context of the ecological crisis? And how can we rethink the relationship between God and the world, in which humans participate integrally?

I start with a brief overview of the ecological problems we are experiencing and in what sense we can talk of a real crisis. We are not just dealing with climate change but also with pollution and the extinction of species. The impact of humans on the earth has become too big to handle. Next, I will show that a practical approach alone is not the answer to the problem. Solutions are often sought in better technology and new products, which overlook the underlying agents: cultural, ideological and religious motives. There is clearly something wrong with our worldview. I will show that the roots of nature's exploitation reach into an anthropocentric vision, the prevailing scientific model, technocracy, the neoliberal market economy, patriarchy and colonialism. The underlying assumption is that men – more specifically western men – exploit the earth.

Christianity has played a role in creating and promoting this worldview, but also in criticising it. I will maintain that theology becomes relevant if it does not acquiesce uncritically in this worldview of modernity and if it does not restrict itself to ethical considerations and the meaning of life, but dares to speak out about how the world works. It can draw from its own rich sources and join in with many other interlocutors. Most interesting among these are certainly those scientists and postmodern philosophers and others who by their position and/or ideas move away from mainstream modern views on men and world.

1.1 AN ECOLOGICAL CRISIS

In 1972, the famous report *The Limits to Growth* commissioned by a thinktank that convened in Rome warned that without any policy change the earth would in the near future be unable to provide for all the needs of the world's population. Although some of its predictions did not come true, the urgency of the report's call has not abated.[5] Problems concerning the using up of natural resources, the extinction of species, pollution increase, climate change, rise of poverty, population growth and overconsumption are so huge and alarming that we can rightly speak of an environmental and ecological crisis. Should the earth provide sustainably for the needs of people, humans have to stay within the boundaries that the earth has set for them, because her carrying capacity is limited and already overcharged. We see the steadily rising number of people individually using more natural resources, which means an increasing burdening of the earth. The more earth's carrying capacity gets overstretched, the more detrimental the consequences will be to us. This is the picture if we only consider what ecological crisis means to us, as humans.

Using the word crisis can be inapt because it suggests that we can return to the stage we were at beforehand. That is not the case, unfortunately. Some things will never be the same; some losses are already decisive. Climate change, for instance, cannot be reversed; what has become extinct will not be seen again, and neither will the eroded layers of scooped-out minerals. This is a crisis in terms of outline and urgency, not in terms of time.

> The sea level will rise for centuries even if all greenhouse gas emissions have come to a halt. If the instability rate of the polar icecaps is in accordance with the latest scientific figures and we do not reduce the greenhouse gas emissions, we can expect within a couple of centuries a sea level rise of up to twenty meters. Even with the most robust emission reductions we may not preclude in two hundred years a rise of three to four meters (The Royal Netherlands Meteorological Institute, KNMI).[6]

1.1.1 Hidden crisis

Still, fifty years after the publication of *The Limits to Growth*, the situation has not become as grim as was predicted. For the majority living in the wealthiest parts of the world, most environmental problems are not plainly visible. A sense of urgency is missing due to lack of sudden change, which would clearly happen during an economic crisis or a calamity such as a pandemic. Nobody's life here in the West is set to change overnight, as would be the case when one faces redundancy or bankruptcy. Summers are perhaps on the whole slightly warmer, showers heavier and droughts longer. There are fewer waders and insects, flowers have disappeared from most pastures, but that seems just about all that matters, although we easily forget that the air that we breathe in the Netherlands is the most polluted in the whole of Europe[7] and causes ever more cases of lung disease. But the country has not become uninhabitable. Because everything happens gradually, changes stay very much under the radar. Some areas are faring better than fifty years ago. Rivers have become cleaner, buses ride on gas and do not stink anymore, and most glass is recycled. Surely other solutions to environmental problems will be found? is what many people think. Recycling refuse and occasionally eating vegetarian, which is something that most people already do, convey a reassuring feeling of contributing to the solving of problems.

The COVID-19 crisis was ascribed to an unhealthy situation in a market in China. Barely noticed was the conclusion reached in a workshop run by IPBES, the UN institution for biodiversity, 'on biodiversity and pandemics': 'The underlying causes of pandemics are the same global environmental changes that drive biodiversity loss and climate change.'[8]

Most of the deterioration of the environment of which we in the West are the agents is hidden from view. The overstepping of earth's carrying capacity has a much bigger impact in other parts of the world. The production of our commodities and the raw material that this involves generally occurs somewhere else. Our refuse is dumped partly in places where we no longer see it.[9] Landscapes dramatically destroyed through mining, cattle raising or agrarian monocultures are also hidden from our view. The poorest in the world suffer most from the environmental deterioration. Where they live, climate change takes the form of extreme droughts, or the opposite, flooding. They lose fertile ground and experience water shortages. Fodder for the cows, pigs and chickens slaughtered for our consumption is mostly grown elsewhere. We do not witness the soya and oil palm plantations for which centuries-old forests are razed. We hear of plastic soup floating in oceans, but we do not see it ourselves. We do not experience first-hand how it disintegrates into small particles and ends up in the food chain.

These aforementioned processes amplify each other. They come by gradually; the results are partial where we live, and still containable. Yet the ecological crisis will certainly become inevitable for everyone. The impact on the whole of the earth has become huge. Once the message of the sheer size of the crisis has sunk in, this may well lead to a feeling of powerlessness. Answering 'it will be not so bad' and 'I cannot do anything about it' are two options that lie side by side.

1.1.2 The growing impact of people on the earth

The earth's climate has changed more than once. The last ice age was just 12,000 years ago. Great geological transformations in the past were the result of meteorite impacts and fluctuations in solar activity, but at the moment we are experiencing the first period in earth's history in which the changes of climate, plant and animal life can be rightly ascribed to one species only – humanity.[10] In a very short time, humans have changed the face of the planet. To emphasise the impact of people on the earth, some speak of a new geological era, for which they have coined the disputed and equivocal term Anthropocene. It marks the sixth time in the four-and-a-half billion years of earth's existence of a mass dwindling and dying out of animal species. The World Wildlife Fund reported an average drop of 60 per cent in animal population sizes between 1970 and 2014. In Latin America, that drop was 89 per cent, in fresh water 83 per cent.[11] Two years, later the average loss amounted to 68 per cent.[12]

The effect of humans on the earth's ecosystem has increased exponentially. As hunters and gatherers, they lived relatively in harmony with their natural environment, although the wiping out of animals, like aurochs and mammoth, began at an early stage in human history. But when people turned to agriculture, they started to bend nature to their will. According to some historians and biological anthropologists, the agricultural revolution during the Stone Age created a gap between humans and non-human nature that also heralded in inequality and violence.[13] In the nineteenth century, Friedrich Engels, Karl Marx's collaborator, followed the same line of reasoning.[14] He averred that agriculture inaugurated private property, having one's own yard and stock, and thus created a difference in property and the urge to retain it. Humans' estrangement from nature and the products of their work could be deducted from this past event. Men, wanting to be sure of their legitimate children and rightful heirs, were prompted then to take control of women's sexuality. According to Engels, the result was patriarchy.

From the nineteenth century onwards, with the Industrial Revolution, the pace of human influence on nature sped up. Some maintain that the Anthropocene era started somewhere in the middle of the 1800s, when natural resources could be mined at a much faster rate, thanks to the use of fossil fuels, which enabled the world population to grow to seven billion to date.[15] The World Wildlife Fund states: 'it has really been in the last 50 years that economic development has driven a phenomenal increase in the demand for energy, land and water that is fundamentally changing Earth's operating system'.[16]

The term Anthropocene has its flaws.[17] One is that it is too broad. Not all people contribute to ecological problems to the same degree. Not 'men' or 'mankind' but a privileged minority gave rise to and fed the ecological crisis. The ever-growing poverty in the world and an ever-smaller group of extremely wealthy people are also factors to take into account.[18]

A model to measure environmental impact per person is the global or ecological footprint.[19] If you divide the available surface of the earth between the total amount of people, you know how many hectares a person may use; the outcome is called Fair Earth Share. At the moment this figure is settled at 1.7 hectares (4.2 acres).[20] In order to figure out how many hectares you utilise, you add up what you actually consume, how much you travel and the energy you spend. In

2015 the Dutch used on average 4.9 hectares (12.1 acres), the Belgians 7.5 hectares (18.5 acres), while in the UK 4.4 hectares (10.9 acres). The USA figure is up to 8.1 hectares (20 acres). People in countries like Burundi use 0.7 hectares (1.7 acres) and Bangladesh 0.9 hectares (2.2 acres); they also pollute less.[21] That the average westerner, and everyone with the same lifestyle, lays claim to so much of the earth is partly due to their meat consumption. For meat production, one needs lots of land. Pasturage takes up a lot of space; the growing of animal fodder demands arable soil. Stock-breeding also requires enormous quantities of water.[22] If the same area were used for growing cereals and pulses, seven times more people could be fed. Seen the other way round, people who eat a vegan diet use around 14 per cent of the earth's surface area required by meat eaters.[23]

Those who are most guilty of creating the ecological crisis are the ones less affected by the direct consequences. As was already mentioned: the poorest suffer the most under nature's demise. And let's not forget how much animals, plants and all other living beings suffer in their own particular way.[24]

1.1.3 Mainstream solutions

There is a lot one can do to reduce the impact of people on the earth. A model to measure their total effect on the earth is the IPAT formula: Impact (I) = Population (P) x consumption/per person (A = Affluence) x impact/per unit of consumption (T = Technology).[25] Environmental effects depend on the world population's size, the consumption per person and the impact of consumption per unit. In other words: impact = population x footprint. To reduce the impact (I) one can reduce the number of people (P) and/or consume less (A) and/or pollute and waste less (T).

Our culture, so shaped by technology and capitalism, looks automatically toward technical solutions and new revenue models. Ecomodernists believe in urbanisation, economic growth and technical possibilities to enable life for everyone on a cleaner planet.[26]

Churches tend to think likewise: sustainability is a task for technicians, researchers and politicians. Using the IPAT model, I will give a quick overview of the practical solutions on offer and highlight their shortcomings.

There are several possibilities for less polluting and wasteful consumption (T). Sustainable sources could be more advanced and made more commercially viable. There is still room for improvement in home insulation. Eco products may serve new markets. Vintage stuff is hot. And many young city dwellers show less eagerness to own a car, at least in the Netherlands, preferring cycling and car sharing. Instead of buying light armatures in company buildings, one might rent light from a company with a vested interest in cheap leasing and energy saving. Recycling garbage may pay off. Products could be made in such a way that parts could be reused.

But all these new products and services are only viable if they are marketable. That is to say, if they are profitable for manufacturers and retailers and if consumers are interested enough to consider purchasing. The slogan 'people, planet, profit' is a yardstick for this practical approach. Is it good for people, for the earth and for profit? Sometimes these elements work together. As long as something is not more expensive or, even better, is cheaper and provides equal or more comfort (as some forms of energy saving do), people are willing to comply. But changing holiday plans by forgoing the use of aeroplane and/or cars does not appeal to many people. Cycling demands more effort; going by train is more expensive and demanding.

What's more, the preservation of plant and animal species hardly fits into technological solutions and revenue models. To assess nature, one can try to price it under 'services of the ecosystem'.[27] This approach has its pros and cons.[28] The advantage is immediately clear because it shows how people are dependent on nature – for instance food, drinking water, coast protection, water management and recreation – and, thus, it becomes also a matter of self-interest to take care of nature. The disadvantage is that nature is only seen in terms of usefulness for people. The intrinsic worth of plants, animals, landscapes and ecosystems is unrecognised. It is not only very difficult to estimate the price of ecosystems – what is the market value of the Cotswolds or of Niagara Falls? – but it also degrades animals, plants and wildlife resorts.[29]

To consume less (A) may not be immediately appealing, but it is without doubt necessary. Those who consume most will have to economise substantially. Recycling seems a solution, but this alone will not be sufficient, because recycling itself takes energy. Even if everything could be recycled – the circular economy – the energy required to make a product has already been used up; more energy will be needed to convert it into something new. Another concern is that recycling often results in a certain loss in quality. Old clothes are not turned into new ones but end up as cleaning cloths or insulation material; plastic can morph into verge markers. It would be a help in terms of debris and energy saving if products lasted longer, did not break easily, and were easier to repair or reuse, but manufacturers clearly have a greater interest in compelling their clients to purchase a new gadget every few years.

Not all necessary changes are therefore economically attractive. Added to this is the so-called rebound effect: 'the financial revenue of recycling or energy saving is immediately spent in more consumption'.[30] Thus, the introduction of the energy-saving lamp did not result in the saving of energy because people switched on more lights and left them burning much longer than needed. With the introduction of LED lamps – even more energy saving – people started to light up their gardens. Environment-friendly products and services often do not generate profit; what is saved by economising lowers the threshold for more consumption.

The ecological crisis is not automatically counteracted by marketing more and better environment-friendly products and services. Finding a solution to the ecological crisis within current capitalism, based on growth, is hardly feasible. Every effort to direct people's behaviour towards less consumption will be countered by economic interests more powerful than all other interests. If everything is arranged to enhance production and consumption, prosperity is measured by gross domestic product, and economic crisis sets in once growth is stagnating or absent. How, within this predicament, may one expect that any large-scale and durable economising is possible? Good examples like eco-suburbs, local vegetable gardens and food co-operatives help to keep the spirit alive, but are nothing more than niches. Sustainable growth is self-contradicting because sustainable implies precisely no growth, and growth is not sustainable.[31] The system itself is the problem, like the worldview that goes with it.

What remains is population growth (P) as a target for ecological action. Even if all available means to protect the environment were set in motion, the question remains as to whether the earth is capable of sustaining seven billion inhabitants.[32] Inasmuch as it is unethical to keep the poor poor in order to keep their ecological footprint small, it is equally hypocritical to tell them that they should have fewer children. One would almost forget that it was the Europeans who in the last couple of centuries spread themselves as eager colonists around the globe.[33] Besides, childbirth prevention programmes have seldom worked. We do know that women have fewer children once their social status improves. Women's emancipation – education for girls, equal rights, economic independence, and women having control over their own bodies – is, therefore, a prerequisite to stem global population growth and to put a limit on the ever-growing exploitation of the earth.

1.2 WORLDVIEWS

As it has become clear that the ecological crisis is more than just a series of practical problems that can be solved by the usual means, it now becomes necessary to look deeper into the more fundamental causes of this crisis. What are the cultural, ideological and religious reasons? What is wrong with our worldview, and do we have an alternative? Is a different worldview, mental model or paradigm feasible?

A worldview is not an idea that hovers above reality, but is always embodied in practices. Our technology, for instance, is a set of opinions attached to engines and technical possibilities. Our market economy, likewise, is a system of money and goods in which certain beliefs function. Practices come from beliefs and beliefs from practices. Changes can start with practices and/or with beliefs, but will always implicate both.

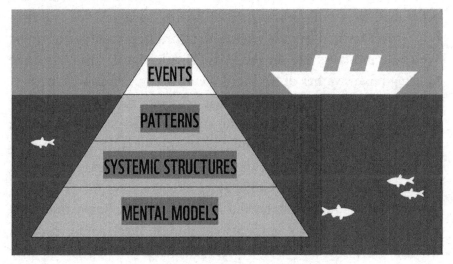

Four levels of thinking[34]

1.2.1 Anthropocentrism and exploitation (White and Morton)

As a historian, Lynn White specialised in medieval technological innovation, but as early as 1966 he opened up a debate[35] that continues to date about the role of religion in the western worldview.[36] He blamed Christian churches for their anthropocentric theology, which, geared up to human interest, had degraded nature to a commodity.

> Especially in its Western form, Christianity is the most anthropocentric religion the world has seen. [...] Christianity made it possible to exploit nature in a mood of indifference to the feelings of natural objects.[37]

29

Christianity had prepared the ground for western natural science and technology, according to White. The churches justified technological dominance over nature as being in line with God's plan. This aggressive approach towards nature set for exploitation started, according to White, in the Middle Ages, although technological means were at this time still limited. The text of Genesis 1:28, giving humans dominion over the earth, played a central role in the process. Animism – the belief that everything is animated or divine – was rejected and thus was respect for non-human reality. The third important factor in the West was monastic life. In the early Middle Ages, cloisters started to bring huge swathes of land under cultivation by introducing new techniques. They made clear in their religious rules that work was as important as prayer. Increasing technological possibilities made them more and more successful at controlling nature. According to White, this all goes to show direct links between Christian virtues, technological advancement and nature's decline.

White also pointed out that the Bible was read in a linear timeframe and not cyclically, as was the case amongst surrounding peoples, which underpinned a belief in progress: the future had to be better than the present. This timeframe, combined with Bible texts that placed humans right in the middle of creation (especially Genesis 1's commandment to subdue the earth), gave rise to an anthropocentric, exploitative worldview.

White was criticised by several theologians who saw taking care of nature as typically Christian and in defence of Christianity brought forth other Bible texts. The Bible was about everything that exists, the whole world, the whole of creation, they said, and men's task was not to waste but to preserve nature. The theological anthropocentrism that White criticised was not the Bible's fault, but that of one-sided biblical exposition and a matching theology that connected God exclusively with humans and ordered them to exploit the earth.[38]

White also encountered criticism from fellow historians and philosophers who questioned his image of the Middle Ages. They alleged that during the Middle Ages nature was endowed with its own quality. Human control over nature was already highlighted in the Classical, pre-Christian, era. Besides, not only Christians harmed nature.

Hendrik-Joost van Soest, who researched the ways Genesis 1:26-28 was interpreted in the Netherlands during the nineteenth and twentieth centuries, also took White to task. He opined that 'dominion over the earth' was not an important theological issue at the time. If this text was mentioned, it was either to justify the cultivation of grounds or to advocate the conservation of wild spaces in the Netherlands.[39] It was not humanity but God that was centre stage, maintained theologians from different backgrounds, a stance promulgated in articles for the general public. Once 'dominion' was severed from its theocentric, God-centred, context, the concept became, according to van Soest, problematic, as it immediately made men lords and masters.[40]

Did White's criticisms really touch on Christianity as a whole or rather the humanistic strand in Christianity? 'Humanism started with modernity and furthered a culture in which humans made themselves lord and master of the world and possessors of the earth.'[41]

Since White's criticism, the relationship between religion/ theology, worldview and ecological crisis has been a point of discussion. Worldview and religion are interconnected, as belief always comes alive within a certain context. In a pre-industrialised agrarian society, one thinks differently about belief compared with someone who lives in a post-industrialised society. Even in the Bible, we find huge dissimilarities between texts from different times and circumstances. The differences between the two first biblical creation accounts, for instance, are mainly due to changes in context, as I will show in the next chapter.

Whether Christianity enabled a worldview that caused the ecological crisis or Christianity was shaped by the world in which it came to maturity is really a chicken-and-egg issue. The only thing that one *can* say is that modern theology and modern culture are

31

interwoven and, therefore, that Christianity is partly to be blamed.[42] Still, White maintains that 'Christianity bears a huge burden of guilt'.

If religion and worldview were both contributors, it is equally obvious that one must find a solution that involves belief or conviction – in our case, one that encompasses Christianity. White put it like this:

> More science and more technology are not going to get us out of the present ecologic crisis until we find a new religion, or rethink our old one. [...] Since the roots of our trouble are so largely religious, the remedy must also be essentially religious, whether we call it that or not.

He took Francis of Assisi as an example in 'his belief in the virtue of humility not merely for the individual but for man as a species. Francis tried to depose man from his monarchy over creation and set up a democracy of all God's creatures'.[43]

Timothy Morton thinks that a paradigm shift is already taking place.[44] The Anthropocene is revolutionising our thoughts. In the act of destroying our planet, we have realised that we are part of the earth. The ecological crisis has made us aware that we have entered the Anthropocene. This new era had already started by the time of the Mesopotamians, but at that time no one had as yet any knowledge of the fact. Morton calls this 'dark ecology': the terrible ecological disaster has already happened, but not all its consequences are visible. We are confronted by the limits of natural sciences and, hence, with the limits of human dominion, because what humans have set in motion has got out of hand – climate change, plastic soup, antimicrobial resistance. He calls these phenomena that are too big to handle 'hyper-objects'; in them, we begin to see our guilt and vulnerability. Like other creatures, we can understand the world only in our own limited way. We have to relinquish the illusion that we exceed all other creatures and are able to control the earth. Morton concludes that our relationship with other entities should change from exploitation through science to agnostic solidarity. This does not just entail loss. It is also a liberation, because we don't have to be in command any longer: we can take pleasure in other creatures and in ourselves.

Morton's thinking is influenced by postmodern philosophers such as Derrida and Said, and he has an affinity with Buddhism. But notions like guilt, vulnerability, solidarity, not-knowing and taking pleasure in other creatures are also important from a Christian point of view. These will return in the next chapters.

1.2.2 Western worldviews through the ages

Through the ages, people have had different thoughts about the relationship between God, humans and the world.[45] The Bible still talks about the whole earth; God does not have a direct relationship with people only, but equally with, for example, animals. I will come to this later on in chapter two. Although the Church Fathers see the relationship between God and world as mediated via people, their worldview is not anthropocentric in the way we take it, because God is still in charge.[46] The Middle Ages also knew a cosmology that encompasses all, in which everything is created according to the eternal ideas (Plato) found in the Spirit of God, and is taken as the image or trace of God. The cosmos is unchangeable and perfect, with the earth and people in its centre. Creation is a book that tells about God. People took the world as a living whole and themselves as mirroring this, a micro cosmos. Humans had to perfect themselves according to the perfect order of the cosmos. With the rise of the city in the thirteenth century, nature received a value in itself, separate from humans; man saw himself as *homo faber*, man at work. Via Thomas Aquinas, Aristotle's philosophy came to the fore in theology: nature's rational order could be fathomed through human reasoning.[47] The same idea was taken up by occultism that mastered the spiritual powers of nature through magical practices. This practical and active attitude vis-à-vis nature was the birthplace of the scientific revolution and capitalism.[48]

The Reformation initially conserved the medieval image of the world as a book through which one could acquire knowledge of God. The *Belgic Confession* (*Nederlandse Geloofsbelijdenis*) is one of the founding texts of Dutch Protestantism.[49] Article 2 speaks of the two sources of knowing God. The first is through 'the creation, conserving and governing of the whole world'. The world is like a book by which one can know of God's power and divinity. To know who God really is, one needs an additional source, the Bible. This confession from 1561 still thinks in terms of the whole world. Nature is not set aside. It is not only 'the book of nature', as it was later called: history was very much part of this book of the world.

The image of the two books of knowledge of God received new meaning in the early modern period. In the seventeenth century, Protestant scientists in particular did experimental research to show how beautifully everything was made by God. All sciences sprang forth from theology.[50] Even Descartes (1596–1650), the radical enlightenment philosopher, does not contrapose mind and God. Nevertheless, the image of the relationship between God and the world is changing radically. The dominant image of God among Protestants becomes that of a clockmaker who has set the world in motion; its smart machinery, once kicked off, is not in need of its maker anymore. Influenced by Isaac Newton's (1642–1726) mechanics, creation becomes an act of God in the past, not something which requires his continuing exertion.[51] The world has become a machine without a soul. God is in the beginning and at the end of time and in between the big clock just ticks away by itself. It takes just one small step to proclaim the idea of 'God' redundant. To study nature, one is not in need of God anymore. The postulation of evolution theory in particular challenges God's role as the great initiator.

The image of the world as a machine is still with us. People talk about their own body as a machine, for instance, a visit to the hospital is likened to taking a car to the garage. If something is wrong with your body, you can take it for repair, so the thinking goes.

Nowadays, the separation of humans and nature, made by the

philosopher Immanuel Kant (1724-1804) is taken for granted.[52] If we talk of nature, we normally mean what is not human and not manmade. We automatically position ourselves outside. This explains also the division between humanities and natural sciences, where the latter have become normative for all science. Theology as a science that studies the knowledge of God is within this worldview simply impossible. Theology has tried to circumvent the issue by not taking God but humans and their beliefs as the object of research. Scholars of religion – and more and more also theologians – make use of methods borrowed from the humanities. Another option has been to look for God in the spaces left vacant by natural sciences. The idea behind all this is, if we don't know how something works, we may there find the hand of God operating. Theology does not necessarily have to go along with this worldview. She can also set her face against it, by returning to an older worldview, or by getting into dialogue with the latest philosophical and scientific insights.

1.2.3 Current natural science

It is interesting to note that recently in some areas of natural science a new worldview has emerged. In others, the mechanistic worldview still dominates, and in theology people are still detached from nature, viewing people as persons and the remainder as things. Current cosmology and biology teach us that everything is interdependent. We know now that the earth is old and the universe even older; people are newcomers. The vastness of the universe is incredible and people are just specks of dust. We know that everything is connected; people are also made of stardust. And we know that the universe is dynamic, and that history does not oppose nature, because nature is also permanently in flux.[53]

The theology–natural sciences relationship has become complex. There are roughly four views.[54] The first is that theology and natural science cover different things and have nothing in common. This opinion prevails in mainstream church life in the Netherlands. One believes for instance that the natural sciences deal with facts and theology with belief and ethics. The second view is that the mechanistic worldview of the natural sciences is normative, which leaves hardly any room for religion and theology. This secular stance considers religion a private thing and, as a matter of fact, outdated. The third option is that theology takes precedence over natural sciences. This is what religious fundamentalism endorses – evolutionary theory is discarded because it runs counter to Bible interpretation. The fourth view considers a dialogue between both as feasible: theology and natural science can learn from each other. Although it is not easy to bring about such a dialogue due to the fact that theologians feel a stronger need for it than most scientists, this last option will yield much more fruit when it comes to the matter of theology and sustainability.

Current theology has taken the divide between people and world so far that it even rubs off on the image of God: one speaks differently about God in relation to nature than God in relation to people.[55] If theology deals with the non-human world, a static image prevails: nature divinely ordered is a thing detached from God and given over to humans to administer. For God's relationship with people, more dynamic images are available: exodus, calling, deliverance. People are seen as on their way to God's kingdom.

It seems more logical, following the insights of current natural sciences, to apply this dynamic model to the whole world. Nature, as we know, permanently develops. 'One of the most remarkable insights of contemporary science is that the whole cosmos is inherently historical.'[56] Even the laws of nature are not fixed but vary according to circumstances. Not only theology but also natural science makes use of stories, and contains a narrative.[57] This dynamic model yields a different image of God. In a changing world, God is the driving and attracting force. God is not the designer but the engine of the world. God calls and invites not only people, but all of reality. Thus, everything is on its way to its fulfilment in God. Creation is not unchangeable, nor by itself good or bad. In all of reality, God is working – that is creation. This is not a new model, but goes back to the work of Thomas Aquinas, and has been explored in a certain way in process theology.[58] God is compared to a choreographer or a conductor: God points out the way and tries to let the musicians/dancers perform as best they possibly can.[59] This dynamic image of God in relation to the world is also biblical, as we will see in our next chapter.

The dialogue between natural sciences and theology will be profitable to both. Theology may even reject certain worldviews cherished by natural scientists, for example, the view that everything is total chaos or that evolution entails the right of the fittest to cast aside the weak.

1.2.4 Technology

Natural sciences and technology cohere as knowledge and application do. Scientists oversee the matter; engineers take action. Alongside modern warfare and the exploitation of the earth, technical developments have also engendered many improvements. One can think of healthcare and the quality of life brought within reach of many and which would be sorely missed by anyone. Nevertheless, the overrated belief in technology is an enormous problem: the illusion that people can take control of the world with technology, and that the world freely provides people with the material for technological development. White showed how a technological worldview and ecological crisis were connected. Pope Francis in his encyclical *Laudato Si'* pointed out that a technocratic worldview – a worldview where technology is in total command – is one of the causes of environmental deterioration. Most important in causing the ecological crisis is the 'techno-economic paradigm', the dominant idea being that people can rule the whole of reality with the help of their technology. A small group usurps the right for themselves to subdue other people and nature to maximise revenues as the highest aim in life. An ideology that places satisfying one's own needs as its sole norm leads to unjustifiable work conditions and food production, like taking fertile land away from the many and giving it to the few.[60] In the ruling western worldview, the natural sciences and technology are not the only agents playing an important role. Equally prevalent is a certain economic model that supports it.

1.2.5 Market economy

The way our economy is organised appears overall as self-evident. Since the fall of the Berlin Wall, hardly any realistic alternative has been found for our present-day market economy. This belief is in the USA even stronger than in Europe. Europe still knows in places the Rhineland model, in which a strong public sector keeps a close watch on the market, protecting the workers, constraining the law of demand and supply and the power of the stockholders. Politicians and policy-makers very often make it look as if economy is all about natural laws and not about values.

The worldview that underpins this economic way of thinking is that of man as an individual and the world as a machine existing of many parts that can be taken apart for closer scrutiny. The aim is growth, and everything that brings in money is good, because it contributes to GDP (gross domestic product). Unpaid work such as managing a household, childcare and volunteering are not included in GDP, in the same way as destruction of nature and society is not reckoned with.

The idea behind all of this is that the mechanism of demand and supply produces the best possible price and the best possible distribution of commodities, which benefits everyone. Who *really* profits from an economic system and whether the earth is able to support it is not part and parcel of this economic theory.[61] The entrepreneur keeps the client satisfied, for instance, with cheap clothes and the client does not ask how a t-shirt can be so low-priced. Many things are not taken into account: the insecticides and the artificial manure used for growing cotton, working conditions in the clothing industry, the plastic fibres that soil nature, the stream of rejected clothing that can be hardly recycled because of the mix of materials.

Income per capita is often used for measuring degrees of welfare, but income level does not reveal everything. Take, for instance, someone living in a shantytown earning five dollars a day, who at the same time must pay a one-dollar bus ticket to get to work, and must likewise pay for food, water and her children's education. This person is certainly poorer than someone who earns just two dollars a day, but grows his own vegetables, keeps some chickens and a goat; nearby is a forest and clean water, and he enjoys free school education and healthcare. Many programmes for stimulating the economy have discarded all these elements.[62] Deregulation, privatising and economising on social welfare have been the current policies for targeting economic growth.[63]

Capitalism's image of man fits well with that of the Reformation: both consider people as free individuals driven by self-interest. But the way this is valued by both is different. From the point of view of belief, self-interest is considered sin; in economics, it is seen as a necessary driver in life. Here, a point of tension arises. Until well into the twentieth century, everyone was considered part of a greater whole, including in politics and church life. Once institutions grow weaker, society's cohesion starts to

What price to pay for development? (poster of the Belgian NGO (C) *Broederlijk Delen* 1989)[967]

crumble, the sense of belonging and dependency gets lost, and the feeling of a shared responsibility becomes vague.[64] The consumer society seems the only thing that matters. Consuming more can indeed make one happier, but this only counts in cases of utter poverty. As soon as wants are provided for, more income and possessions do not bring more happiness. Besides, the current western level of consumption, which overtaxes what the earth can give, engenders dread should all of humanity live in the same way, even if we were capable of reinforcing considerably the sustainability of our products and services.

If the world could be compared to a machine, one might be able to repair it, as one could replace the broken parts. But so-called 'renewable sources' are interdependent: water, air, soil, trees, biodiversity. Replacing them is impossible. They are not products, parts of a machine, but taken together they form our ecosystem. The image of a living organism fits better than that of a machine.[65]

Thus, our economic model has at least two faults: its individualistic image of man and its blind spot for earth's wellbeing. On top of that, it is outdated because it still thinks in terms of local markets. Globalism has turned the whole world into one market, which directs the big money to places where taxes are low (the Netherlands!) and environmental laws are lax or barely enforced. As the biggest companies hardly pay taxes, the costs are paid elsewhere. Trade agreements make it even harder to compel international companies to comply to social and environmental legislation.[66]

The economic theory of market capitalism has become an ideology that turns people into consumers, individuals that only long for more.[67] Unlimited growth is impossible because the sources are limited. If the economy has to find a way to share the scanty goods, the question has to be raised what justifiable sharing entails and what is enough. 'How to share the planet's goods cannot be left to the vagaries of market capitalism, for, as we have seen, the results are neither equitable nor sustainable.'[68]

1.2.6 Patriarchy and colonialism

We have seen that several answers are given to the question of what lies at the root of the way of thinking that legitimises the exploitation of nature. There are several connecting roots: anthropocentrism, scientific model, technocracy and the neoliberal market economy. The general assumption is that 'people' exploit the earth, but people as such do not exist. Not all people exploit the earth to the same degree, as became clear in the model of the ecological footprint. The poor use less than the rich, the non-western world less than the western world, women less than men. Besides, the consequences of ecological deterioration are not felt equally by all people. In 1989 the UN reported: 'It is now a universally established fact that it is the woman who is the worst victim of environmental destruction. The poorer she is, the greater is her burden.'[69] That the impact on women is bigger has to do with the way work is traditionally divided; householding is considered women's work. Ecological hardships make it more difficult for her to get water, food and fuel for sustaining the family. Many development aid projects have devastating consequences for women and nature.

Even in general perception, there are differences between certain categories of people: some are considered as being above nature and others as part of it. Women are traditionally, historically considered closer to nature than men.[70] Nature itself was insistently depicted as feminine: it is mother earth who brings forth life. Women through their menses and pregnancies were seen as standing closer to nature; as the bearers of new life, they were more defined by their body, more earth-like. Cultures where nature was held in high esteem gave women more credit, and vice versa: where women were held in high regard, nature was also well assessed. Western culture did not work out well for women and nature.[71] Both were compared to higher-regarded entities: men and culture. A body of hierarchical dualisms came into being. Inferior were earth, nature, women, body, emotion, wilderness; superior were heaven, culture, men, spirit, reason, civilisation. The idea that civilised rational men should dominate over women, nature and non-western people – the 'savages' – is deeply ingrained in our culture and can be traced back to Aristotle.[72] Women and nature are both still spoken of in terms of conquering and possessing.

The concept of nature as feminine had initially both a positive and a negative meaning: nature was nourishing but at the same time wild and uncontrollable, equally giving and taking life. The negative side got the upper hand and as such became embedded in philosophical, religious and scientific ideas.[73] Thus started an ideology of control that lay the foundation for the patriarchal–capitalist order. This made possible the connection between the mechanistic worldview and modern sciences, the rise of the global market economy, and the exploitation of human and natural resources.

This ideology recurs in colonialism and the agendas of development aid. In the language of colonialism, it becomes the culture which has to be promoted; in the language of development aid, the so-called underdeveloped countries have to rise to the same level as the rich countries. But in order to reach out to a more sustainable relationship with the earth, non-western worldviews and practices should be taken as examples: 'most non-western cultures are rooted in the democracy of all life'.[74]

1.2.7 Postmodernism

The modern worldview of the autonomous man has also been challenged from within. Darwin dethroned men by turning them into an animal species, closely related to apes. Freud showed that people – the well-to-do, white, healthy male included – aren't in charge of their own lives at all. The ego is driven by all sorts of unknowledgeable urges. Marx proved that the unequal participation in production strongly influenced – according to him it even determined the outcome of – who people are and how society functions. Nietzsche put into words the unease felt by humans fully exposed to an unfathomable world.

Following in the footsteps of these thinkers, postmodern

philosophers like Foucault, Derrida, Deleuze and Irigaray continued to destabilise the image of men as autonomous and rational. They reconsidered the relationship between men and world once again. Although postmodernism is a container word for quite a number of thinkers who, among themselves, are more inclined to differ, they do agree in rejecting the presuppositions of modernity. They not only criticise the concept of the autonomous individual but also thinking in dualisms and a belief in irrefutable truths. According to them, there is no solid identity, epistemological certainty, unequivocalness in meaning and historical progress. Truth is always constructed, a combination of language and power. There is no absolute truth that is validated always and everywhere. The 'grand narratives' are exposed as oppressive because they legitimise structures of oppression and exclude everything different.[75]

What is presented as common truth is always conditioned by certain circumstances, the balance of power and the interests involved. The modern idea that people take centre stage and can and must take possession of the world came simultaneously with the rise of the natural sciences and technology. To exploit the earth, one needed a new concept of men that separated them from nature, and reified nature whilst believing that this entailed progress. Postmodern philosophy took this image and other Enlightenment ideas apart. It 'deconstructed' them.

Postmodernism has a bad name because it often seems nothing more than nihilism. If everything is relative, what can one possibly believe? Is cynicism the only option left? But one forgets that the exposition of power play creates room for what has been pushed aside. Postmodernism criticises and opens eyes. If objectivity is impossible, then being involved is not unscientific. Specifying one's own context, position and suppositions becomes necessary for a credible disquisition. If meaning is always relative, new interpretations are at all times possible. If historical progress is debatable, then recent insights are not inevitably better than past insights. If the world stays partly inscrutable, then an all-embracing worldview is no longer necessary. The fissures in seemingly closed systems in particular enable light to pass through and make visible what stayed hidden in the dark.

Some theologians make fruitful use of postmodern insights and methods to understand the situation in the world, to re-read texts and to reinterpret the past in order to gain new insights into God and the world.[76] This theology does not pretend to have a timeless truth, but it knows how conditioned it is by time and situation, and – if all is well – is serious in entering into dialogue with other times and situations.

1.2.8 Language

Language is never neutral. Language mirrors a worldview and also forms the present worldview. The word nature, for instance, is mostly used to point out a reality that is not manmade. This creates a divide between people and the rest of reality. Should we persist in using the word nature? How do we actually use the word?

Nature has many meanings. Nature can mean character. Nature can also signify everything that is studied by natural sciences: atoms, animals and plants, meteorological and geological processes, the cosmos, the material and energy of which everything consists, and the internal connections involved. The concept of nature can signify the animal and plant world and inorganic nature in all its diversity. 'Natural' joined to social theories, norms and values makes them sound self-explanatory. Natural can mean healthy or good. Nature can be set off against socialisation (nature/nurture), technology, the supernatural, culture or manmade creations.[77]

In religious language, nature also has many meanings. Nature can be taken in both a positive and a negative way, either as good creation or as menacing or fallen nature. In theology, nature is often set against grace and, subsequently, has to be corrected or salvaged. If nature is used in a positive way, then it is frequently pictured as something desirable, self-evident or inevitable. 'The "laws of nature" or "natural law" are minefields of religious concepts, biases, and instruments of social organization or control.'[78] In modern theology, nature often opposes history where God is mainly to be found.[79] Sometimes nature is just a synonym for creation.

Eco-theologians and philosophers remind us that people are part of a bigger scheme of earth's biotic community. Some avoid the word nature. Latour rejects the separation of people and nature, of nature and culture, as well as the related partition of subject and object.[80] Theokritoff uses nature to signify the non-human material reality, whereas creation is about all that exists.[81] Keller does not use the word nature, but sticks to creation. Boureux confesses towards the end of his book that he has evaded the thorny subject of what is meant by 'nature'.[82] Elvey calls nature a homogenising term and prefers instead 'matter'.[83]

Because nature is so poly-interpretable and confusing, it seems tempting to discard the word altogether. I do not consider this a serious alternative, because it just shifts the problems and amplifies the confusion. 'Matter' and 'creation' are likewise poly-interpretable. It is important to be aware, from the very beginning, how problematic the term nature is. I will not avoid its use, but neither will I stick to one definition. In general, I will use nature according to the most current meaning of the non-human material world or solely of designating animals and plants, sometimes earth's biotic community, sometimes the whole earth or the cosmos. The meaning will be conditioned by the author and context involved.

Up to now I have used the terms sustainability, ecology and environment indiscriminately. They all have their pros and cons. 'Environment' (milieu) has the disadvantage that in its use as natural background it leaves out people and is strongly anthropocentric. Sustainability has become a catch-all term – there is economic, social and ecological sustainability – by which all emphasis is laid on preserving, especially preserving the living condition of our and future generations of people,[84] clearly making it an anthropocentric term. 'Ecology' is less weighed down with this disadvantage. Initially, it was the name of a field of study within biology. Nowadays, it has a much broader meaning. As a discipline of biology, ecology studies ecosystems: 'Ecology is the science that studies how organisms interact with one another and their environment.'[85] Biologists have pointed out that earth as such can be taken as a one big ecosystem, the biosphere.[86] Outside of biology, ecological has come to signify respect for nature or earth, acknowledging the interconnectedness of everything. It emphasises the cohesion of earth's ecosystem and the inalienable worth of non-human nature. The Pope even calls for an 'ecological repentance'.[87] Ecological has sometimes become nothing more than being friendly to the environment. Although I prefer the word ecologic, I will also use the words sustainable and environment.

Speaking about God is in the same way not without its suppositions. I try to avoid calling God 'he', because I don't want to stress a one-sided image of God. I cannot avoid this completely. Because applying 'she' to God is still uncommon and may create a form of estrangement, I will use 'she' only when the context makes its use obvious, as is the case among feminist authors. The neutral term 'the divine' I find too impersonal and vague.

1.3 THE TASK OF THEOLOGY

Up to this point, the ecological crisis and the worldview that caused it were already connected with theology. Now it is time to look into the precise nature of this connection. What do I mean by theology, and how can theology be of value? As my starting point, I take the classical definition of theology as faith-based thinking about God and everything that is connected with God. In the words of Anselm (eleventh century) attributed to Augustine (fifth century), theology is *fides quaerens intellectum*, faith seeking understanding. Faith-based thinking may take distinctive forms. For me, it consists in particular in a systematic reflection open to academic scrutiny. I will on my way refer frequently to other sorts of texts that reflect belief, such as liturgical texts.

1.3.1 Theology is about the world in relation to God

By being drenched with modernity (the anthropocentric shift, the mechanistic worldview, and a belief in manipulability and progress), theology made itself redundant in the following two ways. In the first place, theology was no longer considered scientific because it could no longer make a valid claim about the whole but was by now restricted to defining morality and a sense of purpose. Theology was reduced to either a type of anthropology that only describes what people actually believe, or a kind of ethics. Anyone wanting to know how the world functions will no longer consult theology to find the answer. But a relevant theology perceives the whole of reality, which includes animals and plants and economic structures, in relation to God.[88] Secondly, modern theology is no longer capable of countering the ecological crisis because it is stuck with the very worldview that was one of its causes. White called this Christianity's 'huge burden of guilt'. Theology that tries its utmost to make itself understood by modern men runs the risk of adapting to what is en vogue and ends up being meaningless.

Once theology does not comply with the dominant worldview but takes a critical stance, it may become relevant again and a factor to take seriously. Theology can do more than just supporting a mentality change or being a source of inspiration for opinions which have already been decided upon. Theology provides not only norms and values, but also real knowledge about reality that differs from natural science.[89] Social sciences may assist theology provided they don't reduce it to one of their sub-disciplines.[90]

1.3.2 Many sources and participants

Does this imply a return to pre-modern times? Of course, there is no option to return to the worldview of the Middle Ages or that of Old Israel.

You can't just turn back the clock – the conditions are simply different – and neither can you change any worldview with a snap of a finger. Staying outside the reigning worldview may be hard to do, but every worldview has its own cracks, fissures through which other possibilities become visible. Our worldview changes as soon as the conditions change. Can we cling to the image of man as ruler of the earth if the ecological crisis makes us aware how dependent and vulnerable we are? Knowledge from other eras and cultures may help us to put our worldview into perspective and readjust it. Likewise, other practices and listening to non-dominant groups (i.e. non-privileged people, powerless to set the agenda) can be of help.

This may take place in several ways, inside and outside of Christianity. Other religions have other insights and practices to offer. For some people, these alternatives replace Christian religion, but they can also confront Christians: witness the legendary speech that Chief Seattle delivered when the American government wanted to buy land from the indigenous people. 'How can we buy or sell the sky?'[91] Such a question rebuts with a notion of holiness the whole idea of the earth being either a supplier of goods or a commodity itself. That notion of holiness is also present in Christianity when it calls the earth God's creation.

Within Christianity you will find many more voices than just the modern western. The Bible, of course, conveys these, but the history of the Church is also full of them, in all its diversity of living faiths of Christians of all cultures and places. Among the Yine, a people in the western part of the Amazon in Peru, communicating with non-human persons plays a significant role in their Christian religion. These persons can be animals, the spirits of the dead, the sign of the beast, God and Satan.[92] Nearer to home, we find other forms of Christianity especially among migrant and intercultural churches. There are also other practices than what the usual economic agenda offers. Although small-scale initiatives like local vegetable gardens and ecological living accommodation are not likely to revolutionise the world, they can provide new experiences and insights, also for theology. Sallie McFague brings up the question of how Christians can love nature.[93] She distinguishes two ways of seeing: the arrogant eye and the loving eye. Those who are able to recognise the trees, the plants, the stones as neighbours can also love them. McFague extends the commandment to love your neighbour to all of nature. To love nature, one does not have to look for a spectacular landscape far from home. Your own garden, the plants on a balcony, the park nearby carry more weight because you can directly relate to them. Those who tend a garden or care for pets know that nature is not a thing, that dogs and cats have their own personalities, that no rose is like another. If you consider everything in your natural environment not as a possession but as fellow creatures, you will behave differently. Touching opens up a different worldview than analysing and using do, because touching implies reciprocating. Touching establishes a relationship. Meditation/prayer and service/ liturgy also create experiences that can divulge a different form of knowledge than the one we are most familiar with.[94]

By the way, listening to non-dominant groups is not easy. The voiceless in our society are only heard if they adjust themselves to what we find acceptable. But these people living on the margin of society may have insights that we miss altogether, for example, about the way our economy functions. And what would it mean if animals had a voice? If we could see the world through the eyes of a pig? One step further and the 'parliament of things' comes into sight.[95] In short, a new theology with a new worldview would be well served with non-dominant insights. Our modern western worldview may be prevailing, but it is never without its cracks. 'Hidden narratives' (Michel Foucault) are always audible for those who can listen. A nice example is *The Hidden Life of Trees*, written by an expert who explains for a wide audience how trees live and communicate.[96]

1.3.3 Bible and tradition

The three sources of theology are usually Bible, tradition and lived religion. Theologians are concerned with biblical texts, theological material in the form of creeds and theological controversies from the past, and cultural material of actual living Christian experience such as liturgy, devotions and social caring practices.[97] These sources need perennial reinterpretation if new situations and opinions bring forth new questions.[98] Reformed, liberal and Catholic theology have to deal with this. A liberal theologian such as Christa Anbeek wants to decode traditional religion as a symbolical language in order to make the experiences behind it and the perspective on offer understandable to secularised people. She calls it a must for the survival of Christian theology to translate theological insights into personal encounters with life's brittleness.[99] The Catholic theologian Erik Borgman reinterprets the thirteenth-century theologian Thomas Aquinas for a theology 'that is authentic in its search in what really happens in the world and contributes to the progress of our culture and considers the problems we face'.[100] Gijsbert van den Brink, who belongs to a traditional brand of the Reformed tradition, takes theology to account for and explain what the Church believes in, as is laid down in dogmas and creeds. He re-read the Bible and some of the authorities in his tradition to answer the question of how orthodox Protestants could relate to evolutionary theory.[101]

Theology is, thus, always the recapitulation and reinterpretation of a mix of elements of the Bible and the tradition in a specific context. Past opinions can never be the only norm for proper theology, because the past encompasses always more and is more diverse than whatever specific imagining of a glorious past suggests, and everything can always turn out different from what one expects.[102] Neither can current opinions and practices be the only norm, as it immediately implies locking oneself in the present. Each perspective is limited. Although God and the world are never completely knowable, historical research of Bible and tradition help to broaden one's horizon. With Kathryn Tanner, I would like to place myself in a broader theological space:

Knowledge of Christianity in other times and places is a way, then, of expanding the range of imaginative possibilities for theological construction in any one time and place, a way of expanding the resources with which one can work.[103]

This is not a restoration of old theology nor its rejection, but 'a creative mobilizing of the Christian tradition in order to say something about God and God's relation to the world'.[104] When Tanner speaks of world, she means above all things the world of people, but if her method is applied to the whole world, the non-human included, it becomes much more relevant.[105]

1.4 THEOLOGY AND THE ECOLOGICAL CRISIS

Relevant theology deals with all of reality, thus including animals and plants and economic structures, everything in relation to God. Theology is, therefore, more than ethics and provides real knowledge about reality. Christian theology is not a repeat or a readjusting of fixed insights, but it mobilises creatively the Christian tradition in order to say something about God and the world. Many other interlocutors are welcome to join in.

Besides constructive theology, we need a form of deconstruction, because theology has all too often supported vested interests and maintained social and ecological inequality.[106] It is therefore necessary to look critically into forms of theology that legitimise the unlimited exploitation of the earth. The same goes for other forms of exploitation, insulation and suppression, in particular of women, the poor and of non-western peoples. Theology is always embedded in some worldview and can at the same time put it into perspective and expose its injustice. Philosophy can be supportive in this undertaking.

The ecological crisis necessitates a deconstruction of the modern worldview. This worldview with its anthropocentrism, individualism, belief in manipulability, and the clear divide of subject and object, of men and nature, has brought us, on the one hand, many good things, like, for instance, scientific research, useful technology and the bringing down of a class-based society. On the other hand, it is perhaps more apt to say that this worldview mutated into a techno-economic paradigm with devastating effects on the earth's biosphere and the lives of many. Theology can do more than just motivate a specific group in our societies, that is to say Christians, to keep in step with the environmental movement's agenda. Theology can contribute from her own resources to earth's wellbeing and that of her denizens by beginning to question fundamental issues, sharpening already existing questions and contributing from her own rich tradition. These insights come often in the form of stories, like the stories from the Bible.

CHAPTER TWO

The different worldview of the Bible

Theology always resumes and reinterprets elements of the Bible and tradition in a particular context. The ecological crisis is such a context, and it urgently questions theology. Lynn White holds the churches responsible for nature's exploitation due to their anthropocentrism and belief in progress.[107] One cannot deny that Christianity is up to a certain degree guilty of the current ecological crisis by upholding theological opinions that confine God's relation to the world exclusively to the world of men. To place men as rulers outside and above nature reduces nature to a resource for human progress. The earth is often seen as God's gift to people to accommodate their wishes. A negative assessment of nature quite often coincides with a negative assessment of women and peoples living closer to nature.

The so-called superiority of (certain) people and the commandment to subdue nature are inferred from the Bible, which for many readers is reason to look upon the Bible as irreconcilable with and ultimately irrelevant for an ecological vision.[108] This is why the Bible is discarded most of the time by the environmental movement. Others, on the other hand, point out the many biblical environmentally friendly texts, which depict clearly and positively God's relation with animals, plants and the earth. They read in the Bible that people are called upon to care for nature.

In this chapter I will re-read the Bible from an ecological perspective. The Bible is, after all, for all Christians an important source and appeals to many non-Christians. I consider the Bible as an authoritative interlocutor. However, I don't want to make this task too easy by highlighting only those texts that prove what I already think. The questions that I will ask dig deeper. How does the Bible consider the correlation of God and the earth and what is the place that humans take up within that setting? And, given this relationship, how is the correlation of human and non-human life depicted?

I will start briefly by summarising several methods of ecological Bible reading and account for my choice of biblical texts. These texts will be listed in the following three categories: (1) texts that deal with creating; (2) texts that speak of animals; and (3) texts about the saving of the earth (eschatology). Re-reading the Bible in this way has a lot to offer. We get a completely different picture from the western Christian worldview that places men above creation.

If not stated otherwise, all quotations and verse numbers are taken from the New Revised Standard Version (NRSV), apart from the divine appellation 'Lord', which I have changed to 'the Everlasting' to avoid the misunderstanding that Lord would be the most desirable translation of JHWH. Quotations taken from biblical books not included in the NRSV are from the New American Bible, Revised Edition (NABRE). I will refer explicitly to the Hebrew or Greek of the source texts if this provides additional clarification. Occasionally, I will suggest another translation if this does more justice to the source texts or reveals another interpretation. Sometimes, I will refer to Dutch translations.

2.1 THE BIBLE IN ECOLOGICAL PERSPECTIVE

An ecological reading of the Bible places certain accents, puts forth particular questions and brings certain texts out in the open. It entails reading through an ecological lens. Everyone reads the Bible through a particular lens, even those who swear that they accept unreservedly everything that the Bible commands. Theological presuppositions, quite often implicitly, determine which texts merit more weight and which less. Luther was looking for the God of grace, whom he found in reading Paul, and who, subsequently, became his main access to understanding Scripture. Liberation theology reads everything largely through the lens of Israel's exodus, the prophets and the gospels finding God portrayed as the saviour of the poor. A psychological reading of the Bible is fashionable nowadays. Many sermons explore the emotions and motives of the biblical characters in a way that listeners can identify with. What will happen if we read Scripture by starting with the questions that the ecological crisis puts forward? This demands a different focus from the all-too-familiar emphasis on individual salvation and personal growth. The first step entails reading better, seeing more sharply what previously remained vague or downright invisible due to anthropocentric prejudices. Reading through an ecological lens means in the first place becoming aware of the non-human reality in the Bible.

2.1.1 Possibilities for an ecological interpretation

Bible interpretation that is relevant to an ecological theology comes in many forms.[109] The authors to whom I refer differ in method, in setting and aim. Jan Boersema tries to prove in his *The Torah and the Stoics on Humankind and Nature* that our western ideas about the correlation of people and nature mainly derive from Greek thinking and not the (Hebrew) Bible. David Horrell, in *The Bible and the Environment*, develops a hermeneutics that may support environmental ethics. Richard Bauckham wants to show in *Living with Other Creatures* that the Bible is about the biotic community of all creatures. Gijsbert van den Brink figures out in *Reformed Theology and Evolutionary Theory*[110] how evolutionary theory can be brought into line with orthodox Protestant dogmatic theology. Ellen van Wolde takes creation stories as myths of origin. Johan Graafland is particularly interested in animal rights. Christophe Boureux maintains with French philosophical flourish in his *Dieu est aussi jardinier* (*God is also a Gardener*) that the Bible is Christ-centred. Catherine Keller, a Protestant systematic theologian, writes within a postmodern feminist frame of mind *Face of the Deep*, which is devoted to just one biblical verse: Genesis 1:2. In *Earth, Wind and Fire*, feminist exegetes and systematic theologians, working on different texts, look for themes for an ecological theology of creation.

In all these authors, exegesis and systematic theology interact. That will come as no surprise, because theological presuppositions always play a role in exegesis in the same way as exegesis does in systematic theology.

Sustainability in the Bible

Reading through an ecological lens can be done in several ways. The easiest method is to search for keywords. Words like ecology or environment do not appear in Scripture. 'Sustainable' is also lacking, but in the sense of enduring, durable and everlasting, the notion does appear in connection with God's faithfulness put into words that will remain whatever may happen. This notion can be interpreted ecologically: God's faithfulness towards the earth will be enduring.

But searching for keywords barely satisfies because the Bible doesn't speak about the ecological crisis of our time. In biblical times the earth was considerably less densely populated than nowadays, and large parts were not or were hardly affected by human involvement. Human refuse was organic and decomposed by itself. Nature was in abundance and often menacing for humans. The sea was dangerous and took many lives. The chances of getting killed by a wild animal were substantial. Growing food involved hard labour and sufficient yield was not guaranteed. The impact of humans on earth was still small. People were not yet capable of making the earth uninhabitable, except in cases of war, but that would always be temporary and local. One can refer here to the cutting down of fruit trees, the stopping up of wells and throwing stones on arable fields to bring the enemy's people to their knees (Deuteronomy 20:19–20 and 2 Kings 3:25).

Green texts

Of course, the Bible cannot provide solutions to a crisis that didn't exist at the time of its writing. But one can look in Scripture for analogies or a broader category within which questions about belief and sustainability are relevant.[111] *The Green Bible* highlighted 'the strongest and most direct passages [...] based on how well they demonstrate:[112]

- how God and Jesus interact with, care for, and are intimately involved with all of creation
- how all the elements of creation – land, water, air, plants, animals, humans – are interdependent
- how nature responds to God
- how we are called to care for creation'.

Extra reading material and assignments that *The Green Bible* provides come up with some slightly different theological notions: 'And it was good', 'Finding God', 'Connected to creation', 'Creation care as justice', 'The full impact of sin' and 'The new earth'.

The Dutch *Green Bible* translation's editorial board made a slightly different choice.[113] Their aim was to highlight texts that propagate green living because they call on respectful dealing with people, plants and animals and are a 'summons that is linked with the belief that the whole of creation is a gift of God entrusted to people'.[114] This idea of a gift of God put under people's care is typical of current Protestant theology[115] and does not do justice to Bible texts about creation, as we will soon see. It has nothing to do with the way God and men deal with nature, because by putting it thus, God, men and nature are treated like three separate entities. The texts marked in green do show, nevertheless, how often animals, plants and earth appear in Scripture.

Ecological and feminist exegesis

Following my analysis of the ecological crisis as a crisis of our worldview, the broader category entails God's relation with the whole world, of which human beings are just a part, as are other creatures. Reading the Bible from within this theological category gives us orientation in the ecological crisis. My leading questions will be: How is humanity depicted in relation to non-human life? How are the relationships between God, humanity and earth understood?[116]

Scripture has all too often been read too anthropocentrically, as if it were a story about God and people, or even a story of men only. Let's take one example from Genesis 9.[117] This section of the Bible is commonly known as 'the covenant with Noah', which so considered reduces it to a covenant solely with Noah and his descendants. But Genesis speaks of a covenant with all living creatures and with the whole earth. Most exegetes completely ignore this fact. This self-evident anthropocentrism can be compared with the equally self-evident androcentrism that places man, and the one-sided male gaze, in the middle.[118] In the same way, one always refers to the Abraham narratives as if Sarah has no significant part in them.

As one was on the lookout for forgotten women in the Bible with the rise of feminist exegesis, one is now often in search of forgotten green texts. Many beautiful things are to be found, as one can see whilst going through the selection made by the *Green Bible*. But more needs to be done. Many thorny texts that have had a negative influence on the way the environment was treated remain unchallenged.[119] One needs a method that looks for texts that both inspire us and enable us to explain other seemingly less attractive passages differently. Feminist exegesis found three approaches that can be combined.[120] They are also useful for an ecological exegesis that:

- reads the Bible from a tradition of liberation, liberating not just for men, but also for women; not only for all humans but for the whole world
- looks for opposing voices in the texts, i.e. voices of women in texts where men are centre stage, and the voice of the earth in an anthropocentric text
- composes an alternative canon consisting of biblical texts that in the context of gender inequality, in this case ecological crisis, are most relevant.

But the comparison between ecological and feminist exegesis goes only so far. In most biblical stories, men take the lead, and Scripture is altogether an androcentric and patriarchal book. According to some, the Bible is also an anthropocentric book because people are seen as more important than the rest of the earth.[121] But the Bible, in comparison with our culture, is certainly much more patriarchal but at the same time less anthropocentric. Many texts are really about the whole of creation. Historical-critical research has unearthed the patriarchal character of the Old Israelite culture, but 'these same historical methods have also uncovered the independent relationship of the ancient Israelites with all other living things' and their 'awareness of their own fragility and dependence, an awareness that led them to respect other parts of creation'.[122]

Thorny ecological texts can be read within the liberating tradition of the Bible by listening carefully to the opposing voices in the texts. Reading these texts within their literary and historical context will very often suffice. Then it will become clear, for instance, that humans are less the focus of Genesis 1, and that the idea that God will destroy the earth, which many fundamentalists take from the Bible, cannot be retrieved from Scripture. Reading in context entails at the same time bringing to the fore lesser-known texts, like the creation Psalms and Job.[123] These very often throw new light on all-too-familiar texts.

2.1.2 Relevant texts

There are many texts that are relevant from an ecological point of view. Some are always mentioned in debates on Scripture and ecology and are, therefore, essential for this book. Genesis 1 and 2 jump out, but there are other creation narratives and texts about the future of the earth and animals. I will also mention texts that I happened upon during my preaching practice and texts that gave me new insights when I started reading from an ecological perspective; the Samaritan woman at the well (John 4) is a case in point.

How God, humans and non-human nature interrelate within the whole picture is a question that comes in particular to the fore in creation narratives. Thus, we will begin by going through a considerable amount of creation texts. In the second part of this chapter, we will explore texts about animals. I would like to take a closer look at these texts because they involve non-human nature. The third part covers texts that we may sum up as 'saving of the world': texts on deliverance, liberation, God's kingdom, a new heaven and a new earth. We will see that the texts falling under this last category are not easily distinguishable from creation texts. Many Bible scholars and theologians hold on to a linear concept of time, using salvation history and eschatology as key concepts.[124] In the great diversity of texts certain trajectories and developments are discernible, but these cannot be arranged in a sequence that runs from primal beginning to the end of time. The frame 'salvation history' is much too linear to organise texts of creation and salvation.[125]

My division is thematic and more or less historical as I go from earlier to later Bible texts, partly following the canonical order. If needs be, I will not hesitate to jump back and forth from the Old to the New Testament, taking their reciprocal continuity seriously. I do not pretend to have given all relevant texts their due. Still, all texts dealt with should be enough to fundamentally question the modern worldview that contributed to the ecological crisis and, subsequently, provide a wider ecological perspective.

Ongoing interpretation

Moving from the context of Scripture to our context always requires a certain amount of exertion. Bible texts were at all times transmitted through a process of ongoing interpretation.[126] Up until their definitive, canonical status, texts were prone to change. A new context prompted an altered way of telling the same story. Differences in situations, interests and opinions ensured a great variety in traditions in the Bible. Texts were continually recycled; there was really no other way.[127] Every text demands interpretation. Exegesis is an ongoing interaction between different texts and contexts. Texts are never utterly new; previous texts will at all times resonate, and the reader re-assimilates them in her or his situation. That doesn't mean that every interpretation is equally true, valuable or meaningful. 'In the Bible books themselves there already is a conversation going on.'[128] Reading the Bible entails participating in this ongoing conversation. Behind the different voices in the Bible I hear God's voice and through that conversation God's spirit blows.

2.2 CREATION STORIES

If, in common parlance, 'the creation story' is mentioned, one generally refers to chapters 1, 2 and 3 of Genesis. These three chapters have had the greatest impact on what most people throughout time have thought of creation. That we actually discern more than one creation story is something on which theologians agree. The chapters just mentioned already contain two different versions. But which other Bible texts could also pass as creation stories is more contested. Do these narratives and poems only explain how it all began or do they also speak about God's relation with everything that exists? Creation is a theological category that cannot be unequivocally defined. Do the following texts, for instance, fit in: Psalm 104 ('You stretch out the heavens like a tent'), John 1 ('In the beginning was the Word') and Romans 8 ('the whole creation has been groaning in labour pains')? I think they do, like all other texts that speak of a beginning or contain the word creation/creating/creator.

The Old Testament uses several verbs that can be translated as creating, each with its own meaning. A separate noun for creation appears only in the New Testament: *ktisis*, which can mean both the act of creating and its outcome (creation/world or creature). Everything that exists, the whole of reality, is being called 'heaven and earth' or – only in the New Testament – *cosmos*.

2.2.1 The coming into existence of the cosmos: Genesis 1—2:4

Creation and evolution, image of the cosmos

> *In the beginning, when God separated heaven and earth,*
> *and the earth was without fundament and ground*
> *and darkness was over the deep,*
> *and God's breath was blowing over the waters,*
> *God said: 'Let light be' and light was.* (Gen. 1:1—3)[129]

The image of the cosmos in Old Israel did not differ from the image that its neighbours upheld.[130] The description of Genesis 1 agrees with Sumerian and Akkadian texts. The shared worldview pictures the earth as a flat disc with water above and underneath it; the firmament with its heavenly bodies is stretched out as a cupola, and the space beyond heaven also contains water. Older biblical texts mention three spheres: heaven, earth and the deep under the earth. Later texts mention a partition in two, heaven and earth. The concept of God abiding in heaven is of a later date.

The biology of Old Israel differs completely from ours. Plants are not counted with living creatures; they belong to the earth, and are scarcely systematically distinguished into separate species. In the Old Testament we find for instance a grouping of trees and low-growing vegetation, but a generic term for plant is missing. Animals are classified in several ways, sometimes according to their habitats, sometimes according to whether they might be eaten or sacrificed.[131]

The creation poem of Genesis 1—2:4 is often referred to in discussions on the connection between creation and evolution. 'Modern readers, unfamiliar with stories as vehicles of serious thought, find it difficult to appreciate the depth and enduring meaning of these chapters.'[132] They take the narrative for a factual report and compare it to modern scientific theories about earth's age and the origin of species. Because of this, many reformed and evangelical Christians reject the theory of evolution as contradictory to the Bible's creationism. Other people following a similar line of reasoning come to the opposite conclusion, namely that the Bible is simply out of date.[133] Apart from the fact that the whole exercise amounts to comparing two incomparable quantities – Genesis is not interested in history and science in the modern sense of the word – many of those wanting to be strictly faithful to Scripture are inconsistent in their reasoning. Earth, for instance, is clearly depicted as a flat disc, yet very few creationists maintain that the earth is flat. Why then do they hold on to the conviction that the cosmos was created in six days or six periods, sticking firmly to the order mentioned in Genesis 1? Trying to read evolution into Scripture, as others do, is, by the way, equally debatable.[134]

Contents and composition

Because Genesis 1 has been so influential, and everyone seems to already have a clear picture of its meaning, it becomes even more necessary to interpret carefully right from the start what the text actually conveys. The majority of creation theologies take only God's speaking as the act of his creating. This entails quite a reduction of the text, which pictures God's creating as far more diverse. Genesis 1 also demonstrates a process of separating and ordering. Creating implies 'making' and 'naming' too.[135] 'Blowing', 'letting it grow' and 'blessing' may also be added to these acts. The whole structure is like a song with its rhythm, variations, intervals and refrain. Genesis 1 is sheer poetry.[136]

The first verse is mostly interpreted as the title of the text that follows: 'In the beginning God created heaven and earth',[137] Another option is 'From the beginning God is creator of heaven and earth'.[138] (The advantage of this last translation is that it prevents historicised reading:

creation is an ongoing process.) The NRSV follows another tradition that translates verse 1 as the beginning of a sentence that continues in the next:[139] 'In the beginning when God created the heavens and the earth, the earth was a formless void.' 'God creates and divides heaven and earth, the heavenly bodies and earth's denizens, everything closely and mutually linked, but at the same time set apart by clearly marked distances.'[140] The starting position of this reading is not that there was previously nothing at all: earth existed already, a formless void, or formless and empty or without fundament and ground.[141] A mass of water is covered in darkness; God's breath/Spirit/wind is present and moves – hovers, blows or breeds. Most expositors allow God's creating activities to begin in verse 3. God acting is described with verbs that signify taking apart (in place) and separating (in time). Light and darkness are in such a way divided, and water is separated in two, one part kept under the earth and one part above the earth. Creating in the sense of making something new starts in verse 7, with the stretching out of heaven's vault. Dry land becomes visible because of the assembling of water. Other texts describe the way God lays the foundation of the earth.[142] The imagery is that of a disc placed on pillars. 'You set the earth on its foundations, so that it shall never be shaken' (Ps. 104:5).

The fifth day, fragment of 'The Tapestry of Creation', Girona, Spain, twelfth century[968]

Then God lets life come into existence and makes the heavenly bodies that arrange life into day and night and seasons. God lets water swarm with living creatures and lets the birds fly high up across the dome of the sky. God creates or divides these animals into three groups: great sea monsters, the living creatures in the water and the birds of every kind. Earth brings forth by itself the plants and the animals. On the same day as earth brings forth cattle, creeping things and wild animals, God makes people. They are blessed and are commanded to be fruitful, like the beasts of the sea and the birds; they are given plants to eat, just as the animals are. They must subdue the earth, rule over the fish, the birds and the beasts that crawl on earth. The huge sea monsters and the wild animals do not fall under their dominion. Humans are made in God's image. A refrain recurs: and God saw that it was good. On the sixth day, when God looks at everything he has made, God closes by saying: very good! On the seventh day God rests and hallows this day. This explains the origin of the Sabbath.

The first to the third day and the fourth to the sixth run parallel.

The beginning: the earth is a formless void; darkness is on the face of the deep. God's Spirit is over the face of the waters.	
Day 1 Day and night	Day 4 Heavenly bodies
Day 2 Sea and heaven's vault	Day 5 Sea life and birds
Day 3 Dry land and plants	Day 6 Land animals and humans
Day 7 God's work is finished. God rests, blesses the seventh day and hallows it.	

'Subduing the earth' and 'having dominion over the animals'?

The importance of Genesis for an ecological theology stands without reason, but what precisely do we learn from it? Traditional exegesis emphasises the uniqueness of humans. Lynn White signalled the effective history (*Wirkungsgeschichte*) of verses 26–28 as fundamental for anthropocentrism in Christianity. But many eco-theologians show that here humans are just part of a bigger picture, creatures among other creatures. Crowning creation is not human beings but the Sabbath. People are created on the same day as the animals of the earth.[143] People share their food with the animals. Life is depicted as being interconnected and reciprocally dependent. Not only humans but nature as a whole is basically good, because God saw that it was good.

But does the notion of dominion not imply human superiority and being the first to be served? Is an anthropocentric approach not backed by Scripture? Verses 26–28, about people, are problematic, viewed ecologically. According to David Horrell, 'This text proves one of the hardest to defend against the criticism that the Bible may generate a view of human superiority and vocation that insufficiently values the rest of the earth community.'[144] From the time of the Church Fathers, this passage has been brought forward to emphasise the uniqueness of people within creation, although this was phrased in a theocentric frame of mind when the anthropocentrism of the Renaissance, the Enlightenment and modern science was still a long way off. That humans were, like God, endowed with reason in contradistinction from 'unreasonable' animals stems from Greek philosophy.[145] In the middle ages, the term *dominium terrae* – the dominion of the earth – came into use, based on Genesis 1:26–28 in combination with Genesis 2:15 ('God, the Everlasting, took the man and put him in the garden of Eden to till it and keep it'), Genesis 9:2–3 ('The fear and dread of you shall rest on every animal of the earth […], into your hand they are delivered') and Psalm 8:5–6 ('Yet you have made them a little lower than God, and crowned them with glory and honour. You have given them dominion over the works of your hands; you have put all things under their feet').[146]

There is some discussion about the exact meaning of the words that are translated as 'having dominion over' and 'subduing'. We have plenty of arguments to counter the subsequent interpretation that influenced these words, because human dominion as image of God can never imply conquering, but signifies caring and allowing something to flourish. In Scripture, a human being, even a king, can never be an absolute ruler, but is always accountable to God.[147] 'Ruling' appears already in verse 16: 'God made the two great lights – the greater light to rule the day and the lesser light to rule the night – and the stars.' According to exegetes, this form of ruling has no specific connotations and is purely functional. Could likewise human ruling be taken as a simple fact, that is, that humans are on the whole the dominating species on earth? As the sun and the moon are domineering of heaven's vault,[148] so are humans dominant on earth. Fear for wild animals in Genesis 9 can also be seen as plain fact. And in Psalm 8, dominion does not entail a commandment. We'll take a closer look into these texts later on.[149] In short, 'having dominion over' and 'subduing' should be put into perspective.

Moreover, one should ask, who or what is being ruled over? The whole earth and all animals? Seen in context, it becomes quite obvious that the earth is the shared habitat of men *and* animals. And there are good reasons to assume that earth specifically refers to land that is owned for growing food and domesticating animals. There are two arguments that favour this interpretation. The first argument considers the time when the text was conceived. When the people returned from exile, their biggest worry was whether the land could again provide for their sustenance. I will come to this in the next paragraph. The second argument is the fact that sea monsters and wild animals are not mentioned in these verses.

There are also reasons that explain the difficulty in countering the longstanding environment-unfriendly impact of this text. The most important is that 'subduing' definitely means 'conquering' and, therefore, in no way can be said to mean caring. To bring under dominion is what kings normally do with conquered territory. Besides, it is not the only text that perhaps not propagates but nevertheless assumes human dominion. For some people, this text expresses the dominating male ego that has caused by now more than enough suffering and, thus, deserves to be ousted from power. At the same time, these verses, which legitimised the exploitation of non-human species, created the very possibility of gender equality between people.[150] It's not just men who are made in God's image, but all people, from the very beginning.

Some voices cry out not to reject the text but rather the ecological approach. They infer from Genesis 1, Genesis 2 and Psalm 8 that men have received the commandment to subdue nature – and thus restore nature and deliver it from its curse – by turning the wilderness into a garden in order to satisfy humans' needs to the full.[151]

No human superiority

A way to take seriously both the text and the ecological approach is reading the text in the context of its time and after that asking oneself what its meaning is for our times. Genesis 1 was written at about the end of exile, when part of the captive people brought to Babel were returning to Judah. Genesis 2 and 3 were written earlier. What could have been the motive for adding another creation narrative to the one already existing?[152]

Genesis 1 is a form of resistance literature and intended to encourage the discouraged. The text reuses the creation myths of their oppressors and comes up with an alternative version. The *Enuma Elish* is the myth that legitimised the status of the Babylonian Empire and its god Marduk. In Genesis 1 humans receive their place among other living species in a world that is centred on Sabbath.

Unlike Genesis 2 and 3, nothing is said about prohibitions and the actual trespassing of these, neither the mentioning of deception nor curses. Guilty feelings after exile were in abundance. Exile was seen as the result of the disintegration of society, as punishment for injustice and idolatry. In that context the authors of Genesis 1 deliver a message of encouragement. 'Being made in the image of God, then, is not an assertion of human rationality and/or superiority. Rather, it declares to a disheartened people that they are worthy after all.'[153]

The emphasis on procreation – an aspect of this text – makes sense and is even a must when a people return to cultivate again a depopulated and devastated land. They have to survive and in order to succeed they have to be with enough people. This is the reason why people are not only compared to God, but also to animals: being fruitful as the sea animals and the birds (Genesis 1:20), as 'males and females'. The Hebrew words in verse 27 are only here used for humans; in Genesis 6 and 7 they are used for the animals in the ark. Subduing the earth and having dominion over the animals can thus be interpreted as a confirmation of people's power in a situation where they feel utterly powerless and useless.[154]

Eating plants signifies what animals and people have in common. In times of utter poverty, it is tempting to slaughter your cattle, but it is wiser to let them be. Animals are yet needed to cultivate the land and as means of transport. Besides, they also provide milk and eggs.

Seen from this context, it is unlikely to assume that the authors looked for a legitimisation of human superiority. They were altogether very much aware of their vulnerability and the reciprocal dependency of all living beings and they emphasised, on the contrary, what was apparently not obvious: people were good in God's eyes and could influence their environment. Current western culture has taken exactly opposite things for granted: hardly a notion of sin and a technocratic ethos of being in control. Moreover, if it comes to population size, there are rather too many people than too few. The commandment of verse 28 to be fruitful and multiply can, if taken literally, do only harm. We may interpret this commandment in the sense of stewardship, responsible management. In chapter three we will say more about this option. Or is it wiser and more in line with the Bible to consider this verse as no longer directed to us, modern people?

As we have put verse 28 in the context of the whole first creation narrative and its time, we can perceive much more clearly what the rest of the story means. We can take advantage of knowing the reciprocal relationship between all creatures and God's approval of the earth and all living creatures. People and animals share the land and the edible plants that the earth brings forth. God tells the people that the plants are also there for the animals in order to make them understand that the earth has more mouths to feed than just theirs. They may use the earth, but not unrestrictedly, and always respectfully towards other creatures. The notion of the earth as one big ecosystem is already apparent in Genesis 1, as is the notion that all creatures have their own value for God, and that a rich biodiversity is important.[155] The value of biodiversity comes to light in the repeated terms 'every' and 'of every kind', said of both plants and animals. Resting on the seventh day is a rule that goes against the grain of an economy that thinks in terms of unrestrained growth and a 24/7 production and consumption pattern.

If we temper the commandment to have dominion, the question remains what responsibility people have within the greater whole. This question will be taken up again and again in what follows. A provisional conclusion could well be 'the human dominion over other creatures is not the domination of superiors over inferiors but the responsibility of some creatures for their brother and sister creatures',[156] following the example of the king in Israel who is bound by all sorts of restrictions, stating 'neither exalting himself above other members of the community nor turning aside from the commandment, either to the right or to the left, so that he and his descendants may reign long over his kingdom in Israel' (Deuteronomy 17:20). Having dominion entails certainly having a role within creation, not being above it, and can signify either intervening or abstaining and letting be.[157] Not just people, but also the earth and the sea animals and the birds are required to bring forth their own species, and to be fruitful and plentiful.

Out of the deep – Genesis 1:2

Verse 2 is at least as influential and difficult to interpret as the verses on humans, but in a different way. As much as the existing translations of verses 26–28 hardly differ, the same cannot be said about this verse. Earth is *tohu wabohu*, waste and void, without form and void, formless void, without fundament and ground, chaos and desert, waste and deathlike.[158] And darkness was over the *tehom*: the deep/primal flood/ abyss. And there is *ruach* (literally: moving air), the breath/wind/Spirit of God, that moves/hovers/blows/breeds asunder (above) the waters. This poetic text can be translated in many ways and be interpreted on many levels. Much has been done with it that contradicts the text. The theological concept of creating out of nothing, *creatio ex nihilo*, became dominant. This may fit with the notions of 'formless void' and with 'darkness', but does not make a lot of sense considering the actual presence of earth and primal flood, God's breath even. Neither do the other creation texts from the Old Testament suggest that absolutely nothing pre-existed before God acted, at the most that nothing was visible. Van Wolde came to the following conclusion:

> Genesis 1,1-2 seems not to be a text about the absolute beginning of time, but about the beginning of a certain action. Subsequently this act that is mentioned in verse 1 seems not to be 'creating' but 'dividing'. And the beginning of this divide causes heaven and earth and not the third cosmic part, the subsoil mass of water or *tehom*, that already existed and continues to exist. Next comes verse 2 that describes the situation that God came upon before he started with this dividing. Earth existed already but was still covered with water and not yet based on pillars. The heaven as dome or vault would be made later on in the mass of water. At this very moment there is only this enormous mass of water shrouded in darkness and *elohim-*God. Later on, it becomes clear that in this mass of water *tanninim* or sea-monsters were there all along.[159]

Many theologians don't read in Genesis 1 a creation from nothing, but assume that what existed before God spoke was entirely bad. They identify the primal flood and darkness with evil. Although the sea is often seen in the Bible as a place of peril and in some other texts God is said to be striking down the monster or the monsters of the sea or will do so in the future,[160] in this verse this aspect seems totally absent. And even then, peril is not necessarily evil.

The New Bible Translation (in Dutch: NBV) initially added to the texts the words 'yet' (*nog*) and 'but' (*maar*) – 'The earth was *yet* deserted and deathlike, and darkness was over the primal flood, *but* God's spirit hovered over the waters' – and created thus an opposition between on the one hand the earth and the flood and on the other hand God's spirit. It gave the text an unjustifiable twist by suggesting a dualism. With the revision of the NBV these additions have luckily been removed. The Bible doesn't offer that dualism between spirit and matter that later became such a dominant feature, also of theology.[161] The first chapters of Genesis make it quite clear that all life comes forth from earth and God's spirit.

Creation from nothing, battle against evil, matricide?

An interpretation that offsets God with the waste and empty earth legitimises all too often a dualistic theology that places earth on the side of evil and sees God acting as freeing people from the earth. It becomes even more dangerous when evil and earth are both labelled as feminine. This, in fact, happened exactly in the Assyrian Babylonian creation myth *Enuma Elish*, to which the writers of Genesis 1 responded with their text.[162] In that myth, the primal state is taken up by big mother *Tiamat*, related to the biblical word *tehom*. She is slaughtered by the young warrior-god Marduk and from her bloody remains the earth is made. In *Enuma Elish* the world starts thus with matricide, the killing of the mother. From hymn 350 in the Dutch Hymn Book (*Liedboek*) one gets the impression that in Genesis also one is killing off the (motherly) womb of the earth ('*de aardse moederschoot*').[163] The first strophe goes like this: '*Het water van de moederschoot, dat is de diepte van de dood*' ('The water of the motherly womb, that is the very depth of death'). It could mean either the primal flood or the deluge. This hymn is very much in line with Karl Barth, who reads Genesis 1:2 as a parody of the image of the heathen mother goddess and the deep as *das Nichtige* (the invalid, insignificant, worthless), to which God answers with a clear no. According to Barth, 'in that monstrous sphere even the Spirit of Elohim ... is condemned to the complete impotence of a bird hovering or brooding over shoreless or sterile waters'.[164] Barth's theology may have been an antidote against the *Blut-und-Boden* ideology of the Nazis; he nonetheless appears to disqualify without batting an eyelid the feminine image of the earth and the feminine aspect of God. If poison is nowhere near, the effects of its antidote can be just as poisonous.

> Before the mountains were born or you brought forth the whole world, from everlasting to everlasting you are God. (Psalm 90:2, NIV)

The spirit is in the Old Testament feminine. There are similarities between the *tehom* – the deep, the primal flood – and the womb. Creating is compared to giving birth in Genesis 2:4. The translation runs: 'These are the generations of the heavens and the earth'. The word that is usually translated as history or generations means literally procreations. Hebrew has just one word, *jalad*, for the way men bring forth – procreate – and the bringing forth of women – giving birth.[165] The Dutch 'Statenvertaling' (1637) translates: '*Dit zijn de geboorten des hemels en der aarde*' ('These are the births of heaven and earth'). Considering the feminine imagery of Genesis 1:2, it is not at all far-fetched to see the universe as God's body, materialised from the deep as a cosmic body born from the deep, out of endlessness.[166] The spirit as a bird breeds not at all impotently – *pace* Karl Barth. The word that is translated in the Dutch NBV as 'hovering' is elsewhere translated as the flapping of wings that a bird does when it balances on the rim of its nest; it is accordingly a powerful moving.[167] The breath of God takes precedence and afterwards comes the word. There is no reason to contrapose in the text breath and word. It makes more sense to see that breath enables speaking. In Psalm 33:6, word and breath are almost synonymous in God's creative activity: 'By the word of the Everlasting the heavens were made, and all their host by the breath of his mouth.' In Genesis 8:1, God's breath makes the water of the deluge disappear.[168]

A dualistic reading of the second verse of Genesis has legitimised a negative image of women and the earth. That this is surely incorrect becomes clear from the verses that follow. God calls the light to come forth: 'Let there be light' [...] 'And God separated the light from the darkness.' Light and darkness are separated as water and land are separated. And as land and water were there all along, so were light and darkness.[169] The beginning as such is not sketching out hierarchical dualism of spirit and matter, good and evil, male and female, for it is from the deep of chaos that everything new comes forth.[170] Not then and never again, but again and again, in a non-historic interpretation.[171] The old image of a God dwelling in heaven who designs and checks the universe's structure and dynamics is surely not what Genesis 1 makes of it.[172] God's activity is partly a making, but even more a calling forth, letting be, making its existence possible: 'it must … come'. The translation 'let it … come' is also possible and even preferable, as it doesn't bring up associations with forcing, and certainly doesn't sound as an order. God lets it be, and it is the earth that brings forth green life and all manner of living creatures (verses 12 and 24). Verse 25 is almost a repeat of 24. 'Let the earth bring forth living creatures of every kind […] and 'God made the wild animals of the earth of every kind […]' are here practically synonymous.

Its refrain is 'And God saw that it was (very) good' – not 'God said', but 'God saw', as if God were happily surprised with what the earth brought forth.[173] God serves out the freedom to be and calls it repeatedly 'tov'.[174]

The following hymn of Iona is very appropriate.[175]

She sits like a bird, brood-ing on the wa-ters, hover-ing on the cha-os of the world's first day; she sighs and she sings, mo-ther-ing cre-a-tion, wait-ing to give birth to all the Word will say.

The primal water is also the water of the womb; everything comes forth from it if the spirit breeds. Something new comes from God's speech: light, heaven and earth, life, we humans. The creation is like a giving of birth set in motion through the Word. In the next strophe the spirit is linked with Noah's dove and Lady Wisdom, who both look on earth for a place to settle.[176] Then the song continues with the Spirit that inspires prophecy, Pentecost, the Trinity and the Church. God's Spirit that creates is the same that inspires prophecy; the Spirit that is 'Gifted by the Saviour in eternal love'.

A new reading of Genesis 1

So, in Genesis 1, everything does not revolve solely around people. It is a hymn that commences with God's Spirit that moves over the primal flood and terminates with God resting after seeing that everything turns out to be very good. Everything revolves around God, and is, therefore, theocentric. Humans have their own part in the greater whole in which everything is connected. They are creatures among creatures. Animals are pictured in all their diversity. Creating is an ongoing movement of God's Spirit that allows life to come into existence from what is undefined (unstable, chaotic, hidden) in interaction with earth and its inhabitants.

2.2.2 Paradise lost? Genesis 2 and 3
Contents and structure (Genesis 2)
The second creation narrative, which starts with Genesis 2:4, is not about the whole cosmos, nor about the waters under, above and around the earth, nor about heaven's vault and the heavenly bodies, but solely about the earth itself. It starts by summing up what is still not yet there: no plants, no rain, no people. And then what is already there: water that wells up from the earth and irrigates the ground everywhere. It commences thus with fertile soil and looks from a farmer's or gardener's perspective to the basis of existence. Then God makes man from earth, breathing life's breath in him, enabling him to become a living creature. God plants a garden and puts man in it to tend and watch over it. God enables trees to grow whilst a river irrigates the garden. Man may eat from every tree, says God, with the exception of the tree of good and evil.

Man needs a helpmate and God makes from earth all wild animals and birds. Man gives them, including the cattle, names. But a helpmate is still sorely missed. A helpmate appears after man is being split into two: male and female. Heterosexual marriage is in this way explained as being a reunion, a two-ness. Surprisingly, it is not the woman who leaves her family, as was common practice in patriarchal cultures and also in Old Israel, but the man who leaves his parents to join his wife.

Humans and animals made from earth and God's breath
This creation narrative underlines the bond between women and men and the rest of creation. Humans and animals – all animals living in the wild and all birds – are all made from dust, formed out of earth. Humans and animals share even the same breath of life: 'then

76

God, the Everlasting, formed man from the dust of the ground, and breathed into his nostrils the breath of life; and the man became a living being' (Genesis 2:7). That even animals are endowed with the breath of life becomes clear somewhat later: 'They went into the ark with Noah, two and two of all flesh in which there was the breath of life' (Genesis 7:15). Humans are ordered to tend the garden and watch over it. Some take Genesis 2:15 as a commandment to take charge of the whole earth. But in the same way as subduing and ruling in Genesis 1 did not involve the whole earth and all animals, there is no need to substitute the whole earth for the garden. Besides, the Hebrew tending – *abad* – means in general serving. And although 'watching over' – *shamar* – may mean keep a close watch (over something valuable against external danger), more often it is used in the sense of keeping, that is to say, the commandments.[177] If this commandment is applied to the whole earth, it is not obvious to accentuate the preparing of wild nature for cultivation, but rather serving and loving earth. The interconnectedness and interdependence of all creatures and the earth are in this story also emphasised.

This account underscores the earthy solidarity women and men have with each other and with the rest of creation. Far from being taken out of the natural world and placed over it, they are made of the same stuff, immersed in a web of reciprocal relations with the land and other creatures, and charged to reverence and serve, to carefully use and protect them.[178] Giving animals names implies recognition and creates trust.[179]

Cursed is the ground because of what you have done (Genesis 3)
In chapter 3, evil turns up for the very first time.[180] Late Jewish tradition and Paul see the 'fall' as of capital importance, as a decisive event between God, humans and the earth. Although some read this story as history and others take it as myth,[181] the interpretation almost always hinges on the question of what went fundamentally wrong or goes wrong in the correlation of God and the world. When this query,

as in the story, includes the earth, it becomes an ecologically relevant question. I will mention three different interpretations.[182]

According to Horrell, the story is about the difference between God and humans – humans are not immortal – and to explain the harshness of daily life.[183] In his exposition, the key passage is not the eating of the apple, but the cursing of the snake and the ground, and the consequences for the woman and the man (Genesis 3:14–19). The suffering, the toil and perils of life are accordingly explained, from the burden of pregnancy to the hard work on the land. Important from an ecological point of view is verse 17: 'cursed is the ground because of you; in toil you shall eat of it all the days of your life'. The ground, the earth from which humans and animals are made, becomes the dust that the snake will eat (Genesis 3:14), the dust to which humans will eventually return: 'By the sweat of your face you shall eat bread until you return to the ground, for out of it you were taken; you are dust, and to dust you shall return.' The cursing of the ground is seen as an outcome of human disobedience.[184] This sounds most timely for our age: the ground is also badly marked by the results of human activities.

Although the text is a realistic rendition of life's burdens, it also implies that it should be altogether different. In the prophecies of salvation of the biblical prophets the ground, the earth, is frequently mentioned. Thus, Joel does not call out exclusively to all the children of Sion to be joyful and to the animals in the fields to be no longer scared, but also the fields: 'Do not fear, O soil; be glad and rejoice, for the Everlasting has done great things!' (Joel 2:21).[185] There is also salvation for the soil. Even the soil has to keep Sabbath, which, according to Leviticus 25, should occur every seventh year.[186]

The agrarian revolution as fall

The authors of *The Good Book of Human Nature: An Evolutionary Reading of the Bible*, biologist Carel van Schaik and historian Kai Michel, also recognise in this narrative a depiction of life's burdens.[187] They read the Bible as rendering prehistoric developments. The fall is taken as a distinct phase in history, viz. the prehistoric agrarian revolution, when humans as hunter-gatherers gradually turned into herders of cattle and farmers and, subsequently, became city dwellers.[188] This revolution, according to the authors, is the biggest mistake that humankind made; it created a lot of hunger, disease and violence. Their misery made people yearn for the time that they were still living in harmony with nature; theirs was a longing for paradise lost.[189] The authors have their own atheistic agenda. Believing in God is seen as an outdated mode to interpret all the problems that we now face. As people in biblical times didn't know anything about the causes of diseases, bad harvests and natural disasters, they imagined an angry God and laid all the blame on women. Positive and negative commandments were necessary to win over God and to keep women at bay, according to the authors.

The amount of theology involved in their approach is quite striking. The classical concept of fall, paradise lost and the sinful state of the world is their outline of the history of humanity up to the present. There are many things to be said against this approach. I will mention just three. The first is that projecting a paradise in a primal era (or in a faraway future) may be tempting but implausible. Although the society of hunter-gatherers was apparently more egalitarian than our modern society, still an estimated one in five died because of violence. In short, this was no paradise at all. Furthermore, in the Middle East this society was already gone 9,000 years before the Bible came into being. My main objection is that the linear construal of history figuring the good lying in the past or in the future does no justice to what the Bible states about God's actual presence in created reality. This, my last, demurral will turn up regularly in this and the coming chapters.

God as gardener

The French Dominican Christophe Boureux reads Genesis 3 not historically but symbolically.[190] He does this with a background in Catholic theology, French philosophy and psychoanalysis. Starting from the ecological crisis, he asks what is fundamentally wrong in the correlation of humans, God and nature. The fall indicates, according to him, that humans are guilty of appropriating life. Humans do get life to look after, but they may not call themselves owners. Life has to be looked after and protected, someone has to take care of it.[191] This is the reason why it is screened off in an enclosed, distinctive, area: a garden. Work is not the outcome and punishment of their sinning. In the garden of Eden people do work, viz. they tend it.

The prohibition not to eat of the fruit of the tree of the knowledge of good and evil is not a restriction of their freedom, but a warning: don't disturb the connection between God and created reality. By eating of the tree, man robs God of his power as the only giver of life. Eating from the tree of knowledge of good and evil is, therefore, like eating from the tree of life: you extricate life from its source. It is in fact one tree, says Boureux, although the Jewish and the Christian traditions take it sometimes as one and sometimes as two trees.[192] Boureux takes it as one that shows itself 'in the middle of the garden' in two ways: as tree of knowledge of good and evil *and* as tree of life. When humans have been found guilty of appropriating life they hide 'between the trees' (Genesis 3:8). But the loss of life cannot be made up by hiding behind the tree of life.[193] Humans are driven out of paradise. Eating from the tree of life would make them like God, and that is what now happens. But humans cannot live with this knowledge. The expulsion from paradise brings them in 'time' (outside of eternity) and teaches them that life is given, and that to stay alive one has to work for it and to take care of it. Humans have to be screened off from the option to live as God in eternity.[194] The tree of life in Paradise 'characterizes God's direct and patent presence and the tree of knowledge characterizes God's presence in our conscious that speaks up, if need be'.[195] Knowing this entails that 'man has not made himself, but he has received life from someone else, that he doesn't exist just for himself but in order to sustain life'.[196]

The garden of Eden falls outside of time (*chronos*) and place.

It has no fixed time or place. Paradise loses, therefore, its traits of utopian fiction, according to Boureux, but stays what Foucault would call *hétérotopie* (another place). It is both place and no-place, like an image that appears in a mirror. One sees oneself in the mirror and also in the room where one is, but located beyond the glass of the mirror. Through the mirror, in the mirror image, you can be seen, but you cannot be found where you are seen. Foucault called these places other places because it suggests order; what is not there is still imagined as real. Thus, the garden of Eden is also the image of a place where something is to be seen that does not really exist, but at the same time cannot be called nowhere. Paradise is a pageant of real life, something that we cannot accomplish on our own.[197]

Boureux draws parallels between the garden of Eden and the garden of Jesus' sepulchre where the risen Christ meets Mary (John 20). The impossible happens right at the moment that Mary Magdalene lives with the certainty of the dead Christ but, whilst standing in front of the open sepulchre – also a *hétérotopie* – all of a sudden, she encounters the living Christ. Appropriating the living is impossible ('do not hold on to me'), but this encounter impels her to give witness to the resurrection.[198] The encounter between Maria and 'the gardener' in front of the open sepulchre gives room to the garden and resembles the enclosed garden of Eden: the angels present at the garden's gate are on the border between divine and worldly territories. The enclosed garden of the sepulchre also mirrors the closed eyes of Mary, who doesn't recognise Jesus because the risen one is unperceivable through discursive reasoning.

> Maria who wants to take Jesus's body as Eve took the fruit, Maria being called by her name as God does when he is looking for Adam, and Christ who signifies the tree of life and the tree of knowledge. These images have been repetitively used in Christian iconography such as the image of the tree of the cross that is planted on top of Adam's bones.[199]

With Boureux, the image of Jesus as gardener coincides almost with that of God strolling in the garden of Eden. God as gardener is a metaphor of the connection between God and creation. Boureux's application of the concept of heterotopy to Genesis 3 generates possibilities. His rendition is a beautiful alternative for the interpretation that takes the narrative as a description of a historical reality or a utopia, projected in the past, or just an explanation of the burdens of existence. The connection with the resurrection narrative according to John fits in with an old tradition and adds depth to the story by giving a role to nature. But there is a clear risk involved in placing all the blame for bringing evil into the world on women again: Eve takes the apple and Mary Magdalene wants to hold on to Jesus.[200]

How green is our couch

Thinking through Boureux, I come up with another connection between the garden and the resurrection, that is, the connection between Mary Magdalene and the woman of the Song of Songs.[201] Both women have lost their lover, are in search of him and want to hold on to him (Song of Songs 3:1—4). The lovers in Song of Songs use plants and animals as images to compare the attractiveness of the other; their love is described in smells and tastes of nature and their couch is green:

> *Ah, you are beautiful, my beloved, truly lovely.*
> *Our couch is green;*
> *the beams of our house are cedar, our rafters are pine.*
> (Song of Songs 1:16-17)

> *As an apple tree among the trees of the wood, so is my beloved among young men. With great delight I sat in his shadow, and his fruit was sweet to my taste.* (Song of Songs 2:3)

There is hardly any Bible book that contains more plants and animals as the Song of Songs. Both in the Jewish as in the Christian tradition, these sensuous songs of love are interpreted allegorically, as an image of the love between God and his people or of Christ and the church. Mystics also borrowed images of the Song of Songs to put into words what they experienced. The song became a way of telling how God and soul vied. A non-dualistic approach has the advantage of not automatically creating an opposition between a 'spiritual' and a 'material' interpretation. Besides, every text has more meanings, and that certainly applies to poetry. The smells, colours and tastes of flowers and fruits and love are connected with God's presence. Moreover, is the Song of Songs not celebrating in song some sort of paradise, perhaps even as heterotopy?

Approaching Genesis 3 by starting with the question 'What went wrong between God, humans and the earth?' served us well. To sum up, this chapter can be read as an explanation of the burdens of our existence. It teaches us that due to human interference the ground/earth doesn't fare well, and that God's salvation also includes the ground. By signalling historic events as fall, we do not take the text seriously; neither would that be the case if we were looking for a historical Adam and Eve. I read the text, like the rest of Genesis 1—11, as a mythical narrative that deals with deep insights into important subjects. The garden as heterotopy confronting us is then a beautiful interpretation. The fact that people are guilty of appropriating life is clearly appropriate to the current exploitation of the earth that does no justice to the correlation of God and creation.

The next chapters of Genesis are about the ongoing deterioration, the wickedness of humans, and how God regrets having made men and thus decides to destroy the whole earth. Important for eco-theology is to note that the deterioration of mankind and the rest of the earth are interconnected, which implies the same for their rescue. There is more about Genesis 6—9 in section 2.3.2 about the end and the new beginning of all living creatures.

2.2.3 Prophet of creation: Deutero-Isaiah

Creation and salvation are intimately connected in Deutero-Isaiah (40—55; the second part of the Book of Isaiah). The prophet resumes the exodus narratives of Exodus and Deuteronomy and joins them to God as creator to encourage the Babylonian exiles.[202]

Isaiah 40:12–31 and 42:5 – a creation narrative

Isaiah 40:12–31 is a somewhat longer text that has similarities with Genesis 1. Likewise, it starts with water: 'Who has measured the waters in the hollow of his hand and marked off the heavens with a span, enclosed the dust of the earth in a measure, and weighed the mountains in scales and the hills in a balance?' (v.12). The foundation of the earth is also mentioned: 'Have you not known? Have you not heard? Have you not been told from the beginning? Have you not understood from the foundations of the earth?' (v.21). And heaven is stretched out like a tent: 'It is he who sits above the circle of the earth, and its inhabitants are like grasshoppers; who stretches out the heavens like a curtain, and spreads them like a tent to live in' (v.22). God weighs the dust of the earth, the mountains and hills in a balance (v.12). God's activities are depicted as something that continues[203] – God stretches out the heavens like a curtain. The words 'who gives breath to the people upon it and spirit to those who walk in it' (Isaiah 42:5) remind us of Genesis 2.

God as maker and ruler reigns from his throne above heaven's vault (v.22). All God's creative activities are framed in the setting of his greatness: 'Who has directed the spirit of the Everlasting, or as his counsellor has instructed him?' (v.13). 'To whom then will you liken God, or what likeness compare with him?' (v.18). 'To whom then will you compare me, or who is my equal? says the Holy One?' (v.25). God's greatness is compared with humans, who are like grass (v.6), with peoples, who are like a drop in a bucket or a speck of dust on a balance (v.15), idols are just pieces of wood (v.19), and princes and leaders wither when he blows upon them (v.24). The 'creator of the ends of the earth' (v.28) gives power to the faint and strengthens the powerless (v.29).

'Thus the disputation brings together the themes of cosmogony[204] and the ongoing creation of the cosmos and of humans in one unified defence of the one God whose power made and sustains the universe.'[205] This is done partly by using the same verbs that appear in the beginning of Genesis: creating/dividing (*bara*') and forming (*yasar*). Nature and history are not opposed. God's activity affects both cosmos – 'He who brings out their host and numbers them [i.e. the stars]' (v.26) – and people.

Creation and salvation

Systematic theology generally dwells upon creation and salvation in two separate sections. In Isaiah, creation and salvation are not fundamentally different categories, no more than nature and history. In the following prophecy of salvation, they are intimately linked. God takes care of the poor and needy through the provision of water in the desert. The verb create (*bara*') is mentioned in this context.

> When the poor and needy seek water, and there is none, and their tongue is parched with thirst, I the Everlasting will answer them, I the God of Israel will not forsake them.
>
> I will open rivers on the bare heights, and fountains in the midst of the valleys; I will make the wilderness a pool of water, and the dry land springs of water.
>
> I will put in the wilderness the cedar, the acacia, the myrtle, and the olive; I will set in the desert the cypress, the plane and the pine together, so that all may see and know, all may consider and understand, that the hand of the Everlasting has done this, the Holy One of Israel has created it. (Isaiah 41:17–20)

In Isaiah 43:1–7, creating and redeeming/ransoming are linked: 'But now thus says the Everlasting, he who created you, O Jacob, he who formed you, O Israel: Do not fear, for I have redeemed you; I have called you by name, you are mine' (v.1). 'Do not withhold; bring my sons from far away and my daughters from the end of the earth –

everyone who is called by my name, whom I created for my glory, whom I formed and made' (v.7). The verb calling in this text is the same (*qara'*) as in Genesis 1:5, 8, 10 and 2:19, 23. God creates a people for himself, as God creates everything when he calls the exiles to return to their land.

Although the islands are called upon – 'Listen to me in silence, O coastlands' (41:1) – people are central in God's creative/salvific acting, according to Deutero-Isaiah. This can be explained due to the circumstances at the end of the exilic period, also the time that Genesis 1 was written, when the people were discouraged and they had to be told that God took an interest in them. Only Israel is the goal of his doing; later on we see how the perspective widens and all people and the whole world come into view. But neither Israel nor all peoples are mentioned as the objective of his creation: this is solely God's majesty (43:7).

2.2.4 The creation sings: the Psalms

In the Psalms, creation is an important motive for thanking and praising God. Praising is not only done by people but by all creatures:

> *Let the sea roar, and all that fills it;*
> *the world and those who live in it.*
> *Let the floods clap their hands;*
> *let the hills sing together for joy*
> *at the presence of the Everlasting* (Psalm 98:7–9)

Creation is a theme particularly in Psalms of praise and thanksgiving, but hardly in Psalms of lament and Royal Psalms.[206] Creation appears here in two fashions: as witness of God's greatness and herald of the praise to God.[207]

Creation as witness of God's greatness

As in Isaiah 40:12–31, some Psalms describe God's creative activities to portray God's greatness. In Psalm 136, creation is a sign of God's faithfulness. After a threefold call to praise God because he performs miracles, there follows:

> who by understanding made the heavens, for his steadfast
> love endures forever;
> who spread out the earth on the waters,
> for his steadfast love endures forever;
> who made the great lights,
> for his steadfast love endures forever;
> the sun to rule over the day,
> for his steadfast love endures forever;
> the moon and stars to rule over the night,
> for his steadfast love endures forever (Psalm 136:5–9)

The Psalm continues by depicting the exodus and repeating the refrain: for his steadfast love endures forever. Creation and salvation belong together, as in Deutero-Isaiah. These are God's wonders.

In Psalm 19 creation bears testimony to God's majesty. It does so without words, simply by existing:

> Day to day pours forth speech,
> and night to night declares knowledge.
> There is no speech, nor are there words;
> their voice is not heard;
> yet their voice goes out through all the earth,
> and their words to the end of the world. (Psalm 19:2–4)

Even as God starts creating with his breath, the Spirit, that carries the spoken word,[208] the creation doesn't need words to answer back. The human voice comes secondary.[209]

In Psalm 104 the earth is described as an ecosystem in which everything is interconnected and depends on God. After a call to praise God (vv.1 and 2) follows a description of the stretching out of heaven's vault like a tent, the clouds, wind and fire, and the putting of the earth on pillars and the separation of the waters (vv.2-9). From then on life appears on earth, in the air and in the sea in all its inner cohesion:

> *You make springs gush forth in the valleys;*
> *they flow between the hills,*
> *giving drink to every wild animal;*
> *the wild asses quench their thirst.*
> *By the streams the birds of the air have their habitation;*
> *they sing among the branches.*
> *From your lofty abode you water the mountains;*
> *the earth is satisfied with the fruit of your work.*
> *You cause the grass to grow for the cattle,*
> *and plants for people to use,*
> *to bring forth food from the earth.* (Psalm 104:10-14)

Verses 14 to 21 talk of woods and mountains and everything living in them, including humans. Then the sea: 'creeping things innumerable are there' (v.25). God sports with Leviathan.[210] It is God who feeds all living creatures (27-28) and through God's breath everything comes to life:

> *When you hide your face, they are dismayed;*
> *when you take away their breath,*
> *they die and return to their dust.*
> *When you send forth your spirit, they are created;*
> *and you renew the face of the ground.* (Psalm 104:29-30)

At the end of the Psalm the psalmist takes pleasure with God in everything God created and the psalm ends as it started: 'Bless the Everlasting, O my soul' (vv.31-36).

Psalm 104 contains the most vivid portrayal of the whole of creation as a community of creatures. Every one has received from God its own place in the world and has been provided for by God. Humans are only one of many creatures; God is of central importance:[211]

> Psalm 104 reserves a humble living space to people in the midst of an enormous variety of living creatures, and shows us the various ways that these other creatures flourish to the glory of God, each in its own way witnessing of his power and wisdom.[212]

People are called upon to praise God and to find joy in God and to take pleasure with God in the goodness of creation:

> *and wine to gladden the human heart,*
> *oil to make the face shine,*
> *and bread to strengthen the human heart.*
> *May my meditation be pleasing to him,*
> *for I rejoice in the Everlasting.* (Psalm 104:14-15,34)

People are not required to rule or manage the earth. The image of the earth is one of a substance that provides food for all its inhabitants, an image that altogether differs from its being cursed in Genesis 3.[213] Food comes from the earth and God, without any hint of an antithesis. There is nothing that resembles our western dualism that separates God and earth.[214] Neither do we see a separation between the act of creating and providing. God brings forth the earth and bestows on it life's breath, then, now and in the future.

Psalm 8 likewise bears testimony to God's greatness. People are just part of the whole creation; they even seem insignificant. But God's power comes to light in the weakest, the infants and babes.

> *O Everlasting, our Sovereign,*
> *how majestic is your name in all the earth!*
> *You have set your glory above the heavens.*

Out of the mouths of babes and infants
you have founded a bulwark because of your foes,
to silence the enemy and the avenger.
When I look at your heavens, the work of your fingers,
the moon and the stars that you have established;
what are human beings that you are mindful of them,
mortals that you care for them? (Psalm 8:1–4)

Following these verses comes the very notion that lends support to the idea that people were above creation, as in Genesis 1:26–28, and subsequently were given permission to exploit it to the full.[215]

Yet you have made them a little lower than God,
and crowned them with glory and honour.
You have given them dominion over the works of your hands;
you have put all things under their feet,
all sheep and oxen, and also the beasts of the field,
the birds of the air, and the fish of the sea,
whatever passes along the paths of the seas.
O Everlasting, our Sovereign,
how majestic is your name in all the earth! (Psalm 8:5–9)

But this Psalm contains wonderment, not permission to exploit. The Book of Job contains the same comparison voiced in the same grammatical construct: 'What are human beings, that you make so much of them, that you set your mind on them …' (Job 7:17). It should therefore be more logical to read the sentence 'you have made them a little lower than God' not as a statement but as part of the question and translate thus the whole thought in the form of a question: 'What are human beings that you are mindful of them, that you care for them, that you have made them almost a god, crowned them with glory and honour?' Then follows the crux: You have given them dominion over the works of your hands.[216]

The motives behind this line of reasoning appear to be the same as in Genesis 1: encouraging people in dire need, emphasising their power in a situation where they feel powerless and useless; they may use the earth whilst keeping in mind that they are very much part of the greater whole of heaven and earth.[217]

The creation brings praise to God

That creation is bringing praise to God is a recurrent theme of the Psalms. And not just there. Joel 2:21–22 has already been mentioned,[218] and Deutero-Isaiah offers texts such as:

> *Sing, O heavens, for the Everlasting has done it;*
> *shout, O depths of the earth;*
> *break forth into singing, O mountains,*
> *O forest, and every tree in it!* (Isaiah 44:23)

A call to the whole earth – and sometimes also heaven – to cry out for joy and praise God can be found in Psalm 66:1–4, 69:35, 96:1,11–12, 97:1 and 98:4–9. A variation on this trope is the call to all breathing creatures to praise God, found in Psalm 103:22 and 150:6. In the New Testament we come upon this notion in Philippians 2:10 and Revelation 5:13.

Psalm 148 is the most extensive Psalm of praise, if not in length then surely in range. It commences in heaven: 'Praise him in the heights [i.e. of heaven]'.[219] The inhabitants of heaven – angels, sun, moon and stars – are all commanded to give praise to God, because God has given them their place. Then follow the earth and what belongs to its sphere. Recall how people in the Old Middle East imagined the cosmos: a flat disc, water all around, and above that the dome of heaven with the sun, moon and stars and beyond that water again, which sometimes pours down through apertures as rain. And above all that water resides God with the angels. The Psalms give a vivid picture of the cosmos, from heaven above to the earth below:

Praise the Everlasting from the earth,
you sea monsters and all deeps,
fire and hail, snow and frost,
stormy wind fulfilling his command!
Mountains and all hills, fruit trees and all cedars!
Wild animals and all cattle, creeping things and flying birds!
(Psalm 148:7–10)

And then we see the people, from kings to young women. People, being part of the earth, are gladly invited to join in this gigantic cosmic song of praise. A special place is given to the people of Israel – Israel, not all humanity – because they are near to God. Heaven and earth are a double choir that encompasses all beings.

Much of this Psalm can be found in the praise of the Burning Fiery Furnace. In Catholic Bible translations it is to be found as Daniel 3:51–90. Protestant Bible translations do not include or list these as additions to Daniel.[220]

Mountains can (not) break out into singing

The whole idea of mountains singing is for modern people scarcely imaginable. Since the Enlightenment we have become accustomed to see everything not-human as things and only people as persons able to act. Wim van der Zee adapted this song of praise from Daniel to make it more acceptable.[221] The Bible text runs as follows:

Mountains and hills, bless the Everlasting;
praise and exalt him above all forever.
Everything growing on earth, bless the Everlasting;
praise and exalt him above all forever. (Daniel 3:75–76 NABRE)

Van der Zee translates these words in the following way: 'mountain and hill [...] resonate loudly the echo of the joy to his honour'. The image is that of a landscape that echoes a song. Not the mountains and hills give praise. Who are the ones who really praise? Only people? In the next strophe the plants are mentioned; it is their turn to praise: 'Be a song of praise', translates van der Zee. That sounds more like a nosegay presented to God. The plants in hymn 154b are likewise no longer in charge of their own song of praise. The animals, on the other hand, do have a voice, in as much as they make a sound. Apparently, we can only figure animals as singers of praise in as much as they resemble us.

There is much to be said for taking the text more literally. Just because nature is figured in such a different way from that we are used to, Psalms can have so much more meaning for eco-theology. The whole of living and non-living nature praises God simply by being there. The clattering of water, the rushing of the trees can sound as clapping and rejoicing, but also the soundless heavenly bodies and the silent plants are parts of the creation that give praise to God. As people, we are part of this bigger whole, to be exact: part of earth's biosphere.

The fact that the psalmist calls all creatures doesn't mean that this calling is necessary in order to hear them praise God. Just by being there, they praise, without needing us to be reminded.[222] The call is grammatically comparable to the call of one's own soul: 'Praise the Everlasting, O mine soul' (Psalm 103:1 and many others), meaning so much as 'I praise the Everlasting.'

The Psalms are poetry and contain much imagery. These passages are also metaphorical in the sense that human imagery is substituted for non-human reality. They refer nonetheless to non-human reality and turn it into a subject in its own right. Nature is not just a metaphor for the human world. In pre-modern times, one definitely had fewer misgivings about non-human subjects. 'Thomas Aquinas (1225–1274) for instance ascribes to everything that lives feeling, desire and imagination, albeit in various grades, and considers their behaviour as clear proof of this.'[223] Think also of Saint Francis, who in the year 1224 or 1225, inspired by the Psalms, composed his Canticle of the Sun or Creation. It starts like this:

Most High, all powerful, good Lord,
Yours are the praises, the glory, the honour,
and all blessing.
To You alone, Most High, do they belong,
and no man is worthy to mention Your name.
Be praised, my Lord, through all your creatures,
especially through my lord Brother Sun,
who brings the day; and you give light through him.
And he is beautiful and radiant in all his splendour!
Of you, Most High, he bears the likeness.
Praised be You, my Lord, through Sister Moon
and the stars, in heaven you formed them
clear and precious and beautiful.
Praised be You, my Lord, through Brother Wind,
and through the air, cloudy and serene,
and every kind of weather through which
You give sustenance to Your creatures.
Praised be You, my Lord, through Sister Water,
which is very useful and humble and precious and chaste.
Praised be You, my Lord, through Brother Fire,
through whom you light the night and he is beautiful
and playful and robust and strong.
Praised be You, my Lord, through Sister Mother Earth,
who sustains us and governs us and who produces
varied fruits with coloured flowers and herbs.[224]

It is telling that in the version of the song that was included in the Dutch hymnbook of 1973, all praising was done not *through* but *for* the creatures. Another adaptation of the Canticle of the Sun appeared in the new hymnbook of 2013 and is more to my liking, but is still not unequivocal in allowing all creatures to go their own way. Many versions translate the Italian *per* as 'for', as, in the opening section of the Dutch version of the *Green Bible*, Liesbeth Goedbloed did in her translation of this Canticle.

Francis understood the Psalms of creation. We lost this notion with modernity. With the help of postmodern insights on being a subject and a person, it becomes possible to understand them anew. In the poststructuralism of Michel Foucault, the subjectivity of humans was relativised: people are not autonomous individuals, but are constantly formed and influenced through their environment.[225] Animals appear, in the meantime, more subject and individual than what was long thought. The behaviourist idea that animals are just driven by their instincts is already rendered out of date thanks to ethological research. Primatologist Frans de Waal showed beyond doubt that traits for a long time seen as typically human behaviour, like self-consciousness, a sense of justice and empathy, were also to be found in animals.[226] In the animal rights movement, animals are recognised as persons. Plants differ far more from people than animals and are therefore seen as the lowest form of life, says plant neurophysiologist Stefano Mancuso.[227] They do not resemble animals and humans, who are undividable organisms with organs and a central command centre (brains), but they can be divided and have a structure like the internet, having a type of swarm-intelligence. According to Mancuso, plants are equipped with more senses than humans. In the social sphere, they resemble people in as much as they are able to orientate, communicate and recognise their family.[228]

In post-humanistic philosophy, man is no longer the measure of everything.[229] Every contraposition of person and thing is negated, in the same way as in current natural sciences.[230] If being a person entails the ability to orientate, handle and develop, and in this to differ from fellow members, the same can be claimed for plants. If a certain accommodation and individuality is enough to be called a person, the boundary between thing and person is pushed even further. The Whanganui, a river in New Zealand, officially received in 2014 the status of a legal person. This happened at the request of the Māori people. Thus, a conflict over the interpretation of an agreement that had lasted from 1840 came finally to an end. The British initially thought that they were the owners of the river. They took advantage of the fact that the Māori didn't know this concept of ownership and thought about nature in terms of relationship, as between people, not in terms of owning. The river as legal person or entity is a compromise between two conflicting worldviews. Guardians are now appointed to look after the interests of the river.[231]

These insights dating from before, after and outside of modernity support a horizontal model of fellow creatures, which is voiced in most Psalms of praise. This model counters within the Bible the ruling of people taken from Genesis 1 and the idea from Psalm 8 that everything was put under the command of people. Each creature praises God in its own way. A voice is as such not obligatory. A beech lives to honour God by growing and to communicate in a way that fits the species and that also differs slightly from its fellow beeches.[232] A frog praises God by croaking, but also by just being there. People are not necessary for nature to phrase its own praise. Our fellow creatures can teach *us* to learn to praise without words, according to Bauckham:

> It is distinctively human to bring praise to conscious expression in voice, but the creatures remind us that this distinctively human form of praise is worthless unless, like them, we live our whole lives to God's glory.[233]

> In fact, it is much more obvious that other creatures can help us to worship God than that we can help other creatures to.[234]

That the world sings God's praise by being there sounds maybe a bit romantic, even too beautiful to be true, as if there were no suffering in the world. It certainly contains some element of wishful thinking, as if to say: Ah, let everything be as God initially had in mind … May your Kingdom come. In the meantime, creation is groaning in labour, as Paul said (Romans 8:22).[235] Praise and suffering are by no means contradictory. Very often people who are experiencing great hardships abide by the song of praise of all creation. Francis of Assisi was, at the time he was composing his Canticle, very ill and on the brink of losing all hope. Even the men thrown in the fire by King Nebuchadnezzar, and, not to forget, Job, in all his suffering, sang hopefully God's praise against all evil and misery.

2.2.5 Job's suffering in context

Creation has a prominent part in the Book of Job, especially in the last chapters. The image of the cosmos is as found in other texts: the earth-disc lying on water with heaven's vault above it. God's activities are described in the same fashion. God divides, makes, limits, measures, founds, moulds and brings forth. Adding to this comes a motive that has not been mentioned yet: God's wisdom. Wisdom, personified as a woman, is also a component of creation.

Contents and structure

Job is listed under wisdom literature.[236] The beginning and the end – Job 1—2 and 42:7–17 – are written in prose and function as story frame. The other chapters are poetry and are from a literary point of view very beautiful.

The story pictures Job as suffering patiently. His sufferings are in the end lifted as in a fairy tale. In the end he receives more than he initially lost. The loss of his children, his belongings and his health are the result of a wager between God and Satan. The bet is: will Job be steadfast in his belief and in his righteousness if he loses everything? In Job 3—42:6 we hear Job, his wife and his friends speaking. Job rejects the explanations of his friends and the consolation they try to offer. He brings a charge against God.

Both Job and his friends refer frequently to the creation, sometimes in an act of praise, sometimes to level an accusation against someone or to reproach, sometimes to support an argument. Thus Eliphaz recommends Job to leave everything to God to judge, whose ways are inscrutable anyway, like his sending of rain (5:8 etc.). In his second discourse Eliphaz wants to silence Job: 'Are you the firstborn of the human race? Were you brought forth before the hills?' (15:7). Job throws this in God's face: 'Your hands fashioned and made me; and now you turn and destroy me?' (10:8). Job also refers extensively to the creation in chapter 28. Men can do much, like digging deep into the earth to extract silver, gold, iron and copper, but it doesn't bring them any nearer to wisdom. God is the only one who knows wisdom, he who was there from the very beginning: 'When he gave to the wind its weight, and apportioned out the waters by measure; [...] then he saw it and declared it; he established it, and searched it out (28:25–27). Through the wind God apportioned out the boundaries of the primal waters.[237] Wisdom is already present before creation. People are wise if they fear God and depart from evil (28:28).

Ecologically speaking, the last chapters, 38—42, are of utmost importance. In the surprising answer that God in the end gives to Job, it comes to the fore how important non-human creation really is. The text is all about nature, which does not reckon with humans. Unlike Genesis, the Book of Job doesn't speak of people having dominion over creation. People simply lack the knowledge, the abilities and the power to do so.[238]

Job 38—42:6 God's answering in the storm, contents and structure

God's answer to Job consists of two discourses, interrupted by two short reactions coming from Job: 'Gird up your loins like a man, I will question you, and you shall declare to me' (38:3).[239]

The first part of the first discourse, 38:1-38, deals with inanimate nature: earth and water, light and darkness, rain, snow, winds and clouds etc. The questions run 'Where were you ..., Who ..., Where ..., Can you ..., Do you know...?' 'Where were you when I laid the foundation of the earth?' (38:4). 'Can you send forth lightnings, so that they may go and say to you, "Here we are"?' (38:35). The image in verses 1–15 is that of God being a foreman giving directions, laying down boundaries, measuring with a rod, placing a cornerstone, hanging a door.

The second part of the first discourse, 38:39—40:2, deals with wild animals, again posing a string of questions. Ten animal species are mentioned: lion, raven, mountain goat, deer, wild ass, wild ox, ostrich, horse, hawk and eagle. What they have in common is their fierceness, freedom and their awesomeness. In old-eastern iconography, they are often depicted in combination with a sovereign, sometimes symbolising harmony, e.g. with a tree of life. A short reaction is given by Job in 40:3–5. Job puts his hand on his mouth and promises to say nothing more.

God's second discourse, 40:6–41:26, zooms in on two animals: Behemoth and Leviathan. They have the traits of the hippopotamus and the crocodile respectively, but from the very description they appear to be mere primal monsters.[240] They are fiercer and more indomitable than the other wild animals: 'Even if the river is turbulent, it is not frightened; it is confident though Jordan rushes against its mouth' (40:23) and 'Its breath kindles coals, and a flame comes out of its mouth' (41:21).

Job reacts for the last time in 42:1-6: 'I had heard of you by the hearing of the ear, but now my eye sees you' (42:5). Verse 6 is difficult to interpret: does Job drop his charge; has he been righted or has the verdict been inconclusive? Is he remorseful, submitting or rather consoled?

Knowledge and battle against evil?

God's discourses are the longest texts dedicated to non-human creation in the Bible. God in his discourses doesn't refer to Satan or Job (the guinea pig), who were the main characters of the first two chapters. The wager between God and Satan is missing altogether. The general assumption is that the first chapters are a later addition to the main story. Still, what remains unexplained is to what extent God's discourses meet the complaints and sufferings of Job. Job has called God to account. Why does God answer in the way he does?

first discourse of God	38:1–38	inanimate nature	cosmogenesis, God as foreman
			earth/water, light/darkness
			weather phenomena
	38:39—40:2	wild animals	
first reaction of Job	*40:3–5*	*Job promises to be silent*	
second discourse of God	40:6—41:26	primal monsters	Behemoth
			Leviathan
second reaction of Job	*42:1-6*	*Job's conclusion*	

According to traditional explanation, God just shows how mighty he is. God subsequently humiliates Job and so silences him. God is, in short, pictured as a powermonger, whilst wild animals illustrate his power; men, in comparison, are just powerless and guilty. Thus, the picture we get is more or less that of a raging God and a human being in the act of submission, while the meticulously depicted animals hardly matter at all. What makes this explanation so unsatisfactory is its macho image of God and the negative part nature plays.[241]

Jan Boersema's approach does more justice to the depiction of nature in the Book of Job. He contends that God shows the way the cosmos is structured, including its innate chaos; God is certainly not the maker of evil but the one who views chaos and fights it.[242] In this scenario, man is not looked upon by an angry God as being insignificant; no, God sides with Job. Once Job has come to recognise this fact, he finds solace. Job finally understands that evil doesn't work according to laws, as his friends were trying to point out to him. They claimed all along that he was to be blamed for being pestered by evil, because God who is good and mighty could never be its instigator. What's more, God proves himself to be a trusty companion in the battle against evil. One lesson that can be learned from Job's history is that there is order and regularity in the cosmos. Although humans can gradually grasp more of this, human knowledge remains limited, and the really big question will equally remain unsolved. Unanswered is also the question about the existence of evil; nevertheless, it is given a new perspective in the recognition of the limitation of human knowledge.

The strength of this explanation lies in the fact that it uses knowledge as the key concept to interpret God's answer to Job. Knowledge, including knowledge of nature, is an important theme in wisdom literature as all knowledge and insight are founded on God's wisdom, residing in creation. It was already said regarding Solomon's wisdom that he was very knowledgeable about nature (1 Kings 4:32–33).[243] People should take pride in being taught by Lady Wisdom. Still, it remains a mooted question what particular insight Job obtains from God. The downside of this approach is that it is prone to dualism, as it equals chaos and evil, and demonises the monsters. As in Genesis 1, this dualism cannot be inferred from Job.

The monsters

Some texts do mention Leviathan or another monster that has to be defeated. In Psalm 74:13–14, sea monsters are beaten by God. Leviathan in this Psalm stands for Babylon, which has come to invade Israel. God's mighty arm brings salvation by crushing the monster's head. Isaiah 27:1 defers the killing of Leviathan to the future: 'On that day the Everlasting with his cruel and great and strong sword will punish Leviathan the fleeing serpent, Leviathan the twisting serpent, and he will kill the dragon that is in the sea.' The imagery fits mythical representations in Syria, Egypt and Palestine of the battle between the gods and serpentine monsters. In Egypt, the crocodile was the sun god's enemy, subjected to Horus and the Pharaoh. It is clear that the author of Job was familiar with these traditions.[244] In Job 40 and 41, God speaks rather respectfully about the hippopotamus/Behemoth and the crocodile/Leviathan. Their strength and mighty appearance are described in great detail. And God's discourse on Leviathan ends in the following way: 'On earth it has no equal, a creature without fear. It surveys everything that is lofty; it is king over all that are proud' (41:25–26 Hebr.; 31:33–34 NRSV).

Thus not in all Bible texts do these primal monsters play the same role.[245] Whether Behemoth appears elsewhere in the Bible is unclear. Behemoth is also the plural of *behemah*, which simply stands for a female animal.[246] But in Job, Behemoth is just one animal. In the last chapters of Job the monsters are dangerous and God seems to be the only one strong enough to finish them off, but surprisingly God doesn't kill them. Even Job in one of his replies to his friends was convinced that God had done so: 'By his power he stilled the Sea; by his understanding he struck down Rahab. By his wind the heavens were made fair; his hand pierced the fleeing serpent' (26:12–13). But God, in his own words, talks rather admiringly, hardly disapprovingly, about these monsters.

The world doesn't revolve around people

In God's discourses one important thing becomes clear to Job and the reader. There are many things that Job doesn't understand, things which are not in his power and are not made by him.[247] 'Tell me, if you have understanding' (38:4). 'Have you entered the storehouses of the snow' (38:22). 'Do you know when the mountain goats give birth?' (39:1). More often, the text refers to Job's impotence, as in the question 'Have you commanded the morning since your days began?' (38:12), 'Can you bind the chains of the Pleiades?' (38:31), 'Can you hunt the prey for the lion?' (38:39), 'Is the wild ox willing to serve you?

Will it spend the night at your crib?' (39:9) and, about the crocodile, 'Will you play with it as with a bird?' (40:29 Hebr.; 41:5 NRSV).

To every question, Job can only answer 'no'. All natural phenomena and animals extensively described do not fall within men's ruling power. Animals domesticated by men are not mentioned, so no cattle, just the wild animals. Humans are not found in the very centre. They are on the whole nothing but admiring onlookers. The world rightfully has a claim to existence and meaning apart from people.

> Who has cut a channel for the torrents of rain,
> and a way for the thunderbolt,
> to bring rain on a land where no one lives,
> on the desert, which is empty of human life,
> to satisfy the waste and desolate land,
> and to make the ground put forth grass?' (38:25–27)

It is not only about God and Job, but also about all of non-human nature. The question is what the role of people is within the whole ecosystem of the earth. People are put in their place.[248]

People don't have the knowledge, the ability or the power to dominate creation.[249] In this way, the Book of Job clearly offers a different picture of men's role in the whole of creation from that of Genesis 1. And it also differs from Genesis 9:2, which says that animals are afraid of people and people have power over animals.[250] In God's discourses, people are not the main focus, and the human will to power is exposed as illusory.[251] Job has no power over wild animals.

These particular ten are selected largely because of their magnificent wildness. They are to remind Job that the world does not revolve around him, that it is full of creatures with whom he has nothing to do and whom he could not dream of controlling. Yet God delights in them.[252]

The magnificent beauty of creation

God is no tyrant who humiliates Job. No. God takes pleasure in the wildness of the animals mentioned. 'Its strength is in its loins, and its power in the muscles of its belly!' (40:16). 'Can one take it with hooks or pierce its nose with a snare?' (40:24).

That all is said in the form of poetry is not insignificant, because it fits the contents. 'The beauty of the divine speeches in Job is not an accidental literary feature or merely a pleasant harmonious aesthetics, but revelation itself.'[253] Job does not receive a ready answer to his accusation, but indirectly he gets something of a response. He is invited to look at the unbelievable beauty of the cosmos. He experiences the world and God as *tremendum et fascinans*, awesome and fascinating; the terminology was used by Rudolf Otto to indicate the outcome of experiencing the sphere of the divine.[254] This experience turns Job into a different person. God reproaches Job's friends and brings a turn in Job's life. Job himself speaks in favour of his friends – he prays for them (42:10) – and his daughters are all summed up by name and receive an equal share of the heritage, as all their brothers (42:14–15), which in the old eastern world and in the Bible was hardly ever a custom.

What Job must have experienced is well illustrated in the experience of a present-day polar explorer. Erling Kagge, a Norwegian lawyer, the first to reach both the South and the North Pole on foot (and also to have climbed Everest, in the Himalayas), said, when asked in what way experiencing the wilderness makes you a better person:

> Nature's greatness, its power and energy, make you feel how small you are, how unimportant your life is, and that makes you in a certain way humble. On the other hand, you become aware of being part of something bigger. And because of that you feel there is something big in yourself. Maybe, from a larger perspective, your life is insignificant, yet it is still *your* life. You are *just* a creature – yet you are part of that tremendous creation.

> Thus, you have also to acknowledge your responsibility towards it. If you are all alone in nature you feel your potentials.[255]

Job starts to know God by looking into creation.[256] The beauty and the freedom of wild animals resemble that of their creator. When the storm has blown away all Job's anthropomorphic projections, he can see God anew because he is now able to see the rest of creation. Then he bows down. And he withdraws. There are many interpretations of this elusive verse 6. Withdrawing has no object. The NRSV adds 'myself' and translates 'therefore I despise myself, and repent in dust and ashes'. In the Dutch NBV, 'his words' is added. But does he really despise himself and withdraw his charge, or are there still other options? According to Job 42:8, Job spoke of God 'what is right', unlike his friends. His friends had even less understanding than Job. Verse 6 may also be interpreted that Job withdraws the dust and ashes – in other words, he goes back on his mourning.[257] It is also possible that he doesn't take back his charge, but has come to acknowledge his situation realistically within the whole of creation.[258] In a place, a situation, where nobody could stand tall, Job endured. Thus, he put a hand on his mouth and he kept silent. He is not shamed but lifted up as part of a still bigger wholeness, humble and self-confident all in one. Everything fell into place in the extraordinary revelation that befell Job.

2.2.6 Lady Wisdom: Proverbs 1—9

Wisdom is both in Hebrew (*chokma*) and in Greek (*sophia*) a feminine noun, and is as such personified as a female character. In the Book of Job, God looks at her as he is setting boundaries to the water. Apparently, she dates from before creation, whereas in Proverbs 8 she is reckoned as the first of all creatures. In all wisdom literature Wisdom is connected with creation; this does not just happen in the older books, as in Job and Proverbs, but also in the deuterocanonical/apocryphal books Wisdom, Sirach and Baruch.[259] The same creation motifs moreover turn up in the other, canonical, books of the Bible.

Contents and structure

It is hard to say when Proverbs was written. It is generally believed that its final editing must be dated somewhere in the fifth century BCE, more or less when the Book of Job was completed. Proverbs certainly contains much older material, even from the tenth and ninth centuries BCE.[260] The more recent wisdom texts are strongly influenced by Hellenistic philosophy; biblical wisdom literature makes use of older traditions. Proverbs consists of three parts. The middle section, chapters 10—29, contains twofold sayings; the third section, chapters 30—31, comprises larger sayings and poems, being one long poetic instruction meant for teaching purposes.

The first nine chapters are of particular interest for eco-theology, because here Lady Wisdom is extensively portrayed and connected with creation. She was already present before anything existed, and she is said to belong to God. She takes the floor with three discourses – 1:20-33, 8:1–36 and 9:1–6.[261]

> *Give heed to my reproof;*
> *I will pour out my thoughts to you;*
> *I will make my words known to you.* (Proverbs 1:23)

These discourses are unique in the Old Testament, but match Egyptian texts in which the goddess Ma'at, child of the god of creation and the goddess of justice, speaks.

Lady Wisdom is endowed with much power. She is always present where power is exercised, in city gates and at crossroads, places where one will normally find prophets and justice being rendered.[262] According to Proverbs, she is the only one who can offer knowledge and insight. She lends prestige and protects those that follow her; kings reign through her. Her other name is Understanding: 'Does not wisdom call, and does not understanding raise her voice?' (8:1). The places where she invites people to learn from her are, by the way, also the places where prostitutes look for clients. Her counterparts are, therefore, both the foolish woman (9:13) and the loose woman (5:2).

Divine

Lady Wisdom can be seen as a personification of a divine characteristic. She is God's wisdom. There are good reasons to believe that she is the remnant of a former goddess. 'Although modern interpreters have often treated her as a literary personification, it can be argued that what later came to be considered a mere figure of speech started its career as a "real" deity.'[263] She is, thus, the goddess of knowledge, intelligence, statesmanship and the writing professions. The wisdom literature of the Old Testament does not write off polytheism so radically as Deutero-Isaiah and the Deuteronomistic revision of the Pentateuch do.[264] Like in some Psalms (95, 96, 97), JHWH is not seen as the one and only God, but of all deities JHWH is surely the highest. All other gods are submitted to him. Lady Wisdom, in Proverbs 1—9, is God's child, witnessing creation, supervising kings and their administrators in the way they must rule, and teaching and coaching young men.

In the apocryphal/deuterocanonical books Baruch, Wisdom and Sirach, Lady Wisdom also plays a role. In Baruch she coincides with the Thora (Baruch 3:9—4:4). In the other two books, coming from the second and first centuries BCE, her role is even more prominent. The influence of Hellenistic philosophy is noticeable; at the same time, she clearly resembles the popular goddess Isis, who also takes interest in kingship and nature.[265] Due to the fact that apocryphal texts are not included in most Protestant Bibles, they seem of less importance; nevertheless, their range of ideas has had a strong afterlife in the New Testament in the imagery of Christ as creator.

Firstborn of creation

> *The Everlasting begot me, the beginning of his works,*
> *the forerunner of his deeds of long ago;*

From of old I was formed,
at the first, before the earth.
When there were no deeps I was brought forth,
when there were no fountains or springs of water;
Before the mountains were settled into place,
before the hills, I was brought forth. (Proverbs 8:22–25 NABRE)

Many expositors and translators wrestle with these verses because they find it difficult to harmonise words referring to pregnancy and birth with a God who is represented as male.[266] Of Lady Wisdom, it is clearly said that she had been begotten (v.22) and formed (v.23) – i.e. in the womb, as is the case in Psalm 139:13 – and born (v.25).[267] The NRSV translates incorrectly: the Everlasting created me (v.22).

Sirach solves the problem of a birth out of a male God by letting her birth succeed by way of his mouth: 'From the mouth of the Most High I came forth, and covered the earth like a mist' (Sirach 24:3 NABRE). This verse combines the creation of Proverbs 8 with both Genesis 1:3 – the speaking of God – and Genesis 2:6 – water wells up from the earth and waters the face of the ground.[268]

Witness of creation

When he established the heavens, I was there,
when he drew a circle on the face of the deep (Proverbs 8:27)

and I was daily his delight,
rejoicing before him always (Proverbs 8:30)

Lady Wisdom is as a child – the word *'delight'* seems to point in that direction – witnessing creation and learns, thus, how everything is as it exists.[269]

In the Book of Wisdom, Solomon says to God: 'Now with you is

Wisdom, who knows your works and was present when you made the world' (Wisdom 9:9 NABRE). Chapter 9 covers almost in its entirety Solomon's supplication for wisdom. He asks, for example, 'Give me Wisdom, the consort at your throne' (Wisdom 9:4), and refers thus to wisdom's divine status.

Besides being a witness, Wisdom is instrumental to creating: 'The Everlasting by wisdom founded the earth; by understanding he established the heavens' (Proverbs 3:19). In the Book of Wisdom, she is called Wisdom 'the artisan of all' (Wisdom 7:22 NABRE).

One aspect of the all-encompassing knowledge of Wisdom is her knowledge of nature: of earth, water and air, with all living beings. Solomon got his vast knowledge of nature from her:

> God gave Solomon very great wisdom, discernment, and breadth of understanding as vast as the sand on the seashore, so that Solomon's wisdom surpassed the wisdom of all the people of the east, and all the wisdom of Egypt [...] He composed three thousand proverbs, and his songs numbered a thousand and five. He would speak of trees, from the cedar that is in the Lebanon to the hyssop that grows in the wall; he would speak of animals, and birds, and reptiles, and fish. (1 Kings 4:29–33)

Intermediary between God and world

Lady Wisdom thus has divine traits and is also intimately connected with creation:

> *Then I was beside him, like a master worker;*
> *and I was daily his delight, rejoicing before him always,*
> *rejoicing in his inhabited world*
> *and delighting in the human race. (Proverbs 8:30–31)*

She also has the role of an intermediary:

For whoever finds me finds life
and obtains favour from the Everlasting;
but those who miss me injure themselves;
all who hate me love death. (Proverbs 8:35–36)

In Wisdom she coincides with the Spirit.[270] She is a power that comes from God and pervades all of creation.

For Wisdom is mobile beyond all motion,
and she penetrates and pervades all things
by reason of her purity.
For she is a breath of the might of God
and a pure emanation of the glory of the Almighty;
therefore nothing defiled can enter into her.
For she is the reflection of eternal light,
the spotless mirror of the power of God,
the image of his goodness.
Although she is one, she can do all things,
and she renews everything while herself perduring
(Wisdom 7:24–27)

She enters the hearts of prophets and leaders and inspires their utterances and deeds.[271]

Wisdom mediates between God and the world. Immanent in creation, she is the source of all meaning in this world. Coming from God, she is also a revelation from God and a call from him to the world. [...] It is a divine appeal through creation which seduces, draws and eventually embraces us. Thus, Christian theology has applied the figure of Wisdom to Jesus who, as the Incarnate Word of God, is the mediator par excellence between God and this world. (1 Cor 1, 24)[272]

People as pupils

Having such a comprehensive knowledge and an urge to share it makes Lady Wisdom a great teacher. Proverbs 1—9 has probably been used for centuries as teaching material for young men trained to move into leadership positions in society. In the time of David and Solomon there was a demand for well-educated people in administrative offices. Although these texts were initially intended for an exclusively male elite, this doesn't mean that they can be put down as condoning the status quo of their society. Nowhere is said that knowledge and insight are strictly there for the benefit of a few privileged people. The only restriction that is set to all forms of knowledge is that its receivers require the fear of God: 'The fear of the Everlasting is the beginning of all knowledge' (Proverbs 1:7). The fact that the initially intended audience consisted of men brings this type of instruction in line with most parts of the Bible. Wisdom, nevertheless, is not only transmitted by fathers but also by mothers: 'hear, my child, your father's instruction, and do not reject your mother's teaching' (Proverbs 1:8).

Although Lady Wisdom talks mainly with men, her femininity clearly does not affirm a male and hierarchical status quo. By being both feminine and divine, and as such present at the time of creation, makes her precisely a perfect counterweight to the image of God as a male ruler over creation. As female image of God she is not just portrayed as transcendent but also as immanent. From every part of creation Wisdom calls out to all:

> But ask the animals, and they will teach you;
> the birds of the air, and they will tell you;
> ask the plants of the earth, and they will teach you;
> and the fish of the sea will declare to you.
> Who among all these does not know
> that the hand of the Everlasting has done this?
> In his hand is the life of every living thing
> and the breath of every human being. (Job 12:7–10)

Everyone can become wiser thanks to her. The role of humans within the entire cosmos is, according to wisdom literature, being a pupil. This significance of the pupil is enhanced in the New Testament, where the wisdom tradition is carried on.

2.2.7 Christ the creator

As Joseph Sittler was addressing the World Council of Churches in 1961,[273] pleading for giving more attention to sustainability in theology, he referred to the hymn in Colossians 1 where Christ is depicted as creator. This hymn has ever since been important for ecological theology. Strange as it may seem, all references to Lady Wisdom in this hymn are often overlooked in exegetical studies.[274] John 1 also refers to her, as we shall soon see.

Apart from these wisdom texts, other texts can be named that show how Jesus is connected with the act of creating. One can think of Mark 4:35–41 in which Jesus, on the sea of Galilee, calms a storm by rebuking the wind and silencing the lake.[275] The passage ends with a question: 'Who then is this, that even the wind and the sea obey him?' The image is that of God who sets boundaries to the primal waters to enable life to be, as happens in Genesis 1 and other creation narratives.[276] The awesome scene on the lake fills the disciples with tremendous fear.

The story of Jesus walking over the water (Mark 6:47–54)[277] can also be seen as referring to creation. Again, we are told about the anxiety of the disciples and the strong wind that immediately calms down when Jesus gets into their boat.

The wisdom of Jesus; Jesus as Wisdom

Elisabeth Schüssler Fiorenza showed in her book *Jesus: Miriam's Child, Sophia's Prophet* how important the wisdom tradition is in understanding Jesus.[278]

The New Testament connects God's wisdom in several ways with Jesus. Luke's childhood narratives say, for instance, about him 'The child grew and became strong, filled with wisdom' (Luke 2:40) and 'Jesus increased in wisdom and in years, and in divine and human favour' (Luke 2:52).

In Matthew, Jesus identifies himself as Wisdom. He says so explicitly – 'Yet wisdom is vindicated by her deeds' (Matthew 11:19) – and implicitly when he presents himself as a humble teacher who cries out for pupils:

> Come to me, all you that are weary and are carrying heavy burdens, and I will give you rest. Take my yoke upon you, and learn from me; for I am gentle and humble in heart, and you will find rest for your souls. For my yoke is easy, and my burden is light. (Matthew 11:28–30)

In lectionaries the text is traditionally linked with Zechariah 9:9–12, probably due to its referring to humbleness. But because of that reference the connection between Lady Wisdom and Jesus is totally lost.

Jesus passes his wisdom on to his disciples: 'For I will give you words and a wisdom that none of your opponents will be able to withstand or contradict' (Luke 21:15), The Gospel of Matthew ends with the commandment to teach what Jesus taught: 'Now

Christ: 'Mathete ap'emou...' – learn from me... (Matthew 11:28)

113

the eleven disciples went to Galilee, to the mountain to which Jesus had directed them [...] And Jesus came and said to them, [...] Go therefore and make disciples of all nations [...]' (Matthew 28:16–19). Whereas in the Old Testament wisdom literature is still exclusively aimed at male members of the elite, at the end of the Gospel of Matthew the reach is broadened in order to invite all people to become Christ's pupils. Jesus' wisdom is not just for kings, administrators and the learned, but for everyone.

Paul maintained that Lady Wisdom was not to be found with the dominant groups in society. In his first letter to the Corinthians, especially in the first two chapters, he contrasts God's wisdom in Christ sharply with the wisdom of the world and its rulers. 'But we speak God's wisdom, secret and hidden, which God decreed before the ages for our glory. None of the rulers of this age understood this; for if they had, they would not have crucified the Lord of glory' (1 Corinthians 2:7, 8). Paul's message – Christ crucified – is foolishness for them. 'But to those who are the called, both Jews and Greeks, is Christ the power of God and the wisdom of God' (1 Corinthians 1:24). Wisdom and Spirit are also closely linked in Paul: it is the Spirit that teaches (2:13) and wisdom is a gift of the Spirit (12:8).

When Paul links Christ and creation, we immediately recognise Lady Wisdom: 'yet for us there is one God, the Father, from whom are all things and for whom we exist, and one Lord, Jesus Christ, through whom are all things and through whom we exist' (8:6).

Firstborn of creation: Colossians 1:15–20

Whether Paul was also the author of the letter to the Colossians is not at all certain. Presumably, the author was either one of his collaborators or a follower. At the time of its writing,[279] the church of the Colossians was strongly divided over Gnosticism. According to the Gnostics, God was only connected with the spiritual world, not with the material world. They didn't believe in God as creator; matter was created by a demiurge. In order to come nearer to God, men had to get rid of everything that attached them to their earthly existence; the human spirit had to free itself from the body. God was for them pure spirit and had nothing to do with materiality. The Gnostics believed that Christ could not be God and human at the same time. If Christ was really God, then he couldn't be a human being. His body might appear as such, but would be no more than a sort of cover. And if he was really human, he certainly could not be God.

In order to gainsay this gnostic separation between God and the sphere of the everyday, the bodily, the material and nature, the author of the letter to the Colossians reverts to an older hymn. The hymn praises Christ as creator and firstborn of creation. Its provenance is unknown. It might well be pre-Christian Jewish, because the motifs are directly borrowed from wisdom literature.[280] Most biblical scholars take the elements of the Church (v.18) and the Cross (v.20) as additions from the author of the letter.

> He is the image of the invisible God, the firstborn of all creation;
> for in him all things in heaven and on earth were created, things
> visible and invisible, whether thrones or dominions or rulers or
> powers – all things have been created through him and for him.
> He himself is before all things, and in him all things hold
> together. (Colossians 1:15–17)

What is said about Christ has been said earlier about Lady Wisdom. 'He is the image of God', not just like the image with which every human being is endowed according to Genesis 1, but fully and unveiled, as was said about Wisdom: 'For she is the reflection of eternal light, the spotless mirror of the power of God, the image of his goodness' (Wisdom 7:26). He is 'the firstborn of all creation' in the same way as Wisdom was called firstborn of creation. 'For in him all things ... were created' in the same way as Wisdom was instrumental to creation and was the maker of everything.

Christ/Sophia – the feminine face of God

The link between Christ and Lady Wisdom is relevant to an inclusive ecological theology for at least three reasons. First, the whole of reality – without distinguishing between material and spiritual, human and non-human – is linked with God. Secondly, the connection resonates similarly in Christ. Thirdly, Christ is being identified with a female figure. This differs clearly from the usual androcentric and hierarchical image of Christ as ruler of the cosmos that legitimises human ruling of the earth.[281] Sophia is God's feminine face which implicates the creation and salvation of the whole earth.[282]

The hymn 'Come and Seek the Ways of Wisdom' takes up these motifs from wisdom literature in the Old and New Testaments and blends them beautifully.[283]

> *Come and seek the ways of Wisdom,*
> *she who danced when earth was new.*
> *Follow closely what she teaches,*
> *for her words are right and true.*
> *Wisdom clears the path to justice,*
> *showing us what love must do.*
>
> *Listen to the voice of Wisdom,*
> *crying in the marketplace.*
> *Hear the Word made flesh among us,*
> *full of glory, truth and grace.*
> *When the word takes root and ripens,*
> *peace and righteousness embrace.*
>
> *Sister Wisdom, come assist us;*
> *nurture all who seek rebirth,*
> *Spirit guide and close companion,*
> *bring to light our sacred worth.*
> *Free us to become your people,*
> *holy friends of God and earth.*

Incarnation of the Word/Wisdom: John 1

At the beginning of the Gospel of John, Christ is presented as creator. A hymn of Lady Wisdom is, according to Ernst Haenchen, directly applied to Christ and connected with the ascendancy of John the Baptist.[284] Jesus Christ as God's Wisdom incarnated resembles God's incarnated Word.

> In the beginning was the Word, and the Word was with God, and the Word was God.
>
> He was in the beginning with God. All things came into being through him, and without him not one thing came into being. What has come into being in him was life, and the life was the light of all people. (John 1:1–4)
>
> He was in the world, and the world came into being through him; yet the world did not know him. (v.10)
>
> And the Word became flesh and lived among us, and we have seen his glory, the glory as of a father's only son, full of grace and truth. (v.14)

The Greek *logos* is usually translated as Word, but can also mean Wisdom, as the German translation *Bibel in gerechter Sprache* does in its translation of John 1:[285]

> *In the beginning was Wisdom*
> *and Wisdom was with God*
> *and Wisdom was like God.*
> *She was in the beginning with God.*
> *Everything came into being through her*
> *and without her nothing came into being.*
> *What came into existence in her, was life,*
> *and life was light for the people.* (John 1:1–4)

She was in the world and the world came through her into existence,

but the world did not recognize her. (v.10)
And Wisdom became matter
and dwelled among us. (v.14)

The margin of this translation provides explicit references to the books of Proverbs, Wisdom and Sirach. The motif of Wisdom, for instance, who is searching for a place to dwell and is subsequently rejected by the world, but against all odds succeeds in finding a place among some people, is borrowed from Proverbs 1:22–25 and Sirach 24:8–12.

Wisdom/Word belongs to God from the beginning. This beginning has not to be taken historically, no more than 'in the beginning' of Genesis 1. Because creation is about God's relation to the world, it is not at all strange that creation and incarnation are so intimately connected in Colossians 1 and John 1.

Matthijs de Jong, an exegete working for the Dutch Bible Company (NBG), seeks an alternative for the translation of '*logos*' for 'Word' in the *Bible in Ordinary Language* (*Bijbel in Gewone Taal*). He sums up some strong arguments favouring the close connection between *logos* and the Jewish wisdom tradition:

By using the term logos the author of the prologue introduces an already existing concept that is rooted in the Jewish wisdom tradition.[286] [...] Just like the logos in the prologue, wisdom is being portrayed as

- a figure;
- being in the presence of God preceding creation;
- mirroring God;
- doing God's creating work and all God's mighty deeds;

- coming to earth and (temporally) finding a place to stay among people.

The use of the term logos (instead of Sophia, wisdom) for this concept, fits in along with an already existing tradition. In the book of Wisdom God's logos appears as an equivalent of wisdom (e.g. Wisdom 9,1, and for the way wisdom functions see also Wisdom 18,15), and in the first century of the common era among Greek speaking Jews it was current to use the term logos in connection with the concept of wisdom.[287]

His first objection against using the usual Dutch translation 'het Woord' (the Word) is that 'woord' is in Dutch a neuter noun and therefore not eligible 'for identifying it with a person', whereas the Greek *logos* is masculine and could be used for word.[288] Besides, he avers:

the rendition of 'the Word' does not comply with the criteria agreed upon for the *Bible in Ordinary Language*, namely that its language should be clear and comprehensive [289]

thus, he states, 'word' causes too much misunderstanding. So far so good. Up to this point I can wholeheartedly agree with him. But when all is said and done and the conclusion should be that 'Wisdom' fits best, he still decides against it.

John 1:1 in the *Bible in Ordinary Language* has become 'In the beginning God's *son* was already there.' This outcome is very odd, because his objections against the use of 'the Word' do not apply if one renders *logos* into 'wisdom'. Wisdom is both in Hebrew and Greek (and in Dutch) a feminine noun and is in the Old Testament portrayed as a person. In the Old Testament Wisdom is not a human but a divine person *and* part of creation. Besides, 'wisdom' is not really too difficult to comprehend.

By translating *logos* as 'God's son', de Jong follows Philo of Alexandria

(20/15 BCE–CE 50), who called the *logos* 'the firstborn son of God'.[290] De Jong, thus, lends a hand to an interpretation that already shoved aside a feminine image of *logos* and traded it for a male image. By using this interpretation, he also legitimises the repressing of one the most significant female images of God. Not being willing to acknowledge this is wasting a glorious opportunity, and it gives the impression that Jesus' maleness is far more important than his humanness.[291]

Wisdom incarnate in Jesus is the wisdom to let the poor be the first to enter God's kingdom, before the rich, and to know that even a sparrow will not fall outside God's care. This wisdom belongs to one who socialises with prostitutes and publicans and dies shamefully on a cross.

> Jesus enfleshes Sophia as she is portrayed in the Old Testament and the intertestamental literature in her prophetic street preaching, her public calls for justice, her befriending of the outcasts, her promise to offer for the heavily burdened rest, her gathering of friends and strangers for an abundant feast, her healing ministry, and her initiation of disciples into friendship with God. Throughout his ministry and in a final and definitive way in his death, Jesus embodies Sophia's compassion for, and solidarity with, the lost and the least.[292]

Creation and salvation

In the same way as the whole cosmos exists through Christ, is the cosmos is also there on behalf of Christ. Source and destination, creation and salvation, are closely interwoven, as we have seen in Deutero-Isaiah. The last part of Colossians 1:15–20 is mainly about salvation:

> He is the head of the body, the church; he is the beginning, the firstborn from the dead, so that he might come to have first place in everything.
>
> For in him all the fullness of God was pleased to dwell, and

> through him God was pleased to reconcile to himself all things, whether on earth or in heaven, by making peace through the blood of his cross. (Colossians 1:18–20)

The redemption through Christ's cross concerns the whole of creation. 'All', 'all things' or 'everything' are mentioned several times in Greek (*ta panta*). The author certainly had by 'all things' something else in mind than we do because his image of the world differs from ours. His first concern was not that humans can place themselves outside creation. His concern was to show that the forces and powers that inform our material world were related to God, contrasting what Gnostics believed. Thus, he emphasises that the forces and powers, i.e. the angels and demons, were also created by God in Christ and would be saved by God in Christ.[293]

This means that in the current context of ecological crisis and a theology that contributes to this crisis, 'all things' receives a whole new meaning. The first thing to conclude is 'Creation is not merely the stage on which the drama of human salvation takes place. These texts support two of the ecojustice principles: the intrinsic worth and the purpose of the earth.'[294] God's salvation involves the whole cosmos. As Moltmann said, 'Resurrection is not just the essence of history but also the essence of nature.'[295]

This salvation is already here and now, and is, at the same time, not fully realised. Christ, as the one resurrected, is the firstborn; the rest of creation has still to follow. He is the first from creation (v.15) and from the dead (v.18). Death that sets his mark on everything on earth, has, in principle, been conquered. Thinking through the imagery of a firstborn, one can picture God as a pregnant woman carrying the world.[296] The world is not full-grown yet. Christ is the only one who is fully grown; he is born and lives. He is the first. What the world has to be has already become visible in Christ. In him dwells God's fullness that someday will be all in all. Through his life, his death on the cross and his resurrection, Christ, in whom

God's fullness dwells, has brought peace. Thus, it is not only the people that will change into God's image, but the whole world.

The role of people becomes visible in the Church, body of Christ, but is not separated from all of creation. The Church as a gathering of all Christ's disciples participates in God's fullness, a fullness for which all of creation is destined.

2.3 GOD AND THE ANIMALS

Not only creation narratives give non-human reality a distinctive role alongside humans. Many Bible texts speak of animals and plants. This is not really a surprise considering the fact that these texts were conceived in a mainly agricultural society where men and beasts lived closely together and cultivating the ground was for many everyday work. In Paul's letters, rooted in urban life, animals are hardly mentioned. The role of animals in the Bible is important for ecological questions like diminishing biodiversity and the treatment of animals is equally important for our food provision.[297]

The particular position of non-human creatures has often been ignored in the interpretation of the Bible:

> References to nature in the New Testament, especially the Gospels, have been persistently understood from the perspective of modern urban people, themselves alienated from nature, for whom literary references to nature can only be symbols or picturesque illustrations of a human world unrelated to nature.[298]

The same goes for the Old Testament. In everyday church practice, the animals in Noah's ark are nice for children, and the raven and the dove that Noah lets loose may in a sermon stand for the ways people behave.

Animals do have a far bigger place in the Bible than in our modern western worldview. We are used to placing animals and plants under the collective heading of 'living world', i.e. flora and fauna, excluding ourselves as humans. The Bible has a different way of distinguishing: plant and earth are lumped together, and animals and humans are often seen as sharing the same fate.[299] Many texts mention animals and humans in one breath:

> Jerusalem shall be inhabited like villages without walls, because of the multitude of people and animals in it. (Zechariah 2:4)

And:

> I said in my heart with regard to human beings that God is testing them to show that they are but animals. For the fate of humans and the fate of animals is the same; as one dies, so dies the other. They all have the same breath, and humans have no advantage over the animals; for all is vanity. All go to one place; all are from the dust, and all turn to dust again. (Ecclesiastes 3:18–20)[300]

But also:

> Your righteousness is like the mighty mountains, your judgments are like the great deep; you save humans and animals alike, O Everlasting. (Psalm 36:6)

Animals can be a plague. Think only of the plagues of Egypt – frogs, gnats, mosquitos, stinging insects, and locusts (Exodus 7—12) – the hornets that will drive out the peoples from Canaan (Exodus 23, 28) and the locusts that will clear the fields of all their crop in Joel's prophecy (Joel 1:4). But animals are not in themselves bad. They can behave as enemies, just like people, but they still remain fellow creatures. A positive assessment of animals is typical of the whole Bible.[301]

The Bible contains several instructions to protect animals. Beasts of burden should not be loaded up too heavily (Exodus 23:5;

Deuteronomy 22:4); sick and weak animals should be spared and helped (Ezekiel 32:2–4) because 'the righteous know the needs of their animals, but the mercy of the wicked is cruel' (Proverbs 12:10). Animals have a right to take their share of the crop (Deuteronomy 25:4) and they must rest on Sabbath (Exodus 20:10 and 23:12; Deuteronomy 5:13–14). Wild animals also deserve some sort of protection. They may enter the ark (Genesis 6—9), they may eat of what the fallow ground brings forth during Sabbath year (Leviticus 25:7), and the mother bird may not be taken away with her eggs (Deuteronomy 22:6–7).[302]

Being compassionate towards all animals – both wild and domesticated – was essential, and agriculture was generally sustainable. The rules concerning the proper treatment of animals were not formulated as rights. The Bible didn't think in terms of animals' rights, but in terms of men's obligations towards animals.

Animals have their own inner value, and not just in as far as they are useful to humans.[303] The rhetorical question at the end of the Book of Jonah makes this point quite clear. God says to Jonah:

> You are concerned about the bush, for which you did not labour and which you did not grow; it came into being in a night and perished in a night. And should I not be concerned about Nineveh, that great city, in which there are more than a hundred and twenty thousand persons who do not know their right hand from their left, and also many animals? (Jonah 4:10–11)

2.3.1 Animals in creation narratives: a summary

In the overview of creation narratives it became clear that not everything is about humans, but about God and the whole earth – the whole cosmos, even. God takes pleasure in his creative work when he sees how good it is (Genesis 1); he sees everything in its interconnectedness, the whole ecosystem with all those animals, each with their own habitat (Psalm 104), when he presents the animals one by one to Adam as possible partner (Genesis 2), and when he pictures the wild animals, even the most terrifying, for Job's mind's eye. God delights in the abundance of animals and their concomitant variety.

Animals appear many times in creation narratives. They are not divided, as in current taxonomy, into mammals, reptiles, amphibians, birds, fish, insects, or into useful/beneficial versus harmful categories, but, for example, according to habitat – land, sea, air – or in as far as they are domesticated or wild. Creeping animals form a separate category.[304] The primal monsters are also seen as belonging to the world of animals.

There are many parallels between animals and humans. Land animals are created on the same day as humans. Animals and humans both partake only of plants; both have to be fruitful. Animals, just like humans, are made of earth's dust and both are animated by life's breath. Both are created for the honour of God. They praise God with their voice and their existence. Animals are not objects, but subjects in their own right. Humans and animals are moreover both mortal.

Humans have their own unpretentious position among a diversity of living creatures, and, yet, they may rule over certain categories of animals. Fish, birds and animals that move upon the earth are under their rule; sea monsters and wild animals are exempted.[305] Animals can be scared of humans,[306] but there are also proud and untameable species[307] that show their rightful place within creation. Cattle are of importance to people, not just for food, but also to assist them in working the soil. Although animals are often mentioned in connection with people, they also have their own direct relationship with God, who gives them life and food. God's wisdom speaks through animals and the earth.

2.3.2 End and new beginning of all living beings: Genesis 6:5—9:17

Many biblical scholars distinguish two sources in the narrative of the great flood and the covenant, which could explain certain internal contradictory sayings.[308] Yet Genesis 6:5—9:17 proves also a well-composed unity. It is structured in layers, like a sandwich. Every layer in the first half is mirrored in the opposite part, the second half. The middle is the turning point and contains its central motif.[309]

a. wickedness of humankind, earth's corruption
   b. destruction
      c. entering the ark
         d. beginning of the flood
           e. rising of the water
GOD REMEMBERS NOAH AND THE ANIMALS
           e. lowering of the water
         d. the earth dries up
      c. abandoning the ark
   b. the earth endures
a. blessing, respecting life, covenant

'The end of all living beings'

After the story of the evil in the world (Genesis 3) the story continues in the next chapters, telling about the ongoing corruption, the wickedness of the people and the animals, and how God is sorry that he made everything and, thus, decides to destroy all living creatures, including the earth. Humans are the first culprits and they are his first choice in deciding their annihilation (Genesis 6:5–6). In the following verses 'all flesh' (Hebrew: *kol-basar*) is blamed:[310]

> And God saw that the earth was corrupt; for all flesh had corrupted its ways upon the earth. And God said to Noah, 'I have determined to make an end of all flesh, for the earth is filled with violence because of them; now I am going to destroy them along with the earth.'

Although Noah and his family have a leading part in this narrative, it does not imply that the story affects only humans. Animals are explicitly mentioned in Genesis 6—9: the birds and all sorts of land animals. The animals do not enter the ark in order to be served up to the humans on board. Food is mentioned separately: 'Also take with you every kind of food that is eaten, and store it up; and it shall serve as food for you and for them' (Genesis 6:21). Plants are stored aboard as food supply. Plants are not counted among the living creatures; they don't belong to what is called 'all flesh'.[311] The assumption is that plants will sprout out again as soon as the earth has dried up.[312] Living on earth has again become possible once the dove returns with an olive branch, which means that plants have returned at last.[313] Noah was responsible for making sure that all animals came in in pairs, in order that they may multiply and check their extinction. All other animals and humans will perish in the flood.

> And all flesh died that moved on the earth, birds, domestic animals, wild animals, all swarming creatures that swarm on the earth, and all human beings; everything on dry land in whose nostrils was the breath of life died. [...] Only Noah was left, and those that were with him in the ark. And the waters swelled on the earth for one hundred fifty days. But God remembered Noah and all the wild animals and all the domestic animals that were with him in the ark. And God made a wind blow over the earth, and the waters subsided; the fountains of the deep and the windows of the heavens were closed, the rain from the heavens was restrained [...] (Genesis 7:21—8:2)

The situation is just like the one described in Genesis 1:2 when the *ruach* (literally: moving air), the breath/wind/Spirit of God hovers over the waters.

It appears that the whole earth and animals in particular are also considered guilty of earth's corruption. This is hard for us to apprehend, accustomed as we are to conceive animal violence as part and parcel of their natural behaviour. Moreover, it sounds absurd to take all the earth as thoroughly bad. But being 'bad' should not immediately be termed a moral category, no more as 'good' in Genesis 1 is deemed as such. Good and bad can, in this context, also mean well or badly suiting God's purpose. In the Old Testament it is not unusual to read that animals are called to account for their actions. Later in the story God says: 'For your own lifeblood I will surely require a reckoning: from every animal I will require it and from human beings [...]' (Genesis 9:5). In the Book of Jonah both humans and animals show remorse (Jonah 3:7–8). In prophetic visions of a new world all animals are herbivorous.[314] From an ecological perspective it is certainly important to note that in the Bible the corruption of people and the rest of the earth is interwoven. The same can be said about their salvation:[315]

> Then God said to Noah, 'Go out of the ark, you and your wife, and your sons and your sons' wives with you. Bring out with you every living thing that is with you of all flesh – birds and animals and every creeping thing that creeps on the earth – so that they may abound on the earth, and be fruitful and multiply on the earth.' (Genesis 8:15–17)

Noah subsequently makes a burnt offering of all clean animals and birds to God. It does seem odd to offer up all these animals after going to all that trouble to save them from certain death and to ensure their future life. But, according to Genesis 7:2,[316] Noah had brought with him not one but seven pairs of every clean animal. Hence, some could be slaughtered and offered up as a sacrifice. The offering of animals in the Old Testament 'had nothing to do with their purportedly low esteem, on the contrary, it showed precisely how highly they were regarded'.[317] You are supposed to give only what is very dear to you in order to procure atonement for God.[318] 'For the life of the flesh is in the blood; and I have given it to you for making atonement for your lives on the altar; for, as life, it is the blood that makes atonement' (Leviticus 17:11).

Life of animals and humans is valuable

Although God said in his heart that the inclination of the human heart is evil from youth, he has decided that he will never again curse the earth on account of them (8:21). God blesses Noah and his sons (9:1) and repeats the command of Genesis 1 that they should be fruitful and fill the earth.[319] The animals are, unlike what is said in Genesis 1, not blessed. According to Genesis 1, humans would rule over the animals, but were not allowed to eat them: both were herbivorous. But as from that day people have permission to eat meat and animals will be scared of people. By not forcing them to be vegetarians anymore, God makes allowances for people's incorrigibility.[320] Animals have from now on good reasons to fear humans. This new relationship between humans and animals is not labelled as good anymore; this fact has simply become reality. In our times of industrial farming and the stark decline both in numbers and in species of wild animals, animals seem to have more to fear from people than in the time of Old Israel.

Yet eating meat is not unrestricted. There is one important qualification: 'Only, you shall not eat flesh with its life, that is, its blood' (Genesis 9:4). Blood is seen as the centre of life's power, its soul or spirit. One has to give special attention to life, animal life included. This commandment lays at the root of ritual slaughtering. Even in the Acts of the Apostles this commandment was still considered obligatory: 'For it has seemed good to the Holy Spirit and to us to impose on you no further burden than these essentials: that you abstain from what has been sacrificed to idols and from blood and from what is strangled and from fornication ...' (Acts 15:28–29).

Religious Jews caring for sustainability stress the importance of these dietary laws. Since the 1970s there has been in the US a strong Jewish vegetarian movement.[321] In the Netherlands there is growing interest in eco-kashrut, which expands and interprets the dietary laws ecologically.[322] The concept of eco-kashrut (eco-kosher) affects the whole process of production and selling, safeguarding it through additional ethical standards. Food that puts too much stress on the environment is accordingly not considered kosher, no more than low-welfare meat or food produced under degrading labour conditions.[323]

Animal blood is forbidden food. Blood of people may not be shed at all: 'For your own lifeblood I will surely require a reckoning: from every animal I will require it and from human beings, each one for the blood of another, I will require a reckoning for human life [...] for in his own image God made humankind' (Genesis 9:5–6). Blood, which means life, of people is even more costly in the eyes of God than the blood of animals. But the difference is proportional rather than essential. The idea that animals are created on behalf of humans is derived from Aristotelian and Stoic philosophy, not from the Bible, although these ways of thinking have left their own traces in Jewish and Christian thought.[324] But Genesis 1 and 9 and the dietary laws still show that eating animals is far from self-evident.

The covenant of God with the earth and with all that lives on it

The making of the covenant as described in Genesis 9:8–17 is commonly known as 'The covenant with Noah'. Calling it thus entailed the exclusion of a great section of God's partners in this particular covenant. God includes in this covenant also all the animals, as they are explicitly mentioned by their separate categories:

> and with every living creature that is with you, the birds, the domestic animals, and every animal of the earth with you, as many as came out of the ark. I establish my covenant with you, that never again shall all flesh be cut off by the waters of a flood, and never again shall there be a flood to destroy the earth. (Genesis 9:10–11)

The covenant implies all of the earth: 'I have set my bow in the clouds, and it shall be a sign of the covenant between me and the earth' (Genesis 9:13). Verses 8–17 mention no fewer than four times 'every living creature', five times 'all flesh' and six times 'the earth'.

The interconnectedness of people, animals and the whole earth of which these texts speak is relevant for eco-theology, as well as the connection between God and all of the earth and all sorts of animals that have to be saved. One can safely conclude that God clearly wants to preserve the earth in all its rich diversity.[325]

2.3.3 Resting in freedom: the laws of Sabbath

A tender handling of animals as norm can be found in the laws of Sabbath. Sabbath affects not only humans but also animals and the land. Humans and animals need a rest every seventh day and the land every seventh year. Added to every seventh and fiftieth year is the remission of debts. Sabbath, the Sabbath year and Jubilee are an important base in the Bible for social and ecological sustainability.

The Sabbath: rest for man and beast

According to both versions of the Ten Commandments, livestock should rest on the seventh day of the week (Exodus 20:8-11 and Deuteronomy 5:12–15):

> Observe the Sabbath day and keep it holy, as the Everlasting your God commanded you. Six days you shall labour and do all your work. But the seventh day is a Sabbath to the Everlasting your God; you shall not do any work – you, or your son or your daughter, or your male or female slave, or your ox or your donkey, or any of your livestock, or the resident alien in your towns, so that your male and female slave may rest as well as you. (Deuteronomy 5:12–14)

The reason for keeping the Sabbath is expressed in various ways. Deuteronomy explains that God is liberator from slavery: 'Remember that you were a slave in the land of Egypt, and the Everlasting your God brought you out from there with a mighty hand and an outstretched arm; therefore the Everlasting your God commanded you to keep the sabbath day' (5:15). Exodus tells that God himself took a rest on Sabbath. On the sixth day, according to Genesis 1, God saw everything he had made and came to the conclusion that all was very good. On the seventh day God took a rest and hallowed that day. Sabbath crowns creation; the goal of creating was the Sabbath.[326] Both traditions – creative fulfilment and rest on the one hand and deliverance from slavery on the other hand – concur and reinforce one another. Housekeepers (men and women seem equally addressed) are held responsible for seeing to it that their family, servants and beasts keep Sabbath. In Egypt, they were slaves themselves and, therefore, they know what it means to be exploited. 'This should never happen again' is the message. No more slavery. This includes the slavery of others, people and animals. Hard labour should not be extorted from them. Likewise, people should not ask the most of beasts in order to maximise profit, because the Sabbath is the pinnacle of creation and animals are fellow creatures. In our 24/7 economy, geared to an ever-increasing output, this message is more relevant than ever.

> Six days you shall do your work, but on the seventh day you shall rest, so that your ox and your donkey may have relief, and your homeborn slave and the resident alien may be refreshed. (Exodus 23:12)

In Babylonian creation myths people are created to take over the work that the gods had to do.[327] In the Bible everything created is to share in the joy of Sabbath.

Jubilee and Sabbath year

> For six years you shall sow your land and gather in its yield; but the seventh year you shall let it rest and lie fallow, so that the poor of your people may eat; and what they leave the wild

animals may eat. You shall do the same with your vineyard, and with your olive orchard. (Exodus 23:10–11)

Exodus contains a shorter version. Leviticus 25:1–7 goes into more detail how the Sabbath year should be kept. Not only the poor and the animals shall eat from what the ground produces by itself, but everyone, men and beast. All distinctions between people are declared null and void, like the distinctions between wild and domesticated animals, and even to some extent between men and beasts:

> You shall not reap the aftergrowth of your harvest or gather the grapes of your unpruned vine: it shall be a year of complete rest for the land. You may eat what the land yields during its Sabbath – you, your male and female slaves, your hired and your bound labourers who live with you; for your livestock also, and for the wild animals in your land all its yield shall be for food. (Leviticus 25:5–7)

Leviticus 25:8–55 deals with the year of Jubilee. After seven times seven years there is a holy year that commences at the Day of Atonement with the blowing of a ram's horn. That year, as in a Sabbath year, people shall not sow and reap; everything that grows on the land is again for everyone's use, people and animals. Moreover, all grounds return to their former owners – 'In this year of jubilee you shall return, every one of you, to your property' (25:13) – and those who fell into debt bondage are set free (25:39–41). The remainder of this chapter explains in detail how this should be done. Who would be willing to buy any land if it has to be given back in the year of Jubilee? That problem is dealt with by setting the purchase price at a much lower rate depending on the nearness of the year of Jubilee. In fact, you are not really purchasing land, but you are just buying the right of usage; the shorter the time of making profit, the lower the price.

The ground cannot and may not be used with impunity. You have to work the ground, as with other people and animals, with care. The reasons given for the year of jubilee are that the land and the people belong to God: 'Speak to the people of Israel and say to them: When you enter the land that I am giving you, the land shall observe a Sabbath for the Everlasting' (25:2). 'You shall not cheat one another, but you shall fear your God; for I am the Everlasting, your God' (25:17). 'The land shall not be sold in perpetuity, for the land is mine; with me you are but aliens and tenants' (25:23). 'I am the Everlasting your God, who brought you out of the land of Egypt, to give you the land of Canaan, to be your God' (25:38). Owning land and ruling others[328] are thus relativised. Caring for the earth and freedom to the people are an expression of respect to God.

Replenishing soil and social relations

The reason for starting all over again every fiftieth year in Israel was to enable each generation to experience a year of Jubilee at least once in its lifetime. There is still some debate whether these Sabbath years and Jubilees were really kept. Yet to maintain that this was utopian fiction is unlikely. A so-called 'clean-slate legislation' existed already in Sumer. The enthronement of a new king often occasioned the promulgation of such laws. A periodic redistribution of land and the remission of debts were important to prevent a growing imbalance between the rich and the poor, and to stem the depopulation of rural areas when, out of land shortage, one could not obtain sufficient sustenance. In Israel, these measures prevented the rise of a landed elite and the depletion of the soil.

Rome was the first great empire in the region that lacked such a redistribution legislation; debts could not be remitted. The context of Roman colonialism under which Palestine suffered puts additional value on one of the supplications in the Our Father prayer: 'And forgive us our debts, as we have also forgiven our debtors' (Matthew 6:12).[329]

Jubilee 2000 can be seen as an update of the biblical year of jubilee in our time. This UN project suggested a partial remission for countries that had no means to pay their current debts without forcing their own citizens to live below what is considered the guaranteed minimum income.

The replenishing of soil is more timely than ever. An estimated one third of all grounds are categorised somewhere between averagely and heavily affected by erosion, depletion, acidification, salinisation, subsidence and chemical pollution, according to a recent UN report, and this is just the start.[330] Some parts of the earth are experiencing a complete depletion of the soil due to monoculture of, for example, soya. Other areas face the opposite problem, viz. the eutrophication by industrial farming. Poverty and depletion of soil are connected issues. The poorest often live on the worst soil.

Land fallowing is still a method for replenishing soil. Two others, often used in organic farming, are crop rotation and once in so many years sowing plants to ameliorate the soil. A further is not harvesting the borders in order to grow plants that attract butterflies and bees.

One of the lessons of the sabbatical laws is that human and environmental relations that tend to inequality can be set straight.[331] The ecological impacts of these laws are extensive. They are beneficial for the soil and give special attention to the feeding of the poor and wild animals.[332] Giving the soil and wild animals their due shows respect to nature.[333] They stimulate an attitude that doesn't measure value only in terms of economic profit and, even more, they comply with another economic order:

Sabbath gives a vision for a world in which such inequities and imbalances are set aright, where all creation enjoys God's abundance and freedom, and where all is in harmonious relation for the praise of God and the wellbeing of all.[334] Sabbath, in this way, takes on a new, eschatological, significance. As a holy moment in time, it anticipates how life should be in the future: 'the joy of right relation that the Sabbath brings is a foretaste of its eschatological completion'.[335]

Sunday rest

At his first public appearance Jesus points out that his mission proclaims the year of Jubilee: 'He has sent me [...] to let the oppressed go free, to proclaim the year of the Lord's favour' (Luke 4:18–19). Although animals and ground are not mentioned, this does not mean that the good news is only meant for people, as we will also see in the next chapter. The fact that Jesus performs healings on the Sabbath is seen by his opponents as an infringement. But in the light of this year of grace these healings are, however, a fulfilment of this commandment, because it is focused on liberation.[336]

The Christian Sunday as the first day of the week, the day of resurrection, is an extension of the Sabbath.

> Therefore, while the promise of entering his rest is still open, let us take care that none of you should seem to have failed to reach it. For indeed the good news came to us just as to them; [...] So then, a Sabbath rest still remains for the people of God; for those who enter God's rest also cease from their labours as God did from his. Let us therefore make every effort to enter that rest, so that no one may fall through such disobedience as theirs. (Hebrews 4:1, 2, 9–11)

Sunday rest can be of great ecological importance by interrupting the economic pressure to produce and consume, fostering an awareness of other values, and offering a foretaste of more just relationships among people and between people and the rest of creation.

2.3.4 Jesus and the animals

The gospels seem to indicate that they are all about Jesus and people. Animals play a lesser role than in the Old Testament, although they appear in parables to clarify teachings about God and people. Yet this is not the whole story because animals are not just illustrations. Jesus embodied in words and deeds the biblical view of God's care for creation, the interconnectedness between humans, animals and earth, and the compassionate treatment of animals and sustainable agriculture.

I will approach this motif in a twofold manner: first from the ecological context of Jesus's appearance, and second by looking into texts gleaned from the synoptic gospels in which animals play a significant role. Animals in the Gospel of John deserve a separate treatment, but I leave this gospel aside.

The ecological context of the gospels

In biblical scholarship, historical–critical research in particular, context is of great importance. To know anything about the gospel, one has to be conversant with first-century Palestine. Attention has been given to the religious and, sometimes, also to the political and sociological contexts, but hardly anything is done regarding the ecological context.[337] However, Jesus's way of thinking and handling are clearly inspired by Galilee's natural world and the way its inhabitants interacted with nature. The natural surroundings and agriculture could be described in the same manner as social relations. Animals and plants are mentioned in the gospels, together with non-living nature. To give just a few examples at random, Matthew 7 and 8 mention dogs and swine, fish and snakes, foxes and birds, a herd of swine, trees with good and bad fruit, grapes and thorn bushes, figs and thorns, a stone, a rock, mountain streams, storms, sand, a mountain, waves and a lake, wind and water, caves and a steep slope. They are meaningful as locations where the gospel takes place, mirroring the relation between God and people, but they are more than just accidental props or fortuitously chosen literary images. More insight into these natural surroundings can deepen our understanding of Jesus' message.

Jesus' theology of creation

Sometimes animals are made an example to humans:

> See, I am sending you out like sheep into the midst of wolves;
> so be wise as serpents and innocent as doves. (Matthew 10:16)

Look at the birds of the air; they neither sow nor reap nor gather into barns, and yet your heavenly Father feeds them. Are you not of more value than they? (Matthew 6:26)[338]

Birds do not organise their lives as people do.[339] Their reliance on the creator is more obvious than people's, because they don't work for a living. Humans might harbour the illusion that they make their own reality, but if you look at birds you can see that this is not the case. Birds remind us that we at a deeper level equally depend on our creator. The disciples don't have to worry because they are in God's care, just like the birds.[340] 'Are you not of more value than they?' is the conclusion that follows logically from minor to major premise. But this syllogism doesn't place people outside creation, nor does it suggest that birds have no value at all.

This type of argument is frequently used:

Are not two sparrows sold for a penny? Yet not one of them will fall to the ground apart from your Father. And even the hairs of your head are all counted. So do not be afraid; you are of more value than many sparrows. (Matthew 10:29–31)[341]

The reason for this comparison is to take away fear from people. The argument runs as follows: even a creature that in the eyes of humans is hardly of any value, like a sparrow, is still valuable in the eyes of God, so, if God is that good to sparrows, how much more will he not be to people?

Jesus compares healing the sick on the Sabbath with treating animals compassionately:

Then he said to them, 'If one of you has a child or an ox that has fallen into a well, will you not immediately pull it out on a Sabbath day?' (Luke 14:5)

He said to them, 'Suppose one of you has only one sheep and it falls into a pit on the Sabbath; will you not lay hold of it and lift it out? How much more valuable is a human being than a sheep! So it is lawful to do good on the Sabbath.' (Matthew 12:11–12)

The presupposition of the comparison between people and animals is always that people are more important, but also that every animal is valuable to God. Paul in his first letter to the Corinthians, at first glance, seems to differ on this point. The commandment that animals must have their share of the harvest is being applied to the apostles, who have to be supported by the local church: 'For it is written in the law of Moses, "You shall not muzzle an ox while it is treading out the grain." Is it for oxen that God is concerned? Or does he not speak entirely for our sake? It was indeed written for our sake, for whoever ploughs should plough in hope and whoever threshes should thresh in hope of a share in the crop' (1 Corinthians 9:9–10). Does Paul suggest that God does not care for the oxen in the Torah?[342] His way of reasoning resembles on the contrary that of the gospels, going from the minor premise to the major, because verse 12 says 'If others share this rightful claim on you, do not we still more?' His argument is thus: if God gives ploughing oxen the right to partake of the crop, should we, apostles, not receive a reward for our work even more?

Another text that on first sight doesn't give much concern to animals is Mark 5:1–20. Jesus gives permission to the demons leaving a possessed man to enter a herd of swine. Are the lives of swine of no value to Jesus?

So he gave them permission. And the unclean spirits came out and entered the swine; and the herd, numbering about two thousand, rushed down the steep bank into the sea, and were drowned in the sea. (Mark 5:13)

Thus, Jesus doesn't actually drive the swine into the sea; the unclean spirits are doing this. There is an interpretation of this story that suggests that the swine co-operate with Jesus in a self-effacing deed to free the man of his demons.[343] The water would signify the primal flood, the chaos of the beginning. It is, thus, possible to take the story as a creation narrative.

'He was with the wild beasts' – Mark 1:13

One text mentions explicitly something about Jesus being with animals. According to the synoptic gospels, just before his public appearance, Jesus stayed in the desert for forty days. Mark mentions that 'He was in the wilderness forty days, tempted by Satan; and he was with the wild beasts; and the angels waited on him' (Mark 1:13). Although this doesn't seem to say a lot, its meaning is profound.

In the first place, one should be aware that the wild beasts Jesus encountered in the wilderness are hardly there anymore. At the time of Jesus, the Palestinian wilderness still contained bears, wild asses, ostriches and several antelope species; all these animals have disappeared due to human interference.[344]

Secondly, it is possible to think of wild animals as threatening, a threat against which angels might have had to protect Jesus. But Jesus appears not to be afraid of them. In the Old Testament the righteous, e.g. Job and Daniel, have nothing to fear of wild animals. In this way, Jesus could be taken as a righteous one.[345]

Thirdly, his stay in the wilderness calls up the visions of Isaiah (Isaiah 11:6–9 and 65:25):

> The wolf shall live with the lamb, the leopard shall lie down with the kid, the calf and the lion and the fatling together, and a little child shall lead them. [...]
> They will not hurt or destroy on all my holy mountain; for the earth will be full of the knowledge of the Everlasting as the waters cover the sea. (Isaiah 11:6–9)

This is an eschatological image of peace of the whole creation: predators live in peace both with their prey and people. Jesus living with wild animals shows that the kingdom of God, which is still to come *and* is sometimes already there, implicates all creation. 'Mark's image of Jesus with the animals provides a christological warrant for and a biblical symbol of the human possibility of living fraternally with other living creatures, a possibility given by God in creation and given back in messianic redemption.'[346] No wonder that there are so many stories about the desert fathers and mothers and other saints who didn't frighten animals and even harboured friendships with dangerous ones.[347]

Animals have their rightful place in the kingdom of God. The Our Father prayer gives witness to this implicitly by stating 'on earth as it is in heaven', which refers to the three preceding petitions about God's name, kingdom and will. Christians everywhere pray that God's kingdom may ultimately be realised for all creation. This is precisely what is meant by 'heaven and earth'.

2.4 SALVATION OF THE EARTH

In the USA, a considerable number of Christians expect the foreseeable destruction of the earth, out of which only a small group of believers will be saved. These are fundamentalist Christians who prepare themselves for the physical outcome of the vision of the Book of Revelation because they believe that after its destruction a new earth will appear that gives room to all true Christians. They even welcome the signs of earth's corruption because they take them as omens signifying the return of Christ, who will save them. Disaster movies and some forms of science fiction are a secular form of this apocalyptic way of thinking. In Europe, many evangelicals and stern reformed Christians hold on to the same destructive image of the end of time. They are not at all worried about the ecological crisis or social justice issues: 'why should one make such a fuss about the earth if soon everything will go up in flames?'[348] This type of thinking is fed by certain biblical texts, such as found in Revelation, Mark 13:31 – 'heaven and earth will disappear' – the second part of Joel and 2 Peter 3:10.[349] For an ecological reading of the Bible, one has to think carefully about these texts concerning the 'last things'. Do they really speak of the complete destruction of the earth? That would be the first question to put forward. The second question would be how 'last things' should be taken with regard to time. Is it about the future or does it rather put the present into a specific perspective? There is much to argue in favour of an interpretation that takes the texts about salvation, outcome, kingdom of God and a new earth as saying something about the present, in the same way as creation narratives are about an ongoing process and not primarily and exclusively about a very first beginning. At the same time, it is almost impossible for western minds to wriggle out of the linear timeframe that permeates our whole culture.[350]

Many liturgical texts voice the hope or the expectation that God's plan with the world will be realised one time: because once everything was alright, and in the future it will be alright again; initially God wanted paradise and, behold, there will be a kingdom of peace and in the Church we cherish this dream.[351] But if this longing for justice, peace and equality can only be found in the future, the present becomes nothing more than an interval. Although this future perspective does not coincide with what happens after we die or beyond the end of time, it is equally far from the good things happening in our life, here and now.

Christians who are involved in social activities, on the other hand, have the tendency to think that they can and must realise God's kingdom on the basis of their strength alone. They run the same risks as fundamentalists with their us-versus-them, dividing sharply between good and evil, and lack of self-critique. If God's kingdom coincides too much with an ideal future society, it starts to resemble utopia with all its pitfalls.[352] As Keller describes it:

A radical demand for justice opens it to faith in a promised outcome. [...] the promise morphs into the guarantee. [...] If the revolution drives not just with determination but with determinism toward the utopic end – knowable to its radical elite – it moves from total certainty to totalitarianism.[353]

Thinking in a time sequence starting with creation and running to salvation that will be fulfilled at the end of time runs counter with present-day theories of a cosmos that is immense, unfinished and interconnected. Taking current cosmology seriously implies seeing creation and salvation in a far more interconnected way, as already happens in the Bible. Cosmos and earth are continually changing. Even though the biblical writers had the image of the earth as a disc on the surface of the water resting on pillars with heaven's vault above, and a seemingly unchangeable flora, fauna and landscape, creation is also presented as an ongoing process that encompasses all of reality. May this also be true of salvation?

The Old Testament contains a whole range of prophetic visions of the near and far-away future. In the New Testament we also find various perspectives on the future, the kingdom of God and salvation. I will discuss a few texts that always appear in the context of ecology: the groaning of creation in labour pains (Romans 8), texts on destruction and peace (various prophets) and the Book of Revelation, and I will add to these a text that is hardly discussed in this context: the woman at the well (John 4).

2.4.1 Salvation, creation and the animals: a summary

Earlier in this chapter we saw that in Genesis 3—9 the decline of humanity and the rest of the earth are interwoven, and the same can be said about their salvation.

In Deutero-Isaiah (Isaiah 40—55) creation and salvation are not fundamentally different categories. God is involved with cosmos and people; nature and history are not in opposition. People do receive more attention in God's creative/salvific work in Deutero-Isaiah than is the case in the beginning of Genesis. Out of concern for the poor and the needy God provides for water in the desert (Isaiah 41:17–20): 'he did not create it a chaos, he formed it to be inhabited!' (Isaiah 45:8). In the Psalms of creation the whole world sings God's praise just by being there, not by denying all suffering in the world, but by being hopeful in spite of all its evils and pains.

Sophia/Wisdom is a feminine image of God in which creation and salvation of all the earth is implicated, as is said in Colossians 1:15–20. The last part of this hymn is about salvation:

> He is the head of the body, the church; he is the beginning, the firstborn from the dead, so that he might come to have first place in everything. For in him all the fullness of God was pleased to dwell, and through him God was pleased to reconcile to himself all things, whether on earth or in heaven, by making peace through the blood of his cross. (Colossians 1:18–20)

Salvation is already there and not yet. Christ as resurrected is the first-born, the rest of creation has still to follow.

When Jesus declares a year of grace (Luke 4:18–19), thus referring to the sabbatical year, he clearly implicates the animals and the ground. God's kingdom is not just for people. Jesus, in being with the wild animals (Mark 1:13), refers to an eschatological image of peace in the whole creation: predators live in harmony with their prey and with people. God's kingdom, both coming and sometimes present – your kingdom come – involves all of creation, just as Isaiah said:

> *They will not hurt or destroy on all my holy mountain;*
> *for the earth will be full of the knowledge of the Everlasting*
> *as the waters cover the sea.* (Isaiah 11:9)

2.4.2 The labour pains of creation: Romans 8:19-23

Paul has had a tremendous influence on Christian theology, especially on the Protestant concept of justification through faith. Only people can believe; thus, by centralising the notion of *sola fide*, salvation seems only a matter between God and humans. That Paul does reckon with the whole of creation becomes clear from the already discussed Christ hymn from Colossians 1 and also from Romans 8.[354]

> I consider that the sufferings of this present time are not worth comparing with the glory about to be revealed to us. For the creation waits with eager longing for the revealing of the children of God; for the creation was subjected to futility, not of its own will but by the will of the one who subjected it, in hope that the creation itself will be set free from its bondage to decay and will obtain the freedom of the glory of the children of God. We know that the whole creation has been groaning in labour pains until now; and not only the creation, but we ourselves, who have the first fruits of the Spirit, groan inwardly while we wait for adoption, the redemption of our bodies. (Romans 8:18-23)[355]

In the first 11 chapters of his letter to the Church of Rome, Paul sets off Christ, who justifies and brings life, against Adam, who brought sin and death into the world. The believers participate in Jesus's resurrection and in this new life. But the whole creation suffers and longs for salvation.[356] Its groaning is a sign of hope.[357]

Salvation with the body and the earth

The meaning of the word *ktisis*, creation, in this passage is contested.[358] Some believe that it refers to people, others that it signifies only non-human nature.[359] Nothing seems to be against the notion that *ktisis* really means all of creation, including people, as is very much the case in other texts. 'For the creation waits with eager longing for the revealing of the children of God' (v.19) does entail also the believers, as we see in verse 23: 'but we ourselves'. The ones addressed have also received 'the spirit of adoption' (v.15), but that is apparently still for the future, because now there is still this groaning, futility and decay. This decay does not have to be solely a result of human sin, which maybe already shows too much anthropocentricity. It does not fit either with 'for the creation was subjected to futility, not of its own will but by the will of the one who subjected it'; the one who subjects is certainly God, not man. All creatures suffer in their own way from the decay of being because suffering is unmistakably part of the whole creation. According to Paul, all creatures are born to be free. God's spirit liberates, and is received in advance, literally, as first fruits of the harvest. God's children certainly prevail; all of creation is focused on their adoption as God's children. The creation participates in this salvation.[360]

The translation 'the redemption of our bodies' (v.23) parallels 'set free from its bondage to decay' in verse 21. This has been taken in a dualistic fashion: the body, the earth-like, versus the spiritual, the divine. This would mean that people should be liberated from their bodies in order to become God's children. But it is not just people but the whole of creation that has to be delivered from futility, hopelessness, nothingness, meaninglessness (v.20: *mataiotes*) and decay, destruction, depletion (v.21: *fthora*).[361] This cannot be the deliverance from the material, because the earth is being delivered as well. Thus, people are also not delivered from their bodies, but *in* their bodies. Being delivered is living in the spirit (vv.15, 16, 23) and that is not an unembodied reality but freedom in the body in harmony with God and nature.

In this text Paul does not speak dualistically, in terms of spirit versus matter or humans versus nature.[362] The hoped-for salvation is inclusive, coming forth from the spirit who is already present.

God's children within the community of creation
The fate of the whole creation is, thus, in Romans 8 connected with the fate of God's children. The question is: in what way? Those who connect

'creation' in this text solely with non-human nature see a link with the ground that is cursed in Genesis 3:17: through men's sin decay came into the world, through the salvation in Christ the world was delivered together with humanity.[363] Paul resumes in this passage a theme found in the books of the prophets: the suffering and salvation of the whole community of creation.[364] 'The prophets, however, announce a future redemption which will revivify the people and the natural world together.'[365] The prophet Hosea has the key to this interpretation.

> Hear the word of the Everlasting, O people of Israel; for the Everlasting has an indictment against the inhabitants of the land. There is no faithfulness or loyalty, and no knowledge of God in the land. Swearing, lying, and murder, and stealing and adultery break out; bloodshed follows bloodshed. Therefore the land mourns, and all who live in it languish; together with the wild animals and the birds of the air, even the fish of the sea are perishing. (Hosea 4:1–3)

It goes badly wrong with the land and the animals because of what people do. The animals that suffer are the same animals that according to Genesis 1 fall under the dominion of humans and, thus, are directly affected by them.[366] In our current era, the Anthropocene, people act upon all of earth's ecosystem. An ecological interpretation of Hosea 4 and Romans 8 could, therefore, be if people behave better, the earth will flourish again. 'Our sinful behaviour has destructive consequences not only for our own kind but for other creatures as well, bonded with us in one community of life.'[367] Creatures need one another. The revelation of God's children is necessary because humans can put words to all of creation's need to live and to give thanks.[368]

2.4.3 Peace or destruction in the prophets

Hosea 4 makes us realise that the prophets were cognisant of what happened to the whole earth. We saw the same in the creation narratives of Deutero-Isaiah. Creation and salvation were clearly not fundamentally different categories, no more than nature and history.[369] Many prophecies of salvation and disaster in the Old Testament do not apply only to the human world. Both the disaster that has been noticed and foretold and the salvation that has been proclaimed affect all reality. The question is how. Occasionally prophecies seem to suggest that the earth should be habitable just for people and nature is accordingly perceived as inimical. Thus, locust plagues are disasters and the chasing away of wild animals is salvation. Does the choice of imagery show after all that the prophets think really negatively about nature? Is it really true that salvation in the near or far-away future, according to the prophets, does not include the earth and its whole community of life? Is it necessary that the old earth has to be destroyed first, as some fundamentalists believe?

Living peacefully with wild animals or driving them away

> I will make for you a covenant on that day with the wild animals,
> the birds of the air, and the creeping things of the ground; and
> I will abolish the bow, the sword, and war from the land; and I
> will make you lie down in safety. (Hosea 2:18)[370]

Just like Isaiah, Hosea describes how humans are at peace with animals.[371] This motif of living peacefully with wild animals is also seen in Job and is connected with this promise: 'At destruction and famine you shall laugh, and shall not fear the wild animals of the earth. For you shall be in league with the stones of the field, and the wild animals shall be at peace with you' (Job 5:22-23). In times of peace, one should also live in peace with the animals.

But there are other traditions in which a future peace is pictured as a land from which all wild animals have been banished.[372] Ezekiel prophesies of David, the good shepherd, and the people as sheep: 'I will make with them a covenant of peace and banish wild animals

148

from the land, so that they may live in the wild and sleep in the woods securely' (Ezekiel 34:25).

These are no visions that provide a blueprint of ecological justice. A wolf laying down at the side of a lamb and carnivores turning into vegetarians are not realistic.[373] We have been quite successful, though, in the other option, viz. the banishing of wild animals in our part of the world, although the whole exercise did not turn out as blissfully as we thought.

It seems to me that what in these Old Testament texts is said about wild animals may parallel the way hostile peoples were looked upon. Either you conquer and/or banish them or you make peace with them. It was all about the liberation of the people of Israel from their enemies, either humans or animals. If peace with people is to be preferred above waging war, this should also be the case with animals. These texts could thus point to a route leading to ecological peace, searching for living conditions for all living beings within the living community of the whole creation.

> The wilderness and the dry land shall be glad, the desert shall rejoice and blossom [...] Then the eyes of the blind shall be opened, and the ears of the deaf unstopped; then the lame shall leap like a deer, and the tongue of the speechless sing for joy. For waters shall break forth in the wilderness, and streams in the desert [...] (Isaiah 35:1–7)

Locusts and God's verdict in Joel

The Book of Joel shows the transition of classical prophecy to apocalypticism. This shift explains the use of even more imagery. It is not clear whether Joel is in itself a unity and when his prophecy should be dated. Most biblical scholars opt for a post-exilic date and point out the clear demarcation between the first two chapters and the last.[374]

The first part contains two descriptions of a disaster followed by a summons to mourn and sing a song of lamentation. The first catastrophe appears to be a plague of locusts, the second an invasion of an army. Still, it could well be that they both point to the same catastrophe that comes either in the guise of real locusts or an army. Either way, the result will be the same: the utter ruin of the land. 'The fields are devastated, the ground mourns; for the grain is destroyed, the wine dries up, the oil fails' (Joel 1:10). The motif of a land in mourning is common in prophetic literature.[375] The state of the land is indicative to the state of the people. If people practise evil and turn away from God, the land immediately deteriorates. If they are righteous, the land will flourish.[376] Joel does not specify their sins, but still calls for repentance. People may take their example from the land that mourns.

God will respond to their act of repentance (2:18–27). 'Then the Everlasting became jealous for his land, and had pity on his people' (v.18). The speech is at first directed to the land, then to the animals, and after that to the people:

> Do not fear, O soil; be glad and rejoice, for the Everlasting has
>   done great things!
> Do not fear, you animals of the field, for the pastures of the
>   wilderness are green; the tree bears its fruit, the fig tree and
>   vine give their full yield.
> O children of Zion, be glad and rejoice in the Everlasting your
> God; for he has given the early rain for your vindication, he has
>   poured down for you abundant rain, the early and the later
>   rain, as before.
> The threshing floors shall be full of grain, the vats shall overflow
>   with wine and oil. (Joel 2:21–24)

However important the land may be in Joel's eyes, all emphasis is nevertheless on what it yields to men. His vision is, therefore, clearly anthropocentric. [377] Surprisingly inclusive is Joel, nevertheless, regarding people – he states in the next verses that God's spirit will be poured out on the sons and daughters, the old and the young, and even on the slaves, male and female (3:1–2).[378]

A new visual language emerges in chapter 3 that is more apocalyptic in tone.[379] 'The day of the Lord' is proclaimed. This day will come accompanied with sun and moon eclipses, dying stars, earthquakes, blood and fire, and pillars of smoke (3:3–5 and 4:14–16). These are images of war and natural disasters like a volcanic eruption or an earthquake.[380] Darkness and light, smoke and fire, are also images of the coming of God.[381] On that day all peoples and their lands will receive an alarming sentence. 'Egypt shall become a desolation and Edom a desolate wilderness, because of the violence done to the people of Judah …' (3:19). But Judah shall have wine, milk and water in abundance (3:18).

Is this 'day of the Lord' in some ways related to the seventh day, Sabbath, and the Sunday? This image leaves room for thinking of the 'last things' not as the end of history but as looking at the present from a specific angle. It is clear that Joel does not speak of a complete destruction. Fields will be razed by locusts and life in Israel will become almost impossible, but they will thrive again the moment God arrives. What was destroyed will be restored. But the countries that abused Israel and its land will turn into deserts.[382]

A new earth in Isaiah

Does Isaiah also take the new earth for the restoration of the earth? 'For I am about to create new heavens and a new earth; the former things shall not be remembered or come to mind' (Isaiah 65:17). These words are the beginning of a passage that ends with a wolf and a lamb feeding together (v.25).[383] The verses between suggest the existence of a city, a new Jerusalem, where people will live long and happily, and see and enjoy the fruits of their labour, where children have a good future and no one dies young.

But be glad and rejoice forever in what I am creating; for
I am about to create Jerusalem as a joy, and its people as

a delight. [...] No more shall there be in it an infant that lives but a few days, or an old person who does not live out a lifetime; [...] They shall build houses and inhabit them; they shall plant vineyards and eat their fruit. [...] and my chosen shall long enjoy the work of their hands. They shall not labour in vain, or bear children for calamity; for they shall be offspring blessed by the Everlasting – and their descendants as well. (65:18–23)

The third part of Isaiah, Trito-Isaiah, is post-exilic and is firmly connected thematically with Deutero-Isaiah. The returning exiles find Jerusalem in a poor state and rebuilding proves to be quite disappointing. Poverty is everywhere; living conditions are precarious. Many infants die, most people don't come of age, others take advantage of the fruits of their labour. It might be possible that Isaiah pictures their situation too bleakly when he talks of 'weeping and crying' (v.19), 'labouring in vain' and 'bearing children for calamity' (v.23). On the other hand, it helps him to sketch more sharply what is really new: they will 'be glad and rejoice forever in what I am creating' (v.18), 'for one who dies at a hundred years will be considered a youth' (v.20), 'a lion shall eat straw like an ox' (v. 25). Thus, Isaiah creates a clear contrast between how it is and how it should be in the Jerusalem of his time.

There is no indication to read anything other than his desiring a better life, criticising the current predicament and believing that a new start is conceivable. Plenty of parallels with our times spring to mind: people dying too young due to poverty; people labouring too hard without really benefiting from what their work yields because most of their profits go to others.

2.4.4 A new earth in Revelation

In the Book of Revelation the motifs of God's judgement and a new earth and a new heaven return. In the New Testament era, prophecy gradually changed into apocalypticism. Whereas Isaiah drew up an altogether recognisable situation and countered it with perhaps not readily realistic but still understandable imagery, Revelation is full of images of angels, devils and weird animals. The primal monsters of the Old Testament have changed into a gruesome beast and a dragon that have lost anything recommendable in themselves, which was not so when they put in their first appearance in Job and Psalm 104. In Revelation, they just represent evil.[384]

> And I saw a beast rising out of the sea, having ten horns and seven heads; and on its horns were ten diadems, and on its heads were blasphemous names. And the beast that I saw was like a leopard, its feet were like a bear's, and its mouth was like a lion's mouth. And the dragon gave it his power and his throne and great authority. (Revelation 13:1–2)

The second beast takes over from the first its power (13:11) and forces people to worship the first beast and let them be marked on their hand or their forehead. In the end this beast will be defeated, and the lamb, symbol of Christ, will be victorious.

The prophets still spoke of a new Jerusalem in terms of a peaceful but recognisable city, in which people were building houses and working, but in the last chapters of Revelation the city that descends from heaven is incredibly rich and glorious, covered in gold and gems. In the description of the new Jerusalem of Revelation 21:1— 22:5 elements from the beginning of the Scriptures reappear. The tree of life, a river, and the end of pain and death seem to refer to Genesis 2 and 3.

> Then the angel showed me the river of the water of life, bright as crystal, flowing from the throne of God and of the Lamb through the middle of the street of the city. On either side of the river is the tree of life with its twelve kinds of fruit, producing its

fruit each month; and the leaves of the tree are for the healing of the nations. (Revelation 22:1—2)

Is the new Jerusalem *paradise regained*?[385]

Transformation of the earth

The Book of Revelation dates from the end of the first century, when the Roman repression of Jews and Christians increased. The readers, whom the Book of Revelation addresses, are the urban churches of Asia, the western part of current Turkey. The use of imagery that was only understood by insiders was to avert any suspicion that the Roman regime might harbour against them. The cosmic battle between, on the one side, God and the lamb, and, on the other side, the dragon and the beast, can be interpreted in several ways. The visions are so rich in imagery that these images have been applied to all sorts of conflicts: the struggle against the Pope, against communism, fascism and capitalism.[386] And why could the beast not equally be taken for 'the fossil-fuel economy that devours lands and peoples'?[387]

Fundamentalists tend to read Revelation as a prediction of the future. 'Then I saw a new heaven and a new earth; for the first heaven and the first earth had passed away, and the sea was no more' (21:1) and 'See, I am making all things new' (21:5) are used to proclaim all care for the earth as irrelevant. There are yet arguments that favour an ecological interpretation of Revelation.[388] God's good future is earthbound; it takes place on earth. The old heaven and earth are not destroyed: 'God doesn't make new things but makes all things new.'[389] The divide between heaven and earth will be suspended. The holy city will be a city of gardens. On the other hand, there will be no more sea and night (21:1, 5). Though Revelation teems with animal life, these creatures are not the animals that the Old Testament calls our fellow creatures (either friend or foe), but they have become symbols of good and evil.[390] On the other hand, we see how all creatures gather round God's throne to sing his praise, just like we read in the Psalms:[391]

Then I heard every creature in heaven and on earth and under the earth and in the sea, and all that is in them, singing, 'To the one seated on the throne and to the Lamb be blessing and honour and glory and might forever and ever!' (Revelation 5:13)

The heavenly woman and the earth

A great portent appeared in heaven: a woman clothed with the sun, with the moon under her feet, and on her head a crown of twelve stars.

She was pregnant and was crying out in birth pangs, in the agony of giving birth. (Revelation 12:1-2)

Revelation 12 portrays very dramatically the image of the liberation of the world:[392] a heavenly woman giving birth to the Messiah is threatened by a dragon. Later she becomes one with Mary, the mother of Jesus, pictured as standing on a crescent moon, stars around her head, and under her foot the head of a dragon or a snake. Mary became the second Eve killing the snake. In Revelation, earth comes to this woman's rescue:

But the earth came to the help of the woman; it opened its mouth and swallowed the river that the dragon had poured from his mouth. Then the dragon was angry with the woman, and went off to make war on the rest of her children, those who keep the commandments of God and hold the testimony of Jesus. (Revelation 12:16–17)

In this chapter the imagery of giving birth and having labour pains reappears, just as happens in Romans 8 and in Old Testament creation narratives. And just like the gospels it mentions 'for nation will rise against nation, and kingdom against kingdom; there will be earthquakes in various places; there will be famines. This is but the beginning of the birth pangs' (Mark 13:8 and Matthew 24:8). Apt for picturing a new beginning is the image of giving birth as an unstoppable process marked by vulnerability and hope. This feminine perspective of the Bible has all too often been snowed under by a language of faith that favoured fathering and being born over giving birth. Unfortunately, in the devotion of the virgin Mary, her act of giving birth was broken away from her physical embodiment and sexuality and earthiness. She was left with the image of an asexual Mother of God.[393]

Counter-image of Roman propaganda

> Then I saw a great white throne and the one who sat on it; the earth and the heaven fled from his presence, and no place was found for them. And I saw the dead, great and small, standing before the throne, and books were opened. Also another book was opened, the book of life. And the dead were judged according to their works, as recorded in the books. (Revelation 20:11–12)

The imagery of Revelation is in the original setting a weapon in the resistance against Roman repression. The image of a throne can also be found with the prophets. Sitting on a throne means having power; God's throne is a counter-image of the powers that be. In Roman propaganda the Roman Empire was an empire without end, Rome an eternal city and the emperor the divine ruler of the world who forced all peoples to subjection.[394] Against Rome's claims to eternity the New Testament brings in the end of times, especially in its books written after the year CE 70, when Jerusalem was conquered and its Temple destroyed: 'the eschatological focus of the Gospels and other post-70 C.E. New Testament literature [...] was aimed at giving people hope for a different future'.[395]

Earth and heaven dissolving into nothingness are thus interpreted as the social structuring of the Roman Empire seen as a colonial dictatorship. And the violence that fills all of Revelation, e.g. 'And these two were thrown alive into the lake of fire that burns with sulphur. And the rest were killed by the sword' (Revelation 19:20–12), may well stand for Roman violence.[396]

The image of God's throne with the dead standing before it waiting to be judged has been linked with the image of the Son of Man, who sits on his throne to separate the sheep from the goats (Matthew 25:31–46). Since the Middle Ages this has become the dominant image of the Last Judgement. Think of the pictures of Hieronymus Bosch, where a select group of the elect ascend to the light, supported by angels, and a group of doomed souls descending into the dark to be tortured by devils. This terrifying image must spur every person to good behaviour. In Revelation, the vision gives hope to a suppressed community. Even those killed by the beast will be vindicated.

The last vision is about a tree of life and a river that springs up from under the throne of God and the lamb. Its leaves bring healing to the peoples (Revelation 22:1–2). The tree of life appears after Genesis in Jewish apocalyptic writings such as 4 Ezra, where it is said that paradise will be reopened for a time, the tree of life will be planted, fruit will not rot and joy and healing will be found.[397] In the beginning of Revelation the tree is called: 'To everyone who conquers, I will give permission to eat from the tree of life that is in the paradise of God' (Revelation 2:7). Since the Fathers of the Church, it has become common to link the cross and the tree of life. The image can be a symbol for both the earth's wounds and its healing.[398]

Revelation can be read both as a warning against self-destruction and an intensification of salvation, a renewal of the earth *de profundis*.[399]

2.4.5 The woman at the well: John 4

The Gospel of John contains, apart from chapter 1 that we have already analysed in depth, many other passages that are interesting from an ecological point of view.[400] Divine and earthen reality touch each other in stories like the marriage in Cana (John 2), where water changes into wine, and in some of Jesus's titles, such as 'bread of life'

(John 6:35).[401] Whereas Paul emphasises what is not yet realised, John is familiar with a more realised eschatology: everyone who knows Jesus enjoys already eternal life.[402] 'And this is eternal life, that they may know you, the only true God, and Jesus Christ whom you have sent' (John 17:3). Eternal life does not mean life after death. Close to the aforementioned text is: 'I came that they may have life, and have it abundantly' (John 10:10). This is not the abundance of taking whatever is in your reach, of consuming to the full, but the abundance of the feeding of the thousands (6:12), of sharing equally what is available.[403]

In Jesus we see the coming of a new reality that has the traits of a new creation. There is no reason to restrict 'the fullness of life' just to people. The whole of biodiversity can be included. In the Gospel of John, Jesus is rightly called the saviour of the whole word.

Saviour of the world

The story of Jesus speaking with a Samaritan woman at a well (John 4:5–42) is in churches' lectionaries hardly ever read to the end; very often, the lesson breaks off at verse 26. That is the moment that Jesus makes himself known to her as the Messiah, after she has hinted at this likelihood by calling him a prophet. But in verse 42, the story reaches its climax when the other Samaritans say 'and we know that this is truly the Saviour of the world'. The recognition of Jesus as the saviour of the world on the part of the Samaritans includes the other expressions of Jesus' significance and functions as their unsurpassable term: 'a Jew' – 'more than Jacob' – 'a prophet' – 'the messiah' – 'the saviour of the world.'[404] Literally, the text says 'saviour of the cosmos' (in Greek, *soter tou kosmou*). This title, which Roman emperors gave to themselves, attaches John to Jesus, and is clearly meant to be a counter-image of the Roman Empire. Again, there is a link with the beginning of the gospel: the one through whom everything came into being (1:2) is also its saviour.

A theological conversation

The gradual insight into who Jesus is gains shape in a discussion about water and food. Jesus is going through Samaritan territory and takes a rest at a well that is named after the biblical ancestor Jacob.

> A Samaritan woman came to draw water, and Jesus said to her, 'Give me a drink.' (His disciples had gone to the city to buy food.) The Samaritan woman said to him, 'How is it that you, a Jew, ask a drink of me, a woman of Samaria?' (Jews do not share things in common with Samaritans.) Jesus answered her, 'If you knew the gift of God, and who it is that is saying to you, "Give me a drink," you would have asked him, and he would have given you living water.' (John 4:7–10)

A Samaritan woman is an equally improbable agent to Jesus as the Samaritan who came to the help of the badly wounded Jewish victim of a violent robbery (Luke 10:25–37). The Samaritan woman and the Samaritan of the parable belong to a people that Jews looked down on. To make things worse, no decent man should be seen talking with a strange woman.

Nevertheless, the two start a deeply engaging conversation. It is a theological discussion about three topics: water, her life, and the correct way and place of praying to God.[405] When Jesus's disciples return with food, they start a similar conversation about food with Jesus. In the meantime, the woman has returned to her city to speak with its citizens about Jesus. Through her testimony, many come to belief. After Jesus has stayed two more days in their city and they have listened to him, the number of believers grows even more. At that point they call him 'saviour of the world'.

This text has often led to a dualistic and sexist reading: the dumb woman keeps on talking about drinking water whereas Jesus speaks symbolically of water as God's word. She has often been called a prostitute because Jesus says 'You are right in saying, "I have no husband"; for you have had five husbands, and the one you have now is not your husband' (4:17–18). Being at the well 'about noon' (v.6) was interpreted as that she was drawing water at the hottest moment of the day, probably in order to avoid being seen by anyone else.[406] But literally, the text says the sixth hour, which can point to the sixth hour of the day, noon, as in the Jewish way of counting the hours, or it could signify the sixth hour of the evening, according to the Roman way of counting.[407] To me, this is not really relevant. Besides, from the story, one cannot deduce that the story takes place in summer when, at noon, it would be too warm. The only other time that John mentions the sixth hour is when Pilate sits down on the judge's bench and says: 'Here is your king!' (19:14). The sixth hour might just indicate the hour of light and insight. If it is the hour of midday, then it stands in opposition to the nightly hour at which Nicodemus, one of the Jewish leaders, comes to Jesus (3:2).

As is often the case with the Gospel of John, the story of the Samaritan woman is about a gradual progression from not knowing to knowing fully; it is a steady turning from misunderstanding and unbelief to confession and the spreading of belief.[408] The woman is not more stupid than all the others who do not understand Jesus immediately. Whilst talking with this woman, Jesus comes to an important declaration: 'God is spirit, and those who worship him must worship in spirit and truth' (John 4:24). In this saying the male image of the Father is enhanced with the female image of the Spirit, the creating and insight-giving power of God.[409] What Jesus knows about her life marks in this story only his prophetic talents; it is not a disqualification of the woman. On the contrary, she returns to the city to testify to her belief, and thus becomes a trusty witness, because many come to belief through her words. John also uses the verb to testify (Greek: *martureo*) in connection with John the Baptist (1:7). She as a witness has become for others a source in her own right, because 'those who drink of the water that I will give them will never be thirsty. The water that I will give will become in them a spring of water gushing up to eternal life' (v.14).

Water of life

Both the woman and Jesus talk about water in more than one sense. For the woman, water is a symbol for the harshness of daily life. Drawing water every day is a heavy chore. It would be nice if one did not have to do it anymore, but without water no one can survive. Jesus agrees that water is essential to life, but also points to himself as life's true source: 'Jesus himself gives water, he is the water of life, the gift of God.'[410] Speaking with his disciples about food brings up the notion of life's privations.[411] They have just returned from the city with food that they have bought and they implore him to eat something. But Jesus sends them away to gather the harvest, for which they did no labour (4:38). Later on, he will pass bread around to the multitude and say about himself: 'I am the bread of life.'

Water is, like bread, a multi-tiered symbol in the Gospel of John. It is important to piece all these layers together and not to play them off against each other. Jesus as water of life doesn't downplay the daily efforts of women to find enough drinking water. This Samaritan woman was busy doing her daily work. This ordinary water does not stand in opposition to the water of eternal life; both are in the scope of one another.

Worldwide, we see that mainly women share the burden of providing clean water and good food for their families.[412] Due to pollution, desiccation and/ or the privatising of water companies, clean drinking

Rev. Kuzipa Nalwamba with a bottle of dirty water symbolising the problem of pollution. Photo: Helen Putsman/WCC

water has become for some hard to obtain. Churches in sub-Saharan regions started a campaign to protect the Zambezi basin that supplies 30 million people (animals and plants not included) with drinking water because it has, through mining activities, become more and more contaminated. A pioneer in this struggle is Reverend Kuzipa Nalwamba: 'Women can bring new energy, insights, and a new basis for harnessing water resources in the region in the quest for dignity, peace and just relationships among people and the rest of God's creation.'[413]

2.5 CONCLUSIONS

It is impossible to put everything found in the Bible under one heading. The Bible is a library containing books from different times and contexts, with different aims and written for different audiences, passed on in a variety of literary genres. The texts were, moreover, handed down and subsequently brought up to date as time went by. We hear different voices through these texts, some clearer than others. The Bible is certainly a coherent collection, but not a homogeneous unity. This is an advantage in our time, when meta-narratives or grand narratives are looked upon with suspicion.[414] But these are mostly the stories that always escape out of the grand narrative they were morphed in. One doesn't do them any justice by homogenising them. But one can ask the question of what they say to us in the current ecological crisis. They get new meaning in this context. Every African woman at her polluted well gives new meaning to the story of the living water encounter in the Gospel of John. The experience of awe and vulnerability of the polar explorer makes God's discourse to Job more timely. Insights of biologists into the life of plants and animals help us to understand the song of praise of all creatures in the Psalms as being beneficial.

The long line of this chapter was a search for worldviews in the texts. I undertook this research to understand them better by asking two particular questions: what is the relation between God, people and world, and what is the relation between human and non-human creation? A few lines can be detected that also encroach upon the image of God.

2.5.1 Worldviews

The non-human reality plays a significant part in the Bible. All sorts of animals, plants and other forms of natural life appear in texts. The Bible certainly does not entail a history of humanity or is solely interested in God's history with people. God is centre stage and takes an interest in all reality. People are part of God's creation; they do not stand above it or take up a position from the outside. They certainly have their own role that is not the same in every text.

The biblical worldview taken literally, viz. as a cosmology of the earth as a disc and water above heaven's vault and under the earth, differs significantly from ours. 'Heaven and earth' is the biblical expression for all reality, not for a division between spirit and matter. That we do not share this worldview anymore doesn't mean that what is said about the relation between God and the world is no longer meaningful. Our image of the developing cosmos and the earth – an expanding universe and evolution theory – helps in many ways to read the Bible even better. The Bible too appreciates the interconnectedness of everything. History is not a closed-off unity, because creation is still happening, and a better future is also continually in the offing. There is no linear timeframe that runs from primal beginning to the end of time: these are just metaphors. The Bible also doesn't distinguish between nature and history: God's activity and presence have to do with both human and non-human developments.[415] The distinction between humans and nature that started in modernity, that made God only interested in us humans and reduced nature to merely a backdrop, is certainly not true to what the Bible says. In the Bible we see how creation and salvation coalesce. God creates and liberates the whole world, and people are part of this world.

2.5.2 The relation between human beings and nature

Very often humans and animals are taken together, e.g. in the expression 'all living beings', literally 'all flesh'. In biblical biology, plants are not seen as living beings – they belong to the earth. But humans and animals belong also to the earth because they are made from earth. Most biblical texts come forth from nomadic or ancient agricultural settings where land and animals are quite straightforwardly part of men's world. The dependency of human life on the earth and other living creatures is taken for granted. Due to mechanisation and industrialisation, which involves also our agriculture, we easily lose this awareness and end up thinking that the earth and the animals are there for the benefit of people. Mainstay exegesis completely overlooks non-human nature or interprets it purely metaphorically, as a symbol of human life. The non-human reality has in the Bible 'its own place, function and value even apart from what they would mean to humans' and their own relation with God.[416]

Thus, wild animals have their own place in the whole, together with the animals that are of use to people, the domesticated animals. Wild animals can even be a threat to people and other animals, a threat that may resemble the threat of other peoples. How they are approached varies: from wiping out via careful handling to peacefully living together. Wild animals can be the object of God's care or sign of God's awesomeness.

The role of people regarding their fellow creatures differs. Some texts speak of ruling over (a part of) the animals and the earth; others talk about tending and keeping. None of these texts can be used to fully legitimise human superiority. Other texts let people take part in the choir of all of creation that sings God's praise, or they make people into learning pupils. Some texts give people a bigger role than others, but always reckon with the fact that people are part of the bigger whole of creation. They are, equally with all the others, made by God and they live through God's breath.

2.5.3 Picturing God

The Bible is theocentric: it is all about God. The whole reality – without making a distinction between matter and spirit, human and non-human – is connected with God. When there is talk about God's relation with all reality, very often female images of God come to the fore. Creating is as giving birth. This puts God not against or above the earth, but links God intimately with it. God brings forth by letting the earth bring forth. Spirit and Wisdom, both female in the Old Testament, play an important role. The New Testament connects Christ likewise with the whole creation, e.g. by identifying him with Lady Wisdom. The image of the word solidified as male authoritative speaking has unjustly pushed aside the more feminine images of God.

2.5.4 Ecological perspective

The Bible offers, thus, another worldview than modernity, in which humans – especially the western male – have become the standard of all things and human history was portrayed as gradual liberation from nature. In the Bible, God is the standard. History and nature are not opposite entities. God is intimately connected with creation of which people are an important part. God is continuously, creatively, liberatingly, present in all of reality.

This is not an outdated worldview. It is a worldview that in current ecological discussions appears timely, because it is so inclusive. People are not put above non-human nature. And equally not beneath it. We are creatures coming out of the earth, and like animals and plants highly valued by God. That biblical cosmology portrays the universe as smaller than we currently think does not make its message less true.

If we translate all this into a secular perspective, we can conclude that the Bible offers an inclusive worldview without despondency, many stories and images, and a meaningful context that doesn't put people above non-human nature, but neither demotes them to a noxious animal species.

CHAPTER THREE
Issues in eco-theology

In the previous chapter we observed that the Bible uses several ways to outline relations between God, people and the world. All these relations are non-dualistic. A large interdependence exists between people and their fellow creatures and, equally, between God, earth and cosmos. When the connection is most apparent God is not just represented with male characteristics but conspicuously often with female ones, to wit, as Spirit and Wisdom.

This chapter deals with the rise of eco-theology and resistance to it. Although my examples are taken mainly from developments in the Netherlands, the issues as such are clearly not exclusively Dutch. The same topics appear almost everywhere where eco-theology comes to the fore. I finish this chapter by summarising the main issues that mark off eco-theology. The expressions 'stewardship' and 'care of creation' predominately recur in this connection. We already explained that both expressions are inadequate in light of the seriousness of the ecological crisis, nor do they do any justice to what the Bible says about our role in the greater scheme of things.[417] Still, I acknowledge that it is wise to accept the term stewardship up to a point, because with all its faults it does impel people to be in favour of sustainability.

Along with enthusiasm for sustainability one encounters strong resistance. Eco-theology appears to many to challenge features that they consider central to Christian faith. Although I am aware that the road I travel is not an easy one, I have not become convinced that apprehension and resistance to it are tenable and justifiable, either from a theological or from a believing point of view. Another obstacle that I signal is that ecological awareness often leads to a practical frame of mind without touching the very heart of church and theology. Orthodox Protestant circles have a strong wish to ground their activities in Bible and theology. But if one moves further towards the more broad church and liberal Protestant communities, ecological activities are generally pigeonholed as diaconal tasks or matters concerning church upkeep.[418] The ecological perspective of the Bible is, thus, unwittingly filtered out from much Bible exposition, liturgical texts and sermons.

What are the forces that resist an eco-theological perspective? An explanation takes our western worldview for the main culprit, as I have already explained in chapter one. But there are also specifically Dutch features to take into consideration, like the huge impact of certain theologians, such as the Barthian Kornelis Heiko Miskotte (1894–1976) and the Catholic poet and hymn-writer Huub Oosterhuis (1931–3). Mistrust of nature and rigid anthropocentrism do not leave much room for ecological theology and spirituality.

I will sketch the rise of eco-theology in the Netherlands by using a document that was promulgated by the Dutch Reformed synod, the encyclical *Laudato Si'*, and three recently published Dutch books. (Two of them are available in English.)

3.1 STEWARDSHIP AND CARE OF CREATION

The word *stewardship* is in the air once Protestants speak of the connection between theology and sustainability. Unfortunately, this term is unjustly presented as biblical and receives, therefore, a higher status than it really deserves. Catholics favour the word *creation*, which is also common practice among Protestants, but it suffers under the misapprehension that creation is at variance with evolutionary theory.

Many other words and combinations of words are in use. The encyclical *Laudato Si'* gave currency to 'our common home' to signify earth. Home is an apt metaphor because the Greek *oikos* (house) connects etymologically with ecology and economy, as well as with ecumenism. Sometimes the term *sacrament* is used. Words such as justice, solidarity and grace have an ecological application in climate justice, planetary solidarity and green grace, for example.[419] Terms like relatedness, care and 'the good life' are also connected to non-human reality. Creation is used in 'care of creation', 'the good creation' and 'doing justice to God in creation' without suggesting that everyone agrees on what creation signifies.[420] Sometimes man is called 'co-creator'.

3.1.1 Master of the household

Stewardship has been the dominant term in Protestant eco-theology since the 1970s. Several theological assumptions are left in the dark regarding this term, but its starting point is clearly that God gave the earth to people to use and take care of. Moreover, people may rule the earth in so far as they do this in the image of God, that is to say, lovingly. Thus, we hear a particular interpretation of Genesis 1:28 joining Genesis 2 in which people receive the commandment to till the garden and keep it, and Psalm 8, which states that God assigns the work of his hands to people.[421] Noah may exemplify such a steward. God as owner of the earth can be traced in the words of Psalm 24:1: 'The earth is the Everlasting's and all that is in it, the world, and those who live in it.' This is roughly sketched the theology behind the notion of stewardship.[422]

A persistent misapprehension takes stewardship itself as scriptural.[423] It is true that the notion shows up in Scripture, but it is never used in dealing with nature conservation or creation. 'Steward' stands for various officiaries in the source text signifying, for instance, a master of the household, a chief chamberlain, a palace master or a head waiter.[424] Stewardship has to do with managing a household or a feast. Sometimes, steward has a more limited meaning. The gospel contains a parable of the unjust steward, and Herod's steward is once mentioned, as is a steward who pays labourers.[425] In these cases, a steward is an economic functionary. The Dutch word *rentmeester* has only this more restricted meaning. The current meaning of *rentmeester* is a manager of agrarian realty. *Rentmeester* is an economic functionary, and this appellation is thus even less apt than steward to signify the relationship between people and the rest of creation. It is not just because stewards or *rentmeesters* do not convey anything related to the notion of creation, but most of all because *rentmeester* is a metaphor that fits an economic predicament that turns nature into a resource and a commodity, controlled by and at the mercy of people. This way of thinking is one of the causes of the ecological crisis.

Stewardship implies that we manage the earth in God's stead. The image of a steward has this advantage – it connects people both with God and nature. But stewards manage a household or a property on behalf of the owner. If the steward received the freedom to act as he saw fit, the real owner would easily slip out of view altogether. In a secular worldview, people managing the earth furtively become its owners.

A steward may in some cases be counted in the owner's possessions, as was certainly the case in biblical times, when a steward was quite often a slave; this equally applies nowadays, when not just non-human nature but also humans themselves are reduced to sheer resources for the sake of higher profits. Thus, one can defend that in all these cases a steward has a role within creation.

For many Christians, stewardship appeals urgently to take up responsibility and be more caring towards nature. Distancing people from the rest of creation is advantageous in as much as it emphasises the unique responsibility of people. Animals and plants are after all incapable of destroying the biosphere, whereas people are not.

3.1.2 Responsibility or control

Where did the term 'stewardship' actually come from if it was not derived from Scripture? Stewardship was introduced in the seventeenth century in England as an addition to and correction of Francis Bacon's view that humans could and should control nature. The term stewardship emphasised the responsibility and the obligation to take care of nature that came with the commandment to rule the earth.[426] The term steward was derived from Calvin's exposition of Genesis 2:15:[427]

And the Lord God took the man Moses now adds, that the earth was given to man, with this condition, that he should occupy himself in its cultivation. Whence it follows that men were created to employ themselves in some work, and not to lie down in inactivity and idleness. This labor, truly, was pleasant, and full of delight, entirely exempt from all trouble and weariness; since however God ordained that man should be exercised in the culture of the ground, he condemned in his person, all indolent repose. Wherefore, nothing is more contrary to the order of nature, than to consume life in eating, drinking, and sleeping, while in the meantime we propose nothing to ourselves to do. Moses adds that the custody of the garden was given in charge to Adam, to show that we possess the things which God has committed to our hands, on the condition that being content with a frugal and moderate use of them, we should take care of what shall remain. Let him who possesses a field, so partake of its yearly fruits, that he may not suffer the ground to be injured by his negligence; but let him endeavor to hand it down to posterity as he received it, or even better cultivated. Let him so feed on its fruits that he neither dissipates it by luxury, nor permits it to be marred or ruined by neglect. Moreover, that this economy, and this diligence, with respect to those good things which God has given us to enjoy, may flourish among us; let everyone regard himself as the steward of God in all things which he possesses. Then he will neither conduct himself dissolutely, nor corrupt by abuse those things which God requires to be preserved.[428]

Calvin's plea for frugality and responsibility touches on private property, which may include realty. But people had to keep in mind that all property was really God's; they could at best manage it. In this sense, Calvin was in step with what the Church Fathers believed within their ascetic and theocentric worldview.[429] On the threshold of modernity, Calvin's stewardship carried still another meaning than what it would entail in our context.

In the Middle Ages the world was seen as complete, and having dominance over it was not taken in as a commandment; at the most, it was just stating a matter of fact. Everything existed for the glory of God; not men but angels were the top-ranked creatures. It was with the Renaissance that one began to think in terms of a human domination that might change the world.[430]

This concept was not immediately embraced by the majority. For the better part of the nineteenth century most people in the Netherlands, as in the rest of the world, had no inkling of the way to keep nature in check. Diseases, bad harvests and flooding made it all too clear how they depended on nature.[431] Besides, nature was not yet a secular zone but still the place of divine revelation. Nature was either a glorious harmony in which people participated, or creation was wrecked and men were sinners before God. Both visions left hardly room for man as earth's ruler.[432]

All this changed at the end of the nineteenth century. The idea of people ruling creation became a strategy to cancel out Darwinism in order to safeguard humans against the evolution process. People were still singled out because they had a specific task in the great scheme of things. This way of thinking was also used to counter the suspicion that Christians were obstructing scientific progress. Later on, stewardship even became an argument against Lynn White to show that Christians clearly take responsibility for nature.[433]

3.1.3 Awkward concept

Stewardship is in our current context an awkward concept. It supports the idea of human control over nature. It fits all too well into an economic–technological paradigm in which business models and improved technology promise to find a solution for the ecological crisis.[434] It fits equally well into a hierarchical positioning of God above men, and men above creation. Because it fits so well into current concepts, this makes it attractive for most people, but also dangerous, because it legitimises a worldview that co-created the ecological crisis.

However, stewardship is also such a motivation for environmentally friendly activities that it seems strategically prudent to opt for a balanced approach and to supplement it with other images instead of disapproving it. It is certainly worthwhile to maintain the idea that people are responsible for the wellbeing of their fellow creatures, but are not their owners, in the same way as to uphold the view that people have to face God and give an account of what they do for their fellow creatures. Accountability implies all the more that non-human creation is valued.

'Care of creation' might prove just as anthropocentric and domineering as stewardship turns out to be, but it may also stress the particular human involvement in the task of caring for our fellow creatures. Stewardship and care of creation are useful terms if they are embedded in biblical notions of reciprocal connectedness of all creatures and the connectedness of all of creation with God.

Popular in liberal theology is the image of man as co-creator or creator next to God. Co-creator is ecologically speaking as risky as the term steward: 'He has become creator himself, gifted with a great intellect and creativity, and can mould nature to his liking.'[435] Although human creativity derails or overplays its hand, as happens in the climate crisis, economic modernising is still seen as the remedy.[436] Liberals envisage God as being creatively present to realise opportunities and call in humanity.[437] I infer from this that liberal theology tends to turn man into the one and only creator and by doing so separates man from creation. Co-creator could be a meaningful term, but only if one doesn't lose touch with the interconnectedness and interdependency of all creatures. This might then lead to calling not just people, but all living and even, perhaps, non-living creatures co-creators.[438]

3.2 PROTESTANT RESISTANCE

A growing interest in green theology and spirituality also faces a huge resistance. Particularly among Protestants, there is a strong tendency to contrapose history and nature, salvation and creation.[439] A positive assessment of nature is invariably greeted with suspicion. This attitude stems from the domineering western worldview of the chasm between God and the world. Theologies that underpinned this chasm, like Karl Barth's, were held in high esteem for most of the twentieth century. They obstructed the approval and acceptance of eco-theology.

3.2.1 Nature in Protestant tradition

The culture of modernity has had a far greater and more lasting influence among Protestants than among believers in other Christian traditions. A succinct overview leads up to the following sketch.[440] Luther and Calvin lived in a pivotal era. Luther, with his nature mysticism, was clearly rooted in a medieval worldview. He gave preponderance to the preaching of God's Word, but nature was still important to him because Luther and his contemporaries shared the conviction that the finite conceived the infinite. To Calvin, nature was 'the theatre of God's glory'. He certainly thought that man was called to change the world, and, therefore, his theology became easily susceptible to ideas about ruling nature. Under the influence of Renaissance thought, men became more and more the centre of everything.

The divide between God and nature became gradually manifest through the culture of modernity. We cannot conceive it differently anymore, however hard we try, because

> divisions – such as on the one hand the world of nature, the body and the material world and, on the other hand, the world of the human spirit, reason, intellect and consciousness – became as time went by part and parcel of our everyday intuitions. The first domain is about objective relations and causal connections; the second is about subjectivity, meanings and reasons.[441]

A century after the Reformers, Descartes divided the world into (human) spirit and matter. Matter was dependent on God as the legislator of natural laws; men had to abide by moral law. Deists continued this divide between spirit and matter and envisaged nature as a God-made machine. God stood at the beginning of everything and at its end, but God was not or was hardly involved on earth.

Pietists emphasised the work of God's Spirit in the human heart. They were simultaneously sensitive to Romanticism, in which nature is valued in itself. Many Protestant theologians were followers of Kant's philosophy: God's role in nature was substituted by that of human spirit. God became exclusively linked to ethics; creation didn't signify more than the human feeling of dependency.

There were exceptions to the prevalent negative image of nature in Protestant theology. Albert Schweitzer confessed his 'reverence for life' and Paul Tillich adhered to Luther's mysticism of nature with his 'salvation of the whole world'.

Karl Barth condemned the emphasis on human experience and the idea that one could know God from nature. That he stood up against Nazism's *Blut-und-Boden* ideology with this theological viewpoint contributed to the great popularity of his theology after the war. Rudolf Bultmann, nevertheless, brought against Barth that he made non-human nature a foil of the God-human drama. On a popular level the reception of Barth's theology often took a deistical form: God had once created the world and, subsequently, didn't have a concern in the non-human world.

The responses to evolutionary theory were varied in Protestant theology. Followers of Kant saw it as a new theory of nature that did not impinge on faith. Followers of Descartes concluded from Darwinism that humans were part of the material, mechanistic world. But for many this idea was simply too outrageous. Fundamentalists saw a way out of this highly charged issue by rejecting evolutionary theory as contradicting Scripture. Theistic evolutionists declared that creation had been in step with evolutionary stages. They were often interested in natural sciences and they found out that according to new physics nature was unlike a machine; it was a living whole. The next step was to take evolution as a process in which God acts, as was voiced in Whitehead's process theology.[442]

The presupposition of western ideology that human history is liberation from nature, one of the root causes of our ecological crisis, contributed to the formation of Protestant theology.[443]

All viewpoints just sketched within their historical developments can still be found among Protestants. In pietistic circles great emphasis is put on how God works in the human heart together with an openness towards nature's beauty. The deistic tendency to pin down God's meddling in the world only in the past and the future, in the Bible and at the end of time respectively, runs like a strong thread through all Protestant churches. 'Dream' and 'vision' are popular terms to bridge past and future, reducing the present and daily life to a sort of interval. For many Protestants faith and nature have nothing in common. Faith is often reduced to ethics that can be targeted both at the individual – 'it all boils down to being a good human being' – and society. 'Creation' only brings up the question of how this relates to evolution.

On Dutch soil the theology of van den Brink and van der Kooi is influential in what is called middle orthodoxy. In their *Christian Dogmatics*[444] they keep in line with the traditional distinction between God's creation and God's preservation, between God and creation, and between humans and the rest of creation. In more liberal circles the distance between God and humans is much smaller. Non-human nature has hardly any part at all. God is first and foremost a God *of* people and a God *in* people. Thus, the regular church service no longer starts with the traditional phrase 'Our help and hope is in the name of the Lord, who made heaven and earth', but with, for example, 'We praise God as light kindled in people.'[445]

3.2.2 Theology of contrast

In her theology Kune Biezeveld (1948–2008) started with human experiences and arrived at a new appreciation of 'nature'. She noted that women didn't recognise their experiences in the churches' hymn book that was published in 1973. In many hymns Biezeveld traced the theology that had formed her, the theology of Kornelis Heiko Miskotte (1894–1976), a follower of Karl Barth.[446] Like many Dutch vicars of her generation, Biezeveld was strongly influenced by his theology that puts God far above the world, assesses nature negatively, and treats human experience with suspicion. She rose against this theology that thinks in contrasts and is hostile to the feminine and the natural. Her analysis was not intended to contribute to eco-theology, but it certainly is of importance to it.

In *Als scherven spreken* (*If Shards Speak*), published posthumously, she takes Miskotte to task.[447] Protestant theology always puts emphasis on the Word that reaches us from beyond. This emphasis is directly borrowed from the biblical prophets with their condemnation of idols and the worship of nature. But it shows a rather one-sided use of Scripture. The shards to which the title of her book refers stand for everything that literally and figuratively was smashed to pieces due to the zeal of Israel's prophets directed against the worshipping of idols.

These shards equally symbolise how, in the sixteenth century in the Low Countries, Catholic churches were violently stripped of their statues, paintings and sacred relics by angry mobs. Didn't we lose, in these demolitions, something that we couldn't miss, she asks herself, viz. the link between God and daily life?

Miskotte thought in contrasts, carrying on what Karl Barth and reformed theology maintained.[448] To Barth, biblical belief clearly opposes what the peoples surrounding Israel believed in: Scripture views the salvific and liberating history of God with people whereas the heathen nations imprison people in nature's circle of life. Miskotte equates the terms natural and heathen and contrasts history and nature.[449]

> The world, 'heaven and earth', do not change anymore, their 'births' have taken place. The essential becoming is henceforth an earthen, human occurrence that goes on, while the world remains something like a foil.[450]

When Miskotte's book *Edda en Thora* was reprinted in 1970 it was enthusiastically received by theologians and read eagerly for many years at theological faculties in the Netherlands. This book was tailored to the way the experiences of Second World War were assimilated:

> Here was a book that, on the one hand, sounded the motives of the national socialist and, on the other hand, explained the specialness of Judaism. On top of that, the book was written before the war in Dutch. Moreover, the book demonstrated how national socialist ideas were slyly part and parcel of belief and theology.[451]

Whoever begged to differ with theology students and university lecturers could easily be accused of not taking seriously fascism's threat or Judaism or Scripture.

3.2.3 Paganism, fertility and the prohibition of images

Biezeveld shows that this theology is not as biblical as it purports to be. She takes a few key concepts – paganism, fertility and the prohibition of images – and puts these to the test by looking at insights culled from current biblical research. She concludes that those professing to let the Bible speak for itself are being falsely led by what was thought about biblical times during the nineteenth century. Systematic theology prolonged this bias in its way of looking at the peoples surrounding Israel, a view that thanks to new research has already for a long time been proved dated.

'In protestant systematic theology, based on outdated Biblical research, Canaanite religion is characterised as fertility religion at its purest, and this is, understandably, not really an endorsement.'[452] The veneration of goddesses would stand for fertility religion in which sexuality and procreation were of central concern, and temple prostitution a key cult form. Biezeveld demonstrates that this identification of women – and thus also of goddesses – with corporeality and fertility tells us more about the researchers' biased image of femininity than the alleged religions.[453] In all ancient religions, also in those found in Israel, fertility played a significant role – fertility of people, animals and land. The Bible has not set itself against nature. All Jewish and Christian festivals take us back to nature festivals. Easter, for instance, was and still is also a spring festival. To Miskotte, these characteristics were just heathen remnants. Biezeveld argues for recognising the fact that what happens seasonally has also its bearing on human life with God. God acts also in nature. She wants to reverse the process of image building, going back to before the time when God and our earthen reality were contrasted.[454]

The prohibition of images plays a significant role in Protestant theology to prevent God being confined in some earthen reality. The assumption is that all images pin God down whereas words do not. Biezeveld had already demonstrated in her doctoral thesis that a one-sided male-centred language equally confines God.[455] To do justice to

God one needs a range of metaphors. Pagans, likewise, didn't identify their gods with their idols, as all researchers of comparative religions will tell us. They too had an awareness of transcendence.[456] Moreover, the Old Testament does not summarily forbid images, solely cult images. The Protestant tradition has misread the Ten Commandments, alleges Biezeveld, because it separated the prohibition of making images from the prohibition of venerating other gods, dividing them into two separate proscriptions.[457] Biezeveld agrees with the Jewish, Roman Catholic and Lutheran interpretations, namely, that it is really one injunction: make no images for the purpose of their veneration. Many archaeological finds seem to acknowledge the fact that, during the Babylonian exile, having idols was more rule than exception. The Bible has left similar traces of these customs.

The Deuteronomistic historiography rewrote drastically Israel's history during and after its return from the Babylonian exile.[458] Protestant theology in the main joins the Deuteronomistic theology and, thus, ignores important parts of the Bible. The priestly theology of God's glory in the temple, the Psalms and wisdom literature like Job and Proverbs receive less attention.

This tension, already felt in the Bible, between God's presence in earthen reality and God's otherness resurfaces in talking about liturgy, especially in discussing the precise relation between word and sacrament. Is God in the liturgical service purely present in the Word, or can we equally experience God in the signs of water, bread and wine? Does God act equally in nature's blossoming as in the liberation of people? Kune Biezeveld argues for acknowledging human experience, corporeality and nature as places where God may be found.

3.2.4 Cyclical mirror of human experience

Biezeveld looked beyond the biblical text into the history of its beginning and into what archaeological sources tell us. To look that far is not really necessary for an ecological approach. The Bible texts in their current form provide enough counter-weight to an anthropocentric, exploitative worldview as was demonstrated in chapter two.

Although Biezeveld mentioned nature as a place where God may be found, she generally adopts Miskotte's concept of nature: 'Nature is everything through which people experience rhythm and regularity; and procreation and decline.'[459] She identifies nature with 'the cycle of the seasons',[460] 'the blossoming of trees and flowers',[461] with all thing that people cannot grasp, 'the way of nature',[462] with its limits and all its tragedies.[463] She pits nature against history. Nature is also, according to her, cyclical and limited; the non-human world has no value in itself. She only differs from Miskotte in the fact that by connecting nature and human experiences she doesn't contrapose God's liberating actions. She also calls creation God's saving work.[464]

Biezeveld's theology was a source of inspiration for the pioneer project of the Protestant Churches in the Netherlands (PKN): the Festival of Earth and Heaven. In 2009 three liturgies celebrating seasonal changes were developed. The goal was to 'build bridges between believers, other-believers and non-believers'.[465] The changing of the seasons served as a mirror for human experiences:

> Every season has its own qualities. The dark winter months connect us with our dreams and visions and our hope in renewal. Autumn with its falling leaves brings us nearer to our vulnerability and mortality, with the concurring worth and care that we need. The autumnal storms bring us air to breathe. The summer sun connects us with our vitality. Spring, finally, connects us with birth and personal growth. Giving more attention to the seasons helps to give room to human experiences.[466]

3.3 CATHOLIC RESISTANCE

The Protestant tradition, according to Biezeveld, emphasises the prophetic, ethical and historical, being particularly attentive to the word, being read and preached, and to the act of listening. The

Catholic attitude is rather priestly, aesthetic and mystical, with a particular interest in images and seeing. Creation is not set off against evolution; nature is not distrusted; God is less 'being over against' and more experienced in the material reality. Sacraments, as earthly signs of God's presence, are important. That being said, this doesn't imply that there is no resistance in the Catholic Church to eco-theology.

3.3.1 *Nouvelle théologie* and the social teaching of the Catholic Church

The Catholic Church went equally along with modernity, albeit at a much later date than the Protestant churches. Thomas Aquinas's theology (thirteenth century) had been the norm for quite some time, its interpretation being adjusted as time passed. Neo-Thomism, in the first half of the twentieth century, distinguished strongly between the natural and the supernatural: God belonged to the supernatural, not to the natural world; earthly life was just a time of preparation for real life; bread changed in substance in the Eucharist. During the 1950s converting Catholics questioned 'Does the real life of people happen here on earth?' and learned 'No. Life here is just a time of preparation. Real life starts after this life, and lasts evermore.'[467]

Nouvelle théologie wanted to bring God and the world closer together. It managed to do so by bringing in a new perspective on sacramentality.[468] Theologians like Henri de Lubac and Yves Congar 'emphasized the sacramental presence of the supernatural, divine grace in the natural reality. They were convinced that theology had to be connected with human experiences in daily life.'[469] The Second Vatican Council (1962–1965) picked up most of their ideas. The Church had to be brought up to date; the '*aggiornamento*' was an assignment that was subsequently taken up with great gusto in the Netherlands.

The environment was not an issue at the Vatican Council. The Pastoral Constitution *Gaudium et spes* emphasised human superiority over the rest of nature. Submitting the earth was alright as long as it didn't benefit the rich but catered fairly for the needs of all people.[470] This way of thinking was in line with Catholic social teaching, earlier Vatican documents, and the theology of Augustine and Thomas Aquinas.[471] *Rerum Novarum*, the first encyclical from 1891, had already brought to attention the predicament of the poor and weak and argued for a just income and a better use of the land in order to meet the wants of people.[472]

During the 1960s the majority of the Dutch Catholics, stimulated by the Vatican Council and supervised by the bishops, went keenly ahead in the modernisation of church and society.[473] But the Vatican thought they were rather too keen, and, thus, decided immediately to put on the brakes, considering its own council as the termination of this process of updating, whereas many Dutch Catholics had grasped it as a starting point. Pontifical measures like the prohibition on contraceptives,[474] unfavourable episcopal appointments[475] and sanctions against progressive theologians[476] caused such an amount of aggravation that many Catholics thought that from Rome nothing good could be expected anymore. Thus, when Catholic social teaching under several popes gradually changed into something more positively ecologic, it fell on deaf ears in the Netherlands. It was Pope Paul VI who wrote in 1971, eighty years after *Rerum Novarum*, 'Man is suddenly becoming aware that by an ill-considered exploitation of nature he risks destroying it and becoming in his turn the victim of this degradation.'[477] And John Paul II observed in 1990 in *Peace with God the Creator, Peace with All of Creation*:

> In our day, there is a growing awareness that world peace is threatened [...] also by a lack of *due respect for nature* [...] It is my hope that the inspiration of Saint Francis will help us to keep ever alive a sense of 'fraternity' with all those good and beautiful things which Almighty God has created.[478]

Pope Benedict XVI spoke on several occasions in a similar vein. The encyclical *Laudato Si'* stood in the same pontifical tradition,

182

and possibly because of that, Dutch Protestants were initially more receptive to its message than Dutch Catholics.

3.3.2 Rapid modernisation

The Dutch Pastoral Council held in 1967 and led by Cardinal Alfrink to implement the decisions of Vatican Council II in the Netherlands worked on the modernisation of Church and theology. Leading sociologist Walter Goddijn 'thought in terms of delayed modernisation'.[479] The Flemish–Dutch theologian Edward Schillebeeckx argued unsuccessfully for an approach in which belief and theology would have their own domain vis-à-vis modernity.[480]

The influential *De Nieuwe Katechismus* (translation: *A New Catechism: Catholic Faith for Adults*) of 1966, which generated interest from all over the world, mirrored a swift turn towards modernity and a strong anthropocentric worldview.[481] The appending press notice at the time of its presentation stated '*A New Catechism* starts with man in search of God. It finishes with God in search of man. It departs from human life and shows where the longing for God commences.'[482] Even if it speaks of creation, it refers almost exclusively to people.[483] Creation is first and foremost creation of man, and creation through human labour:

> God did not create the world long ago. He *is* in the act of creating the world, and he also does it through us. It is not of course true that God makes the countryside and man makes the cities. They are almost even more his creation, because man, the climax of God's creation, expresses himself in them. What man makes is God's creation.[484]

Salient Catholic differences with concurring Protestant developments are the speedy acceptance of evolutionary theory, the positive assessment of natural theology, and the starting out with human experiences.[485] Creation is everything that exists, human culture included. Non-human nature was not suspect but simply irrelevant. *A New Catechism* mentions under the heading 'the becoming world' that people do not only exist with other people, but also 'with the things of this world', are 'part of the material world [...] made of the same material as the earth and plants and animals', are themselves 'part of the universe'[486] and that 'The life in my body comes from the beasts.'[487]

Faith as a system of eternal cosmic truths, as it was before the Vatican Council II, had given way to the acknowledgement of historical development, respect for living faith and societal relevance. This widening of the horizon led however also to a foreshortening of perspective: the whole world shrank and became the world of people, and the present became the norm for judging history. Before modernity took root, faith and theology, just like philosophy, had been in touch with people, society and cosmos, now this perspective on the great whole was all lost.[488] God became God of men. That the 'new theology' returned to its pre-modern sources did not make any difference in that sense. The Bible was still being read as the history of mankind.

Schillebeeckx became the theologian of modern Catholics, not just in the Netherlands: 'His influence has been especially strong in North America and north-western Europe.'[489] His bestseller *Jesus: An Experiment in Christology* (*Jezus, het verhaal van een levende*, 1974), founded on sound historical–critical exegesis of the New Testament, made a profound impact particularly in the way it spoke of the historical Jesus. Jesus was called the 'parable of God and paradigm of humanity'.[490] Huub Oosterhuis wrote poetry in that vein. Schillebeeckx and Oosterhuis then were spokesmen of faith and theology for a whole generation of Catholics, and were at least as important as Barth and Miskotte were for Protestants. During this time of polarisation, which kept the Catholic Church in the Netherlands busy for decennia, both provided texts for the progressive part of the Church. Schillebeeckx drafted a theology that reflected on Jesus, the Church (offices and sacraments) and our human predicament. Oosterhuis wrote many hymns.[491] All his hymns are about the salvation of people, and Scripture is a book concerning people.[492] Now and again Oosterhuis borrows beautiful imagery from nature, but it remains simply imagery. Light and water and trees are not in themselves important. They are just decorative to illustrate, poetically, how one becomes human.

3.4 ECOLOGICAL AWARENESS

The 1980s saw a rising interest in ecology in the churches of the Netherlands.[493] The 'Conciliar Process for Justice, Peace, and the Integrity of Creation' of the World Council of Churches (WCC) was a stimulus for many practical initiatives and ecclesiastical publications. The universities followed in the 1990s.[494] The impact of these publications on the churches and the academic world was not that great.

One of the forerunners of the PKN, the Dutch Reformed Church, published in 1990, instigated by the Conciliar Process of the WCC, a synod document to animate the discussion on the ecological crisis. The title *The Garden a Desert?* (*De gaarde een woestijn?*) refers to Isaiah's prophecy 'Then the desert will become a garden'.[495]

3.4.1 The garden a desert?

This document is thirty years of age, but well thought out and still surprisingly refreshing. *The Garden a Desert? The Environmental Crisis and the Responsibility of the Church. An Exploration for the Benefit of the Discussion in the Congregations, Presented by the General Synod of the Dutch Reformed Church* was published in 1990. The outline of environmental problems, government policy and the environmental movement would certainly be sketched differently now, but the theological reflection is not one-sided and is still cutting-edge. I will start with a brief overview of this document and will then expound the seven theological motifs that are mentioned.

The synod stated that 'The environmental crisis touches us in the deepest core of our faith'[496] because 'our environmental estrangement is a sign of our estrangement of God. Our carelessness in relation to the dying environment shows our lack of love towards God.'[497] The document sketches the connection between this crisis and the modern western worldview and concludes with a quote from a report of the WCC: 'Ever since the marriage of science and technology in the industrial revolution, western culture has arrogated to itself the power to rule creation as if it was its God given right and duty.'[498] The synod criticised the current economic predicament, technology, and underlying norms and values. Because its technique creates its own targets and does not further the good of God and our neighbour, the economy equally reduces nature to a commodity and forgets that *oikonomia* originally meant 'care for our common housekeeping'. These developments are tentatively linked to sin: 'All current environmental crises, economic growth and technological progress considered, how one-sided is one really if one denotes them as structures of sin?'[499]

Seven biblical motifs

Subsequently, seven biblical motifs are treated, seven motifs that 'live in the congregations [...] in order to be involved with environmental issues'.[500] These are covenant, creation, stewardship, liberation, redemption, Sabbath and ethics.

The Noahic *covenant* is mentioned, which implies: 'God has promised to be forever united with people, animals, plants and the earth. That is our hope.' The covenant with the rainbow is a sign of promise and puts a commitment on acting responsibly towards all living beings. Some members of the synod found fault with any emphasis on the general covenant as being too arbitrary. The more specific biblical covenants with Abraham, on the Sinai and the new covenant in Christ's blood should not be left out of the discussion.[501]

Creation is quite a thorny motif. Genesis 1 and 2 are summarised in the following way: 'God has made out of the flood and the darkness of the earth a beautiful place to live for all living beings' and sees that it is very good.[502] Our existence is not founded on fortuitous evolutionary processes, but is willed by God. Psalms 148 and 104 are mentioned to demonstrate that God and creation are reciprocally involved. The current significance of the creation narratives is that

> the extra-human creation is not just there for the benefit of men, but man is also there for the benefit of extra-human creation and both are there for God. [...] The notion 'wholeness of creation' signifies reciprocal dependency of humanity and its ecological environment.[503]

Although creation and evolution are not direct opposites of one another and Genesis 1 and 2 are not read historically, the question of the relationship between evolutionary theory and Christian belief is avoided. Creation is explained as a term of faith that is used in the churches to denote every living and non-living reality as called up by God. This term of faith is apparently not the same as the biblical notion of creation: 'The word creation can exegetically mean several things, it either points to a particular deed of God at the beginning of history, or points eschatologically to the future.'[504] It seems to me that the first meaning is not just a term of faith; it has also a scriptural significance, as I explained in the previous chapter. The eschatological meaning of creation is in line with Moltmann's theology. I already pointed out the dangers of an arbitrary linear model.[505]

The relationship creation–evolution is not an explicit theme. There are other problems connected with the motif of creation that are dealt with, such as the relationship between creation and salvation: 'Does the end of time coincide with primal time?' Via a concept like 'natural laws', current societal opinions and institutions may get legitimised: 'in as much as something (e.g. labour, marriage, family, government) is regarded as an arrangement of creation it may acquire an unassailable value as natural law and in the salvation in Christ seen as a definitive affirmation of the original arrangements.'[506] Barth and his adherents were downright critical about the existing social order and denoted creation solely in terms of the salvation in Christ. According to them, creation hinges on man and 'nature is bound to stay completely in the background'.[507] Process theology, on the other hand, takes the whole of reality (nature and history) as a unified history of becoming in which God too is in the process of becoming. This offers ecological perspective and attention to the dynamism of the whole of human and non-human history. But terms such as God, sin and salvation have to be radically recalibrated, is what the synod document states, and it wonders whether 'this isn't much too high a price?'[508] I will come back to this question in my next chapter when I go into Catherine Keller's theology. From a feminist perspective the recalibration of central theological issues is certainly mandatory, whether in the way of process theology or not.

Stewardship as summing up what people's task is on earth is the third motif. The synod puts this motif in the context of the first creation narratives: dominion over the earth emancipated humans who were weak against the forces of nature; ruling in the image of God signified caringly.[509] One is clearly aware of both the alluring power and the dangerous aspects of this concept. Ruling can equally be seen as subduing (see Lynn White), it mirrors androcentrism (putting male in the centre: there is an explicit reference to Catharina Halkes), and may suggest – if put at the same level as the term *earth-keeping* used in the environmental movement – that the future of the earth is in the hands of people. Besides, stewardship tends to anthropocentrism instead of theocentrism if it lacks the awareness of being accountable to the real Owner.[510]

The motif of *liberation* is equally prone to anthropocentrism. In liberation theology attention is more focused on equal sharing than on environmental care. It focuses on the liberation of people, although there are theologians who relate liberation to nature, as Dorothee Sölle does: 'creation is a project of liberation that has not yet been carried through but waits for the liberating participation of people'.[511] After 1990 more liberation theologians came forward with an ecological interest, like Ivone Gebara, whom I will discuss in chapter four, and Leonardo Boff, who is quoted in *Laudato Si'*. The risk remains that injustice to people is set against injustice to non-human nature.

Redemption, the fifth motif, nearly always concerns God and people. The synod document states that the cosmic Christology of Colossians 1 is of particular importance to the Eastern Orthodox churches, not to the western churches. The whole creation is involved in the act of redemption, and is not just a foil, as is so often the case in the West. Remarkably, this document connects Christ with the motifs of covenant and liberation, but not with creation.[512] The motif of wisdom is missing altogether.

Sabbath is the sixth motif. Sabbath as 'resting in the sense of pausing, to breathe up, to gain new energy' is linked up to joy and liberation, recuperation and renewal.[513] The sabbatical year and the year of Jubilee are set in an ecological perspective and stand for carefully dealing with the earth, and rest and redistribution for people. The document admonishes that it involves more than just keeping Sunday rest and that the concept of Sabbath should not be spiritualised, as is the case in the adjectival use of *sabbatical*.

Ethics, the seventh and last motif, takes us to another level. From the aforementioned biblical motifs, several are distilled for ethics,[514] with the recommendation to make additional use of some Franciscan thoughts and Albert Schweitzer's 'ethics of respecting life'.[515] We 'are in need of repentance' because 'the earth groans under human violence'.[516]

Undigested and forgotten?

The Reformed synod called for public comment from all local churches and promised to use their feedback to bring out in due course a definitive publication. But it never went that far. Has this document really been talked over in the local churches? Perhaps many were at that time simply too busy organising the merger of several Protestant churches in the Netherlands. In his pamphlet *Pulling Knives on Rembrandt's Night Watch* (*Messentrekkers bij de nachtwacht*) Koos van Noppen writes: 'I was appalled by having to conclude that this document and others have been turned over undigested to oblivion.' He ruefully adds:

> Often I feel extremely uncomfortable when I hear all those Christians carelessly talking about their last (or next) faraway holiday destination or the umpteenth budget city trip. You don't want to pass off as a grumpy old man or spoiler of their fun – but if you hear someone cursing in church you surely would say something about it, wouldn't you? Do we not all too eagerly enjoy the fruit of western industry that misuses the earth as a big conquered country for our benefit? Should we be counted among the big spenders who use the Third World as their dustbin?

He appreciates the measures taken by 'green churches' – sun panels on the roof, Fairtrade coffee and doing business with sustainable banks – but 'with all due respect, it does seem like a "modern indulgence". Because in how many of our churches does the care of creation really dictate the daily lives of the majority of their members?'

The same could be said about the policy of the PKN. Hardly anything was said about ecological sustainability, although the climate summit of Paris in 2015 was an impetus to put 'climate and sustainability' on the agenda of the synod's gathering of that year. Afterwards, a synod letter went out to all local church boards. In the policy document 'Church 2025'[517] one could find on the agenda, under the heading 'Around the diaconal and societal presence' and at the very end, 'Climate: maybe the biggest challenge that humanity is facing now. Given the ongoing global warming care of creation should be one of our top priorities.' What in this policy document was called 'maybe the biggest challenge that humanity faces now' was given a very poor treatment. In the policy plan of the central bureau of the PKN and Church in Action, 'care of creation' has become even more marginalised. The organisation 'Green Churches' is shoved in somewhere among problematic issues pertaining to refugees and migrants. Climate change is mentioned as one of the causes of refugee streams.

In 'Yours is the future', a sequel to 'Church 2025', creation has become an important word.[518] The paragraph 'Yours is the Kingdom' speaks about more than just our human society:

> The heavenly light over our reality, the concentration on God's kingdom, enhances the way we are responsible for our neighbour, the creation, the way we live. All of creation is according to a saying of Calvin, 'the theatre of God's glory'; 'Heaven and earth sing together and praise the Lord's name' (Hymn 149,5). We are invited to hear this song of praise and to join in with our head, heart and hands. The whole world is God's creation. We are aware that we are called to keep this song of God's creation going, especially in life's margins where people suffer through injustice, being discarded, and their deepest worth violated.[519]

And – what a nice surprise – Genesis 1:2 is quoted at the beginning of the last chapter and two verses of Hymn 701 are written out: She sits like a bird …

The Dutch Council of Churches pays attention to sustainability among other things via some of its websites. In 2009, the Council published a brochure on climate change in which 'vulnerability', 'responsibility' and 'courage' were the key terms of what the churches could contribute to the battle against global warming. These three virtues are related to theological categories such as sin and guilt, creation as dependency and connectedness, covenant and life in abundance. Some Bible texts are referred to, such as, most explicitly, Genesis 9 (God's covenant with people, animals and the earth) and the Gospel of John (life in abundance); implicitly, there are references to Genesis 1:26–28 and 2:15 (ruling supportively, care for creation) and the prophetic tradition.

Ten years later, the Dutch Council of Churches published a new brochure: *Van God is de aarde en al wat daar leeft. Waarom duurzaamheid tot het hart van kerk en geloof behoort (The earth is the Lord's and all that is in it, the world, and those who live in it. Why sustainability belongs to the core of church and faith)*.[520] The 'Biblical and Christian notions' that are mentioned are 'covenant with the whole earth', 'love thy neighbour', 'the promise of the kingdom', 'the earth is a gift'. Moreover, the brochure gives an update of the things connected with church and sustainability. It provides an outline of what the churches contribute to society at large and subsequently gives a few practical suggestions for all areas of church life.

That the Dutch Council of Churches is geared to sustainability is certainly due to the involvement of the Catholic and Eastern Orthodox churches. If it comes to the level of administration within the Dutch Roman Catholic episcopacy, one bishop is actively engaged in this field.[521] Religious orders, particularly Franciscans and Poor Clares, are also renowned for their caring of creation, and they have the people and the means to act accordingly.

3.4.2 Laudato Si'

"'Laudato si', mi' Signore" – "Praise be to you, my Lord [...] through our Sister, Mother Earth, who sustains and governs us."' With these words from the Song of Creation of Francis of Assisi commences the encyclical *Laudato Si': On the care for our common house*.[522] Up to 2015, when this encyclical was promulgated, I had never imagined that I would really enjoy reading and almost unreservedly concede to a Vatican document. The Pope quotes his name-giver to express his concern over environmental pollution, climate change and other ecological threats and to search for a believing way of looking at the environment. His approach immediately betrays his indebtedness to liberation theology. He mentions the preferential option for the poorest as they suffer most from environmental problems. He states that 'the earth herself, burdened and laid waste, is among the most abandoned and maltreated of our poor; she "groans in travail" (Rom 8:22)'.[523] Set against capitalism with its belief in economic growth, its culture of waste and consumerism, he holds on to a belief in the reciprocal connectedness of all creatures, and in God's presence in nature and all things. He condemns fundamentally the technocratic–economic paradigm of our culture, which he points out as the cause of the environmental problems. His awareness of daily life and his non-dualistic worldview seem to be in part borrowed from feminist theology.[524]

Content: ecological repentance

In the first chapter, Pope Francis sums up the threats of 'our common home': pollution and climate change, exhaustion of natural resources, lack of clean drinking water, loss of biodiversity, social deterioration in the form of, for example, unhealthy cities and inequality. An ecological and a social approach, in his opinion, go hand in hand 'to hear both the cry of the earth and the cry of the poor'.[525] In his search for a response to this crying, he doesn't think in terms of technological and economic progress, nor of subordinating humanity to the global ecosystem, but of a life of sobriety and humility.

In the second chapter he looks into the biblical sources about the care of nature and the poor. In his exposition of the creation narratives in Genesis he contradicts the view that humans in the image of God have absolute power over other creatures. That all living and non-living beings have their own value before God is what he reads in the Psalms. Man is 'a personal being within a material universe',[526] not the final goal of creation or evolution, but a creature with a mission, namely to bring all creatures back to their creator. The Pope says of

Jesus: 'He was far removed from philosophies which despised the body, matter and the things of the world.'[527] One cannot infer from Jesus the dualism of later times. God chose even to enter into the created cosmos through him.[528]

In chapter three he identifies the underlying cause of the ecological crisis as 'the dominant technocratic paradigm',[529] which is the dominant idea that humans can master the whole of reality through technology. A small group of people appropriate the right to subdue other people and nature in order to reach their highest goal: the maximisation of profit. An ideology that takes as normal the satisfying of its own needs leads to abuses in labour conditions and food production, as happens when ownership of fertile land is concentrated in the hands of a few.

Chapter four presents an 'integral ecology', that is to say, a vision of the interactions between natural systems and social systems. Everything is indeed connected with everything. Not only our natural heritage, but also our historic, artistic and cultural heritage are in danger. Economic globalisation, which basically considers people consumers, is a threat to cultural diversity and in particular to the original population of, for instance, Latin America. In some parts of big cities daily life is full of violence and estrangement; rural areas are often neglected. More should be done for public spaces, housing and public service. Apart from justice for the poor there is a need for justice between the generations: earth is not just for us but is also given to future generations.

Chapter five contains some rules for politics and sciences. Conferences on environmental issues have hardly been successful, says the Pope. Politics should be more transparent, and certainly more local and with long-term views. He distrusts companies showing off sustainable growth: 'It absorbs the language and values of ecology into the categories of finance and technocracy, and the social and environmental responsibility of businesses often gets reduced to a series of marketing and image-enhancing measures.'[530] He relativises empirical sciences. They cannot explain all of reality.

They can be more profitable if they take in what religions drawing from their own sources contribute to the protection of nature and the defence of the poor.

The sixth and last chapter is on education and spirituality. Another lifestyle is necessary, but will not be easy, because the market forces us to consume as much as we can. Environmental education is more than just providing information for raising awareness. It has very much to do with supporting the growth of solidarity, responsibility and care. This requires the appropriation of virtues and the cultivation of a good conscience, according to the encyclical. Family and church have a say in this. We are in need of an ecological repentance. This requires a basic attitude of thankfulness and impartiality, being aware that every creature mirrors something of God, sobriety and humility, an attitude of attentiveness and love for everything existing, and brotherhood and sisterhood with all our fellow creatures. The paragraphs at the end of the encyclical concerning the sacraments, the Trinity, Mary and the last things appear to be treated rather perfunctorily.

The encyclical closes with two prayers, the first meant for praying with people of other religions; the second is a Christian prayer.

Critical observations: gender and population growth

Apart from all the good things that should be said about this encyclical, there are a few caveats. One is that it lacks gender awareness.[531] The Pope could have learned from Latin American feminist theologians like Ivone Gebara that women, among the poor, suffer most from environmental problems.[532] And the fact that the church for centuries has done little to counter the exploitation of the earth has partly to do with its theology that placed the feminine and the earthen on one side and the masculine and the divine on the opposite side.[533] He also skips over an important Bible text, viz. Proverbs 8,[534] important to most eco-feminist theology, in which God's Wisdom personified as female is present at the creation as its firstborn.[535]

This document doesn't refer explicitly to current theologians, but it

195

does quote many papal writings, documents from episcopal conferences and Patriarch Bartholomeus. It is a typical Vatican document in as much as it carries on what previous ecclesial proclamations have already stated. Just a few theologians from longer ago are explicitly mentioned, e.g. Romano Guardini (1885–1968) and Bonaventure (1221–1274).[536] It's a pity that Hildegard of Bingen (1098–1179) has been left out. She has been officially declared, quite recently, a Doctor of the Universal Church and has, thus, theological authority. In her theology, creation was just as vital as with Francis of Assisi.[537]

More detrimental is the way nature is regarded implicitly in this encyclical. Being connected with nature sounds all right, but nature is a varied and also, at times, devious concept.[538] As Protestant theology uses God-ordained institutions to give what is culturally defined a self-evident appearance, so does the Roman Catholic Church in its application of the term natural law. Rules of sexuality and procreation would belong to the natural order of things, like moral laws engraved in human nature. Thus, the encyclical mentions abortion several times as an example of a technocratic way of ruling nature. In dealing with abortion the Pope stays within traditional moral confines. He does not show any awareness of the connection between abortion and poverty.

He asserts also that population growth is not a cause of the ecological crisis. He certainly has a point when he says that the West sometimes all too easily blames the world's problems on population growth, as if people in developing countries are the biggest polluters and not the westerners who spread themselves around the globe. He justly points out though the unequal sharing of goods. But even if this sharing were more equal, population growth would still be a problem. Population growth damages the environment, just as the ever-growing economy does.[539]

Proceeds: earth, poor and theology

Laudato Si' makes ecological insights from Latin America available to a wider public, presenting a non-dualistic worldview in which the suffering of the earth and the poor are connected, condemning the economic and technocratic ruling of the world by a few people, pointing out globalism as a threat to cultural diversity and indigenous people in particular. The encyclical shows that standard theological terms like creation and incarnation are really relevant to current environmental issues. The Pope's critique of culture and his emphasising the reciprocal connectedness of all creatures are connecting points for (eco-)feminist theologians to carry on their analysis of gender. They show that the technocratic paradigm is a patriarchal paradigm as well.

3.4.3 Evolution, ecological crisis and humanity's place in the scheme of things

Since the beginning of modernity, theology has not dealt with the greater whole anymore, as we observed before. 'Modern' theology is no longer about the whole world in relation to God but only about people and God; the non-human world is entrusted to the natural sciences.

In recent years, nevertheless, some Dutch books have been published that without passing for eco-theological make a study of humans within the bigger whole from ideological, cosmological and ecological perspectives. I will discuss three of these publications. Two are available in English. They are *Nietzsche and the Earth: Biography, Ecology, Politics* by Henk Manschot (2016),[540] *Reformed Theology and Evolutionary Theory* by Gijsbert van den Brink (2017)[541] and *Het Epos van de Evolutie en de vraag naar de zin van ons bestaan* (*The Epos of Evolution and what the Meaning of Our Life Entails*) by Taede A. Smedes (2018).[542] I start with the most philosophical and finish with the most theological of the three books: first Manschot, then Smedes and lastly van den Brink. What is their view on the world, on humans, on the relation between humans and non-human nature, and their image of God?

Earthing people

Although philosopher and humanist Henk Manschot does not write about theology, his book is relevant for our theological reflection because it deals with modernity's unjustifiable perspective on humans in view of the ecological crisis. Man as ruler and master of the world and owner of the earth is the persistent image of man in humanism and modern Christianity whereas the ecological crisis calls for a radical new paradigm. Manschot is in search of a 'new humanism' grafted on Nietzsche's *superman*, only one that doesn't put man of reason at the centre, but earth.[543] This requires a cultural U-turn by 'overcoming a human-centred way of thinking and creating a future in which real people turn into responsible residents who share the planet with all other life on earth'.[544]

A humanism without anthropocentrism seems a contradiction in terms. But, according to Manschot, this is possible. When in 2004 he was asked what his views were as a humanist on sustainable development, he felt embarrassed because he couldn't give an answer.[545] He wondered: 'Which ways of thinking and doing, which art of living should we develop in order to get physically involved again in the whole process of life?'[546] He went on a trip in Nietzsche's footsteps who, in search of a better health of mind and body, went to the mountains and the coast. By doing so, Manschot arrived at an art of living that is oriented towards the earth. He maintains that the relationship between people and the bigger whole in which they participate should again become a central question of philosophy.[547] This was the case with the philosophers in Antiquity, who had three basic themes: 'the relationships that one had towards oneself, other people, and the cosmos'.[548] Since the time of the Renaissance the cosmos was no longer the basic principle of everything – the individual human being had taken over.[549] That this picture could have been different altogether is already known from anthropological research. Modern western culture is the only culture that separates humans radically from non-humans.[550] Non-western cultures express their way of dealing with nature in terms of a relationship: 'Animals and plants, woods and lakes are for them partners in all sorts of relationships, even family relationships.'[551] Earth is for them a life-giving entity and the forces of nature are depicted and celebrated in their cultures in a rich variety of forms. Manschot is bent on showing that 'the images of the particularly utilitarian relationships between living people, animals and plants, that we take as self-evident, are equally a cultural construct, a construct that, compared to others, caused ecologically a tremendous amount of damage'.[552]

The western divide of nature and culture is an obstacle to seeing what is actually happening, says Manschot, following Latour. An ecological criticism of science is necessary, because ecologising and modernising do not go together. We have to find ways of treating the earth other than scientifically, by humanities, politics, art, philosophy, religion and ethics. Scientific information about the state of the earth is not enough to mend our link with the earth.[553]

Manschot does not focus on the cosmos but on the earth. Evolutionary theory changed our awareness of space and time. We happen to be latecomers in the life-span of the earth, just residents of a tiny planet in an enormous universe. Astronauts told how when they saw earth as a blue globe from outer space, its atmosphere thinly veiled around it, how they began to realise that it is our indispensable but vulnerable home.[554] Manschot zooms even further in on what is local. People should again become 'locals' (*inlanders*), that is to say, they should be ecologically engaged in their locality. This is a vision inspired by the experiences of indigenous peoples that contraposes the vested values of globalism and neoliberalism.[555]

His starting-point is, like Nietzsche, not modern people, not individuals stripped from their body and local context, defined by general concepts as freedom, reason and autonomy,[556] but 'human being seen as always and concretely bodily, fruit of a long evolution, who just by his food and his bringing into culture of his surroundings is entwined with many threads with his habitat'.[557] This theory of human dignity differs fundamentally from Kant and Hegel who, referring to classical antiquity's heritage, linked human dignity with freedom and rationality and not with earthy matters such as growing and preparing food.[558] Man, who has become 'un-earthy', has to be faithful to the earth again.

One may question whether Manschot's philosophy is still humanistic or rather post-humanistic.[559] It is certainly humanistic in as far as it starts from man able to design himself. But from an earth-centred postmodern philosophical position it is not immediately evident to consider people rulers and masters of themselves. Are people not designed by evolution, history, their habitat, and their social position, and/or – from a Christian perspective – by God?

To question our modern western worldview as Manschot does, with the support of philosophers of antiquity, indigenous cultures and Nietzsche, is also of importance to an ecological theology. Philosophers like Manschot can be of help also to criticise modernity's presuppositions within Christian theology. Christianity is less intertwined with modernity than humanism and finds ample support in the Bible and a great part of the history of the Church. In the Bible we also find the image of people 'as bodily persons entwined with their habitat' rather than as rational, autonomous individuals. The 'Man of Reason' of Enlightenment[560] is not a human being as a creature or Jesus's disciple. Ecological criticism of science is also important from a Christian viewpoint.

Evolution as meaningful narrative

Philosopher of religion and theologian Taede Smedes subscribes to Kant's and Hegel's views of man and world.[561] He makes much of man who, even though an insignificant part of the cosmos and coming from earth's ecosystem, is probably the only intelligent being in the universe that is able to think. Man is, according to Smedes, the 'universe's own mirror', because 'through man the universe becomes aware of itself, its own existence and history'.[562] This mixture of dependency and intelligence makes people responsible for life on earth. Evolutionary theory is for Smedes a new meaningful narrative in as far as 'the "great narrative" that was linked with Scripture and that explained how God made the world especially for humans' has turned out incredible.[563]

The stimulus for writing his essay was a question that was put forward to him: What is the meaning of our existence if we may conclude from evolutionary theory that our existence is fortuitous? Smedes had already become fascinated with the history of the cosmos and life on earth whilst following a college course entitled The Living Universe. In line with religious naturalists, he speaks of 'the epos of evolution', and by doing so he makes much more of evolutionary theory than just a scientific theory. The interweaving of man and universe – everything comes forth from the expanding universe, thus, even humans are made of stardust – and taking the fact that man comes last in the line of life that started on earth gives meaning to it.

> We are thoroughly connected with nature that brought us life. This causes in religious naturalists feelings of respect, awe and wonderment and simultaneously makes one humble being aware of one's dependency [...] One can learn to perceive the voice of suffering nature and its creatures.[564]

People can develop an ecologic sensitivity by listening to nature. This quote could well illustrate what is said in Job or Psalm 104. But Smedes doesn't go into dialogue with the Bible or pre- and postmodern theology. If he starts to answer the question about human dignity he brings up the image of men taken from Enlightenment and the philosophy of antiquity. He observes that biologically speaking humans are not more important than other beings and that only from a philosophical, theological and ethical point of view one can say anything about human dignity.[565] Humans derive their uniqueness, according to him, from their thinking, consciousness and knowledge.

People are to him 'the chroniclers who analyse, fathom and write down the history of the universe and of life, keeping alive the past by passing on that memory to next generations [...] that has become the meaning of our existence.'[566]

The 'epos of evolution' is for Smedes the narrative that links believers and non-believers. Respect and connectedness transmit 'a feeling of (horizontal) transcendence',[567] the sacred is manifest in reality.[568] This is, thus, 'not something divine'[569] – anyone may freely add her or his personal belief to it. He calls himself 'a post-theistic thinker' whose disquisition is nonetheless 'drenched in theology'.[570] He concludes with his personal credo: following Jesus in giving a voice to those who are not listened to, 'detecting the trace of God [...] in the countenance of the other'.[571] He feels sympathy for what Rabbi Jonathan Sacks says about God, who, in the Bible, gradually withdraws to make room for people who receive a task to improve the world, 'building a house for God, for a God who is no longer there or is not there yet'.[572] He calls out: feel and show your responsibility for life on earth.[573]

Smedes' essay is indeed drenched in theology, in particular in modern theology that puts no serious value on biblical exegesis or theological tradition, and takes 'god' for a code. He doesn't feel the need to test his thesis that 'the great narrative' that was linked with Scripture and that explained how God made the world especially for humans could rightly pass for biblical. He could have thought for himself whether the Bible really is about the 'how' of creation. The fact that the Bible contains more creation narratives that do not have a unified theory about the 'how' might have been a clue that creation is really about something else. Moreover, he could have read in the Bible that God also has a relationship with non-human reality, not just with people. He could have thought about the relationship between God as the Other and the sacred in reality.

His call on Jesus falls short of solidity and appears to float out of a sheer lack of some embedding of Scripture and tradition. In so far as he takes cognisance of Scripture it is only in ethics. Natural sciences tell us how reality ticks; faith just guides us morally, in line with Kant. But even for morality God is in the end no longer necessary; faith is reduced to a possible source of inspiration of one's own volition.

Inspired by evolutionary theory, Smedes nevertheless brings up one corrective to the image of man in modernity, i.e. man is not autonomous but dependent, but at the same time he holds on to the image of men crowning creation, in the guise of evolution's absolute summit. Man as image of God from Genesis 1 fits perfectly into Smedes' theory. But that is no longer how Scripture takes it. The image is reduced to 'god's eye point of view'[574] in scrutinising the whole. According to Smedes, the narrative of evolution becomes a 'grand narrative' to which everything either has to be adjusted or left out.[575] It is a theology that is shoehorned into the zeitgeist without asking difficult questions. Being sensitive to the suffering of all people and other living beings is his personal creed that cannot be inferred from his premises. Man as such is 'rational man' who oversees everything; it is not in man suffering, not even suffering people in all sorts of circumstances, or suffering creation in all its diversity in which God lets himself be known.

God and the earth

Theologian Gijsbert van den Brink looks, like Smedes, into the relation between evolutionary theory and faith, and brings ecology up for discussion. His point of departure is his belief that God did make the world and, he adds, not just for the benefit of people. He asks

> whether evolutionary theory can be chimed in with the orthodox interpretation of faith that reads Scripture as the authoritative rendering of the concrete–historic trajectory that God follows with people from the time of creation via original sin towards redemption and fulfilment.[576]

He answers in the affirmative, although with some amendments. Accepting evolutionary theory does not automatically lead to liberal thinking or atheism. But what about the position of people? People don't have any properties that animals lack, but they are unique, theologically speaking: they, created in God's image, are called upon to share love with one another and God, caring for creation.

Van den Brink doesn't make things easy for himself. His book caused much anger among some of his orthodox supporters. Only recently has he become convinced that evolutionary theory offers the best explanation for biodiversity and he wonders: if evolutionary theory makes sense, what would this imply for reformed dogmatic theology? He takes his starting point in what is commonly seen as the standard version of the evolutionary theory, viz. the modern evolutionary synthesis. He distinguishes three levels: the geological timescale (the age of the universe and the earth), the concept of a common descent (all life goes back to one or a few ancestors) and natural selection through random mutations.[577] At first, he saw the last level as the biggest problem: how does randomness go with God's providence? He puts this randomness into perspective by pointing out that the current version of Darwin's theory is not monolithic and that according to some evolutionary biologists evolution is internally directed. Thus, natural selection can be seen as the instrument that God uses to keep diversity afloat, says van den Brink.[578] But the geological timescale and the birth of new life forms are gradually seen as really causing reformed theology headaches, especially for covenant theology and challenges to God's goodness. Suffering and death existed already before humans appeared on earth. This seriously questions a direct historical line running from Adam via original sin towards redemption through Christ. Van den Brink goes deep into all the theories held by creationists, evolutionary theists and those who plead agnosticism if it comes to thinking about a beginning. There are several ways to unite creation narratives and evolutionary theory. In Genesis 1 earth brings forth plants and animals, and people are made on the same days as land animals, appearing at the last moment. Thus far we see resemblances. But focusing on resemblances and ignoring the differences is not really an option, says van den Brink: 'we should not read scientific results into the Bible as if it had been concealed there all the time'.[579] He differentiates between the *scope* and the message of the biblical writers and their outdated worldview.[580]

Van den Brink expects that, as it took some time before all Protestants accepted that the earth circled around the sun and not the other way around, the same will happen to evolutionary theory. Protestants, especially orthodox and evangelicals, have more problems in accepting evolutionary theory than Lutherans, Catholics or Eastern Orthodox. Roman Catholic theologians have developed some form of constructive theology concerning evolution and belief. He explains orthodox resistance from the way they read the whole Bible as their only source and norm of faith and practice (*sola Scriptura* and *tota Scriptura*), and the fact that they emphasise 'specific general Christian teachings': covenant, sin and grace.[581] Covenant starts according to orthodox Protestant thinking with an historical Adam and Eve and original sin as an historical fact. He tries to give this notion its due and at the same time to hold on to evolutionary theory by choosing a middle ground between a non-historic and a literal explanation of Genesis 2 and 3. He turns Adam and Eve into 'federal heads' of that humanity that comes to a stage of discernment and, from then on, becomes answerable to God. That point had been reached around 45,000 years ago.

Evolutionary theory does not only impinge on van den Brink's biblical interpretation. His ideas about God's goodness, history of salvation, his anthropology and theory of revelation are all enriched by it – so he writes in the concluding chapter. He concludes that, as the created world had not been perfect from the beginning, Christ's word of redemption did not 'just rectify what went wrong, nor was it just liberating us from the domination of sin, but it was also fulfilling God's creative work by banning from natural reality all suffering, pain and death'.[582] And the 'miraculous complexity of the natural world' makes clear that 'the awe inspiring character of the natural reality […] helps us to see that the book of nature is "written" by God whom we know even better through Scripture'.[583] Natural selection enriches the

205

image of God the Creator. That religion and morality have come all the way through evolution throws a new light on revelation, says van den Brink.

He wonders if there are more Christian notions that have to be adjusted to evolutionary theory and sums up a few of such adjusted examples. The theologian Hendrikus Berkhof (1914–1995) saw Jesus as a decisive jump in human history, a new sort of human being.[584] This idea is rejected by van den Brink. According to the teaching of Christ's two natures, Christ is both God and man, thus, accordingly, simply *homo sapiens* evolving from apes. He mentions another example: 'The Spirit as God's life giving presence in the world easily fits the scientific rendering of a dynamic and ever-changing world.'[585] 'Process theology and related forms of panentheism – that take God, so to speak, as pulling from within at the world towards the future instead of acting from without – have been attractive options for many thinkers in the fields of sciences and religion.'[586] He warns us that we shouldn't Christianise evolutionary theory, because worldviews come and go, and Christianity is really about something else. His reformed tradition centres around human weakness and sin over against God's glory and grace.[587] Van den Brink sharply counters some Christians' worry 'whether humans are indeed the summit of God's creative work' – mind that this was the answer that Smedes came up with in his book – with saying that this is not biblical (see Job 38—41, Psalm 104 and Genesis 1).[588]

It is a pity that van den Brink so doggedly clings to an historical Adam and Eve. With some artificial reasoning, he can hold on to a belief in an historical Adam, what in orthodox circles seems to be a shibboleth signifying that you are one of them.[589] That doesn't make his discourse more convincing, though, whereas he has so much more to say. He doesn't seem to be consistent either. He doesn't want to read scientific insights into Scripture but at the same time he uses a way of Bible reading that is driven by what has been considered scientific since the time of the Enlightenment: only facts that are historically verifiable are real facts. This opinion is, by the way, equally shared by most liberal Christians. But they end up by concluding the opposite: the Bible is for them not true because it is for the most part not historical in the modern sense of the word.

An important question that van den Brink asks is whether Christian views should be brought into agreement with evolutionary theory. The force of his book lies in the fact that he contraposes Christian belief and evolutionary theory without giving up one for the other. The evolutionary theory brings about certain changes in some of the things he believes in, but it doesn't become the substitute of his faith. He alleges rightly that faith is about other things than what evolutionary theory is about. Therefore, there is no need to reduce both to the same denominator. Christianity went through several worldviews without losing itself in or escaping from them. Meanwhile van den Brink has hardly an eye for the fact that all theology is in one way or another affected by worldviews. If he were aware of this fact, he would see that his emphasis on sin and grace was typical of the late Middle Ages and subsequently gained substance in pietistic strands of Protestantism.

Through fissures in beliefs and worldviews other creative forms of theology may develop.[590] Where there is a rub – evolutionary theory and Christian belief, lived religion and the Bible – anything new may arise. The doctrines of Christ's two natures and Trinity could play a role, likewise classical biblical and theological notions as sin, grace and covenant. This may even happen within a panentheistic theology, as we will see in chapter four when we discuss several eco-feminist theologians.

3.5 ISSUES

The Dutch eco-theological discussion is, on the one hand, limited in scale; on the other hand, it is multifaceted, as the aforementioned publications clearly demonstrate. In several places, some try to animate a broader ecumenical get-together,[591] but there we sometimes see these discussions coming to a halt due to conflicting theological presuppositions. A term like *creation,* for instance, means different things to Catholics, liberal Protestants and orthodox Protestants alike. There is not one single point in Dutch and Flemish eco-theology on which everyone agrees, although there are similarities in themes that always recur. I will list these, and I will start taking a stand.

3.5.1 Nature: sacred, fact or threat?

The thorny, poly-interpretable, perhaps even superfluous term *nature* is a real minefield.[592] Nature brings out strong positive or negative associations and emotions. For one, it is the place to find God and the sacred; for another, nature is awesome provided one keeps a clear distance between God and nature; again, there are people who immediately smell out paganism in every associative linking of God with nature. Sometimes non-human nature is valued on its own terms; sometimes nature is just considered as building material or resource, or as mirroring or symbolising our human experiences. Some take everything as nature, including humans and their culture. Then, nature becomes almost equal to reality. Others take nature as background for what is really important: the history (of salvation) of God and people. Some take sustainability solely as thinking about how the earth can be habitable for people; others worry most about the exploitation of nature.

Nature can function as in natural law to legitimise certain social conventions. Some point out a risk when nature's liberation is played off against the liberation of people.

I would prefer to treat non-human nature as we would treat people: as being valued, not sacred in itself, but sacred as being the place where God can be found. From a biblical perspective one can maintain that nature as such is not sacred, but nature is equally not just matter for human use. Human and non-human nature is sacred in as much as it belongs to God; it exists for God's glory and mirrors God's glory. People should not venerate (non-human) nature; they should, in harmony with nature, venerate God.[593]

3.5.2 Creation: non-human nature or everything; past, present or future?

Creation is also poly-interpretable. Catholic theology generally links ecology with theology of creation; Protestant theology hardly takes this road. Sometimes creation includes everything, in as much as it relates to God or puts everything in a particular light. Sometimes non-human nature is singled out as creation, or people are the only ones being labelled as creatures. The question of how God relates to creation always plays a major role: is God the force within creation and/or transcends creation, or does God even stand over against creation? This is the question of the relative proportion of immanence and transcendence. Another issue is whether everything carries God's image or only humans.

Creation may refer to a beginning, whether taken temporally or not, or creation has to do with the present and, thus, with the ongoing relation between God and everything existing. We are always reminded of the relation between creation and evolution. For Protestants, this relation is a thorny issue; Catholics grasp it more in a unifying sense. All sorts of questions come into the game with a changing perspective on time and space, questions about chance and purpose, fortuitousness and providence, how people and their belief match evolution, perceiving respectfully how wonderful the universe is versus the image of an utterly disinterested universe. The evolutionary theory may function as the competitor of a belief in creation, but it may also be a self-evident background of a belief in creation or the current source of giving meaning to life. It is a moot question whether theological opinions should comply with evolutionary theory. Behind all this lies the question of how theology and natural sciences relate.[594] For some theologians the natural sciences are normative; others, on the contrary, take them to task.

I would desist from swapping creation narratives for evolution as a meaningful narrative, as Smedes does. Maintaining that the earth is not flat and was not formed in six days does not make the creation stories a load of rubbish, nor does the fact that we now 'know much more'. We should not leave the scripting of a meaningful narrative, 'storytelling, meaning-making powers', 'to science, to experts, to the rational certainty of modernity'.[595] The narrative of evolution and, fuelled by this, cosmologic narratives tend all too quickly to 'totalising and oppressive strategies' of an grand narrative that holds all other narratives in contempt.[596] Christianity has a treasure trove full of stories worthy of telling in order to nourish our collective imagination, very often and particularly as a counter-weight of the narrative that natural sciences and modernity suggest.

3.5.3 Earth: ecosystem, home, stage, suffering, poor?

Earth can be interpreted in all sorts of ways and from differing perspectives. From the perspective of liberation theology earth can be seen as the most discarded poor, from a biological perspective as an overarching ecosystem or biosphere, cosmologically as an insignificant part of our universe. The earth may happen to be a vulnerable home in an utterly uninhabitable universe, our common home or workplace. The earth can be seen either as active or passive, procreator, revenger, herald, suffering under people's violence or the future dwelling for God. What is said of the earth is partly said also of the cosmos: the cosmos is the greater whole, brings forth, is background or workspace.

Important to me is to acknowledge that we humans are part of the earth. We do not have to pretend that we can have a clear overview over the earth, let alone that we can rule her. It is convenient to make use of different metaphors because images can help out one another. Anyone taking earth just as workspace or a backcloth does her an injustice and clearly doesn't take non-human reality seriously enough. Earth as our common home is a much more positive image, turning us into fellow residents instead of rulers. Christ as cornerstone fits in equally well with this image. Home as a metaphor also has its drawbacks. It might be used to implement patriarchal family values.[597]

3.5.4 Humanity: central or non-central, one or diverse, responsible?

The place of people in the scheme of things has been important in this chapter for all the authors mentioned and discussed, sometimes as a question to be answered, sometimes as supposition. People are described as entwined with the cosmos, image of God, estranged from creation and thus from God, existing fortuitously or willed, latecomers, insignificant and dependent, biologically indistinguishable from other animals, responsible for (life on) earth, persons versus matter, cosmopolitans or earthlings. Human beings are detached from other living beings, marked off in being accountable, called or intelligent. People are considered as the summit or goal of creation or evolution, as in-between stage or as humble part of the bigger whole. Some position humanity right in the middle, but others opt for the cosmos, the earth, all living beings and/or God/Christ taking centre stage. Human beings have been driven from the centre by Copernicus, Darwin, and Freud, if ever they were. Population growth is equally a relevant topic or it's not.

Besides thinking about humanity in general, the question arises whether one reckons with the great differences existing between people. 'People', 'human beings' or 'humanity' may signify a general category, but there are great differences among people on account of their ethnicity, gender or social status. People as a general category very often and implicitly means western, white males. Humans are either seen as modern autonomous individuals, or as concrete individuals linked up with the place where they happen to live. People can be either rulers or the ones being ruled over, privileged or poor. Economy, technology and ecology can be studied in the way these groups interact.

Human responsibility can be assumed in several ways. It can be directed towards one's habitat, all living beings, the earth, suffering nature, the cosmos, God, all other people, the poor and underprivileged, or just oneself. If one asks how far our human responsibility reaches, one should also ask whether people are able to design and develop the earth and themselves.

The question of who people are impinges on Jesus's humanity. Christ as human being may be seen as a new phase in the history of mankind or as an ordinary human being evolved from apelike creatures.

I would support – in the context of the ecological crisis and following the biblical image of humans – the view that people are part of the greater whole of creation, just like everything that is made and exists by God's life-giving breath. While sympathising with other forms of life, some measure of anthropocentrism is unavoidable in as much as humans can only picture the world with human eyes, but questioning our own perspective is still required, as well as seeing our own shortcomings. This same need to relativise our way of seeing and our status should also be taken into account if we consider our fellow human beings, because people among themselves are very different too.

3.5.5 God: in or in opposition to the world?

If we maintain that God is linked with this world, how should we conceive this? Can God be found in our earthen reality or should God be seen in opposition to it? Or is God not in opposition to the world but of an altogether different order? May we connect God with what is awesome in nature? Is believing just a personal choice within a generally accepted worldview or is belief in God typical for someone's worldview? Does the acceptance of the evolutionary theory lead to atheism, is God's spirit the force that drives evolution or should one clearly separate any thinking about God from evolutionary theory? Are there other ways to develop theologically the theory of evolution than in the way process theology does? Is God in the first place creator or keeper of the covenant, and how do these two concepts relate to one another?

I am sure that the evolutionary theory could help us out in

rediscovering the biblical image of God as being enduringly active in the world (and not just in people). This does not automatically imply that evolutionary theory becomes normative for theology. The question is still relevant in what way God's relation to the world should at best be seen, without either coalescing God and world or putting God and world far apart. This is the tension between immanence and transcendence.

Substituting theocentrism for anthropocentrism falls equally short of an answer. Eco-theology must certainly speak also about the image of God: who is God and how does God relate to the earth? In the next chapter eco-feminist theologians will discuss and criticize the separation between God and the earth and come up with different solutions.

CHAPTER FOUR

Insights from eco-feminist theology worldwide

This chapter deals with eco-feminism. If eco-theology is aware of earth's plight and yet ignores gender,[598] it runs the risk of disregarding women's rights, which includes very often the poor's and, subsequently, the earth's.

One of the snares eco-theology may get trapped in is substituting theocentrism for anthropocentrism without changing the traditional image of God. One may emphasise that God is in charge, not humans, but still cling to the overall masculine images of ruling: almighty father, king and saviour. These images certainly censure human ruling, but they have ever so often supported one particular type of ruling and of being ruled: humans ruling earth, men ruling women, western people ruling non-western people.

Another snare is that one talks about human responsibility towards nature or fellow creatures without correcting the image humans have of themselves. One should at least bring up the question: to whom does this ruling concern? Does it also include women, poor people and non-western people? And again: how does she matter in the greater whole

214

and on this tiny speck where she happens to spend her life?

A third snare is that eco-theology stresses the glory of an expanding universe without giving thought to the ambivalence of an earthbound bodily existence. Evil and suffering then go unheeded.

Eco-feminism is needed to keep us out of these dangers. That feminist theologians were well represented among the first eco-theologians is, thus, not accidental. Contrasting God and nature and people and nature is not gender neutral. Since antiquity, women have been associated with nature.[599] At times this benefited them, but more often it was detrimental. Although eco-feminism appears in many guises, and not all eco-feminism pays enough attention to the non-western world and suffering worldwide, it is involved with fundamental issues concerning the images of God, people and the world. Eco-feminist theologians, in particular, disparage the ideology of ruling outright, and introduce alternative concepts and perspectives.

In the past, eco-theology was western, Catholic and Anglo-Saxon, with Mary Daly and Rosemary Radford Ruether at the forefront, followed by many female religious.[600] But its diversity has steadily grown. For this chapter, I have picked a few important eco-feminist authors from different churches and from different parts of the world, known for their expertise in systematic theology. They are Ivone Gebara (Catholic and Latin American), Catherine Keller (Protestant and North American) and Elizabeth Theokritoff (European and Eastern Orthodox).[601] They all have in common that they want to stay within the confines of Christianity and deal with traditional Christian issues. I will discuss each of them in chronological sequence, that is to say, in the order in which they published their most important eco-theological books.[602]

I start with a brief introduction to the theology of another theologian, Sallie McFague, because she is one of the founding mothers of eco-feminist theology. Two of her subjects have had a great impact on eco-feminist theology, viz. that language about God is always figurative and that the world is God's body. McFague also coined the term *earth others* for non-human nature and fundamentally criticised the role of market economy.

The great appeal of Ivone Gebara is her involvement with the daily lives of poor women in Latin America, her particular interest in how we come to understanding (epistemology) and her surprisingly inclusive image of humans. Contrary to the patriarchal theology and structure of her Church, she develops an image of humans, God and the world in which being related is an essential notion. She finds inspiration with the Jesus movement, hardly with the Bible as such, and not with tradition.

Catherine Keller, on the other hand, decides to go into dialogue with the Bible and tradition. Combining this with postmodern philosophy and physics, she develops a form of eco-feminist process theology in which the world is seen as coming forth from chaos and creativity. In this endless process of becoming, Keller compares God with the strange attractor in modern physics.

Elizabeth Theokritoff remains loyal to her Eastern Orthodox tradition. This tradition is much less influenced by modernity than western Christianity. The Church Fathers and the liturgy are her most important sources for celebrating God's presence in every creature. Asceticism is to her the key to open up the way to ecologic Christian living.

I evaluate their separate opinions and assess their relevance to a European eco-theology. I complete this chapter by arranging an imaginary dialogue between Gebara, Keller and Theokritoff.

4.1 SALLIE MCFAGUE: THE WORLD AS GOD'S BODY

McFague showed that it is impossible to speak of God other than metaphorically. Even commonly used terms like 'Lord' or 'Father' are metaphors, not descriptions.[603] In her book *Models of God: Theology for an Ecological Nuclear Age,* she is in search of a theology that speaks out in an age of ecological crisis and nuclear threat, that is to say in a situation in which the world could be destroyed by humans.[604]

Monarchical images of God such as 'Lord', 'King' and 'Almighty Father' carry, thus, a great risk.

> [T]he king as dominating sovereign encourages attitudes of militarism and destruction; the king as benevolent patriarch encourages attitudes of passivity and escape from responsibility. [...] The monarchical model is dangerous in our time: it encourages a sense of distance from the world; it attends only to the human dimension of the world; and it supports attitudes of either domination of the world or passivity toward it.[605]

The image of God as an almighty father turns people into infants and confirms at the same time the power of fathers over their wives and children – in general, the power of certain men over other people and the rest of the world.

New models are needed, she avers, and non-hierarchic inclusive images. These images must also be personal in order to be really appealing. She doesn't want to call God a 'person' because of all the misconceptions that this involves; nevertheless, images should be 'personal'. She tries out three such images: mother, lover and friend. The model that carries the lot is that of the world as God's body. McFague emphasises that because one cannot make such a clear divide between God and the world anymore, this doesn't imply that God and world automatically coalesce. God still transcends the world in the way a human being transcends her body. McFague calls God, thus, radically transcendent *and* radically immanent. She connects creation and incarnation: God incarnates in the world, not only in Jesus. Creation as a whole is a sign of God's presence; Jesus is the first paradigm of God's love. Many eco-feminist theologians adopt this image of the world as God's body and enhance it.

4.1.1 Neighbourly love for all creatures

In *Super, Natural Christians: How We Should Love Nature*, Sallie McFague wonders how we may look after nature with more loving

Caspar David Friedrich, Wanderer above the Sea of Fog (Der Wanderer über dem Nebelmeer)

care.[606] She summarised this a few years later succinctly in *Life Abundant*: ' We live to give God glory by loving the world and everything in it.'[607] 'Salvation means living in God's presence, in imitation of divine love for the world.'[608]

In *Super, Natural Christians*, she distinguishes two ways of looking: the Arrogant Eye and the Loving Eye. The first looks at everything as a ruler, from a distance, and perceives reality either as useful or inimical. We are used to this way of looking at nature. The loving eye is the way one looks at one's friends: they are different and, still, one loves them. What would it mean if we would be looking at nature with this loving eye? McFague introduces the concept 'earth others'. She wants to extend the notion of neighbourly love to all living beings and even to dead nature. A tree, a goldfish or a river is also a neighbour. Thus, she tries to make us look differently at nature, not as an indifferent onlooker, as if we are not a part of it, but involved, participating within a loving relationship.

She asserts that many people are hardly in contact with nature, least of all poor children. We are also hardly prone to consider nature in cities as really nature, because romantically speaking nature is never as ordinary as the tree that grows in front of our home, but majestic, wild and far from the city (see image). She calls the divide between the human world and nature a dangerous dualism because it is important for city planning to create spaces for nature. And in wildlife reserves one should allow for living space for local people.

By experiencing nature – not majestic, but plain and close to home – and through our knowledge we can experience earth others as subjects instead of objects. Since the time of the so-called 'scientific revolution of the seventeenth century' we have come to see nature as a thing to be used.[609] McFague uses the evolutionary theory to correct this image: the earth is an organism in which everything is interconnected. Each part has its own intrinsic value apart from its usefulness to people. She points to Genesis 1 where the refrain is: 'And God saw that it was good.' Knowledge of nature captured through personal experience, science and art can help us to be more aware of the subject-status of our fellow creatures.

4.1.2 An ecological economy

Having arrived at this point, McFague suddenly becomes aware that she has overlooked something very important: the great role of economy.[610] A few years later she will publish *Life Abundant: Rethinking Theology and Economy for a Planet in Peril* as a supplement and correction of her previous book.[611] Living in a loveable relationship with nature, life abundant, has to do with the way the earthly commodities are allocated. Economy deals with the allocation of scarce resources. The theory of market economy dons the mask of self-evidence, as if it is a natural law, she contends. But it is an ideology that turns people into individuals who believe in unlimited growth and only want more. The worldview of market capitalism starts from quite a few very dubious presuppositions: man is driven by self-interest, the world is a machine with replaceable parts, what brings in money is good, consumerism makes everyone happy, the mechanism of demand and supply creates an optimum price and amount of goods. The question of who makes profit in an economic system and whether earth is able to carry the weight is not part of neoclassical economy. The system is detrimental to the earth and the poor and results in an allocation that is neither just nor sustainable.[612]

Another worldview asks for another economic model. Market

economy takes the world as a company, a collection of individuals that unifies its members to make profit by optimally using natural resources. In the Netherlands, some politicians even speak of 'the Netherlands Company' (BV Nederland), in which higher education is assessed on the basis of its earning capacity, municipal information desks for residents are turned into city shops for clients and nature areas are useful for creating a good investment climate, and for the tourist industry.[613]

More in tune with who we are is the more ecological image of the world as an organism or community that survives by being interconnected and dependent on its many – human and non-human – members.[614] An ecological economy pays attention to this connectedness and dependence, to earth's carrying capacity and the wellbeing of all living creatures.[615] For wealthy westerners this entails self-restriction.

4.1.3 The Triune God in times of climate change

Self-restriction is not only a must for the affluent part of mankind in our time: it also distinguishes God. In *Blessed are the Consumers: Climate Change and the Practice of Restraint,* McFague develops a theory of God that starts with *kenosis,* the old notion that by becoming a human person God emptied himself.[616] The kenotic model is a model of self-sacrificing love, of God giving himself up to the world, which contrasts with an ideology that puts consumerism first. McFague avers that the common Protestant image of God and world as two opposing entities has become incredible. The sacramental model of the Catholic tradition has more to offer than the Protestant tradition in terms of speaking of God as intimately connected to the world, as transcendent and immanent. But all Christian traditions have this option because they all believe that God becomes visible in Jesus: 'The question of who God is starts with what Jesus did in his life, teaching, and death.'[617] Thinking about God starting with the love of Jesus on the cross changes the monarchical image of divine power. McFague maintains that the eastern thinking about Trinity is more helpful than the western. The western view of Trinity is more static due to the emphatic stress on the separateness of the three persons. The eastern vision focuses on the process of giving and taking, and on relations. The accompanying image is that of a dance, *perichoresis*. God's movement incorporates the world: 'It is a sacramental vision in which the world is a reflection of the divine in all his trillions of individual life-forms and species.'[618]

You suspect, says McFague, that believing that God is embodied would lead to an appreciation of the body, and of earthen life in general. That this didn't occur may be explained because earthly existence was on the whole bleak. One good reason to put one's hope in another world. Protestants have been particularly anxious to consider anything in this world as divine.[619] Longing for another world diverts one also from demanding justice for all creatures in this world. The insights of 'new materialism' help to overcome the traditional divide between subject and object and to see all aspects of nature as agents.[620] Postmodern ideas assist in finding another image of God and another vision of power.

McFague resumes her image of the world as God's body. The image of God as father does suggest some form of intimacy and caring, but it also makes us toddlers having to take everything on trust. The world as God's body makes all aspects of nature, us included, into parts of this body and, thus, into participants. Kenotic love is another model of God's power: 'Christianity is one form of this kenotic paradigm [...] creation of the world as the body of God [...] Jesus as the "face" or image of God in his life of self-emptying love [...] the Trinity as recycling self-emptying love for the other.'[621]

4.2 IVONE GEBARA: THE DAILY LIFE OF POOR WOMEN

Ivone Gebara is, like McFague, one of the ancestors of eco-feminist theology. She, likewise, wants to develop a non-dualistic and non-patriarchal theology and shares with McFague the emphasis on corporeality, the critique of market economy and the vision of the world as God's body.

She doesn't want to rewrite traditional theology because that would be arrogant and impossible, even, but what she takes on is certainly all-encompassing and fundamental: 'My task will be to point to the possibility of reinterpreting some key elements within the Christian tradition for the reconstructing of Earth's body, the human body, and our relationship with all living bodies.'[622] If the notion of God, Jesus and humans does not change, all protests directed against the hierarchical system of power remain confined to the system, Gebara maintains.

4.2.1 Latin American context

Gebara's context differs from McFague's. She calls herself a city dweller with hardly any experience and knowledge of nature.[623] She is a member of a religious congregation and belongs to the Catholic church in Latin America, which is still very hierarchical and patriarchal. Priests are in charge and female religious are at best recognised as assistants in parishes. A lively popular devotion co-exists with rigid church doctrines in a culture marked by *machismo*. It was on this continent during the 1970s that liberation theology became popular. Liberation theology supported the poor, but had less affinity with women and the earth. It is still adamant in pursuing fundamental social changes, but loses ground among the poor who find their way in evangelical and Pentecostal churches.

Latin America is experiencing an ecological crisis that mainly hits the poor. They are driven from their land due to mining, logging, large-scale cattle breeding and erosion. They suffer from air and water pollution and poor healthcare. Environmental issues present themselves in their struggle for basic needs in a context of ecological destruction. Almost all religious groups, with the exception of the evangelicals, condemn the neoliberal model of development as a new form of colonialism. Most people mix elements of several religions:

there is syncretism of indigenous and Christian practices with those of enslaved African people.[624]

Gebara's context is that of a slum in the Recife metropolitan area in Brazil where she lived for many years. She is actively involved in international theological research. In her way of theologising, she tries to combine these two worlds.

I always asked myself how my theology relates to the experiences of women from the poorer classes – a question that is invariably subjective. It is as if the warmth of the surroundings in which I live and the noises and my neighbours' voices that I hear early in the morning commingle with my own life. [...] Being with my neighbours and the women in my neighbourhood I don't bother about theology, to be honest. Trying to see how they live influenced my way of looking into theological issues. It is as if they let me know through their tears, joy and questions that we have to adjust our insights, as is equally the case with all theories about the divine mystery which is in essence the mystery of human being. Several situations affect me, anger me, move me and give me food for thought.

Let me give you an example. Recently I walked through the main street in my neighbourhood. It was six o'clock in the morning and the sun was already shining fiercely. 'Good morning, Ivone, are you going for a stroll?' In some places the sidewalk is broken up and covered with a lot of dirt. I have to be careful that I don't fall into one of these holes or stumble over a dirt heap. All of a sudden a horse jumps up right in front of me, a bit further down the road I see a donkey and some bitches in heat. I go on and from a distance I see four year old Luan waiting at the corner of the street. I have to take ten minutes of my time tossing a ball between us or playing together with his toy vehicles, whilst his grandmother with a great smile on her face watches over him closely from behind her snack stall. After ten minutes I have to move on again. A bit further I come across the kitchen chef of the crèche. She lets me share in her difficulties. Still further I see Betty with her crippled son. She stops for a moment and tells me about his health and that she lacks the means to look after him. Then I come back home. Heaven has turned bright blue. I live with the women in my neighbourhood and am thankful to be living, although that moment of intimacy is suddenly interrupted by the roaring motor and diesel fumes of an overloaded bus passing by. [...] There are days that one hears stories of murders, births, people suddenly fallen ill, or stillbirths. There are rainy and cloudy days. There are days that there is no water supply and women are almost at the brink of collapsing. There are days that it is very quiet in the neighbourhood because we rise with a power cut.

All those things touch me profoundly and do not allow me to give voice to the patriarchal thoughts in which I was raised and educated.[625]

Gebara opposes the traditional Catholic theology that she had to learn and the hierarchical patriarchal structure of her Church. She engages in the fate of the suppressed and the earth, both victims of the destructive behaviour of mankind: '[...] earth, which is bought and sold and prostituted for the sake of easy profit and the accumulation of wealth by a minority'.[626] Among the human casualties are women and men. In Latin America the indigenous people living closest to nature are subjected to ongoing extinction, according to Gebara; the black population, with their religious tradition of connectivity of all human and natural powers, are the poorest and the most excluded; women belong to the ones most deprived of their civil rights.[627]

Poor women do not see a connection between the garbage in the streets, the lack of clean water and sanitary facilities, and their

Road-sweeper in Lima, Peru. Photo: Trees van Montfoort

children's poor health, Gebara observes. They see the street as public space that is not theirs. Rich neighbourhoods are much cleaner, so she notices. There you find poor people, mainly women, doing the cleaning. Although the streets are dirty, most garbage is not produced by the poor. They do not own the polluting industries and they are not the biggest consumers. They are the workers who cut down the trees, but they are not the ones ordering the large-scale logging of the rainforest.[628]

Gebara's life and teaching

Ivone Gebara's theology and life are thoroughly entwined. She was born in 1944 to a middle-class Catholic family living in São Paulo.[629] Her parents were immigrants from Lebanon who gave her a very protective upbringing. Whilst studying philosophy she got to know some female religious who were actively engaged in politics. Inspired by them, she joined the Sisters of Notre Dame at the age of 22. In this congregation she sought and found the freedom that she would never have found with a husband or a family of her own. She studied theology in Leuven, Belgium, and became in 1973 the first female professor in theology and philosophy at the Catholic theological institute of Recife, northeast Brazil, that was headed by Dom Hélder Câmara and was later

225

closed down by order of the Vatican. These were the years of dictatorial repression that went on until 1985. Gebara was involved with liberation theology and the rise of base communities in Latin America.

Listening to workers' stories, she found out that the experiences of women were hardly picked up by liberation theology. Her eyes were opened when a woman said to her 'You talk like a man and what you say doesn't involve us.' Apart from the same bad working conditions that they shared with their male colleagues, female workers encountered specific problems such as being prevented from breastfeeding their children during work, sexual harassment and submission to men. An economic analysis was not enough to explain their subjugation; cultural circumstances were and are still part and parcel of the whole mechanism. Gebara started to delve into feminist theology and from the end of the 1980s she began working from a feminist viewpoint, taking the broken bodies of women as point of departure: 'I began seeing what I never saw before: that the female body, my own female body, is a space of social and cultural oppression.'[630] In liberation theology, she called for more involvement in their direct material and physical needs. Being short on food for their children, lack of clean water, being subjected to violence and poor health were the daily cares of poor women. Through these cares she uncovered the importance of an ecological perspective. 'I have begun to see more clearly how the exclusion of the poor is linked to the destruction of their lands.'[631] The link between both is the global industrial exploitation that is connected with racism and militarism and fits into the patriarchal system in which nature is separated from humans and dependent on their will, whilst women are identified with nature, she avers.

Gebara got into trouble with the Vatican when in an interview in 1993 she argued for legalising contraception and abortion. She said that abortion for poor women was not in itself a sin, given the overpopulation in the *favelas* and the plight of many women. As a result, in 1995, a two-year gag order was issued against her, a time she used to catch up on theology in Belgium, making a virtue of this need. She then earned her PhD summa cum laude in Louvain-la-Neuve.[632]

After her banishment, she returned to Brazil to continue writing articles and giving many courses and workshops. She stood at the beginning of the Latin American eco-feminist collective 'Conspirando'. Her ecclesiastical conviction had an adverse effect. She became well known all over the world. In 1999 she published *Longing for Running Water* in which several of her articles on eco-feminism and liberation were brought together in translation. It became a primer of eco-feminist theology. She deals with fundamental theological themes such as anthropology, God, evil and Christology. In everything she stays close to what poor women in Latin America experience. The book's aim is to contribute to the repair of earth's dignity and the dignity of women and men who have become estranged from earth's body and their own bodies.[633]

4.2.2 Another way of knowing

It is important to uncover the thought structures of Christian tradition in order to make changes because the way we know and what sort of knowing counts and what is discarded are linked with ethical judgements and with interests. Thus Gebara starts with a theory of knowledge – epistemology.[634] 'Working on epistemology [...] is working towards changing the hierarchical power structure itself.'[635]

A masculine monopoly on knowledge

The dominant epistemology is anthropocentric, androcentric and Eurocentric. 'Real' knowledge, scientific knowledge, always refers to knowledge that is collected and arranged by men. What remains for women, black people and indigenous peoples is knowledge culled from experience, knowledge from a lower echelon. Their ways of seeing and feeling of life are often ignored, both in the media and in the social and historical sciences. Theology and philosophy are no exception. Ideological presuppositions and sexist tendencies determine what counts as real knowledge. Gebara maintains that a male elite has the monopoly on knowledge and power.[636]

Typical for patriarchal epistemology, in particular in the Roman Catholic tradition, are, according to Gebara, essentialism, monotheism, androcentrism and Aristotelian Thomism. Essentialism is the idea that humans and things have a constituent essence, an ideal that lies either in the past or the future and that has to be realised in the ups and downs of life. '[T]hese ideals are often sought in the biblical tradition, as revealed data above and beyond empirical reality.'[637] In the image of the one God – monotheism – we can recognise the values forwarded by men with a specific social status.[638] The centre of all theological knowledge is situated in masculine experience. History is seen as dependent on 'the will of a Supreme Being whose historical image is masculine', all big social and political decisions, all the great works of justice and mercy are attributed to men.[639]

Aristotelian Thomistic epistemology, based on the ideas of the classical philosopher Aristotle and the medieval theologian Thomas Aquinas, is dominant in the Roman Catholic Church and distinguishes between rational and revealed truths. The latter are God's gifts for the salvation of people, unchangeable and fixed in 'dogmas'.[640] The Church clung to this epistemology paralleling the rationalistic and mechanistic epistemology of modernity. Liberation theology, according to Gebara, introduced some new elements, in particular Marx's mechanistic idea about historical change, but at the same time liberation theology upheld the distance and the discontinuity between God's and people's lives.[641]

A broader eco-feminist view

The elite, western, masculine view provides a far too narrow image of reality, according to Gebara. 'Ecological problems urge me to search for a more inclusive style of thought, so that bit by bit people can feel the real connection between the issues of work, unemployment, hunger, and pollution, on the one hand, and the patriarchal image of

God on the other.'[642] The seemingly untouchable theological truths 'are experiences some people have had and have tried to express within their own cultural settings'.[643] We should not adopt these casually, but ask ourselves '[t]o what human experience do we refer when we speak of God, of the incarnation, of the Trinity, of the resurrection, and of the Eucharist?'[644] Knowing consists of experience in the first place. It 'is the most plausible way we have found to say something to one another about the mystery that we are and in which we have our being.'[645] Recognising our experience and starting to relate this with the experience of our ancestors means that we position ourselves and battle against the estrangement that is caused by an authoritarian system. Gebara looks for a new epistemological frame taken from the experience of the Jesus movement then and now.

> If you take a look in the way Gebara suggests, you will immediately find those movements, collectives, groups from the past. There is not just one prophet doing his job, or one evangelist writing a gospel, but a group that searches for a way of expressing experiences of suppression, resistance and the surprising presence of a God who longs for liberation.[646]

'The central assumption of eco-feminist epistemology is the interdependence among all the elements that are related to the human world.'[647] Just think of our body: 'the animal, vegetable, and cosmic forms of consciousness are also a part of our makeup'.[648] We are part of a bigger body. That means that knowledge is not born out of controlling and conquering, but rather more out of a community that goes beyond the separation of subject and object.

Patriarchal epistemology acknowledges knowing as following a causal course, a linear process in which commencement receives a special meaning. Gebara uses for her epistemology the image of a kaleidoscope: rotating the coloured glass inside entails a continuing change of imagery and there is no moment, either from the past or the future, that serves as a paradigm for all ages. Beauty is also there in the passing, the fleeting and the fortuitous. Justice and intimacy belong to life now; they don't have to be adjourned until tomorrow. In eco-feminist perspective there is a unity of matter and energy, no separation of body and mind.

Introducing a gender and ecological perspective in epistemology is needed in order to understand the world better. This means that 'we should abandon the universalization and the overgeneralization of the masculine at the expense of the feminine'.[649] The official way of writing history has fallen short in understanding women and suppressed peoples.

> The masculine can no longer simply be the synonym of the human, and earth's ecology can no longer be regarded as a natural object to be studied and dominated by humankind. Opening up epistemology to gender and ecological issues brings in new frames of reference for our knowing, broader ones than those established by patriarchal epistemology.[650]

This implies for theology that 'an absolute divinity whose image reflects that of his human and historical male "double" can no longer stand up', nor 'uphold a masculine-imaged divinity that dominates and presides over all natural phenomena, altering them according to his will'.[651] People of other religions also have a right to speak, says Gebara.

Eco-feminist epistemology emphasises that knowledge always comes forth out of local historical circumstances and they open up from there towards a global perspective. A certain tension always exists between local and global perspectives. Apart from being contextual, this epistemology is also holistic, that is to say, Gebara acknowledges that we are part of a bigger whole and that this bigger whole is likewise part of ourselves. That certainly differs from the Cartesian epistemology that confines knowing to certain capacities within us that extend towards the so-called objective reality. There are many ways of knowing and we have many cognitive capacities, according to Gebara.[652] Reason has had a far too dominant place, being severed from the totality of our existence on which it depends and feeds, and has turned into a cold, rigid figure bound by strict rules that smother creativity.[653]

The eco-feminist epistemology that Gebara defends tries to be inclusive 'in recognizing the diversity of our experiences'[654] and 'speaks of the reciprocal interdependence in which we live and have our being',[655] is simultaneously not-knowing, and 'relativizes our ambition to dominate the world through the development of the sciences'.[656] Behind this multiplicity of religious experiences is a search for the meaning of our existence, she maintains. 'An inclusive epistemology welcomes the great multiplicity of all religious experiences as different expressions of a single breath, a single pursuit of oneness.'[657]

4.2.3 The human person

Central to Gerbara's theology is anthropology.[658] This doesn't mean that her worldview is anthropocentric. Her view of people is cosmologic: who people are is determined by the fact that we are part of the 'Sacred Body'. In this, she clearly builds on McFague's image of the world as God's body.

> The Earth groans in a plurality of pains. Sufferings of many types are expressed without our being able to understand them in their entirety or to relieve them as we would like. As humans, we are conscious of sorrows and pain, as well as joys and happiness. All that is good and bad is interconnected, touching our human condition and shaping our perceptions of the world. We are the ones who suffer it in our flesh, feeling the pain of others and the suffering of the planet.[659]

The value of every human being

Gebara starts her research into what constitutes the essence of personhood once more with the experience of poor women. She observes that it is not self-evident in Latin America to consider a human being as a person. Being a person is identified with complete citizenship and this is something that has to be acquired, and something many groups fight for.[660] On the other hand, Gebara heard from a group of poor women that they regarded themselves as persons, and not the men who were in charge – the dictators and the generals. The women had taken responsibility for their families when their spouses had left them, and from this they gained their dignity. Owing to this, they called themselves persons.[661]

Gebara tries to disentangle this intricate concept of being a person philosophically with a historical analysis. She sets out her argument that insights that were initially positive, radicalised and morphed into a negative value. In the beginning, the Christian notion of the autonomy of every person was very unusual, because the common understanding was that our lives were subjected to fate, which we could not alter. By defending the autonomy of the human person, Christians underlined the value of every human being in a society that treated disabled, strangers, women and children with contempt. Christians even said that God was present as a person and recognisable for everyone, in particular in slaves, the sick, prostitutes, public sinners, and those who were normally not considered persons.[662] But:

> [t]he notion of a free and autonomous person has been co-opted by the ruling classes, and by neo-colonialism, by the capitalist free market [...] in promoting rivalries and eliminating poor people, especially blacks and native peoples, in order to uphold a power elite as it takes advantage of all the good things of the earth.[663]

That the Christian tradition connected the personhood of all people with the personhood of God – as God's image and likeness and the incarnation – made people the centre of all creation, beings who, in the hierarchy of creation, stand nearest to God. It underlines the transcendental destination of human persons and takes down our link with the earth.[664] This teaching, codified in the Catholic Catechism, testifies of a hierarchic and dualistic way of thinking that is not in essence Christian, according to Gebara.[665] It seems to me that this is an example of radicalisation of an initially positive value turning into its opposite. Gebara doesn't draw this conclusion. She simply rejects the notion of God as a person.[666]

Relatedness

For a new concept of person, Gebara takes as a starting point that she wants to do justice to the interconnectedness of all beings and the call for just relations of women, the poor and the ecosystem.[667] Relatedness is a key term, because relatedness constitutes all that exists. Relatedness is characteristic for being a person and encapsulates for Gebara more than just the individual human being that relates to her surroundings. It is part of our human condition and goes beyond our consciousness.[668] We are also related to our ancestors from long ago who learned to walk upright. In Latin America, consciousness raising was in the past an important aim of the liberation movements. But it was the leaders who determined their objectives, and this model was western, rational, masculine and white. The raising of consciousness doesn't automatically create the desired transformations and it is just one particular form of human presence in the world. 'We are more complex than our consciousness, more unpredictable than our plans, more unreliable than our decisions, and more heavily influenced by our fears and laziness than we realize.'[669]

Relatedness goes beyond rationality because there are so many other forms of knowing. The emphasis on rationality coincided with the partition of gender, separating between rational men and emotional women, and gave us the idea that because of our reasoning powers we were superior to other beings. We have to overcome this divide.[670]

Relatedness also means that we have to return to our material connection with the earth, the soil on which we live, and with our bodies, beyond the classical Christian opposition between the earth on which we live and the heaven for which we are destined. For the ethical dimension of relatedness – respect for all living beings – Gebara refers to the wisdom tradition of the Old Testament.[671] Relatedness is also a religious experience and has a cosmic dimension. Religious language – not just the Christian – very often speaks of the unity with the divine or with the whole. It 'requires us to give up some of our anthropocentrism and some of our imperialism vis-à-vis the rest of the cosmos' because we are part of 'the story of the universe'.[672]

Openness, evolution and mystery

We humans are part of an ongoing evolutionary process. Taking this for granted implies that the idea of an originally good human being who became corrupted through sin or society and was in due course saved by God's grace has become untenable, according to Gebara.[673] In our everyday experience we encounter suffering, death and an uncertain future. Putting 'the certainty of faith' against all this is a dualistic viewpoint echoing Plato's metaphysics.[674] 'What we call Christian revelation cannot be reduced to a kind of static metaphysics that assumes we already know what human beings are and who God is' because we are and stay involved in an ongoing process.'[675] Looking for the origin of evil and asking whether people are inherently good or bad does not make sense, according to Gebara. We can only try to escape from the destructive processes in which we are involved. The divine milieu itself is affected: 'our Sacred Body is bruised and mortally wounded'.[676] We can no longer speak of an original or final paradise and should not go along with 'a naïve naturalism [...] of some ecological organizations and in movements that seek to revive primitive cultures [...] Opening and evolution are two processes in which all beings, including human beings, are involved.'[677]

There is no original perfection, personified in an all-powerful being as a separate person who competes with people.[678] The way to perfection is a gradual, dialogical process in space and time. The beginning of everything is a mystery and this knowing allows for ecstasy, admiration, surprise and wonder. We can open ourselves to praise of the universe, says Gebara.[679]

> In this sense, the human person is a kind of 'word' capable of allowing other words to resonate within it, as if it could hear in itself the voices that draw it forth and remain in silence in the presence of its own mystery.[680]

4.2.4 God as relatedness

Gebara links the human being so strongly with both all that exists as well as a mystery that her vision of humanity incorporates divinity, so to speak:

> To seek God is to seek our own humanity, in an attempt to speak of ourselves beyond our own limitations and contingencies and to heal a kind of wound that we feel within us always. To seek God is to seek meaning, a meaning that is expressed in a thousand different ways and always demands to be expressed anew, because no language is able to exhaust this meaning.[681]

Gebara would like to avoid the word God, but cannot do so because of her background and her Latin American context, in which belief in God is self-evident.[682] She calls the Christian image of God dualistic because God is both pure spirit and incarnated and she prefers seeing God as relatedness to express an experience beyond all experiences, a possibility, an opening, the unsuspected and unknown. In this connectedness we are both creatures and creators because the cosmos is God's body. God is not a pure essence existing in itself, but the relationship.[683] 'Relatedness is not a discourse about the person or the being of God, but about what we perceive of the mysterious Body of the universe to which we belong.'[684]

God without a visible face?

Gebara's way of speaking about God encounters much resistance not only – as could be expected – from leaders of the church and traditional theologians, but also from fellow liberation theologians and the women who are part of her frame of reference. The latter tell her, for instance, 'How can I tell my children about God? I can't ask them to pray and to obey a whole without a visible face.'[685] Theologians warn against pantheism. Some liberation theologians reproach her that she 'fails to stress the image of a God of Life committed to the poor'.[686] This preference for the poor is missing, according to them, and eco-feminism would be too 'new age'. Gebara sums up all these critical questions and goes deeply into the difficulties involved.

Gebara can easily counter the reproaches that position her somewhere in the new-age movement. Her eco-feminism is not romantic; it is about violence directed against the earth and violence against women. Why is it that the 'God of life' of liberation theology has so seldom condemned this violence? she asks rhetorically.[687]

The reproach of pantheism is not so easily rebutted. Gebara refers to McFague: eco-feminism is not pantheistic, but pan*en*theistic – not everything-is-God but everything-is-in-God because the universe is dependent on God in a way in which God is not dependent on the universe.[688] God is not necessarily and totally dependent on the universe, whereas the universe is necessarily and totally dependent on God. Transcendence does not mean to her that God is totally different from all that exists, 'Being in itself' as the Catholic teaching calls it. Transcendence means that the possibilities of the universe, of life and people are not fixed.[689] Reality is defined by openness. Personally, I am left with the question of whether Gebara lets God and all that exists still coincide completely.

More troublesome for Gebara is the objection that the poor need concrete images of God. Eco-feminism argues against 'an extremely paternalistic tradition that has unconsciously cultivated dependency among the poor'.[690] She agrees that churches do try to help the poor, but the symbolic world that the Catholic Church offers to the poor, who look for certainty, identity and consolation, is still very patriarchal, dualistic and hierarchical. The economic system impoverishes the poor, but the religious world has all too often contributed to maintain the status quo.[691] The image of an almighty Father – or an almighty mother Mary – gave a sense of security, but keeps people down too. Leaders of sects use these to manipulate people: God alone knows and does everything.[692]

Most people don't see a connection between religion and the image of the world and of people that they take as self-evident, she concludes. If our experiences change, then our language of faith changes likewise. The old image of God as a superior, masculine being ruling everything is still strong because we have not yet digested the fact of the interconnectedness and interrelatedness of everything and relativised people's autonomy.[693] Clinging to God's personhood runs the risk of confirming the old image of God. In the light of an analogous approach of knowing you might say that God is as a person and you could maintain the word 'God' indicating the surpassing reality that is the sustaining source of all life.[694]

Gebara says that praying is a human need to get in touch with the source of life, the mystery. Nothing is wrong with that. But what is wrong is the form that it took on, that is, the form of mortifications and whippings. Praising, worshipping God and begging God that he may answer certain needs she counts as traits of dualistic and patriarchal traditions. One needs to give up the old image of God and the old forms of prayer. The alternative for the prayer of supplication to an almighty Father is not a prayer of supplication to an abstract stream of energy. There is another form of prayer too:

> Prayer is a moment of gratitude, of silent contemplation of the simple fact of being here, of being part of this immense web of relationships, of breathing within the bounds of the world's breathing of living [...] Prayer is our personal and collective

preparation for acting in solidarity and respect, for awakening feelings of tenderness and compassion for persons and for all living things.[695]

This form of praying Gebara also notices in Jesus, in the way he retreats into solitude and from there throws himself again into the struggle to restore the dignity of the poor and the outcast.

With her emphasis on thankfulness, contemplation and compassion as characteristics of prayer, Gebara corrects in an important way certain traditional prayer practices. But she still does not answer the question of how one can pray to a God without a visible face, unless she means to say that praying is the same as meditation in the Buddhist tradition. That Jesus calls God Father, she simply discards. But I think rather that one could change the meaning of 'father', because changing language changes the experience. As she writes herself: 'Even if we continued to use the same words, they would not have the same meaning.'[696] If father stood for intimacy and caring, then it could be an image among other images.[697] But to Gebara, living in the patriarchal ecclesiastical and social context of Latin America, holding on to a word like father is inconceivable.

Trinity and evil

Speaking of God's absence or silence, as is often done in the theology of the twentieth century, bears witness to a too anthropocentric image of God, according to Gebara a projection of human individuality on onto God.[698] Suffering – suffering of earth, animals and the cosmos, beside the suffering of people – does not mean that God is absent. She even says 'God is in all and all is in God – including suffering, dirt, and destruction.'[699] Thinking about God as absolute goodness which leaves evil outside is not a satisfactory explanation for all existing violence and dearth, she states. 'The benign will of God seems irrelevant to the struggle for survival and the spirit of unrestrained profiteering.'[700] She distinguishes between 'the creative and destructive process that is an essential aspect of the evolution of life itself' and moral evil, that is to say, evil caused by people. The first form is unavoidable; the second form comes, according to tradition, from egoism, greed and arrogance. As we formulate our own identity in such a limited fashion, we have invented systems to protect us from others, systems based on greed and the supposed superiority of those who think of themselves as being the best or the strongest. We idealise the individual and consider the mightiest, richest, smartest individuals as some sort of gods who should protect us. Starting from this concept, we developed an image of God as a person who presides over history. 'This God, who is also an "individual", is always just, strong, and good – the very opposite of our fragility and depravity.'[701]

Eco-feminism does not in the least mean the canonisation of the world of nature or the world of women. The human, animal and physical worlds are simply ambivalent.[702] God is not beyond that as a person who presides history against our vulnerability. This image of God simply leads us into dead ends, says Gebara, and she refers to the discourses of Job and his friends. Evil is an enigma of the cosmos itself.

Thus she takes a stand in the ongoing debate about God and evil. She doesn't believe in an original good reality that was entered by evil, but takes reality as being ambivalent, and since God isn't found outside of reality, this applies also to God. Evil remains an enigma.

Our image of God has been developed by people, she says, but we can change it too. This also applies to the idea of the three persons in one God, as a perfect harmony of Father, Son and Spirit. She opposes a certain model of Trinity, a static thinking about Trinity, as a community of three separate persons who relate to each other perfectly, which people should emulate. The more dynamic model of Trinity as God's self-effacement in Jesus through the Spirit is sadly left out of the discussion.[703]

Gebara wonders which experience is being expressed in this 'doctrine of belief'. It implies more than just how Jesus relates to God and the Spirit, and is thus more than Christology. She links the idea of multiplicity and unity in God to our experience with multiplicity and 'our desire for harmony and communion with all that exists'.[704] The first experience of every human being is being separated from the dyad with the mother to become part of a community. '[E]verything is Trinity […] all things are part of that vital and intimate relationship between multiplicity and unity […].'[705] The universe is Trinity because it 'is a single, multiform energetic unfolding of matter, mind, intelligence and life'.[706] Earth brings forth in one process an enormous variety of life. Human relations are also threefold, because even in the experience of solitude the 'I' is a plurality 'of persons, experiences, traditions, and stories' and always connected with a bigger whole, despite our present illusion of individual omnipotence.[707] We cannot contain the unavoidable cosmic and moral, human, evil by creating an image of omnipotent individuals and project this onto God.

> The two-faced evil is part of the Trinity we are and of humanity and divinity we also are. […] We ourselves, and the whole universe, are made up of the same energy – an energy that is both positively and negatively charged. This very energy continually creates and re-creates the earth and human life.[708]

Thus Gebara reformulates – without mentioning it as such – the doctrines of Nicaea–Constantinople, namely of the Trinity of Father–Son–Spirit and of Jesus's two natures, divine and human. Beside this, she redefines creation and situates evil within. 'Love your neighbour as yourself' she considers as the way back, allowing a threefold balance between I and you, I and we, we and the earth, in order to let everything flourish.

4.2.5 Jesus as symbol and inspiration

Although Gebara does not sever all ties with the Christian dogmas of Christ's two natures and the Trinity, she nonetheless considers them as fossilised and of no use for saying anything significant about Jesus. She goes her own way with Jesus, the gospels and the Jesus movement 'to express my relationship with Jesus in the light of the challenges of our time'.[709]

From obedience towards liberation

Gebara starts by sketching her own journey with Jesus.[710] As a child and a youngster, her leading question was 'What would Jesus have done?' She felt guilty very often. As an adult, she discovered that the moral teaching she had received did not always comply with the gospel. The emphasis on Jesus's obedience to the father legitimised a culture of obedience to the system; however, Jesus was quite often disobedient to the system. As Gebara was a religious confronted by persecution due to her struggle for a just society, Jesus was her role model in the way he spoke up for the poor and oppressed. Liberation theology showed the importance of the body, especially the bodies of the poor. Incarnation started to signify God's presence in suffering and oppressed bodies. Her encounter with feminist theology enhanced her distrust towards traditional Christology and the dogmas. Still, she never calls herself post-Christian, but she does call herself post-dogmatic and post-patriarchal. Her belief doesn't hinge on Jesus anymore but on the Jesus movement. Other persons are also of importance. Jesus never points to himself but to the poor.[711] Liberation is a process in people's daily lives.[712] Jesus is at the moment to her:

> [...] a man who was extremely sensitive to human suffering, who was inspired by the prophetic and sapiential tradition of the Jewish culture [...], Jesus always insisted that people believe in themselves, and taught that their belief in themselves was an expression of faith in God's power. Jesus's actions were aimed at the recovery of health and dignity [...] To Jesus' humanistic perspective, we need to add an ecological perspective.[713]

From the perspective of the body – his awareness of health, food and drink – and from Jesus's practical wisdom we can introduce the theme of ecological liberation, she maintains, referring to Sallie McFague.

Living symbol

Gebara doesn't put faith in re-reading the dogmas of Nicaea and Constantinople – these she takes for the framing of the ruling powers. Whoever starts from these dogmas authorises only patriarchal christologies that picture Jesus as lord in the image of the lords of this world, or authorises his self-denial as an example for women and the poor, she says. Gebara wants to return to the image that the gospels portray of him. Jesus is to her a symbol. Jesus represents what we are looking for and is in this sense an example to emulate. There are more persons with symbolic potential, like Mary and Mary Magdalene.[714]

She wants to revitalise non-dogmatically the values that Jesus stood for, his words and deeds – his openness to dialogue, his mercy, his criticism of oppressive powers, his concern for the sharing of bread and wine, his delight in the flowers of the countryside. 'Jesus is the symbol of the vulnerability of love, [...] being killed ... and which then rises again in those who love him.'[715]

In liberation theology orthopraxis, doing what is right, is more important than orthodoxy, the correct doctrine. In this way, the symbol of Jesus gets changed by women's groups in particular and groups engaged in ecumenical and ecological issues. These communities find their inspiration in Jesus 'who taught his disciples to take notice of the many occurrences in daily life, of the suffering of marginalized bodies, of the community among all beings, and the mystery of life itself'.[716]

4.2.6 Religion as personal experience and social institution

Religion is always there, according to Gebara, and it always has a personal and an institutional side. Nowadays the market economy is a sort of meta-religion, a violent individualistic religion that we nonetheless have to practise in our daily struggle to survive. All institutionalised religions lend support to this system up to a certain point, even though it is not in harmony with what they preach.[717]

Many of our values and symbols are no longer rooted in lived experience. In many places 'the lilies of the fields' have disappeared; we do not find the sources of living water anymore, nor do we remember what it means to share our bread in our community. In Latin American cities people are afraid of street children and their violence and, thus, 'being like little children' is no longer an example.[718] How can truth make us free if we are forced to live by lies? Markets' morals are being ruled by 'cheating, completion, lying, backstabbing, and shameless robbery'.[719] Many forms of religion offer instant salvation, they trace evil back to occult powers and being possessed, not to our collective historical responsibility.

In the everyday life of poor women one sees how suspicion and fear determine more and more the relations between neighbours and between people in the same quarter. Sometimes churches and chapels are alternative communities, but many mothers do not know how to speak with their children about God due to a lack of support from their community. Base communities too are directly or indirectly controlled by priests, and have become marginal or have lost their vitality. Many Christian groups are content with the traditional forms.[720]

Gebara diagnoses the impressive growth of fundamentalist, charismatic and Pentecostal movements as a symptom of a crisis: 'New gods and new demons struggle in the public forum to separate the damned from the elect, the impure from the pure, and the masters from the slaves.'[721] New groups without any formal theology rise up and go into the immediate needs that people feel, they do what the state neglects on a social level, but the hierarchical societal structures go unchallenged. Unemployed men dress up on Sundays in suit and tie, and enjoy for a moment the fleeting taste of dignity and feel as if they are candidates for full citizenship. Women stay put in their submissive roles. Many Pentecostal churches on television 'take money from people to do miracles and exorcize the devil: that is no religion, that is market, trade'.[722] Another development among the poor is that many combine several religions – Catholicism and Afro-Brazilian Candomblé, for instance.

Eco-feminist deconstruction has not many supporters, Gebara avows reluctantly. It would be good if one would integrate into the eco-feminist project the poor's needs of social identity, full citizenship and recognition. She argues for religious biodiversity, comparable with the biodiversity of the earth and the cosmos. This biodiversity is stalled once religion claims imperialistic universality, as 'the new divinity in the image of the "consumer market"' is doing.[723] This divinity entices us with dreams and promises paradise.

'Did you know that religion is a language? A style of speaking about the world [...] Religion as the tapestry hope weaves with words.'[724] Tapestries don't last forever. Sometimes the tapestry has to be rewoven 'to build an ethics based on respect for the activities of our bodies',[725] a broader understanding of 'universal brotherhood/ sisterhood and a devotion in all the manifestations of this one and multiform Sacred Body'.[726] Religions are indispensable, because they 'have an undeniable social role in helping us to develop the sensibilities we need in order to love the earth and the human community in the light of the indissoluble communion among all beings'.[727]

Within patriarchal religions she sees alternative spaces too. She ends with a cry from the heart that is also an explanation of the title of her book, agreeing with the words of Psalm 42: 'As the deer longs for running water'. 'It is a song of an exile who longs for return to her land, her God, and to her loves',[728] a song of hope mixed with pain and confusion.

From where shall our salvation come? […] Who will save us from unlimited progress, from the idols of money and power? […] Even the green things we eat have been poisoned as they grew! […] And yet the flowers go on budding, and birds and children still come forth … The sun shines again today, and last night the moon swept the sky with its silvery light … Once again, I smell the tempting aroma of the kitchen, and the hope of tender meetings pervades my body. […] To seek living waters is to prefigure our hope …[729]

4.2.7 Eco-feminist liberation theology in context

Gebara's theology cannot simply be transposed to a western European context. That demands an effort in translating, comparable to interpreting biblical texts that also come forth from a different context.

Difference in context

The situation of poor women in a Brazilian metropolis is not ours. We are of course connected by means of the same global world economy, its values and systems. That is our dominant 'religion' too. We are also connected as people living in the greater whole of earth's ecosystem. The differences are yet huge, especially in terms of welfare: the profit of the economic system ends up where we live; the loss is for them. But in culture and religious beliefs there are many differences too. The images of a crucified Jesus covered in blood and the immensely sad Marys in Latin America stand clearly apart from the way we express our feelings. The unquestionable position of Christian belief – in whatever form – cannot be compared to our context of secularism. The *machismo* is different from the more subtle form of sexism where we live. Priests and pastors have in general not the same amount of authority in our part of the world. Perhaps they have some informal power but certainly not much power. The Catholic theology primers with which Gebara struggled have since the 1960s in the Low Countries been pushed to the background through the theology of, for example,

Schillebeeckx, in which present experience is considered important and Christology is being first and foremost studied starting with the historic Jesus.[730]

If one takes Gebara's opinions out of context, they start to mean something else. That she wants to see God not as a person appears to indicate the same as what one currently hears mentioned in the Netherlands if one vaguely believes in 'something'.[731] Her idea of God as connectedness and mystery is certainly not belief in an unspecified something. Gebara's and liberation theology's emphasis on the preferential option for the poor is sometimes adopted without real interest in the different situations of the poor in the world. Thus one starts to speak in general terms about the poor, as if all poor people are the same, and they end up as subjects to collect money for, or a theme of harmless political correctness. 'The poor get cleaned up and homogenized as saintly martyrs and victims [...] suffering in faithful and solidaristic anticipation of God's new creation.'[732] They hardly speak for themselves unless to say thanks. Smells, noises and differences are left out.

Gebara's contribution in our context

Taking cognisance of the differences in context, we may chart what Gebara contributes to an eco-theology in the context of western Europe. I will make some suggestions.

Gebara criticises fundamentally how so-called trustworthy knowledge is being culled from facts. She rejects the patriarchal epistemology that is hierarchical and dualistic, in which humans and males in particular take centre stage, and knowledge coincides with ruling over and thinking in essentials and so-called everlasting truths. This epistemology is moreover linear and attaches much importance to the knowing of an origin. A more inclusive epistemology is needed to broaden the one-sided western masculine view on behalf of women, poor and the earth. Taking in a gender and ecological perspective in epistemology is essential to understanding the world better.[733] An eco-feminist epistemology engenders knowledge out of connectedness and the acknowledgment of a diversity of experiences. It is not the search for an origin that gives meaning, but being part of a greater whole. That means that the image of God as a masculine ruler who with his will directs everything is in need of a drastic revision, as is the case with the image of people and world from which this image of God originates.

Gebara's criticism of the current epistemology satisfies, but the theological conclusions that she draws from this are less convincing. Does the rejection of a patriarchal epistemology and a matching theology automatically lead to a rejection of monotheism, and the adoption of inter-religiousness and process-thinking? Starting from her premises there are other options than a radical break with all classic theology and philosophy.

Her theology comes forth from a specific context. She doesn't shy away from bringing in her own experiences and divulging her own identities. She is an urbanite, a woman, a Catholic theologian and philosopher, and she doesn't fit in with the background and schooling in the neighbourhood where she lives. She takes account of all these features that also impinge upon her theology. We learn from Gebara and other feminist theoreticians that every theologian should give an account of his or her personal social context. It would be equally important to western eco-theology to chart its own context, as I have tried to do too.[734]

It strikes me that Gebara gives such a central place to anthropology in her cosmological theology. Her approach throws a surprising light upon theological discussions concerning the place of humans in the greater whole of creation. She starts off with human experience but at the same time she broadens it in such a way that humans are no longer at the centre. The cosmos, evolution and God are included in her anthropology. This results in a completely different image of people than was typical for the Enlightenment. Relatedness is the key word. Human dignity does not compete with God or with the earth, but is embedded within, and vice versa.

But taking it the other way round is not unproblematic. Doesn't

God coincide too much with the world in Gebara's approach? And does not the same question rise with a creation that is creator too, and with the relational web of the cosmos? She denies this and refers to mystery and hope as places of transcendence. God is the meaning of existence, embodied in the cosmos. She rejects an image of God as person on account of the definition of person as being an individual. But if relatedness is a characteristic of being a person, as we say of human persons, it should still be possible to use personal imagery for God. It is a challenge to do this in an inclusive, non-dualistic, non-patriarchal way. It is in fact the very concept of Trinity that creates these possibilities, as McFague shows, if not taken ontologically as a community of three individuals.[735] Gebara too as far as I can see provides openings to continue speaking about God in terms of Trinity in such a way that it expresses the experience of the tension between plurality and unity, in reality and in God.

Gebara says that she doesn't want to dispose of tradition because she herself is part of it. But at the same time she is very negative about 'dogmas' and everything that is being presented as everlasting truth. She uses the term dogma for every ecclesiastical doctrine and is not very clear in what she means by tradition, except when she mentions the Catholic catechism and the dogmas of Nicaea–Constantinople. All in all, 'the reader is left to wonder if Gebara finds anything affirming and salvageable within the history of Christian thought for eco-feminist theology'.[736] Tradition seems for Gebara to equal what has been solidified in theological primers in which she has been educated. Tradition is yet much broader and richer than this and others show that tradition doesn't need to be written off as renewable resource for eco-feminist theology.

Gebara does not very much hold with the concept of revelation either. In her opinion revelation brings about the patriarchal doctrines and the church organisation that are represented by church leaders as if coming as everlasting truths from outside. One wonders whether she opposes revelation and experience too much because she thinks so statically of revelation.

She says important things about Jesus. She wants to show that the gospels were not just interested in Jesus, but also in the Jesus movement in general. That implies that all other personages in the gospel stories are of importance and that this movement continues up to the present.[737] Bible texts came up and were passed on in communities. Another important point is that Jesus was clearly interested in physicality and daily life: suffering, the daily needs of eating and drinking. What he did was geared to the restoration of health and dignity. It is good to hold on to these points in an ecological Christology. Gebara does not want to spend any energy in re-reading Christological dogmas. But in my opinion the doctrine of the two natures of Christ – Jesus as God and human – is very timely provided Jesus's earthen corporeality is not set against the cosmic Christ of, for example, 1 Colossians.[738]

A last point that I would like to take with me from Gebara's theology is her emphasising orthopraxis. I presume that wherever Christian communities are involved in developing more just relationships between people, and between people and earth, new images of God and Jesus may come about.

Our context is not that of a poor neighbourhood in Latin America and our churches are different from those in Brazil. Still, we can learn a lot from what Gebara has to say. We can ask whose experience and what sort of experiences count as valued, and, likewise, make use of mainly masculine hierarchical images as we speak of God; we too know of gender and other forms of inequality. We as privileged westerners in particular perceive the world and God in a biased way. Experiences from other parts of the world and the voices of poor women and the earth should be a wake-up call to us to acknowledge that we are not the centre of the cosmos.

4.3 CATHERINE KELLER: CHAOS AND CREATIVITY

Catherine Keller is professor at Drew University in Madison, New Jersey. Just like Gebara and other eco-feminist theologians, she battles against the suppression of women and the earth and distances herself from a partitioning of people and nature, and God and world. Her engagement with eco-feminist theology is also driven by her longing for justice: social justice, gender equality and ecological justice. She joins in with Gebara's criticism of the patriarchal, dualistic epistemology in theology, in which God turns out as a masculine omnipotent ruler, and a linear view of history in which all meaning is found in a primal cause. Gebara 'moves beyond the androcentrism and anthropocentrism of most liberation theology', says Keller. She agrees with Gebara's 'embodied panentheism of God in the world and the world in God' because 'any theo-politics of omnipotence, left or right, will gravitate toward a theology of machismo'.[739]

Keller is more broad-based than most North American theologians and goes into dialogue with a whole range of thinkers, past and present. She studied in Heidelberg, Germany, and is at home in the German theological tradition but also in postmodern French philosophy. She has been influenced by feminist theology, process theology and postmodern philosophy. She is at the same time a typically classic theologian in the sense that the Bible, the history of dogmatic doctrines and theological insights from the past are her materials.

4.3.1 Theology as recycling

She studies, just like Gebara, the way injustice is rooted into our way of thinking. But Keller makes use of Bible, dogmas and traditional theology differently. She looks carefully into these in order to unravel and reprogramme them, because in and beside the 'dominological discourse' there were always counterflows. She doesn't cite Augustine, Calvin and Barth as timeless authorities, but reads them within their historical contexts. What were their motives, what were they afraid of, what did they try to keep in custody? She distils important insights from these theologians and draws very often different conclusions from their premises. On top of this, she draws insights from many lesser-known sources within the broad Christian tradition, such as the Christian mystic Nicholas of Cusa, and from outside Christianity, including the Jewish scholar Nachmanides and the novels *Finnegan's Wake* and *Moby Dick*. She regards it as a duty to constantly 'recycle' Bible and tradition.[740]

Being Protestant and North American, Keller's context differs from Gebara's. She is in dialogue in particular with many Protestant theologians and her reading of the Bible is meticulous. She challenges the opinions of evangelical and fundamental Christians who in the US have a tremendous influence on politics and for whom key issues include creationism and apocalyptic scenarios.[741] Keller develops in her eco-theological book *Face of the Deep: A Theology of Becoming* a (creation-)theology that provides new interpretations for the relation between God, world and humans. Postmodern philosophy plays a major role in this.

Big Bang and primal birth

A big divide between God and world characterises most Protestant theologies. The image of a male God who without being bothered by matter creates from nothing by sheer speaking is deeply rooted, says Keller. In opposition to the Catholic and Eastern Orthodox traditions, Protestant theology, in general, does not attach any sacramental value to earthen reality. In *Face of the Deep*, Catherine Keller is in search of a way of thinking about God and the world that does more justice to diversity, corporeality, gender equality and ecology. In this way she comes up with an alternative for creating from nothing, *creatio ex nihilo*, namely *creatio de profundis*, creation from the deep. This is the deep about which Genesis 1:2 speaks. The 'face of the deep' is the literal translation of the Hebrew *penee tehom*. It is from the deep that everything continually comes into existence:

> *When in the beginning Elohim created heaven and earth, the earth was tohu va bohu, darkness was upon the face of tehom, and the ruach Elohim vibrating upon the face of the waters ...*

The undertow has gripped the wave. The salt washes the wound. We begin again, or not at all.

What if *beginning* – this beginning, any beginning, The Beginning – does not lie back, like an origin, but rather opens out? 'To begin' derives from the old Teutonic *be-ginnan*, 'to cut open, to open u,' cognate with the Old English *ginan*, meaning 'to gape, to yawn,' as a mouth or an abyss (OED).

We gape back. We make brilliant machines for gaping. They inscribe a universe that appears to open endlessly. Indeed, its speed of expansion now seems, stunningly, to be accelerating – as though replaying the initial surge into materialization called the Big Bang. Or more suitably: the Big Birth. A strange 'dark energy' pushes the universe infinitely out. In a centrifugal expansion that is paradoxically without centre, glamorous conflagrations of star death glide along on the same momentum with nurseries of nebulae incubating fetal stars. The galaxies interlace like a circulatory system: the nonlinear geometry of chaos is figured everywhere. Astronomers, who had once focussed upon 'jewel-like lights that moved in eternally recurring patterns,' must confront the possibility that the starry galaxies and their creatures are 'barely more than flecks of froth on a stormy sea of dark matter.' Darkness upon the deep.[742]

With this evocative text starts *Face of the Deep*. Keller shows how Genesis 1:2 – about the earth being formless void, darkness upon the face of the primal flood and God's Spirit on the face of the waters – is of utmost importance to understand the relation between God, earth, matter and the feminine. Her commentary on this verse appeared already in chapter two. It is revealing that in many biblical commentaries Genesis 1:2 is either skipped or demonised.

Constructive theopoetics

Keller practises 'constructive' theology. Constructive theology is not entirely the same as systematic theology or dogmatics. If one speaks of dogmatics one usually starts from dogmas and doctrines from the past. 'Systematic theology' emphasises the systematising of theological insights. Keller questions dogmas and doctrines: how did they come into being; what lay behind them? She doesn't look for an all-inclusive system, and she doesn't try to morph it into a logical and easy whole of beliefs. This is something she learned from postmodern philosophy and mysticism. Construction signifies the ongoing process of building that will never end in a finished building. Constructive relates to deconstructive too. Theology is according to Keller an ongoing process of deconstructing and constructing: taking apart in order to see how everything fits together, to see what the separate parts look like, in order to construct something new from the old and new parts. In this respect she differs from Gebara and many other feminist theologians who see classic theology as hopelessly patriarchal. She also differs from more traditional theologians who regard only certain sources, texts and traditions as authoritative. Her philosophical orientation too differs from Gebara's. While Gebara looks phenomenologically at what occurs in people's experiences, Keller seeks her philosophical base in postmodern philosophy that deconstructs experience as well.

Applied to the doctrine of *creation ex nihilo*, the creation from nothing, the constructive method that is used by Keller looks into the way this idea arose, what interests were at stake, how this idea was discussed and what other discussions were going on at the time. Then she starts to build everything up again. Assisted by a thorough exegesis of Bible texts, elements taken from the whole history of theology and philosophical insights, she comes up with another theory: everything that exists is becoming in relations. God is interwoven with the internal relations of all creatures without coalescing completely. This idea is not something new, which shows that theology, according to Keller, cannot be a creation from nothing either.

253

For Keller theology is not a pure rational activity. To do justice to what is important for theology, that is God, Keller needs much more than just rational, linear prose. One can speak of God only in metaphors. The pre-rational, the symbolical and the narrative are also important for theology. 'Theopoetics' is how this theology, bordering on poetry, is named. It cannot easily be summarised without losing most of its characteristics – its fleeting, imaginative, evocative character. Its form and content are inseparable.

Feminism, postmodernity and process

Keller is involved in a feminism that does not favour the ending of inequality by upending differences, as classic feminism wants to do. It also differs from radical feminism that puts the feminine above the masculine, by replacing, for instance, a father god with a mother god. But if the underlying thought structures remain the same, nothing changes, Keller would say with Gebara. Postmodern feminism starts from differences but takes account of more than just bipolarity. For instance, if you think about gender and sexuality, you don't have to be either man *or* woman, homosexual *or* heterosexual.[743] There are so many more differences that go without bi-polar ordering, going from the one into the other is rather by degree. In this manner, Keller deconstructs the oppositions man–woman, cosmos–chaos, and subject–object.[744]

Keller borrows many insights from postmodern philosophers. Postmodern philosophy reacts to modernity and thinkers influenced by the Enlightenment.[745] Postmodern philosophers criticise the concept of the autonomous individual,[746] thinking in dualities and being focused on the spiritual in detriment to the material. And they show that what is considered truth is a construction, a combination of language and power. The enlightened image of people does not encompass all people. The western healthy heterosexual male is the norm and one who does not comply is more or less the 'other' deviating from normal man. A postmodern approach will never try to develop a universal theory, because that is impossible, but it will always try to see who and what according to a certain opinion is made into 'the other'. Something is always silenced or made invisible.

A text hasn't a fixed meaning either: meaning depends on context, for example, other texts and situations that resonate within. One can also look at what a text doesn't say. Another context can bring about new meanings. Other questions bring about new movements in a text. Every text contains contradictions and loose ends. One can take these up to deconstruct a text and thus, also to delve even more into it, revealing new meaning. This is the way Keller uses Bible texts. Derrida's and Deleuze's methods of postmodern philosophy are her greatest sources of inspiration. But she doesn't go along with everything postmodernism does. She criticises postmodern philosophy whenever it denies the possibility of all reality outside of language. Deleuze asserts that meaning is always produced, whereas Keller maintains that meaning can be discovered.

Process theology is a third important factor in her thinking. Keller studied under John Cobb and it was due to him that she found a way of thinking that emphasises not being but becoming, interrelatedness and reciprocal influences. In process theology God is challenging what exists, enticing everything to develop within their own conditions as well as they can. God creates through evolution, and is dynamic and relational too.

Process theology rests on the cosmology of the philosopher and mathematician Alfred North Whitehead. Process-thinkers – influenced by evolutionary biology, quantum theory and certain forms of religious experience – see nature as an ongoing creative process, both on a cosmic and an earthen level, of which people are an integral part. All living creatures, and plants, animals and sometimes even ancestors and spirits, are considered subjects who take part in a community. Relatedness is a key concept: every living being is part of the web of life and the whole cosmos. The cosmos has been unfolding in steadily higher forms of creativity reacting on its environment. Cobb applies these principles to Christian theology. God or the divine embraces the whole and is present within as lure for further expanding possibilities, both of individual beings and the whole, without disturbing natural causes. Thus, God shares in the joy and the suffering of everything that exists. Evolution knows some form of tragedy in the very act of dying to ensure new life. Process-theologians do not see this dying as sin. Sin is for them the unnecessary violation of creation. The goal of the unfolding cosmos is fullness of life and in that process people and other living creatures are co-creators. Liberation is not something that happens from outside, but is transformation. From a process-theological perspective spirituality is not exclusively human, because every living creature has its own relation with the divine and tunes in with this divine embrace. Humans take part in this non-verbal consciousness of connectedness. Christ is the one who optimally responds to God's creative lure.[747]

4.3.2 The fiction of the separated self

In her first book, *From a Broken Web*, Keller criticises the western idea of the autonomous subject.[748] People are interwoven with each other, God and the earth, but a lot of these relations are disturbed. In the West, the dominant idea is that in order to be someone, a self, yourself even, one has to be independent of everyone else, an individual in opposition to the world and God. She calls this the fiction of the separated self. This image works out differently for men and women. It is easier for men than for women to deny their dependency; still, both have a contorted self-image. The story of Odysseus is typical: Odysseus is a hero who goes forth; Penelope, woman, stays at home and waits for him, weaving a cloth that she unravels again by herself. He is the prototypical male ego, autonomous relative to the world; she is the– the prototype of female dependency dissolving in her surroundings.

Using myths, Keller tries to unravel the patriarchal structures that form the male and the female. There are many myths in which a male hero slaughters a female monster. One that found its way into the Bible is the Babylonian–Assyrian creation myth of the hero Tiamat.[749] In such myths, the female is identified with chaotic primal power, which is still shapeless, an oceanic connectedness that threatens male autonomy. Psychoanalysis takes these myths prototypically for patricide or matricide. In order to become someone, one has to separate oneself from the father, and certainly from the mother. Keller accuses Freud of not distinguishing between undifferentiated narcissism and the liquid, often labelled as feminine, experience of relatedness.

Theology, particularly the Reformation's, has also stressed the importance of separateness: God over against the world; humans over against God. Keller appreciates rather the notion of relatedness. She finds supports for this view in Whitehead's process-philosophy. Everything is a process, there are no isolated identities, and everything is always in the process of becoming and exists in relations. She constructs a notion of the self as existing in a web of connections, a connected self that transcends the separated masculine and the dissolving feminine self.

4.3.3 Counter-apocalypse

Keller wrote two books about the apocalyptic thinking that, she says, is deeply rooted in our culture.[750] It comes forth from an interpretation of the Bible in which one reckons with an absolute beginning and an absolute end of history. This makes history into a closed linear whole. Many conservative Christians are inspired by the coming of Christ at the end of times. They prepare themselves for the fulfilment of the visions of the biblical apocalypse because they believe in the destruction of the earth and the coming of a new earth in which there will be only room for Christians. Some even welcome the signs of corruption of the earth because these will speed up the outcome, so they say.

Progressive Christians often hope that God's kingdom will be realised in the future. They tend to think that they themselves can and must realise God's kingdom. This hope and urge may even degenerate into utopic thinking when one loses the notion that this kingdom is already present, here and now. Their thinking starts to resemble what fundamental Christians maintain, with all the risks that it entails, sharply dividing good and evil whilst lacking self-criticism. If justice, peace, equality and everything else worth pursuing are only found in the future, although not beyond death or at the end of times, its perspective still lies just as far from the good and normal life, here and now. Keller argues for a less linear way of thinking that is aware of new possibilities that happen continually. Thus the title *Apocalypse Now and Then*. She takes history as an ongoing process with an open ending. There are constantly openings for a new beginning. In this way she differs from defeatists who don't see any future ahead. Keller wants to hold on to resisting destruction without expecting a triumph.[751] This is what she calls anti-apocalypse and, in that way, she reads the biblical apocalypse too. The book is mostly read in a linear way, whereas it consists of a collection of visions. She takes them as images of an end in which there is constantly an opening towards a new beginning. It does not deal with an end of time, but with the way the Spirit works. There is not really any difference between creation and eschaton: on the very edge of chaos something new starts ever again.[752]

4.3.4 Creation from the deep

Face of the Deep is an important book for eco-theology. In this book about creation Keller expands the insights of her previous publications. Using just one Bible verse, she puts many fundamental questions forward about the relationship between God and world. I will not try to set out her argument in full. Some of her insights have already been dealt with in chapter two.[753] She shows that a masculine divine creator creating from nothing cannot be inferred from Scripture. The often ignored or demonised second verse of Genesis describes on the contrary what creation entails: out of the uterine chaos has the universe been born.

In this chapter I will focus on her creation theology, her image of God, her worldview and on her method that is closely intertwined with her theology.

Deconstructing creation from nothing

Keller starts by asking herself how on earth the chaos and the deep disappeared from the theology of creation, or were sublimated or demonised. *Tehomophobia* is what she calls the fear for the deep that led expositors over many centuries to oppose chaos and cosmos and identify chaos with nothing or evil. *Creation ex nihilo*, creation from nothing, was thought up to reinforce God's omnipotence and, likewise, the omnipotent power of the masculine word and mighty men over the world.[754] This ideology of dominion, in which God/He does not accept any other, is detrimental, according to Keller, to everything and everyone that is considered the 'other', but is also at the cost of the profundity of theology. Still, the excluded chaos reappeared time and again in the imagination, often judged unfavourably and linked with water and the feminine, as we see in the fascination for mermaids and sirens. Keller maintains that it was not at all accidental that during the first feminist wave such stories were popular.[755] This provided the suffragettes' opponents with some ammunition. Augustine, in the fourth century, is ambivalent about the primal flood. On the one hand, he sees *tehom* as product of human sin – with an odd image – coming forth from Adam's womb. Without this flood of salt water, creation would have remained wonderful.[756] On the other hand, Augustine sketches God as an ocean and the cosmos like a sponge fully soaked in God.[757] In the tradition of the church there have been theologians who never shut out the other/ Other, seeing God also in darkness. Gregory of Nyssa (fourth century) and the Methodist Charles Wesley (eighteenth century) are just a two examples that she mentions.[758] Next to *tehomophobia* there was also *tehomophilia*, love of the deep. Keller calls her own thinking *tehomic* theology.

She uses Gilles Deleuze's philosophy to reach a less negative understanding with the inordinate. To Deleuze, the deep 'Is not an undifferentiated chaos, but a chaos from which difference unfolds a cosmos. Thus the multidimensional surfaces of heaven-and-earth – its water, earth and atmosphere, its multiple species and societies – disseminate the deep.'[759] A new reading of the Bible supports this vision. When chaos and cosmos do not have to be opposites, theology may receive more profundity and the deep becomes more visible as place of creation. Depth is where it all takes place; it is not the Creator as such. God creates in conjunction with created beings. Not just people are co-creators; earth and sea equally create in conjunction with God. The image of the universe as God's body agrees with McFague's and makes God and world inseparable, undividable, but not identical.

God the Manyone creates

God as the Manyone is not the One over against the many, as in classic theology, but the creative power within the world. In her explanation of God's name Elohim, Keller follows medieval Jewish thinkers like Nachmanides: it is all about heavenly powers or the angels or the assembly of the gods, a sort of committee. Contemporary exegetes too are convinced that in Genesis 'apart from the one God there were other gods'.[760] God does not work alone but with others. Nachmanides concludes that people created in God's image should not think that they can decide everything on their own if even God does not do so. For Keller, God is a pluri-singularity, a manyone. God as the One does not stand over against the plurality of the world, but is the creative power within the world. Elohim creates because creatures create themselves and each other. God and creation are not the same, but they are very neatly interwoven. The *tehom*, the deep, is the matrix of possibilities out of which everything in interconnectedness comes forth, and God is the creative agent within. 'Creation signifies not a zap in the void but a decision within a plenary of possibilities.'[761]

God as Manyone bursts the dogma of the Trinity: there are many more possible ways of thinking of God in plurality than just as three-in-one.[762] She refers to the Kabbala. The ten *sefirot* from that Jewish mystical movement show God as male/female (*bi-gendered*) plurality.

Some people think that Keller says that God is just a word standing for the totality of the reciprocal relations of all creatures. Or even, anthropocentrically, God is a word for the connection between people. But that is not what Keller says – at least not in *Face of the Deep*. God is, according to Keller, not above or beyond the world, but you cannot do without God. This is because, she says,

> if we delete the *theos* from theology, what does it leave? A logos alone, a regime of secular monologoi, from which mystery, prophecy and the love that is stronger than death have evaporated? An elite post-theism, which shuns all theologies of social and symbolic struggle?[763]

In other words: if you leave God out of theology, you end up with a secular form of scientific knowledge that is acceptable for the posh, but does not leave any room for the struggle for just relations, nor for mystery, prophecy and love that is stronger than death. Then one is left with a form of knowledge, a type of logics, in which many things are left out that are difficult to define but are still of great importance.[764] Keller's image of God is 'apophatic panentheistic' – God is mystery and God is in everything and everything is in God. Not only God but our world is a mystery.

Order by self-organising from chaos

The *tohu wabohu* of Genesis 1 is according to Keller not the same as the deep, the *tehom*, but is materialisation, unformed matter, the *chora* of Plato,[765] the not-something (*nihil-aliud*) of Augustine, between being and non-being. There is a rhythm in *tohu wabohu*, a repeat that is never the same. With this assertion she coincides with both postmodern philosophy and the theory of chaos.[766] She searches for another notion of order than replacement of chaos because she wants to get rid of a single negative opinion of chaos that has had such a devastating impact on the image building around women and nature.[767] If 'God's creation' is denuded of 'omnipotence, linearity, even of His grammatical masculinity, what remains of the work of *ordering*?'[768] The language of natural sciences does give clues to construct order differently. The theory of chaos from physics comes namely with another image of order: from fluctuation. Fluctuations can become so strong that they reach a tipping point in which the system disintegrates into chaos or reaches a new, higher level of order. According to this theory order starts spontaneously out of chaos through self-organising: 'I am invoking the metaphor of "self-organizing" as a transcoded theological equivalent to the "order" of creation. Such order maintains itself *within* instability.'[769] Complex systems are dependent of the chaos from which they derive and to which they attribute. The order of Genesis 1 is not a replacement of chaos, as classical theology wants.[770] Order and chaos are not opposites – they need each other. To put it very simply, without ordering nothing exists; without chaos, nothing changes.

Inherent to this theory is that everything is continuously in flux. Evolution goes with the becoming of earth because the development of species is a 'natural expression of a universe that is not in equilibrium [...], there are *differences, potentials, that drive the formation of complexity*'.[771] Keller interprets this process theologically: 'In theology we call this nonlinear might-not-have-been "grace".'[772]

God as 'strange attractor'

To picture the order of creation as self-organising does not comply with the image of God as a ruler from outside. Order in the chaos, self-organisation, makes a supernatural Creator as origin of the universe superfluous. Calvin – with his concept of the world as theatre of God's glory – resisted this notion of a self-creating world because he was afraid that God the Creator would become redundant because human beings would consider themselves as creator. Keller understands this fear.[773] I too think that what Calvin foresaw at the beginning of modernity did become reality: *homo deus*, man considering himself to be as god.[774] Keller considers this as human arrogance that stems from a wrong and unwished-for image of God. Self-organisation demands another discourse on the divinity and humans: 'It looks neither for Creator nor for the human creature outside of the ecosocial web of all life.'[775]

God has not become redundant in Keller's thought. The role of God is, according to her, comparable to the 'strange attractor' of the theory of chaos. A normal attractor is for example the sun, who keeps the planets in their orbits. Complex systems have a so-called strange attractor. A strange attractor does not create fixed trajectories, such as those of the planets round the sun; their paths are labyrinthian. The starting point is important. With some starting points the system will move to infinity, but is kept imprisoned by the attractor. A strange attractor may look like this:

The Clifford attractor, commons.wikimedia.org

Strange attraction looks like what Whitehead called 'Divine Eros, with its lure towards actualization [...] The action of God is its *relation* – by *feeling* and *so being felt*, the divine invites the becoming of the other, the *divine becomes itself*.'[776] Keller sees an oscillation, a vibration, between divine attraction and divine receptiveness: in other words, between invitation and sabbath.[777]

> The strange attractor of chaos theory can serve as another figure for the natural law, logos or Torah, that permits genesis at the edge of chaos. It describes a labyrinthine but limiting path – for a path is always a track of decisions – within the ever-incomplete infinite.[778]

Theology can feel at home here, says Keller. The 'sensitive dependence on initial conditions' resounds with the image of the Spirit that goes up and down in the turbulence. Elohim, Creator, Word or Wisdom remain beautiful names for God.[779] The classical confession of 'God almighty Father, maker of heaven and earth' still sounds through but, yet, differently.

The dynamic model of rhythm and repetition but always different, of instable or disturbed equilibrium, fits also the biblical tradition of exodus, she avers. Exodus, liberation, to be on a journey, return from exile, new beginning, is a recurrent theme in the Bible. Exodus, always again and always different, is not linear nor cyclical. No linear movement towards a being at home in the future of a kingdom or heaven. No eternal return of the same that is imprisoned by the world. God's people are at home in the nomadic.

Strange ways of love: Hadewijch

By using the image of the strange attractor Keller seems to picture God in a very abstract and unpersonal way, almost cold. She herself puts the question forward whether this could be an image of God's love. She finds a provisional answer in the thirteenth-century mystic Hadewijch from Brabant, who speaks in terms of strange ways. For her, God is *minne* (medieval Dutch for *love*), a feminine word. Not a love that gives protection:

Alas! On dark roads of misery
Love indeed lets us wander,
In many an assault, without safety,
Where she seems to us cruel and hostile;
And to some she gives, without suffering,
Her great and multiform joy:
For us these are truly strange manners,
But for connoisseurs of Love's free power, they are joy.[780]

Hadewijch had, like many mystics, not an easy life, but on dark roads, in the *tohu wabohu*, she found yet God's love and hence joy, not an unpersonal fate or an inconsiderate nature.

Darkness as infinite light: Nicholas of Cusa

Keller borrows a lot from the mystic Nicholas of Cusa, who wrote 'this whom I worship as inaccessible light is not light whose opposite is darkness but is *light, in which darkness is infinite light*'.[781] She quotes him to counterweigh the celebration of light in western civilisation. This celebrating is not at all innocent, she says, because it makes life for dark-skinned people harder. They are made into 'the other' because of light's supremacy. 'Early western modernity systematically encoded ignorance, inferiority and evil as darkness.' The Enlightenment brandished the higher light of reason. The flesh-colour of 'white' people became neutral, incorporeal, pure light in opposition to the black other.[782] Negative theology, mystical revelation and prophetic iconoclasm are counterflows. In Genesis, light doesn't stand in opposition to darkness. Light is being separated from darkness (Genesis 1:4) and is, thus, a possibility within darkness.

Negative theology 'would articulate a faith with which to face uncertainty, not a knowledge with which to eliminate it'.[783] Negative theology has a social liberating potential because it is a language lacking oppression. The darkness of our ignorance is in Nicholas's theology not a mistake or a sin. Denying darkness is in fact sin, because then

God would not be honoured as the infinite God, but as a creature. The impossibility of knowing does not only involve God, according to Nicholas. Not by singling out one name but by using a whole range of names means understanding comes about, says Nicholas. The *coincidentia oppositorum*, the coalescing of opposites, provides an alternative for 'the dichotomous regimes of a knowledge that separates God from the world, the One from the many, rational light from unknowable dark'.[784] He thinks pantheistically: everything is in God and God is in everything by way of *complicatio* and *explicatio* (enfolding and unfolding) of God and the universe in one another. Thus, within God is difference, and everything is radically joined. The infinite of God is iconoclastic, it dashes all images to pieces, because God is so much greater than we can say. Contextual and liberation theologies would really gain a lot by negative theology, Keller says, in not falling prey to identity politics. A dark from which light has not been abstracted is a third space between light and darkness in which the whole chromatic spectrum becomes visible.[785]

Not only human creativity

Keller says little in this book about the place of people in the greater whole. People are mentioned only as part of the whole creation, and what applies to the whole creation applies, of course, to people too. The deep is not just in the infinity of the universe but also in every human being. All human sorrow, all love is likewise pluriform and fluidic and of an unplumbed deepness, essentially unfathomable.[786] She makes plausible that Augustine's *Confessions* does not split up into two parts – one about his own history and the other about the cosmos – but that all amounts for him to one thing only, namely, God's wisdom. He is in search of God's wisdom both in the chaos of his own inner being and in the cosmos.[787]

She quotes the seventeenth-century mystic Silesius: 'In a droplet – say how can this be? – the whole ocean of God flows into me.' In this passage she recognises the *kenosis*.[788] God empties himself into one drop of my existence. There is a reciprocal dependence of God and human being, but also of God and the whole cosmos. 'Not just human creativity, we have stressed, from the vantage point of our primitive text: the earth and the sea "bring forth" in response to a permissive invitation.'[789]

Keller turns against the human dominion that is projected on God. That is what she holds against Karl Barth. Her analysis brings out that what modern people appropriated was subsequently put at God's feet: God is the absolute proprietor and originator of everything. 'In the attempt to put Modern Man in his place, Barth seems to have transferred to the Lord's account our most modern claims to certainty and property.'[790] Only in Christ is God, according to Barth, part of the world, immanent. Such an image of God's love Keller calls 'intimacy of domination'. The analogy is, to her, that of a jealous man who drives his wife to the shelters. Keller states that we should pick a better image for God than human dominion. Too often God's omnipotence is shored up to replace human responsibility.[791]

She finds the image of natality appropriate to express the fact that people are at home in the world.[792] She quotes Arthur Peacock, theologian and physicist, who reasons that female images of God fit the universe much better as a matrix of the birth of new forms of life: 'God creates a world that is in principle other than himself, but creates it within herself.'[793]

When Christ's body opens up

Panentheism takes creation as incarnation, that is to say, that God becomes matter in everything existing[794] – 'The all in the divine and the divine in the all.'[795] If that is so, what does Keller think about the singularity and the role of Christ? She says that 'Christ was then deployed to restrict divine incarnation to the singularity.'[796] This way of thinking started very early in church history. The discussion about creation surfaced in the context of the Christological discussion of the Church Fathers about the divine nature of Christ, resulting in the dogmas of the Trinity and Christ's two natures. In other words, the *ex nihilo* came up in the struggle against a 'heresy' in which creation mattered only 'as the arena of salvation – as the eschatological theatre of patristic Christianity'.[797] The beginning of the Gospel of John, as a midrash of Genesis, supplants *tehom*, the deep, with the *logos*, the Word, as the only eternal other of God, says Keller. The Gnostics argued that any uncreated being next to God would diminish God's divinity. Matter was something negative in their eyes, made by a lesser deity. In the second century, Irenaeus postulated creation from nothing to defend creation's goodness and integrity against the Gnostics with their second god and evil matter. His motive could be called ecological, but at the same time it displays a dualism that degrades matter. God acts through *logos* and *Sophia*, but the imagery is one of a 'unilateral, linear and masculine dominance'.[798]

Incarnation has become discarnation, says Keller, through the 'invention of the Incarnation as the God-Man, an exclusive subject to be worshiped rather than an inclusive possibility to be actualized'.[799] To put it in other words: as Jesus was made into a temporary God-Man, he became an object of veneration instead of an example of God being present in the world. Still, the message that God is present in the material, corporeal, has always been passed on through history, for instance, in the belief that liberation in the biblical tradition always promises bodily resurrection. And the liturgies of Christmas are filled with images of birth in which Christ's divine and human nature coalesce.[800]

After the deconstruction of Jesus Christ's incarnation, Keller happens upon a construction due to the rhetorical question 'what if the body of Christ opens up? Into its own tehomic indeterminacy?'[801] Even in the hardened heart of orthodoxy one may find panentheism, the intuition of a complex mix of Creator and creature, says Keller. 'This God-in-all and all-in-God suggests a divinity irreducible to unitary simplicity or self-contained triunity.'[802] A tehomic theology would deduce incarnation from the width of creation. 'Christ would represent the flow of a word that was always already materialised, more and less and endlessly, a flow that unblocks the hope of an incarnation [...] It takes place within the shared, spatiotemporal body of all creatures.'[803] Incarnation is an ongoing process.

In *Intercarnations*, Keller collected her essays in which she amplified her ideas about incarnation.[804] They are echoes of the doctrine of incarnation and go into the divine that becomes corporeal in all sorts of bodies voiced in all sorts of ways within several religions.

Let me relate the question 'what if Christ's body opens up?' to my own experience as a minister. When I'm conducting the Eucharist and I utter the words 'body of Christ', do these words, thanks to Keller's theology, receive more depth? That might be so, provided they remain attached to the life, teaching, suffering and dying of Jesus of Nazareth. But if the body of Christ opens up too far, it might end up being so wide and indeterminate that every distinction between creation and incarnation disappears, that Christ's body encapsulates everything and, thus, nothing at all, that in the end it does not obtain profundity, but dissolves.

4.3.5 Postmodern theology in context

Keller's theology is not special thanks to her image of God. That image does not really differ from many other eco-feminist theologians. Rick Benjamins summarises her theology as follows: 'God is the name for our intertwining with all of life, in whom all is encompassed, whom we cannot fathom and about whom we only speak unknowingly.'[805] Gebara says more or less the same. It's Keller's method that makes her so special, in particular the way in which she applies the insights of postmodern philosophers to understand and reinterpret Bible and tradition. She knows how to demolish the hierarchical dualisms of God–world, man–woman, and so on, with the postmodern concept of difference, that is, giving free rein to the many differences without order. Postmodern too is her dealing with meaning, intertextuality and history. All sorts of texts, broadly speaking, interlace, by which meaning comes into being, but is never tied down. She has a clear eye for the aspect of power in every text, and the way meaning arises.

Endless speculation?

Does Keller's thinking provide a useful theology or is everything possible if meaning becomes so fluid? Some people reject her theology as being 'endless speculation'.[806] I do not know what this objection exactly conveys. Keller is certainly not presenting new dogmatics – which sounds to me quite a relief – but she clearly takes sides, although she gives her opinion until something better comes along. Still, Keller's creative openness has nonetheless its limits. What matters to her is that justice is being done, first and foremost, to gender and ecology. Struggle belongs to theology, 'social and symbolic struggle' that is to say, both on a social and a theoretical level.[807] The main part of Keller's work is about the struggle for justice within Christian theology.

Keller opposes strongly the idea of the *creatio ex nihilo*, creation from nothing, that supports an image of God as masculine ruler. According to Kathryn Tanner this doctrine was precisely intended to counter the hierarchical and coercive relation of God to the world. Tanner's analysis of these intricate philosophic–theological debates from the first centuries differs from Keller's. She concludes that God's absolute transcendence was just the very thing that made a very close relationship between God and world feasible.[808] We will come back to this opinion when we look into Elizabeth Theokritoff.

A related objection towards Keller's theology – and other process-theologies – is that such an approach necessitates the reformulation of current expressions of belief and theological concepts.[809] Process theology has the great ecological advantage that all of reality is seen as a process of becoming in which God is involved; process theology does justice to the dynamics of the human and the non-human history, as is acknowledged by the synod document *De gaarde een woestijn?* and by Gijsbert van den Brink. But then both, slightly worried, wonder whether process theology is needed for that, because recalibrating words such as God, sin, salvation would be too high a price.[810] Leaving process theology aside for a moment, it has become all too clear that much is already out of joint in the current way of speaking of God and world or nature and history. Images of God and the world solidified into fixed concepts turn insights from a certain situation into everlasting truths and naturalise, thus, patriarchal and anthropocentric opinions.[811] One needs another worldview to do justice to God, people and the earth. In the following we will see that there are more options available than just process theology.[812]

Another point in which Keller might be criticised is that she hardly allows for hope in her non-linear view of history. Some forms of process theology take on a linear development of history, for instance, by starting with the Big Bang, continuing via the beginning of gradually higher developing forms of life and finishing in something like an optimum unfolding of the world.[813] God is then "'the creative aim" or "lure" persuading the world towards higher levels of self-actualisation'.[814] Keller argues for leaving history open. She doesn't think in terms of a predictive ending or a steady upgoing line in history towards a new earth, a kingdom of God, final salvation or an optimum self-actualization. But does she deprive us of all hope? Living with uncertainty is asking a lot of anyone. On the other hand, the perspective of a history without a predictive ending makes way for what doesn't fit in a linear concept of a history of salvation, surprises, unexpected grace. This certainly does more justice to our complex reality. Such a vision fits moreover better in the non-linear perspective of Scripture, in which salvation happens time and again. Hope is not linked up with the certainty of a happy end.

Keller 'recycles' Bible and tradition is what we concluded. She is far less negatively set against traditional truths of faith than Gebara. She nevertheless works from a certain ideological suspicion,[815] but reuses many fragments that she was left with after her deconstruction. Keller takes insights from the past seriously by approaching these critically whilst making room for new meanings. She unravels the mechanisms of oppression and exclusion in order to reprogram them. Her way of working creates space to help us in discarding unusable images without breaking radically with all classic theology.

Keller's contribution in our context

Keller's method is a way to continue thinking through, creatively and critically committed, the relation between God and the world, from the Bible and the tradition and many other sources. Keller's theology is not easy; 'due to its breadth of sources relatively few readers will have the expertise to follow the entire argument'.[816]

I too wouldn't be surprised if I have missed out a few things, and in this subparagraph I have consciously and unconsciously left out many. It is tempting to encapsulate Keller's insights into a collection of concepts, a few new images of God, humans and the world. But this would extract all the dynamics and wouldn't do justice to her way of theologising. It seems to me more fruitful to use her method to think further creatively about the big questions involving God and the world. 'Keller constructs (both on the page and in the reader's imagination) a new place to begin thinking about the deepest questions of life and essence.'[817]

This is not easy but neither is it boring, because 'the more we recognize oppositions and contradictions and do not shrink back from these, the more truth will shine in darkness'.[818]

These words are again a fine motto for a discussion on sustainability in which the participants differ considerably, for instance, because they start from diverging theological traditions. Keller shows how you can understand thinkers in their own context, people with whom you, initially, are in complete disagreement, but whom you may appreciate and to whom you even may start relating, without giving up your own theological involvement.

4.4. ELIZABETH THEOKRITOFF: THE GIFT OF GOD'S OWN LIFE

Catherine Keller and many other eco-theologians and feminist theologians draw their inspiration gladly from the tradition of the Eastern Orthodox churches.[819] There one finds a way of thinking about God and the world that is hardly influenced by the modern worldview. God and the earth are closer connected; nature is regarded positively. It matters, therefore, to take a closer look into orthodox theology. (In this part of chapter four, I frequently condense 'Eastern Orthodox' randomly to 'orthodox' or 'eastern'.) I will do this with the support of Elizabeth Theokritoff's theology. She is a Greek Orthodox theologian, associate lecturer and director of the Institute for Orthodox Christian Studies in Cambridge. She also translates theological works from modern Greek. She did a PhD on liturgical theology and has specialised in creation theology and ecological theology ever since she began teaching in 1988–1989 at the Ecumenical Institute in Bossey, Switzerland, for 'Justice, peace and the integrity of creation'.[820] I am not sure whether she could be categorised as an eco-feminist theologian. She doesn't put gender on her agenda, although the experiences of women do appear in her work.[821] She clearly stands for her tradition and hardly criticises in public its patriarchal character. In a Church that is plainly dominated by black-cloaked men, a big cross on their chest, clad in richly ornamented liturgical attire gathered around the altar, her influential voice rings out clearly.

Theokritoff also co-edited the *Cambridge Companion to Orthodox Christian Theology* and wrote *Living in God's Creation: Orthodox Perspectives on Ecology*, which was published in a series of the foundations of Eastern Orthodox theology.[822] With her many courses, lectures and workshops on orthodoxy and ecology she reaches a large audience.[823]

4.4.1 Context Eastern Orthodoxy

Current orthodox churches spring from the churches of the East Roman Empire, to which Constantinople (now Istanbul), Alexandria,

Antioch and Jerusalem belonged.[824] Due to missionary activities and migrations, churches took root in Russia and other East European countries, and later on in the rest of the world.[825] The eastern and the western church, i.e. the church of Rome, separated officially in the eleventh century, but there were conflicts long before. Greek, not Latin, was the common tongue in the churches of the East Roman Empire, which gave cause for many misunderstandings. Both sides did not accept the same theologians as authoritative. The churches grew apart politically and historically, and this had an impact on the way the churches were organised. In the East, before the fall of the East Roman Empire in 1453, the church and the state were united, although this Christian empire became gradually smaller due to the Arabic conquest and the Islamisation of these conquered areas. The fall of the Roman Empire contributed to the increasing power of Rome (the Pope). The East lacked a central power, even though the patriarch of Constantinople had a special position as ecumenical patriarch.

Belief was thought through in an intellectual dialogue with the Greek philosophic tradition. This happened – among other things – in the seven ecumenical councils (325–787), where the decisions were acknowledged by most churches in East and West. Christology was the main issue of these church meetings. The dogmas that subsequently were promulgated about God as Trinity (Father–Son–Spirit) and the two natures of Christ (divine and human) are very often disdainfully regarded as power politics, misjudgement of biblical thinking or outdated metaphysics. In their contexts, these dogmas were nonetheless well-thought-out answers to questions about how lived religion drawn from biblical sources could be formulated in contemporary language. Some churches dropped out at a very early stage. The churches of Antioch and Alexandria could not accept the two-nature doctrine (at Chalcedon, 451) and, thus, caused a schism within the eastern churches.

The fall of Constantinople in the middle of the fifteenth century heralded a period of stagnation that prolonged up till the end of

Ottoman occupation in the nineteenth and the beginning of the twentieth century. The focus of the church was initially very much on surviving in an environment in which Christians were considered second-rate citizens.[826] When, finally, a more peaceful era set in, one could start setting up theological institutions. This was often modelled on western examples with subsequent western influences. The theological revival started in Russia with the development of 'sophiologia' – God as Wisdom.[827] Another important aspect of current orthodox theology is its resourcing through the reinterpretation of authoritative theologians and monks from the past, the 'fathers', such as the so-called eastern Church Fathers, and desert fathers and mothers.[828] The monasteries have always had a big influence on church and theology. They preserved the inheritance of the fathers and mothers, and provided scholars, spiritual guides and missionaries. Mount Athos, the peninsula filled with monasteries of monks, was in the middle of twentieth century on the point of breathing its last, but is now a centre of spirituality where around 1,600 mostly well-educated monks live.[829] The spirituality of the monasteries 'helped to drive the Orthodox vision of theology as a living encounter with God'.[830]

A difference between the eastern and western churches is that the first were not to the same degree influenced by the Enlightenment as the latter were, with all the entailing disadvantages that in some cases turn out as advantages. The individual is not the focus of attention, but the church with all its old liturgical text and rituals, buttressed by a theology that appears static in its repetition of the Church Father texts, but doesn't shy from regular updates of these. The world is not the backdrop, even less the property of humans, but the whole cosmos is sacred. History is less seen as linear: creation, incarnation and fulfilment are not marked on a timescale. God is steadily, actively present. In the centre of theology, we find the unity of the divine and the human, the heavenly and the earthen in Jesus Christ and in the Eucharist.[831] This unity discloses a way towards deification (*theosis*) of all people and even for everything that exists.[832] Transformation is a key concept. Next to the *kataphatic* or positive theology, the knowledge of God, there is the *apophatic* of negative theology, the awareness that God cannot be known fully, neither with reason, nor captured in language. The opposition between knowing and unknowing is transcended by mystical experience.

The eastern churches dwelled more or less in a postcolonial situation after the fall of the Ottoman Empire and – later on, for Russia – of the Soviet Union. On the one hand they were depending on the western models to revive their churches and theology; on the other hand, they sought their own voice and stressed their own particularity over against the West. This was not really a situation in which there was much room for critical evaluation of their own tradition. Some theologians diametrically oppose the eastern against the western way of thinking, for instance about the image of humans, and the Trinity. Others refer to the resemblances, such as in the importance of the sacraments that Orthodox and Catholics equally endorse. At the World Council of Churches, the orthodox were in dialogue and co-operating with Protestants.[833] Anyhow, they find common ground in Bible, the Early Church with its ecumenical councils and the sacraments. Precisely because eastern theology has developed differently from western theology, it is able to shed new light on controversies that in the West played around the role of Bible and tradition, ecclesiology and belief, immanence and transcendence, Christology, and so on. 'Orthodox theology basically does not fit into western concepts. It transcends our differences.'[834] The orthodox contribution to ecumenical contacts was a reminder for other churches of the common heritage of the Early Church: it contributed to the renewal of liturgy and liturgical theology and helped to rediscover the early Christian spirituality.[835]

Orthodox ecology

Bartholomew I, since 1991 the 270th ecumenical patriarch of the Eastern Orthodox churches, also known as the 'green patriarch', is, also in the West, a highly appreciated speaker.[836] The Greek Orthodox Church to which he belongs pays a lot of attention to ecology. In 1845, the church promulgated an encyclical that condemned the burning and demolishing of woods. Patriarch Bartholomew organised several campaigns to draw attention toward environmental problems in European waters, such as the Aegean Sea, the Black Sea and the Danube.[837]

Orthodox theology may appear at first sight dualistic and unworldly and even not at all ecologically minded with its emphasis on eternity, liturgy and asceticism. But it is always concerned with eternity in the world, not hereafter or beyond. Whereas the West emphasises history, a timeline from creation, via covenant and incarnation towards redemption and fulfilment – the history of salvation – the East thinks meta-historically: the eternal and the spiritual are always present in the world.[838] God is present in the whole of nature, '[e]ach place and each moment is a sacred space and time; each can serve as a window into eternity.'[839] The whole world is an icon: an entry into a new reality. The whole word is sacrament of God.[840]

> Were God not present in the density of a city, in the beauty of a forest, or in the sand of a desert, then God would not be present in heaven either. [...] God is present 'in all things' (Col. 3:11). In other words, there is an invisible dimension to all things visible, a 'beyond' to everything material. All creation is a palpable mystery, an immense 'incarnation' of cosmic proportions.[841]

According to Orthodox Christianity the world is both good and beautiful (not separate from God) *and* fallen and sinful (due to human failing) *and* saved (because everything has received the fruits of salvation in Christ). If one of these three aspects of reality is forgotten, theology derails.[842] The whole creation is charged with divine energy according to the often-cited Gregory Palamas of the fourteenth century. He distinguished between divine essence and divine energy and developed a form of panentheism.[843]

In the liturgy, God's presence in the whole creation is proclaimed and the connectedness with all of existence celebrated. It is, thus, no flight from reality into a heavenly reality, but an acquiescing with the liturgy of the whole cosmos.[844]

Asceticism, sobriety and fasting are ways to preserve creation with care. Asceticism is often taken for being hostile towards the corporeal, but from an ecological point of view it is rather a way of life that enables one to become free from the powers that abuse the world, free from consumerism for instance.[845] The orthodox reality is, by the way, often less beautiful than it preaches. There are eco-monasteries, but Athos, for instance, does not shine out in environmental friendliness with its marked reduction of biodiversity, the amount of tarmac and its streams of waste.

4.4.2 Living in God's creation

If you want to live a truly Christian life, you must inhabit the earth in a way that is mindful of the whole of creation – humanity in particular, but also the entirety of non-human creation, spiritual and material, apart from which humanity is inconceivable.[846]

These words, taken from the foreword of *Living in God's Creation*, summarise the thesis of the book. Theokritoff presents in this book a Christian ecology from the orthodox tradition. She perceives the ecological crisis as a cultural and spiritual crisis that asks for a reorientation in thought and deeds. Creation theology from an eastern perspective offers not only a diagnosis but also such an orientation.[847]

It is, however, to suggest that environmental responsibility begins with living our faith in the most mundane details of everyday life. It begins with the realization that nothing is un-spiritual and unworthy of God just because it is physical. The housewife making the sign of the Cross over a loaf before cutting it, or the grandmother censing the livestock of her evening prayers, show an awareness of God's presence in his creation that we would do well to regain.[848]

From control to responsibility

The degradation of nature of the past centuries is according to Theokritoff a result of a culture of control, which she calls a dangerous illusion; 'it is profoundly problematic from both a practical and a theological point of view'.[849] Environmental problems cannot be solved with technology because our attempts to control nature create results that ask for more controlling and, thus, aggravate the problem. The modern worldview lacks the insight of the whole picture – to wit, the creation – and takes nature as a collection of resources and possibilities. 'Unfortunately, our capacity to *affect* the world as a whole is not matched by our capacity to *think in terms of* the world as a whole.'[850]

This worldview, according to Theokritoff, could only arise in a society where Christianity was already waning: it is still sufficiently Christian to conceive the world as not full of gods, but sufficiently unchristian to conceive the world apart from God the creator and from Christ who was born within the creation. A Christian worldview was not the main cause of the ecological crisis, she maintained in reply to Lynn White, but its very fall.[851] She considers the Reformation as a phase in this fall of Christianity. She is so negative about the Reformation because its many resultant church denominations contributed to the ongoing fragmentation of the Christian tradition, and it emphasised the individual as the place of God's activity, thus driving out of view the greater whole.[852]

The Christian ecology that she conceives involves both the *ecumene* – in the sense of the inhabited earth or the human community – and the *eco-system*, and concerns the relationship of the whole to God, its Creator.[853] Leading questions are:

- How does the Orthodox Church's tradition and teaching provide the framework for the necessary changes?
- How does it shape us – if we allow it – into people able to break the vicious circle?[854]

Ecological problems incite among many a sense of paralysis or denial, she states. She therefore seeks support from the thinking of Maximus the Confessor (580–662) as a starting point for her theology. His vision of human being as linking figure in creation helps to find a way out of this stand-off. 'It is necessary to accept that human beings *are* the cause of the world's plight; and that we are *also* God's chosen instrument through which all things are to be brought to fulfilment in Christ.'[855] She wants to replace the culture of control with a culture of responsibility.[856]

God in all things

Theokritoff does not start with the Bible but with the Church Fathers. It's a typical orthodox reflex immediately to read Scripture in the way it was always read and interpreted. 'An idea may be found in Scripture, but actually have played little part in shaping the Christian world view.'[857] Views on people and the world of the fathers are her spiritual compass.

The impression of Christian belief as purely interested in the spiritual and averse to the material is incorrect if it comes to the Early Church, she says, and her first argument is Christ's resurrection. Believing in the resurrection of the body is in flat contradiction with both the Platonic idea of salvation of the spirit from the body as the idea of reincarnation of the Far East, where the liberation of the soul from the cycle of rebirth is the goal. According to the fathers, humans are liberated with body and soul.[858] The whole of creation has a value that is eternal and Christianity proclaims even that God has become part of his own creation:

God the Word has become part of the world created through him; and this is the crucial event that enables creation to be not only a means of physical life, but also the gift of his own life to us.[859]

The fathers didn't argue from nature to God, but looked theologically to nature, says Theokritoff.[860] God is present in creation, in human nature and in the Eucharist; on a different scale, the same pattern recurs.[861] Nothing exists outside God and God is at the same time distinct from all creation because God is being itself. God is, thus, transcendent *and* immanent. People are images of God, but all other creatures are too, in as much as they are images of the *logoi*, the divine words or energies in everything. 'The *logoi* of things can be thought of as exemplars in the divine will for created things, "blueprints" in accordance with which the actual creature comes into being at its appointed time.'[862] Everything that exists takes part in God by existing. According to Isaac the Syrian, we have two spiritual eyes. With the one we see the glory of God's own nature; with the other we see aspects of his glory hidden in the creatures.[863] Maximus called the latter 'book of nature'.[864]

Now surely, not everything in nature testifies of love and wisdom. Sin is the absence of divine presence, says Maximus.[865] God is all, but not all is God. The goal of creation, salvation, is that God will be all in all. Humans play in this deification of the universe an important role.[866] Human acting must be in harmony with the goal of creation. If we want to ameliorate elements of nature, we shall have to do so according to the logos that is inherently present, thus, in dialogue, 'dia-logos'.[867] Gregory Palamas explicitly formulated in the fourteenth century the distinction between God's essence and his uncreated energies. He emphasised that God is separated from creation and, simultaneously, the vital principle of all that exists. Theokritoff stressed that the Eastern Orthodox view of the relationship between God and creation differs from the view of process theology, but also from the deists (God as the great watch-maker who sets everything going)[868] and the theistic idea that God would act from outside. To put it briefly: 'matter is shot through with spirit; all things resonate with the creative Word of the God who is also beyond all things'.[869]

People as kings and priest

In Scripture all creatures have a relationship with God, even without human involvement, as we have seen in chapter two. The fathers, notwithstanding, stress the role of humans as mediators between God and their fellow creatures. That is not to say that the fathers are anthropocentric, says Theokritoff, because they don't put humans but God in the centre. Every other centre would be an idol, whether it is people, the earth or matter. Therefore, she equally rejects an eco-centric theology. The goal of everything is God becoming all in all. People are not the goal but the 'mid-point'.[870] According to Gregory of Nyssa, spiritual and material nature is united in humans. Because of that, people resemble a microcosmos that is able to bring everything in relation with God. They have a key position in creation.[871] People are even kings in creation, according to the fathers, but a king defined by a constitutional monarchy of which God writes out the constitution. People may partake of the world and may use it – the world is even made for that reason – but always according to God's rules and for the glory of God. '[T]o partake in the kingly dignity of the prototype, man must be arrayed in the purple of virtue and the crown of justice.'[872] If people abuse the earth, they infringe not only God's commandments, but they cease to be humans, because they do not answer for what it means to be human: created in God's image and likeness.[873] Without love, the image is lost.

To rule is integral to people as free and rational beings, according to the fathers. Theokritoff concedes that this opinion is problematic from an ecological point of view.[874] Reason, so Theokritoff, is the ability to disown our instincts and to keep ourselves in check, which is really an altogether different stance from the so-called freedom of choice of consumers surrounded by all their must-haves.[875] She hastens to add that the fathers lived in a totally different world from ours. Controlling nature meant essentially surviving by tilling the ground and making clothes and building houses. That the creation was made for humans, as the fathers often say, must be seen in that light.[876] The responsibility that goes with this ruling of people is not in the first place governing but praising God.[877]

Abuse of creation

The fathers have given thought to what is going wrong in the way people use the world. They do not speak of the fall or a fallen world, but of 'the world of the fall'. This distinction is important, because when one takes the world as fallen, one may easily get the idea that the world is of no value and an impediment to spiritual life. Or taking the opposite view that cultivating the earth is required and a Christian virtue in itself. This last opinion legitimised exploitation and colonialism.[878] The fathers intended with 'the world of the fall' that the world was tarnished by the rupture in the relation between God and humans, whereas there is no rupture in the relation between God and world.[879]

This vision of the father returns in the exposition of Genesis 3 of John of Damascus (676–749). He stressed that humans were allowed to eat of every tree.[880] Eating of the trees is equal to getting to know God through his creation, and for that reason humans were made.[881] The one tree that they were not allowed to eat of, the tree of knowledge of good and evil, stands for physical, hedonistic eating that causes us to lose sight of God. Through eating of this tree men fell. Theokritoff brings his exposition up to date: through the fall humans have become top predators, consumers.[882]

The cursing of the ground in Genesis 3:17 does not include the whole earth, but the earth in as much as she is tilled by people. As in Byzantium, civilians had the right to rebel against the emperor when he turned into a tyrant; thus became the earth inimical to people when they no longer obeyed God.[883]

It turns out, then, that the fall as the Fathers interpret it in a key to understanding human abuse of the created world. The Fathers' vision of creation is one in which everything has its origin in God; it is created to reflect him, to relate us to him, and ultimately to be filled with him through our agency. The world of the fall, however, is one in which this constant reference to God is banished from the equation. Creation is there to satisfy my wants [...] Man's original fateful choice is compounded through the ages and generations, until it hardens into a world view.[884]

The fathers regarded greed as personal moral failing because they did not experience its current institutionalised attitude, in which all things of the world are seen as commodities and commercial goods.

Ascesis as the correct use of things

Theokritoff observes that the fathers' theology was put into practice by ascetics and saints and in the orthodox liturgy. Here we encounter the practical perspectives on daily life to experience the world as related to God. They 'enable us to relate to God through creation and bring it to full unity with him'.[885]

It is a common misunderstanding that asceticism is a negative attitude towards the world, the body and nature. It is just the opposite, according to Theokritoff: asceticism shows respect to the world and leads to a more just use of things. Whenever the fathers decry nature, they mean human nature that is corrupted by possessiveness. A negative assessment of 'the world' has to do with something like mundanity: 'the flesh' does not stand for the body, but for a particular way of life.

Ascesis signifies distancing ourselves from people and things, starting with what is nearest to ourselves, our own body. Ascesis is geared to God in a lifelong exercise of body and soul. It leads to a freedom to love the world without the urge to possess. Fasting is a way to return to the paradisiacal state.[886] Care of the soul entails care of oneself, including the body and the material creation to which it belongs.[887] As both Seraphim of Sarov (1754–1833) and Amma (mother) Theodora (fourth or fifth century) said:

> The aim of ascesis […] is to make the body a friend and helper, ready and able to perform virtuous deeds.
>
> Give the body discipline, and you will see that the body is for him who made it.[888]

The body is our interface with the material world.[889] If the fathers and mothers speak of despising of the body, they mean detachment. Ascetics go about caringly in a way one rarely finds in our materialistic society. Materialistic persons value things in relation to their own desires; detachment makes it possible to value things for themselves, as parts of God's creation. Asceticism is not a personal case of self-denial, but has to do with the way we use the gifts that are reserved for the common good. Seraphim says: 'True fasting consists not only in overcoming the flesh [to wit "the desire"] but also in taking that piece of bread which you would like to eat yourself, and giving it instead to one who is hungry.'[890] Praying, fasting and caring for the poor are one. The goal of ascesis is inner freedom. 'The physical discipline qualifies as true Christian asceticism only if it enables us to despise wealth, put away anger and free ourselves from vainglory and envy.'[891]

The correct use of material things roots into the conviction that the created world is a gift of God. Not in the sense that once given the receiver may use in whatever way he likes; it is still God's property. This makes all personal property into a common property. If all things are recognised as gifts and tokens of God's love, they will not be wasted. 'Look upon all the tools and all the property of the monastery as if they were sacred altar vessels', says Benedict's rule.[892] Self-limitation with the fathers does not suggest that food, sexual relations or other things are not good, because creation is good.

Ecological asceticism is urgent as self-limitation focused on God and for the benefit of other creatures because they are objects and instruments of God's love and not of our desires. On a practical level, it is not enough to know that less flying and driving, eating less meat and using fewer fossil fuels are needed: 'it is also necessary to challenge the lie that self-indulgence is the key to a fulfilled and happy life'.[893]

The world as an icon

The lives of the saints and their images on icons tell us a lot about the place of humans in creation. 'The saint is a person in whom the original beauty of the divine image is being restored.'[894] The saints are like Adam before the transgression, who gave the animals their names.[895] There are stories of animals that come to a saint and obey him or her. Animals help and protect the saint, and he or she protects them.[896] But there are also stories of saints who chase away or even kill a wild animal that threatens people.

Animals recognise authority of people to the degree that the image of God in human beings is restored: in other words, in as much as they have grown into Christ, the image of God in full.[897] For sceptical modern minds, Theokritoff proffers a current example of a glimpse of paradise, nature paying respect to an exceptional person.

The following story is told of a saintly priest's wife in Alaska, Olga Michael, who died just a few years ago and is already said to have worked miracles. The night of *Matushka*[898] Olga's death, in November, a strong southerly wind blew forcefully and continuously, melting the snow and river ice – this enabled neighbours to arrive by boat, normally quite impossible at that time of year. The day of her funeral was like spring; the procession was even joined by a flock of birds, although by that time of year, all birds have long since flown south. The birds circled overhead, and accompanied the coffin to the grave-site. Because of the unprecedented thaw, the usually frozen soil had been easy to dig. That night, the ground re-froze, ice covered the river, winter returned.[899]

Seraphim of Sarov feeds a bear. Fragment of a lithography Way to Sarov, 1903

If creation is there for human beings, then it is not just for our comfort, warns Theokritoff, but to serve our basic needs. Creation, moreover, is given to us 'not as a commodity to use at whim, but as a pattern for our own relationship to its Creator', a pattern of co-existence and interdependence.[900] We grow spiritually by seeing and emulating God's beauty and wisdom that are mirrored in creation.

The term animal rights is not relevant, says Theokritoff. It is all about voluntary compassion in God's image that reaches out towards everything made by God. Animals do not have rights as such, but they do have a rightful place in the created order: 'The integrity and unique quality of other creatures, animate and inanimate, must be respected: it is precisely through this unique quality that we glimpse "the divine wisdom invisibly present" in them.'[901]

With saints, the whole perception of created reality has changed. 'Just as the transfigured Christ does not change in himself, but simply allows his disciples briefly to perceive him as he is, so it is with creation's praise of God: it becomes perceptible only when humans have ears to hear.'[902] It is the reality of a world that is created in order to praise God just by being there, and to lead us to him.[903]

What a legend of a saint does in words, an icon does visually and practically: picturing a godly human being and the transformed reality surrounding him or her. An icon is a window onto God and shows that matter is no barrier between God and us, but a fitting medium to transmit his glory onto us. The base for this is that God entered his creation, and that the image of God in human beings is restored in Christ.[904] Light plays an important role in the visual world of icons: everything is illuminated from within by God's light. Non-human nature is hardly ever depicted. Does that show an anthropocentric vision? Well, yes and no, says Theokritoff. Man is 'the focal point *through* whom all things are led beyond the confines of their createdness', but nature too is in the same way being called upon to deification.[905] All elements of this world carry the stamp of the divine Word, thus, 'the created world is *already* an icon'.[906]

The icon gives a vision on the world that is totally different from, for example, the world as a battleground of selfish genes. 'It is the world with its potentials fulfilled.'[907] 'The ultimate contrast is not between shaping our environment or preserving it in a pristine state. The choice before us is whether or not we will embrace its potential, as the saints have done, so that natural and humanmade features alike become a sacrament of divine presence.'[908]

Liturgy and sacramental living

Celebrating liturgy is the heart of orthodoxy, and liturgical texts are an authoritative source of theology. Theokritoff cites an old motto: *lex orandi est lex credendi* (the rule of praying is the rule of believing), that is to say, that prayer moves to belief and liturgy precedes theology.[909] Orthodox theology knows many mandatory texts. In the daily cycle of worship praise is sung for, with and in name of the whole creation. Each evening the Vespers commence with Psalm 104 on the diversity of the created world, its interconnectedness and its dependence on the Creator.[910] Every morning Matins ends with Psalm 148, the praise of heaven and earth.[911] The praise in the liturgy makes people into a part of the cosmic hymn of praise of all creatures. People are unique in their way of expressing this praise, and at the same time they are the only creatures who can refuse to join in.[912] When one brings up theology and ecology one often emphasizes the importance of wonder.

Wonder can certainly lead people to God, but it can also become a substitute for God, says Theokritoff.[913] The daily prayer of the Church affirms our natural wonder at the created world and transforms this into praise for the Creator.[914]

The liturgical year links creation and salvation as parts of the same plan. Theokritoff cites many liturgical texts, amongst which many texts from Scripture, to show that there is a pattern of 'humans and other creatures responding to Christ side-by-side'. Thus in the Holy Friday Vesper: 'The whole creation was changed by fear, when it saw you, O Christ, hanging on the Cross. The sun was darkened and the foundations of the earth were shaken; all things suffered with the Creator of all.'[915] In this text it becomes clear how the suffering of the world coincides with a loving God, so says Theokritoff. In the resurrection too creation responds to the creation as a whole. She refers to Christ as the firstborn of creation. Salvation is there for people and other creatures.[916] The original beauty of creation is restored at the coming of Christ.[917] That accounts for all of creation and subsequently to every separate element of creation: water is cleansed through Christ's baptism in the river Jordan; the tree of the fall becomes the saving wood of the cross: 'One tree in Eden brought death to man, but another on Golgotha granted eternal life to the world.'[918] People abused the tree as an instrument of torture for crucifixion, but God's use of the tree discloses it as being the tree of life. 'The tree's natural functions – providing food and shelter, purifying water, enriching and stabilizing the soil – are thus revealed to have a spiritual counterpart, cosmic in scope.'[919] The Christian vision is that the earth is being sanctified, not sacred in itself, separate from God. Everything is charged with divine energy, but we humans have through our sin – that is to say, through our estrangement of God – severely scarred the earth. 'The breakdown of natural systems that we are seeing today cannot therefore be seen simply as a set of physical problems to be addressed by technological solutions, or even by changes in outward behaviour: it also carries a spiritual message.'[920]

Worship gives us no blue prints for what we must do and avoid doing to keep the land from 'mourning'.[921] Instead, it gives us a powerful and profound vision of the sort of world we live in and use every day. Everything in the natural world praises God, speaks of him, and draws us to him as the star drew the magi. And as we look at the natural processes of the world, the work of water in the environment or the growth of trees, we see more than marvels of physics and chemistry on which our lives too depend: we perceive the patterns of God's work of salvation. It becomes hard to use such a world wastefully or thoughtlessly.[922]

This restoration of the original beauty of creation is expressed best in the sacraments and even better in the Eucharist. In every baptism water becomes sacred.[923] With baptism the prayer connects our normal, everyday water with the water of the primal flood, the Red Sea and the Jordan. Water, bread and wine are not just symbols in the sense of reference. Bread and wine come to their destination when they are given back to God. Eucharist means thanksgiving – *efcharistó* is the common word for thanks in everyday Greek. This offering of thanks sanctifies the whole created world.[924] People offer their gift and express, thus palpably their thankfulness, 'And in return, we receive God's Gift of himself in tangible form.'[925] Current orthodox theologians speak of the priestly role of people in creation 'to underline man's unique responsibility for bringing the material creation of which he is a part to its fulfilment in Christ'.[926] In offering them to God, things receive their true meaning. A sacramental ethos is an antidote against a way of life that destroys nature.[927] Everything we do can be an offering to God once we start to see the sacramental dimension of the ordinary: 'beneath the surface lies a mystery of relationship with the Creator'.[928]

The bread of the Eucharist is made by people from normal ingredients such as grain and water. But the making of bread is not a purely human activity.

From one point of view, our transformation of the natural world [...] is only a tip of the iceberg of transformations going on all the time in nature. The eucharistic bread, which is a human offering, is totally dependent on the activity of yeasts, the physical and chemical processes that provided nutrients to the soil, and the unremitting labour of microorganisms that create humus, to name but a few essential contributors. On a purely physical level, the Eucharist is a cosmic celebration on an awe-inspiring scale.[929]

We do not have to ameliorate the world in order to make her God's instrument. She is already God's instrument and we should work in the world as God does.[930] That is the case when we decipher God's 'words' (*logoi*) in all created things and thus discover his wisdom.[931] Contemplation is part of it, but is not enough. 'If God can be glorified only in a few peaceful enclaves of contemplation, the world of our daily work will speedily fill up with altars to rival deities such as wealth, power, or convenience.'[932]

The Eucharist joins people not only with the material reality, but also with other people, especially with the poor. The community reminds us that all we have is a gift of God, received for the benefit of all.[933] The Eucharist has also to do with our attitude to time. Whereas the daily prayers are linked with specific times of the day, the Eucharist is not tied to a particular hour.[934] The 'Divine Liturgy' helps in 'escaping the domination of time; it opens the way to experiencing in every moment the working out of God's eternal Kingdom'. That is no time that can be bought, no time that is money and can be saved; it is time that is redeemed, an eschatological time, 'a present reality that is grounded in the future'.[935] The sacramental awareness of time is on the one hand 'the dynamic reality which "transvaluates" everything around us' and on the other hand makes us aware that 'this liberation is still a work in progress'.[936] It is not looking back to a paradise long lost in the past or in the future, but it is a transfiguration of all things, in which we may co-operate in doing God's will.[937]

If we participate in the Mysteries of the Church and then abuse the created world in our everyday life, we are living a contradiction. The sacramental life of the Church culminating in the Eucharist, is the supreme revelation of the nature of creation in itself. The Eucharist is a 'moment of truth' in which we see the world in Christ; the blessing of waters makes the world and all creation what it was in the beginning.[938]

4.4.3 Celebrating, fasting and *Sophia* in our context

As of now, I discussed Theokritoff as representative of her tradition, something I did not do with Gebara and Keller. This can be partly explained by the fact that I am very familiar with Catholicism and Protestantism, to which the latter belong, but not with Eastern Orthodoxy. But is has also to do with the fact that Theokritoff presents herself as a representative of her tradition, whereas Gebara and Keller are much more critical of their traditions. Now, of course, there is no such thing as *the* Orthodox theology and, even less, as *the* Catholic or *the* Protestant theology. Theokritoff too makes a stand against certain opinions in her tradition, for instance when she rejects the sophiology, wisdom-theology from nineteenth-century Russia. She says of the theologian Vladimir Soloviev (1853–1900) that he 'attempted to express the unity of all things in terms of 'Sophia', or divine Wisdom personified; his speculations on this mysterious figure took him well beyond the traditional bounds of Orthodox theology.'[939] The importance of Lady Wisdom as a biblical figure does not seem to bother her. Theokritoff is part of a movement that wants to resource theology by reverting to the Church Fathers.[940]

Image of God, worldview and anthropology

Through these fathers and mothers, she turns out a theology that is in many ways closer to the Bible and more ecological than modern western theology. The biblical notion of the praise of all creation in which people participate has been better preserved in the East than in the West. Those not shying away from the (perhaps for contemporary western readers) all-too-devotional language will find with Theokritoff a non-hierarchical image of God that doesn't situate God outside of the world, but neither defines God from the evolutionary theoretical viewpoint as force in the unfolding cosmos. Nothing in the world is separate from God and, at the same time, God is totally different from everything in the world. God is, thus, fully immanent and fully transcendent. This approaches the classical Catholic theology of Thomas Aquinas, in which God is being as such that gives all beings their existence.

Creation is with Theokritoff everything that is not God in himself, as the Nicaea–Constantinople creed says: 'heaven and earth', 'everything visible and invisible'. Thus, not only the animate and inanimate nature are part of creation, but also people and what they make, and even the invisible beings which are called in biblical and liturgical parlance dominions and powers.

The notion of the Church Fathers that the creation is made for people needs quite some explaining and nuancing so it does not fall into the trap of current anthropocentrism. God is pivotal, Theokritoff emphasises, and humans are also there to serve creation, namely to lead everything to Christ.

The goal of creation should not be taken linearly. The orthodox tradition does not reckon with the beginning and ending of time, but with eternity, here and now, experienced in the liturgy, in the lives of the saints and icons. There is the ever-recurring pattern of God giving himself: creation, incarnation, Eucharist. Christ is, according to Theokritoff, first and foremost, the cosmic Christ, born in creation, in whom the original beauty of creation is restored, present in the Eucharist. Historical and symbolical are not contrasts, as is often the case in the West where conservative Christians take 'real' to mean 'really happened' and liberal Christians interpret as 'of real value'. Orthodox theology has no axe to grind with the Cartesian and Kantian divide of spirit and matter, people and nature. Bread and wine of the Eucharist are for Theokritoff part of the pattern that in different shades shows God's presence in the world.

Theokritoff's notion of creation and time does not really differ that much from Keller's. The force of her image of God, if compared with the aforementioned theologians in this chapter, is that God is not only completely connected with the world but also utterly different. And in a way, that it is not detrimental to women and non-western peoples, because the image of God is non-hierarchical and not as such masculine – although she speaks of God in masculine terms.

Celebrating and fasting in our context

Those who do not believe that market economy and the technology will solve the ecological crisis must come to the conclusion that frugality and downsizing are part of an ecological way of life. But frugality is not highly esteemed in our culture. 'Enjoying having enough' is a slogan that tries to deflect the negative connotations of holding in check this urge to consume. Theokritoff shows that, in the Early Church and in Eastern Orthodox tradition, ascesis is a positive way of self-restriction. This tradition as a counterweight to consumerism has not only a personal but also a social component. Ascesis, the reining in of desires through fasting and praying, leads to a freedom to love the world without possessiveness. It relativises property by regarding the world as God's property and God's gift to everyone. Things are only used correctly if their use enhances everyone's wellbeing.

Ascesis is an exercise of body and soul that differs from the exercises of body and soul in our culture, such as fitness, dieting, zen meditation and yoga. These go with some form of 'exertion', too, but are geared to physical fitness, a slim body, and one's own spiritual wellbeing. These are forms of 'indulging yourself', giving yourself a treat. But the essence of ascesis is being focused on God. This orientation has more to offer in terms of freedom than hedonism does, and it enables one to value things as they are – part of God's creation. Ascesis is founded in God giving himself. Self-restriction is even one of God's traits, as McFague shows.[941]

Liturgy is essential to seeing self-restriction in this enhanced perspective. The ancient words and the celebrating are asceticism's meaningful and festive frame in which prayer is its base.[942] Fasting cannot come alive without praying and celebrating.

The link between ascetism and prayer is also found with Sarah Coakley, an Anglican theologian and priest. In her book *The New Asceticism* she assails the churches' sex abuse cases and discussion on homosexuality of the foregoing years.[943] She does so by explorations into the term *desire*. Although ecology is not on her agenda, her insights are certainly applicable to ecological matters. She takes ascesis to find a way out of the deadlock between people in favour of or against sexual freedom, between libertinism and repression. The libertine ethics that allows everything provided all parties involved agree is just too minimal to be acceptable for her. Desire, lust, falls short of measuring correct behaviour. Desire has to be purified and that is possible the moment one acknowledges that all our desires are rooted into the desire of being with God. God desires us and this engenders our desire, says Coakley. Therefore, we have to adjust our desires to God and bring them in line with God's desire. To illustrate this, she borrows a model from mysticism: the first level is the purification through concrete rules of behaviour; secondly, enlightenment through the rule of serving, community and prayer (so the Rule of St Benedict); and, thirdly, unification through contemplation in everyday existence. The highest level, the unification, being absorbed in the life of the Trinity, doesn't follow from the two other levels but accompanies them.

Materialistic desires are in my opinion comparable to sexual desires. To indulge in them shamelessly is very much stimulated in our culture, whereas reining them in is really what we are in need of. The tradition of ascesis is of utmost importance. Ascesis helps us to be neither greedy nor indifferent towards our properties. In ascesis a change of lifestyle is embedded in rules of community and service, and a practice of contemplation. This contemplation does not lead us away from but connects us with the place where we live. In western Christianity the contemplative tradition is still kept alive by monks with their vow of poverty embedded in a practice of celebration and prayer. The famed Protestant sobriety of former times, too, was linked with prayer. I just have to evoke the memory of my grandparents with their robust furniture that lasted almost a lifetime. Celebrating was, alas, among Protestants not much fostered.

Sophia/Wisdom

Sophiology may be out of place in orthodox tradition, according to Theokritoff; in our context this image of God as Wisdom proves very helpful to integrate Eastern Orthodox insights precisely because it is for us not a strange but even a very biblical image. We can retrieve the idea of the *logoi* as God's words in the whole reality in the presence of God's wisdom in all of creation.

Wisdom makes a panentheistic image of God feasible without the risk of process theology that coalesces God with reality or even dissolves God in it. A clear distinction between God and creation that is not detrimental to women remains. God is not banished to the future as a vision of a better world, as happens in some feminist and liberation theologies. Celia Deane-Drummond refers in her argument to revalue the wisdom tradition as seen by Sergei Bulgakov (1871–1944): 'his sophianic vision of God offers a way of bringing the idea of the feminine into a transcendent vision of God, rather than reducing God to human visions of an idealistic de-patriarchal society'.[944]

4.5 WHAT GEBARA, KELLER AND THEOKRITOFF WOULD SAY TO ONE ANOTHER

Gebara, Keller and Theokritoff think through their theologies in different continents and Christian traditions. They also happen to differ starkly in method and in the degree of their loyalty to their church. Gebara is very critical of the Roman Catholic Church and puts the experiences of poor women in the centre, whereas Keller departs from postmodern philosophy and recycles knowingly the Christian tradition, and Theokritoff draws on the sources of her tradition to show how appropriate they are.

They also have much in common. All three dissociate themselves from modernity's worldview in which man, getting pride of place, understands the world rationally and does as he pleases. All three maintain that God is a mystery closely linked to the world.

Imagine how they could strike up a conversation. What would they say to one another?

Gebara would ask the others in what way they are engaged with situations of poverty. Keller could say that she stands up for anyone and anything that is made into 'the other' and is excluded from all dominant discourses and economic systems. Theokritoff may argue that the fathers both in word and deed declare their solidarity with the poor and are still an example for us. Gebara might reproach that she is far too uncritical of her tradition, which is overall very patriarchal. Theokritoff may reply that in the orthodox tradition the corporeal and the earthen is valued positively, that God is pivotal and present in all and that this image is not at all patriarchal. She might add that all people – men and women – are seen as priests called upon to unite the whole creation with God and that the priest's role in the liturgy is inferred from that very idea. Gebara would not be convinced and object that the real power of the spiritual leaders in the Eastern Orthodox churches is at least as formidable as in the Roman Catholic and the evangelical churches.

Theokritoff and Gebara could both say to Keller that she uses the tradition in a very selective and creative way, and by doing so may go every which way. Keller may answer that, in fact, all theologians do so, even Theokritoff, but that she herself does it more in the open and more explicitly. She might say that she, like Gebara, wants to show that injustices are always anchored in the way we think, and that it doesn't work to reject the whole tradition, because then we will soon be confronted by the same oppressive ideas reappearing, this time in a secular outfit.

Theokritoff could say to them both that they should not make theology dependent on scientific theories, but should start with God's glory visible in the whole creation. If Christian belief has to adjust to a scientific worldview, it will lose its transcendence. Gebara might argue that evolutionary theory clarifies the relatedness of everything that exists and, therefore, supports an inclusive theology and that she is even downright critical of a lot of scientific thinking in as much as it degrades other forms of knowledge. Keller would agree with that, taking note that current scientific theories happen to resonate beautifully with the insight of, for instance, the Church Fathers. She would say to Gebara that Theokritoff is right in that in the Early Church and among mystics there was always an undercurrent of knowledge that was not linear and not just based on experiences of men.

In this way they could go on for quite some time and disagree on many things – the importance of other religions, dogmas and doctrines, church and liturgy, Christology and politics. And they would agree on some fundamental issues – some form of panentheism, a perspective on humans as part of creation with a certain responsibility for the whole, a whole that in the end remains unknowable. They would agree that not a primal beginning or an end of history gives meaning to what exists, but God's presence or activity (although Gebara might rather prefer another word instead of 'God').

CHAPTER FIVE

The harvest

In writing this book I had two aims in mind: to render theology greener and show the environmental movement how theology substantially contributes to ecological sustainability. After having queried the worldview that allows the world to be exploited, I looked into the specific task of (systematic) theology, both in ecological issues and in general. I searched for another view on the relation of God–people–nature in Scripture and sketched the rise of eco-theology and resistance against it. Finally, I presented the insights of important eco-feminist theologians to fuel a theology that is just and green.

5.1 SUMMARY

Green theology or eco-theology is not a subdiscipline of theology but the rediscovery of the breadth of theology. Green theology corrects the reduction of theology to an area of study about God and the human world or what people believe. Theology should not hand over all thinking regarding the earth and the cosmos to natural sciences. In dialogue with other disciplines, theology may draw on its own broad tradition to contribute substantially to ecological discussions.

The Bible (see chapter two) counterbalances the reduction of theology in modernity and uncovers a worldview that is extremely relevant in current ecological discussions because of its inclusiveness. It is not solely interested in people. God is central and engaged in all of reality. God creates and saves the whole earth, of which humans are an important part. The linear concept of a history of salvation makes the divide between creation and salvation far too big. According to Scripture, the role of humans in the greater whole has several aspects: humans should be wary in using the earth (ruling, tilling and keeping), they should participate in the choir of all creation singing God's praise, and behave as disciples. The theme of creation appears again and again in Scripture, in various forms, often linked with Lady Wisdom. Christ, too, is connected with all creation. The image of the Word depicted as masculine authoritative speaking has unjustifiably ousted the more inclusive images of Wisdom and Spirit.

The resistance to eco-theology is partly due to a vigorous anthropocentrism and a resistance against any positive assessment of nature (see chapter three). This might explain the fact that in the Dutch-speaking countries the debate on theology and ecology is still in its infancy. In a related field of interest, the relation between God and the whole reality does feature, to wit in discussions about the so-called contrast between belief in creation against evolutionary theory. The way one speaks of creation is so varied that it generally leads to much misunderstanding. Appreciating nature in itself and valuing the relationship of God and the world are important issues. But there is a great fear that by shortening the gap between God and the world one risks merging God too much with the world.

The three eco-feminist theologians (see chapter four) whom I discussed, resist this absolute separation between God and world that proved so detrimental to the earth and women. In the end, Gebara, Keller and Theokritoff all share some form of panentheism and acknowledge relatedness as a significant trait of the whole reality. They all work within the context of their tradition and the way we happen to live. We can learn from Ivone Gebara that without gender and an ecological perspective our way of knowing remains confined to a western masculine way of perceiving the world. Gebara shows clearly, from the perspective of poor women, that human dignity is pivotal. This human dignity does not compete with God or the earth but finds its embedding in them. This becomes visible in the Jesus movement.

Catherine Keller has a very creative way of theologising in which postmodern questions, insights from modern physics, and different voices from the Christian tradition get involved in a lively exchange. Theology does not have to distance itself from scientific insights or to submit to these. She shows how reality is always in flux, a flux that is neither linear nor cyclical. The alternative to a God–human liberating history from the Big Bang to the end of time is not the endless repeat of nature, but an ongoing unfolding of possibilities in the whole cosmos.

Elizabeth Theokritoff makes clear that traditional theology can be extremely relevant. She doesn't start with current experiences of people or with philosophy or with natural sciences, but with the Church Fathers, in particular those who are established authorities in the Eastern Orthodox tradition. This tradition depicts God who is both intrinsically connected with the world, yet at the same time is totally different. People are special within this greater whole, commissioned to join the liturgical praise of creation and to practise ascesis as a positive way of self-restriction.

In churches, sustainability is too often limited to activities focused on diaconal work and church management, as I stated in my preface. Making your church carbon neutral, for instance by installing solar panels, is very popular locally. If my eco-feminist panel would be asked to give their opinion on the matter, what sort of advice would they give? Gebara could ask: Who produced these solar panels? What are the living conditions of the factory workers? And do you take into account that new technologies are affordable often for the more affluent and that those living at the bottom of the income scale are burdened with higher energy costs whilst the biggest polluters are kept out of harm's way? Keller might add: Yes, I agree with that, you certainly have to do more than making your buildings more sustainable because by doing so you remain caught in a frame constructed by men in power who solve all global problems with technological means, and we know by now where that leads to. Theokritoff might say: Precisely, our whole attitude toward God and creation is involved. You will have to tap into the sources of your liturgy again and start behaving less like consumers.

5.2 CHRISTOLOGY AND ANTHROPOLOGY

Green theology is *theology* and is, thus, about God. As *Christian* theology, this theology is about Christ. In thinking through the relationship between God and the world, Christology is indispensable. As God is visible in Jesus, as all Christians believe, Jesus must be an important link between God and the world. In the current western context this relationship is mostly limited to that between God and the human world. For instance, discussions tend to revolve around how unique Jesus is as a human being: is God only in Jesus (completely) visible or in (some) other people, too? Feminists have queried the relation between Jesus' humanity and his maleness. In an ecological theology this question is widened into the relation of God in Jesus with all reality; is God primarily incarnated as human being or as 'flesh', i.e. corporeal, creature amongst creatures? The translation 'the Word became flesh' or even 'the Word became human' for 'the Logos became flesh' (John 1:14) narrows the meaning,[945] even more so, if one translates this phrase as 'God's Son became man'.[946] The wisdom tradition has become invisible in these translations and all emphasis was put on Jesus' maleness through the use of the word Son. Lady Wisdom is certainly very important for a Christology that is biblical and takes cognisance of women and earth.

5.2.1 The Wisdom of God

The Christ hymn of Colossians 1 – Christ as firstborn of creation in whom all things have been created – played an important role in developing an ecological Christology. Christ as logos, thus, as Word/

302

Wisdom, is present in all things and all things are present in him.[947] This notion of panentheism – God is in everything, but does not coincide with everything – has left its mark on the dogma of the two natures of Christ:[948] Jesus Christ has a divine and a human nature, which are distinguishable but not divided. According to the dogma of Nicaea-Constantinople, creator and creation, God and matter are distinct but not divided. This is important to ecological theology as it links not only people but the whole world in Christ with God.

I've come to the conclusion that the dogma of Nicaea-Constantinople is key for an ecological theology in the heart of church and belief because it keeps apparent opposites together. Without this key concept Christology might derail in several ways. A Christology that stresses the cosmic Christ is in danger of describing Christ as ruler and, thus, to create again an enormous distance between God and the earth and legitimise all kinds of domination. This happens sometimes in evangelical and orthodox Protestant theologies and can come with an apocalyptic worldview. Another risk of a cosmic Christology is that Christ and cosmos coincide.[949] This risk is apparent in some forms of process theology, in which there is barely a difference between Christ's body and the evolving universe.[950] A Christology that starts from the earthbound life of Jesus seems to bring Christ closer to earth, but runs the risk of sketching him as the (or an) ideal human being and, therefore, severing people from the context of all creation.[951] An ecological Christology focusing on Jesus' way of handling nature may turn him into a model of stewardship and, thus, condone a distance between humans and the rest of creation.

The link that Scripture forges between Christ and Lady Wisdom is important to keep the human and the divine, the earthen and the cosmic side of Jesus together. Wisdom joins apparent opposites. The Word is Mary's child, who lived 2,000 years ago in present day Israel/Palestine, but is also the saviour of the world. Jesus as incarnation of God's wisdom and as teacher of wisdom is important for an inclusive ecological theology for at least three reasons: 1. All reality, material and immaterial, human and non-human, is linked with God; 2. Christ is connected with all reality without dissolving into it; 3. It renders Jesus both masculine and feminine. God's wisdom in creation makes human knowledge important, but it sets, at the same time, against the dominant knowledge – e.g. western masculine monopolised knowledge – the wisdom of the cross. Creation and resurrection belong together, as illustrated by the image of the garden of Genesis 2 and the garden of John 20. Sin and suffering – just as redemption – not only touch upon humans, but upon all creation.[952] God's kingdom, too, touches upon all creation.

5.2.2 Humans as disciples

In Wisdom Christology, humans are above all defined as disciples: disciples of Jesus, part of the Jesus movement, and disciples of God's wisdom in all creation. Discipleship is different from stewardship. It may go together with the image of people caring for creation and even of being co-creator, but always as part of creation, not above or outside it. Participating in the praising of all creation in word and deed is equally fitting to disciplehood.

Eastern Orthodox theology goes beyond the dualism that is inherent to western theology without sacrificing God's transcendence. Divine and human, heavenly and earthen come together in the person of Jesus Christ, in the liturgy and in particular in the Eucharist, and in the deification (theosis) of all that exists, humans included. This non-linear notion does not reduce (divine) incarnation to singularity.[953]

5.3 THE FRUITS OF THE EARTH IN A CHURCH SERVICE

Local historical circumstances differ, and theology is never exempt from this. All theology is contextual.[954] Church services have played a role in my search as one of the many places where theology is tested and developed. Every liturgy uses rituals, formularies and standard prayers, but at the same time varies according to time and place. If the rule of praying is the rule of believing (*lex orandi lex credendi*), if lived faith – in, for example, praying together – takes precedence over doctrine, liturgy is an important place to search out theology and serves as a breeding ground for theology. As Marianne Moyaert said:

> Material and ritual practices do not simply express or transmit truths that already exist *apart from them*, they are truly *creative: they can alter understanding and generate new insights and even criticize tradition.* Participating in ritual activities can sometimes generate new thoughts and bring about change in tradition. Rituals can be pioneering, rather than simply expressive; they can be the starting place of imaginative and creative thought, which may even challenge and contradict tradition.[955]

Let me give an example.

On Sunday 4 November 2018, I was conducting a church service in Boxtel, a township in the south of the Netherlands. We were celebrating Harvest Thanksgiving because the following Wednesday was officially Thanksgiving Day. They had invited me to lead their service because they knew I was doing research on green theology. Boxtel is very much engaged in sustainability issues and quite a few members of the small Protestant community are involved in Boxtel as a *transition town*, a worldwide movement of communities to promote a smooth transgression towards a sustainable society.[956] Members of Transition Town Boxtel had in the past successfully organised resistance against drilling for shale gas (fracking) in its immediate vicinity. They educate the public on how to diminish one's global footprint, for example by eating less meat and making a start with energy transition. They initiated a so-called repair café and encouraged use of shared vegetable gardens.[957] How do you get all these things into church life? Not by saying 'We already know what to do and we are just searching our belief to find a bit of inspiration to act accordingly,' as if nothing new can be expected from the rich sources of Christian belief.

5.3.1 Preparation

From the start, I had asked for volunteers to help me in preparing the service. This would help me to connect with what people happen to think in Boxtel and also to broaden the support at the base. The turnout at the preparation meeting, the previous Monday, surpassed expectations. Some Catholics attended alongside members of the Protestant congregation. The initiators had asked everyone to bring along some vegetables and fruit harvested from their own vegetable gardens or foraged from somewhere in the wild. The yield lay in our midst. I had brought some *sterappeltjes* (star apples, an old Dutch apple variety) because they smell so nice. But my apples also led to the question why they are so difficult to get nowadays, and they provided us with an opportunity to start a conversation on food production. After I told them something about my research, I read aloud some of the verses of the gospel reading of Thanksgiving Day, Mark 4:26–34, with the pivotal phrase 'The earth produces of itself, first the stalk, then the head, then the full grain in the head' (v.28). I asked them how they saw the relationship between food, God, the earth and themselves. And I paused for a moment to give them the chance to write down their own answers.

Someone saw a link with the supplication from the Lord's Prayer, Give us this day our daily bread; another brought up the feeding of the multitude, because food is a gift that you should share in order that everyone has enough.[958] Someone connected the beauty of creation with God and mentioned the wonderment of all living. Stories were told about harvest festivals in former days. The elderly among us recalled how the church was packed out on those days. Another told how she, on Palm Sunday, walked with her father on his grounds to stick palm branches into the soil, expressing the hope for a good harvest. And statues of Mary were carried around across the fields, added others. Some attendees were really worried about the impact the rise of consumption would have on the environment and pointed at the importance of clean agriculture, fair prices for farmers, being more aware of what you buy, eating food in season and doing something about the dominating power of supermarkets. The star apples lay in our midst as silent witness to a vanishing diversity as supermarkets all through the year constantly supply the same apple varieties, regardless of the season. We talked also about the enjoyment of eating and how to cook delicious food with grains and pulses and vegetables of the season. One related how much she enjoyed working in her kitchen garden because it was so relaxing; how she relished beautiful raspberries and putting her hands in the bare soil. After spending a week in her garden, she found that she was more receptive to God and that she prayed differently, not asking anymore, but worshipping.

I continued by reading a part of Genesis 1 with the key phrases 'The earth brought forth vegetation' and 'Let the earth bring forth living creatures of every kind' (Genesis 1:12,24). Without earth, no food, no life and no dying, said someone, and another that God gave us the earth and it should be looked after carefully. Another stated that many people fear nature. They only want to eat wild brambles or sweet chestnuts if they are purchased from a proper shop. I told of the Noahic covenant as a covenant with the whole earth and how Jewish dietary laws have been turned into eco-kashrut.[959] Those interested could think further about ecological dietary laws in a smaller group, looking for an answer to the question of what sort of things would have to be taken into account. These were some of their observations: farmers should receive a fair price for their products; less energy should be used for tilling and tracking; no food should be thrown away; the soil should not be exhausted and polluted; meat production puts a heavy burden on the earth because of the enormous amount of fodder and water; and cattle is a source of greenhouse gasses.

They came up with seven regulations to think about seriously:

1. Introduce a Friday without fish and meat – 'Veg Friday'.
2. Eat meat in small amounts or abstain altogether.

3. Eat vegetables and fruit of the season, preferably from your own country.
4. Eat varied and unprocessed food to experience how it should taste.
5. Eat more pulses.
6. Teach children where food comes from.
7. If your financial means permit, buy fairtrade and eco products.

Others were busy selecting hymns or composing a prayer. The results became building stones for the church service.

5.3.2 Praying, learning, celebrating and sharing

On this particular Sunday, the church contains more people than usual. In front, for all to see, there is a huge display of vegetables and fruits that several people have brought from their own vegetable gardens. We lay the liturgical table with grapes and figs picked from the church garden; these we will share out with all present later on in the service. The fig harvest is impressive. Is this a good omen, or is it the outcome of a summer that was too warm and too dry? We begin with the hymn that commences 'God who gives life in the womb of the earth' and continues 'But we the rich, alas, remain callous and indifferent. Open our ears, Lord, that we may hear the call for help at the porch.'[960] In the Kyrie prayer, I refer to the earth crying out, and the cry of the poor.[961] The song of glory is Psalm 145, one of the psalms of creation.[962] The first lesson is Genesis 1:11–25, about plants and animals, a passage that is usually skipped in sermons as one jumps furtively from primal chaos to the land of people.[963] Our culture has become so anthropocentric that we have begun to consider non-human reality as matter, as background, as a resource for human existence. We handed all knowledge of non-human existence over to the natural sciences, and the humanities were left with thinking about the meaning of life and dealing with ethics. This divide has been disastrous, because it suggests that the natural sciences are value-free, and the humanities, which include theology, should have no say in the whole of reality. As if theology does not provide knowledge about the world. Theology should, again, be relevant for all reality. Natural sciences should be questioned more critically about their presuppositions.[964] These are not exactly the words that I convey at that moment. In my sermon I say:

"The earth brought forth and God saw that it was good. "The earth brought from itself fruit." Here lie the fruits of the soil on which we live. Our little piece of earth has brought this forth and God sees that it is good. […] We forget how we depend on plants and animals. We lose our sense of wonderment for everything living on the earth, for all the animals that live in the water, on the land and in the sky. It is good when the earth is swarming with living creatures. The earth is not just for us, humans. The Bible states clearly that the earth is God's and we may use what it yields, but we have to share this with other living creatures.'

And I tell the congregation that the idea that people can and must rule the earth is taken from Scripture. When, in Genesis 1, people enter the scene, on the same day as the animals on the land, they are commanded to have dominion over the earth. In the context in which this story was told, this commandment should be taken as an encouragement to till the earth and keep cattle. For many centuries, it was read as an assertion. As sun and moon rule the time and the seasons, in the same way humans should rule the earth. But in modern times these verses have legitimised human domination of the earth. This was the start of an interaction between advancing technological possibilities, economic expansion, colonialism and an image of God as a mighty father. Almighty man becomes creator himself, ruling the earth and his less-powerful neighbours. When God vanished from our culture as a factor to be taken seriously, the dominion of people – some people – became absolute. I say:

We have subjected the earth, not just our piece of land to eat from it, we subjected all earth to take more than we are in need of. And without regard for other living beings. [...] The last fifty years we allowed a 60% decrease of animals.

I tell everyone what was said during our preparation for the service about wonderment and connect this to the growth of the mustard seedling, the subject of the lesson from the Gospel. I mention the connection with the earth in contrast with the ignorance of not knowing where our food comes from. And I conclude with the dietary laws that were thought out by those who had a say in preparing the church service. To avoid being too pushy and moralistic, and to force people into the role of consumers and discard the political and economic structures involved, I amplify:

These laws are personal choices that you can make. In Christian terms you can call them a form of fasting, a voluntary self-restriction on behalf of God and creation. These are intricate issues, because it's not just a matter of personal but also of political choices, of jointly organizing things differently. It all starts with looking differently at the world. God does not give us the earth to do whatever we want; God does provide us with a place to live among our fellow creatures. God loves all living beings, all of earth, let us do as God does, and become ever more an image of God. If we do so we will be able to yield fruits, just like the earth.

After singing the hymn 'What are the good fruits' and the collecting of money, we pass the dish round with figs and grapes.[965] I see some people carefully tasting; the atmosphere is joyful. The prayers of thanks and intercession were made by the people who prepared the service:

God of all life, we thank you for life, for the ground under our feet, for our dear mother earth. We ask you that all living beings may safely and peacefully live with one another. We thank you for our food; in our country and in our neighbourhood, there is food in plenty. We ask you to teach us to share, to teach us to eat in such a way that the earth is not overtaxed and that there is enough for everyone. Good God, we are just specks in the universe, yet we may shine, each one of us. Let our contribution be significant where we happen to live. Make us serviceable to one another, that we may bring peace. Teach us to live filled with wonder for our earth.

After the closing hymn about 'the earth with her good and sorrow, the steep mountains, cool lakes, the trusty land, and the uncertain sea' that all proclaim God,[966] and after the blessing, we end with a surprise gift from the children. The Sunday school leaders had asked them to bring along some vegetables. Just before the reading of the Scripture, they come forward with a cauliflower, a leek, and other such vegetables. In the room next to the church the children had made soup from the ingredients. They talked about the same issues that we grown-ups dealt with during the service. They had a very nice talk about food, the leaders said, whilst cutting up the vegetables. And there is enough soup for everyone. Some weeks later someone tells me that the church has decided to reinstate a harvest service and celebrate it annually.

5.3.3 Knowing

Knowledge that is highly valued in our culture is very one-sided, geared towards ruling, commencing with creating a large gap between people and the rest of reality. Eco-feminist theology starts from connection as source of knowledge, or, even better, relatedness. Everyone and everything exists within a web of relations. I am completely dependent on plants for food; people could not survive without animals too. Compassion is requisite for gaining knowledge. Without being aware of relatedness and, thus, of compassion – the strong feeling of sympathy for the suffering of others – I cannot understand the world, and I become alienated from the earth, ignorant of the places where my food comes from and of who I am. It is necessary to appreciate other knowledge than the knowledge that is cherished by those in command – the knowledge of indigenous people, poor women, knowledge coming from belief in God, local knowledge that cannot be generalised, premodern and postmodern knowledge.

The Harvest Thanksgiving in Boxtel is an example of the coming together of several sorts of knowledge. It rejoices in earth's fruits gathered locally, experiencing connection with the ground on which you live, with the people and animals around you, and with God who is present in everything. Celebrating this connectedness makes it feasible to face the gigantic problems of the mass extinction of animals and plants without losing hope. Christian belief is not a path to a future that we can yet sketch out, but it entails the ability to improvise each time, co-operating or obstructing, without overseeing everything. It is acting without a ready-made blueprint. It involves all our senses, our whole body in the place where we are, connected with all that is.

BIBLIOGRAPHY

Abbreviations

CCFT – Frank Parsons, Susan (ed.), *The Cambridge Companion to Feminist Theology* (Cambridge, Cambridge University Press, 2002)

CCOT – Cunningham, Mary B. and Elizabeth Theokritoff (eds), *The Cambridge Companion to Orthodox Christian Theology* (Cambridge, Cambridge University Press, 2008)

DDD – Toorn, Karel van et al., *Dictionary of Deities and Demons* (Leiden, Brill, 1995)

ERN – Taylor, Bron (ed.), *Encyclopedia of Religion and Nature* (London, Continuum, 2005)

EWF – Dempsey, Carol J. et al. (eds), *Earth, Wind, and Fire: Biblical and Theological Perspectives on Creation* (Collegeville, Minnesota, Liturgical Press, 2004)

LPR18 – Grooten, M. et al. (eds), *Living Planet Report – 2018: Aiming Higher* (Gland, Switzerland, WWF, 2018, www.WWF.org)

LPR20 – Grooten, M. et al. (eds), *Living Planet Report – 2020: Bending the Curve of Biodiversity Loss* (Gland, Switzerland, WWF, 2020, www.WWF.org)

LS – *Encyclical Letter Laudato Si' of the Holy Father Francis on Care for our Common Home*

NJBC – Raymond E. et al. (eds), *The New Jerome Biblical Commentary* (London, Chapman, 1989)

OHRE – Gottlieb, Roger S. (ed.), *The Oxford Handbook of Religion and Ecology* (Oxford, Oxford University Press, 2006)

PS – Kim, Grace Ji-Sun and Hilda Koster (eds), *Planetary Solidarity: Global Women's Voices on Christian Doctrine and Climate Justice* (Minneapolis, Fortress Press, 2017)

Literature

A New Catechism: Catholic Faith for Adults (London/New York, Burns & Oates/Herder, 1967; first published as *De Nieuwe Katechismus: Geloofsverkondigning voor volwassenen*, *De Nieuwe Katechismus: Geloofsverkondigning voor volwassenen* (Hilversum/Antwerpen, Paul Brand, 1966)

313

Anbeek, Christa, 'World-viewing Dialogues on Precarious Life: The Urgency of a New Existential, Spiritual, and Ethical Language in the Search for Meaning in Vulnerable Life', *Essays in the Philosophy of Humanism* 25:2 (2017), pp. 171–186

Armstrong, Karen, *A Short History of Myth* (Edinburgh, Canongate, 2006)

Baker-Fletcher, Karen, *Sisters of Dust, Sisters of Spirit: Womanist Wordings on God* (Minneapolis, Fortress Press, 2009)

Barad, Karen, 'Posthumanist Performativity: Toward an Understanding of How Matter Comes to Matter', *Journal of Women in Culture and Society* 28:3 (2003), pp. 801–831

Bauckham, Richard, *Living with Other Creatures: Green Exegesis and Theology* (Waco, Texas, Baylor University Press, 2011)

Bauer, Walter, *Wörterbuch zum Neuen Testament* (Berlin/New York, Walter de Gruyter, 1971)

Beentjes, Panc, *De wijsheid van Jezus Sirach: Een vergeten joods geschrift* (Budel, Damon, 2006)

Beentjes, Panc, *Happy the One who Meditates on Wisdom (Sir 14:20): Collected Essays on the Book of Ben Sira* (CBET 43) (Leuven, Peeters, 2006)

Benjamins, Rick, *Catherine Keller's constructieve theologie* (Vught, Skandalon, 2017)

Bennet, Jane, *Vibrant Matter: A Political Ecology of Things*, (Durham, North Carolina, Duke University Press, 2010)

Berkhof, H., *Christian Faith: An Introduction to the Study of the Faith* (Grand Rapids, Michigan, Eerdmans, 1979; first published as *Christelijk geloof: Een inleiding tot de geloofsleer*, 1973)

Berlis, Angela and Anne-Marie Korte (eds), *Everyday Life and the Sacred: Re/configuring Gender Studies in Religion* (Leiden/Boston, Brill, 2017)

Bernstein, Ellen, 'Creation Theology: A Jewish Perspective' in *The Green Bible* (New York, Harper One, 2008), Introduction pp. 51–57

Berry, Thomas, *The Great Work: Our Way into the Future* (New York, Random House, 1999)

Betcher, Sharon V., 'Sabbath–Jubilee Cycle' in ERN, pp. 1442–1444

Bibel in gerechter Sprache (Gütersloh, Gütersloher Verlagshaus, 2007)

Biezeveld, Kune, *Als scherven spreke: Over God en het leven van alledag* (Zoetermeer, Meinema, 2008)

Blowers, Andrew et al., 'Is Sustainable Development Sustainable?', *Journal of Integrative Environmental Sciences* 9:1 (2012), pp. 1–8

Boersema, Jan J., *The Torah and the Stoics on Humankind and Nature: A Contribution to the Debate on Sustainability and Quality* (Leiden, Brill, 2001; first published as *Thora en Stoa over mens en natuur*, 1997)

Boersma, Hans, *Nouvelle Théologie and Sacramental Ontology: A Return to Mystery* (Oxford, Oxford University Press, 2009)

Boff, Leonardo, *Cry of the Earth, Cry of the Poor* (New York, Maryknoll, 1997; first published as *Ecologia: Grito da Terra, Grito dos Pobres*, 1995)

Borgman, Erik, *Edward Schillebeeckx: A Theologian in His History* Vol. I: *A Catholic Theology of Culture* (London/New York, Continuum, 2003)

Borgman, Erik and Thijs Caspers, 'In dienst van een zoekend geloof: Edward Schillebeeckx en de na-conciliaire periode in Nederland', *Tijdschrift voor Theologie* 54e jaargang, nr 4, winter 2014

Borgman, Erik, *Want de plaats waarop je staat is heilige gron: God als onderzoeksprogramma* (Amsterdam, Boom, 2008)

Boring, M. Eugene, *Revelation* (Louisville, Kentucky, Westminster John Knox, 1989)

Bouma-Prediger, Steven, *For the Beauty of the Earth: A Christian Vision for Creation Care* (Grand Rapids, Michigan, Baker Academic, 2001)

Boureux, Christophe, *Dieu est aussi jardinier: La création, une écologie accomplie* (Paris, Les Éditions du Cerf, 2014)

Bowe, Barbara, 'Soundings in the New Testament Understanding of Creation' in EWF, pp. 57–67

Braidotti, Rosi, *Patterns of Dissonance: A Study of Women and Contemporary Philosophy* (Cambridge, Polity Press, 1991)

Briggs, Sheila and Mary McClintock Fulkerson (eds), *The Oxford Handbook of Feminist Theology* (Oxford, Oxford University Press, 2012)

Brink, Gijsbert van den, *Reformed Theology and Evolutionary Theory* (Grand Rapids, Michigan, Eerdmans, 2020; first published as *En de aarde bracht voort: Christelijk geloof en evolutie*, Utrecht, 2017)

Brown, Raymond E. et al. (eds), *The New Jerome Biblical Commentary* (NJBC; London, Chapman, 1989)

Brugmans, George and Jolanda Strien (eds), *IABR – 2014 – Urban by Nature* (Rotterdam, IABR, 2014)

Burrus, Virginia, *Ancient Christian Ecopoetics Cosmologies, Saints, Things* (Philadelphia, Pennsylvania, Press, 2018)

Bustamante, Pedro, *El imperio de la ficción: Capitalismo y sacrificios hollywoodenses* (Madrid, Ediciones libertarias, 2015)

Byrne, Brendan, 'Creation Groaning: An Earth Bible Reading of Romans 8.18–22' in Norman C. Habel (ed.), *Readings from the Perspective of Earth: The Earth Bible Volume 1* (Sheffield, Sheffield Academic Press, 2000)

Calvin, John, *Calvin's Commentaries (Vol. I)* (Grand Rapids, Michigan, Baker Books, 2003)

Carbine, Rosemary P. and Hilda P. Koster (eds), *The Gift of Theology: The Contribution of Kathryn Tanner* (Minneapolis, Minnesota, Fortress Press, 2015)

Castiñeiras, Manuel, *The Creation Tapestry* (Girona, Catedral de Girona, 2011)

Christie, Douglas E., *The Blue Sapphire of the Mind: Notes for a Contemplative Ecology* (Oxford University Press, 2013)

Chryssavgis, John, 'The Earth as Sacrament: Insights from Orthodox Christian Theology and Spirituality' in OHRE

Chryssavgis, John, 'Christianity (6b1) – Christian Orthodoxy' in ERN, pp. 333–337

Clines, Jeremy Mark Sebastian, *Earthing Common Worship: An Ecotheological Critique of the Common Worship Texts of the Church of England* (Diss.; University of Birmingham, 2011)

Coakley, Sarah, *Powers and Submissions: Spirituality, Philosophy and Gender* (Malden, Massachusetts/Oxford, Blackwell, 2002)

Coakley, Sarah, *God, Sexuality and the Self: An Essay 'On the Trinity'* (Cambridge, Cambridge University Press, 2013)

Coakley, Sarah, *The New Asceticism: Sexuality, Gender and the Quest for God* (London, Bloomsbury, 2015)

Conradie, Ernst M., 'The Earth in God's Economy: Reflections on the Narrative of God's Work', *Scriptura* (2008), pp. 13–36

Conradie, Ernst M., *The Earth in God's Economy: Creation, Salvation and Consummation in Ecological Perspective* (Wien/Zürich, LIT Verlag, 2015)

Conradie, Ernst M. and Hilda P. Koster, *T&T Clark Handbook of Christian Theology and Climate Change* (London/New York, Bloomsbury T&T Clark, 2020)

Cook, Joan E., 'Everyone Called by My Name: Second Jesaiah's Use of the Creation Theme' in EWF

Cornell, Colin, 'De Engelstalige receptie van K.H. Miskotte', *Ophef* (November 2019)

Cunningham, Mary and Elizabeth Theokritoff, 'Who are the Orthodox Christians? A Historical Introduction' in CCOT

Cunningham, Mary B. and Elizabeth Theokritoff (eds), *The Cambridge Companion to Orthodox Christian Theology* (CCOT; Cambridge, Cambridge University Press, 2009)

Daly, Mary, *Gyn/ecology: A Metaethics of Radical Feminism* (Boston, Beacon Press, 1978)

Daszak, P. et al., 'Workshop Report on Biodiversity and Pandemics of the Intergovernmental Platform on Biodiversity and Ecosystem Services' (IPBES, 2020), https://ipbes.net/pandemics, accessed 21 January 2021

Deane-Drummond, Celia, 'Creation' in CCFT

Deane-Drummond, Celia, 'Sophia: The Feminine Face of God as a Metaphor for an Ecotheology', *Feminist Theology* (1995)

Deane-Drummond, Celia, *Eco-Theology* (London, Darton, Longman & Todd, 2008)

DeHart, Paul, 'The Instance of Pattern, or Kathryn Tanner's Trinitarism' in Rosemary P. Carbine and Hilda P. Koster (eds), *The Gift of Theology: The Contribution of Kathryn Tanner* (Minneapolis, Minnesota, Fortress Press, 2015)

Dempsey, Carol J. et al. (eds), *Earth, Wind, and Fire: Biblical and Theological Perspectives on Creation* (EWF; Collegeville, Minnesota, Liturgical Press, 2004)

DeWitt, Calvin B., 'The Scientist and the Shepherd: The Emergence of Evangelical Environmentalism' in OHRE

Diamond, Jared, *Guns, Germs, and Steel: The Fates of Human Societies* (London, J. Cape, 1997)

Eaton, Heather, 'Ecofeminism and Globalization' in *Feminist Theology* 24 (May 2000), pp. 41–55

Eaton, Heather, *Introducing Ecofeminist Theologies* (London/New York, Bloomsbury, 2005)

Elvey, Anne, 'Matter, Freedom and the Future: Reframing Feminist Theologies through an Ecological Materialist Lens', *Feminist Theology* 23:2 (2015), pp. 186–204

Encyclical Letter Laudato Si' of the Holy Father Francis on Care for our Common Home, http://www.vatican.va/content/francesco/en/encyclicals/documents/papa-francesco_20150524_enciclica-laudato-si.html

Engels, Friedrich, *The Origin of the Family, Private Property and the State* (1884)

Frank Parsons, Susan (ed.), *The Cambridge Companion to Feminist Theology* (CCFT; Cambridge University Press, 2002)

Frank Parsons, Susan 'Feminist Theology as Dogmatic Theology' in CCFT Gebara, Ivone, *Longing for Running Water: Ecofeminism and Liberation* (Minneapolis, Minnesota, Fortress Press, 1999)

Gebara, Ivone, 'Women's Suffering, Climate Injustice, God, and Pope Francis's Theology: Some Insights from Brazil' in PS, pp. 67–81

Generale Synode van de Nederlandse Hervormde Kerk, *De gaarde een woestijn? De milieucrisis en de verantwoordelijkheid van de kerk. Een verkenning ten behoeve van het gesprek in de gemeenten, aangeboden door de Generale Synode van de Nederlandse Hervormde Kerk* ('s-Gravenhage, Boekencentrum, 1990)

Gesenius, Wilhelm, *Hebräisches und Aramäisches Handwörterbuch über das Alte Testament* (Berlin, Springer-Verlag, 1962)

González, Michelle A., 'Review of *Longing for Running Water: Ecofeminism and Liberation* by Ivone Gebara (Minneapolis: Fortress Press, 1999)', *Journal of Hispanic/Latino Theology* 10:3 (February 2003), pp. 78–80

Gottlieb, Roger S. (ed.), *The Oxford Handbook of Religion and Ecology* (OHRE; Oxford, Oxford University Press, 2006)

Greer, Germaine, 'Ecological Feminism', *Resurgence & Ecologist* (May/June 2014)

Grooten, M. et al. (eds), *Living Planet Report – 2018: Aiming Higher* (LPR18; Gland, Switzerland, WWF, 2018, www.WWF.org)

The Green Bible: A Priceless Message that Doesn't Cost the Earth (London, Collins, 2008)

Hadewijch and Columba Hart, *Hadewijch: The Complete Works* (Mahwah, New York, Paulist Press, 1980)

Haenchen, Ernst, *John 1* (Philadelphia, Pennsylvania, Fortress Press 1984; first published as *Das Johannesevangelium: Ein kommentar*, 1980)

Halkes, Catharina, *… en alles zal worden herschapen: Gedachten over de heelwording van de schepping in het spanningsveld tussen natuur en cultuur* (Baarn, Ten Have, 1989)

Hallonsten, Gösta, 'Ex oriente lux? Recent developments in Eastern Orthodox Theology', *Svensk teologisk kvartalskrift* 89:1 (2013)

Harari, Yuval Noah, *Homo Deus: A Brief History of Tomorrow* (London, Vintage, 2017)

Hart, John, 'Catholicism' in OHRE

Heuvel, Steven Christian van den, *Bonhoeffer's Christocentric Theology and Fundamental Debates in Environmental Ethics* (Eugene, Oregon, Pickwick Publications, 2017)

Hilkert, Mary Catherine, 'Creation in the Image of God and Wisdom Christology' in EWF, pp. 147–163

Hof, Eleonora Dorothea, *Reimagining Mission in the Postcolonial Condition: A Theology of Vulnerability and Vocation at the Margins* (Utrecht, Boekencentrum Academic, 2016)

Horrell, David G., *The Bible and the Environment: Towards a Critical Ecological Biblical Theology* (London, Equinox, 2010)

Hulbert, Steve and Jeanne Sletton, 'Poetics Post-Structuralism, and Process', *Newsmagazine of the Center for Process Studies* 29:1 (Summer 2006)

Iersel, Bas van et al. (eds), *Evolution and Faith, Concilium 2000/1* (London, SCM Press, 2000)

Jenni, Ernst and Claus Westermann (eds), *Theologisches Handwörterbuch zum Alten Testament* (THAT) (München, Chr. Kaiserverlag, 1978)

Johnson, Elizabeth A., *She Who Is: The Mystery of God in Feminist Theological Discourse* (New York, Crossroad, 1992)

Johnson, Elizabeth A., *Women, Earth, and Creator Spirit* (*Madeleva Lecture in Spirituality*) (New York, Paulist Press, 1993)

Johnson, Elizabeth A., 'Women, Earth and Creator Spirit', lecture 1993

Johnson, Elizabeth A., *Quest for the Living God: Mapping Frontiers in the Theology of God* (New York, Continuum, 2007)

Johnson, Elizabeth A., *Ask the Beasts: Darwin and the God of Love* (London, Bloomsbury Publishing, 2015)

Johnson-DeBaufre, Melanie et al. (eds), *Common Goods: Economy, Ecology, and Political Theology* (New York, Fordham Press, 2015)

Jones, Serene, *Trauma and Grace: Theology in a Ruptured World* (Louisville, Kentucky, Westminster John Knox Press, 2009)

Juffermans, Jan, *Sustainable Lifestyles: Strengthening the Global Dimension to Local Agenda 21 – a Guide to Good Practice* (The Hague, Towns and Development, 1995)

Kamp, Merel, 'Niet hergebruiken, maar dóórgebruiken', *Trouw*, 26 October 2017

Karras, Valerie A., 'Eschatology' in CCFT

Keller, Catherine, *Face of the Deep: A Theology of Becoming* (London, Routledge, 2003)

Keller, Catherine, 'Dark Vibrations: Ecofeminism and the Democracy of Creation', lecture 6 April 2005, www.users.drew.edu/ckeller/Dark-Vibe.pdf, accessed November 18, 2020)

Keller, Catherine, *On the Mystery: Discerning Divinity in Process* (Minneapolis, Minnesota, Fortress Press, 2008)

Keller, Catherine, 'Returning God: The Gift of Feminist Theology' in *Feminism, Sexuality, and the Return of Religion* (Bloomington, Indiana, Indiana University Press, 2011)

Keller, Catherine, *Cloud of the Impossible: Negative Theology and the Planetary Entanglement* (New York, Columbia University Press, 2014)

Keller, Catherine, *Intercarnations: Exercises in Theological Possibility* (Minneapolis, Minnesota, Fortress Press, 2017)

Keller, Catherine, *Political Theology of the Earth: Our Planetary Emergency and the Struggle for a New Public* (New York, Columbia University Press, 2018)

Kim, Grace Ji-Sun and Hilda Koster (eds), *Planetary Solidarity: Global Women's Voices on Christian Doctrine and Climate Justice* (Minneapolis, Minnesota, Fortress Press, 2017)

Klein, Naomi, *The Shock Doctrine* (New York, Alfred A. Knopf, 2007)

Klein, Naomi, *This Changes Everything: Capitalism vs. The Climate* (New York, Simon & Schuster, 2014)

Kooi, Cornelis van der and Gijsbert van den Brink, *Christian Dogmatics: An Introduction* (Grand Rapids, Michigan, Eerdmans, 2017; originally published as *Christelijke Dogmatiek: Een inleiding*, 2012)

Korpel, Marjo and Johannes de Moor, *Adam, Eve, and the Devil: A New Beginning*, 2nd ed. (Sheffield, Sheffield Phoenix Press, 2015)

Korte, Anne-Marie, 'Reflections of Interdisciplinarity Feminist Systematic Theology in the Netherlands', paper, Groningen, 2011

Koster, Hilda P., 'Creation as Gift: Tanner's Theology of God's Ongoing Gift-Giving as an Ecological Theology' in Rosemary P. Carbine and Hilda P. Koster (eds), *The Gift of Theology: The Contribution of Kathryn Tanner* (Minneapolis, Minnesota, Fortress Press, 2015)

LaCugna, Catherine Mowry, *God For Us: The Trinity and Christian Life* (New York, HarperCollins, 1991)

Laffey, Alice L., 'The Priestly Creation Narrative: Goodness and Interdependence' in EWF, pp. 24–35

Latour, Bruno, *Facing Gaia: Eight Lectures on the New Climatic Regime* (Cambridge,

Polity Press, 2017; first published as *Face à Gaïa. Huit conférences sur le nouveau régime climatique*, 2015)

Latour, Bruno, *We Have Never Been Modern* (Cambridge, Massachusetts, Harvard University Press, 1993; first published as *Nous n'avons jamais été modernes*, 1991)

Leezenberg, Michiel and Gerard De Vries, *Wetenschapsfilosofie voor geesteswetenschappen* (herziene editie) (Amsterdam, Amsterdam University Press, 2012)

Liedboek. Zingen en bidden in huis en kerk (Zoetermeer, BV Liedboek, 2013)

Lorentzen, Lois Ann and Salvador Leavitt-Alcantara, 'Religion and Environmental Struggles in Latin America' in OHRE, pp. 510–534

Makrides, Vasilios N., 'Christianity (6b2) – Greek Orthodox' in ERN, pp. 338–341

Mancuso, Stefano and Allessandra Viola, *Brilliant Green: The Surprising History and Science of Plant Intelligence* (Washington DC, Island Press, 2015; first published as *Verde brillante: Sensibilità e intelligenza del mondo vegetale*, 2013)

Manschot, Henk, *Nietzsche and the Earth: Biography, Ecology, Politics* (London, Bloomsbury, 2020; first published as *Blijf de aarde trouw: Pleidooi voor een nietzscheaanse terrasofie*, 2016)

McFague, Sallie, *Models of God: Theology for an Ecological Nuclear Age* (Philadelphia, Pennsylvania, Fortress Press, 1987)

McFague, Sallie, *The Body of God: An Ecological Theology* (London, SCM Press, 1993)

McFague, Sallie, *Super, Natural Christians: How We Should Love Nature* (Minneapolis, Minnesota, Fortress Press, 1997)

McFague, Sallie, *Live Abundant: Rethinking Theology and Economy for a Planet in Peril* (Minneapolis, Minnesota, Fortress Press, 2000)

McFague, Sallie, *A New Climate for Theology: God, the World and Global Warming* (Minneapolis, Minnesota, Augsburg, Fortress, 2008)

McFague, Sallie, *Blessed Are the Consumers: Climate Change and the Practice of Restraint* (Minneapolis, Minnesota, Fortress Press, 2013)

McFague, Sallie, 'Reimagining the Triune God for a Time of Global Climate Change', in PS

McFarland, Ian A. et al. (eds), *The Cambridge Dictionary of Christian Theology* (Cambridge University Press, 2011)

McGinn, Sheila E., 'All Creation Groans in Labor: Paul's Theology of Creation in Romans 8:18–23' in EWF, pp. 114–124

McManus, Kathleen, 'Reconciling the Cross in the Theologies of Edward Schillebeeckx and Ivone Gebara', *Theological Studies* 66 (2005)

Meek, Hans, *Ecologica: Waarom verkleining van de menselijke impact op de biosfeer moeilijk maar onvermijdelijk is* (Delft, Eburon, 2017)

Miller-McLemore, Bonnie J., 'Embodied Knowing, Embodied Theology: What Happened to the Body?', *Pastoral Psychology* 62 (2013), pp. 743–758

Mills, Sara, *Discourse* (London/New York, Routledge,1997)

Moltmann, Jürgen, *God in Creation* (London, SCM Press, 1985; first published as *Gott in der Schöpfung: Ökologische Schöpfungslehre*, 1985)

Moltmann, Jürgen, *Sun of Righteousness, Arise! God's Future for Humanity and the World* (Minneapolis, Minnesota, Fortress Press, 2010; first published as *'Sein Name ist Gerechtigkeit': Neue Beiträge zur christlichen Gotteslehre*, 2008)

Montfoort, Trees van, 'Geboeid door Kune Biezeveld: Ook in de natuur is God te vinden', *Soteria* 2 (2017), pp. 49–53

Montfoort, Trees van, 'Green Theology: The (In)visibility of the Non-Human World' in Agnethe Siquans et al. (eds), *Gender, Race, Religion: De/constructing Regimes of In/visibility* (Leuven, Peeters, 2020), pp. 279–284

Morton, Timothy, *Being Ecological* (London, Penguin, 2018)

Munteanu, Daniel, 'Elizabeth Theokritoff Living in God's Creation: Rezension', *International Journal of Orthodox Theology* 1:2 (2010)

Nalwamba, Kuzipa M.B. and Johan Buitendag, 'Vital Force as a Triangulated Concept of Nature and s(S)pirit', *HTS Teologiese Studies/Theological Studies* 73:3 (2017), p. 4506, https://hts.org.za/index.php/HTS/article/view/4506, accessed 21 January 2021

Nash, James A., 'The Bible vs. Biodiversity: The Case against Moral Argument from Scripture', *Journal for the Study of Religion, Nature and Culture* 3:2 (2009), pp. 213–237

Navarro, Mercedes and Pilar de Miguel (eds), *10 palabras clave en teología feminista* (Estrella, Navarra, Editorial verbo divino, 2004)

Neuhoff, Klaus Heinrich, *'Gott alles in allem' (1Kor 15,28): Theosis, Anakephalaiosis und Apokatastasis nach Maximos dem Bekenner in ihrer Bedeutung für die Kosmische Christologie* (dissertation), Tilburg, 2014

Newsom, Carol A. and Sharon H. Ringe Fontaine (eds), *The Women's Bible Commentary*, expanded ed. (Louisville, Kentucky, Westminster John Knox Press, 1992)

Noble, Ivana, 'Embodied in the Landscape: How Places We Inhabit Shape Our Theology', *Communio Viatorum* (2017)

Nogueira-Godsey, Elaine, 'A History of Resistance: Ivone Gebara's Transformative Feminist Liberation Theology', *Journal for the Study of Religion* 26:2 (2013)

Nutt, Aurica, 'Eine theologische Praxis des Recycling: Ökologie, Gott und Geschlecht bei Catherine Keller' in Stefanie Schläfer-Bossert and Elisabeth Hartlieb (eds), *Feministische Theologie Politische Theologie: Entwicklungen und Perspektiven* (Sulzbach, Taunus, Ulrike Helmer Verlag, 2012)

O'Collins, Gerald, *Jesus Our Redeemer: A Christian Approach to Salvation* (Oxford, Oxford University Press, 2007)

O'Connor, Kathleen M., 'Wild, Raging Creativity: Job in the Whirlwind' in EWF

Oomen, Palmyre, 'De verzelfstandiging van de natuurwetenschap: Theologische en natuurwetenschappelijke achtergronden', *Tijdschrift voor Geestelijk Leven*, jrg. 72:4 (juli–augustus 2016), *Geloof en wetenschap. Vijanden-vreemden-tochtgenoten.*

Oomen, Palmyre, 'Schepping', *Tijdschrift voor Geestelijk Leven*, *Tijdschrift voor Geestelijk Leven*, jrg. 72:4 (juli–augustus 2016), *Geloof en wetenschap. Vijanden-vreemden-tochtgenoten.*

Oomen, Palmyre, 'Theologische perspectieven op de natuurwetenschap' *Tijdschrift voor Geestelijk Leven*, jrg. 72:4 (juli–augustus 2016), *Geloof en wetenschap. Vijanden-vreemden-tochtgenoten.*

Oomen, Palmyre, 'IV Fragmentation and Specialization: Theology and Interdisciplinarity – Theology in Relation to the Natural Sciences', *Concilium* 2 (2006), p. 111

Opas, Minna, 'Mutually Exclusive Relationships: Corporeality and Differentiation of Persons in Yine (Piro) Social Cosmos', *Tipití: Journal of the Society for the Anthropology of Lowland South America* 3:2 (December 2005)

Opas, Minna, *Different but the Same: Negotiation of Personhoods and Christianities in Western Amazonia* (Turku, Finland, 2008)

Papanokolaou, Aristotle, 'Orthodox Theology' in Ian A. McFarland et al. (eds), *The Cambridge Dictionary of Christian Theology* (Cambridge University Press, 2011), pp. 358–360

Piketty, Thomas, *Capital in the Twenty-First Century* (Princeton, New Jersey, Harvard University Press 2014; first published as *Le capital au XXI siècle*, 2013)

Pineda-Madrid, Nancy, '¡Somos Criaturas de Dios! Seeing and Beholding the Garden of God' in PS, pp. 311–325

Primavesi, Anne, *Cultivating Unity within the Biodiversity of God* (Salem, Oregon, Polebridge Press, 2011)

Raworth, Kate, *Doughnut Economics: Seven Ways to Think Like a 21st-Century Economist* (London, Random House Business Books, 2017)

Reid, Barbara E., 'Sabbath, the Crown of Creation' in EWF, pp. 67–77

Ress, Mary Judith, *Ecofeminism from Latin America: Women from the Margins* (Maryknoll, New York, Orbis Books, 2006)

Ribla. Revista de interpretation Biblica Latinoamericana, no. 21 *Ecotheologia* (Quito, Ecuador, 1996)

Richardson, Alan and John Bowden (eds), *A New Dictionary of Christian Theology* (London, SCM Press, 1983)

Robb, Carol S., 'Resources for Eco-Theology: Projects of Retrieval within Christian Traditions', *Journal for the Study of Religion, Nature and Culture* 6:1 (2012)

Rojas Salazar, Marilu 'La "Ecosofía": Una propuesta Ecofeminista liberadora desde América Latina', http://donesesglesia.cat/documentos/ecosofia.pdf, accessed 24 January 2015

Rolston, Holmes III, 'Science and Religion in the Face of the Environmental Crisis' in OHRE

Rooda, Clary, *Eco-Kashrut and Jewish Tradition: How the Food on our Table Can Atone for Us* (Master's thesis, Levisson Institute, October 2013)

Rossing, Barbara R., 'Reimaging Eschatology: Toward Healing and Hope for a World at the Eschatos' in PS, pp. 325–340

Ruether, Rosemary Radford, *Sexism and God-Talk: Toward a Feminist Theology* (Boston, Massachusetts, Beacon Press, 1983)

Ruether, Rosemary Radford, *Gaia and God: An Ecofeminist Theology of Earth Healing* (London, SCM Press, 1993)

Ruether, Rosemary Radford, 'Religious Ecofeminism: Healing the Ecological Crisis' in OHRE

Ruether, Rosemary Radford, 'Ecology and Theology: Ecojustice at the Center of the Church's Mission', *Interpretation* 65:4 (2011), pp. 354–363

Santmire, Paul H. and John B. Cobb Jr, 'The World of Nature According to the Protestant Tradition' in OHRE

Sassen, Saskia, *Expulsions: Brutality and Complexity in the Global Economy* (Princeton, New Jersey, Harvard University Press, 2014)

Schaab, Gloria L., *The Creative Suffering of the Triune God: An Evolutionary Theology* (Oxford, Oxford University Press, 2011)

Schaik, Karel van and Kai Michel, *The Good Book of Human Nature: An Evolutionary Reading of the Bible* (New York, Perseus Books Group, 2016)

Schillebeeckx, Edward, *Jesus: An Experiment in Christology* (London, Collins, 1979/New York, Crossroad, 1981; first published as *Jezus, het verhaal van een levende*, 1973/1975)

Schreiter, Robert J. and Edward Schillebeeckx, O.P., *Constructing Local Theologies* (Maryknoll, New York, Orbis, 2003)

Schreiter, Robert J., 'The Relevance of Professor Edward Schillebeeckx, O.P. for the Twenty-First Century', lecture, Tulane University New Orleans, Louisiana, 8 October 2009, https://schillebeeckx.nl/wp-content/uploads/2008/11/Lecture-on-relevance-Schillebeeckx.pdf, accessed 21 January 2021

Schüssler Fiorenza, Elisabeth, *In Memory of Her: A Feminist Theological Reconstruction of Christian Origins* (London, SCM Press, 1983)

Schüssler Fiorenza, Elisabeth, *Jesus: Miriam's Child, Sophia's Prophet – Critical Issues in Feminist Christology* (New York, The Continuum International Publishing Group, 1994)

Schüssler Fiorenza, Elisabeth, *Changing Horizons: Explorations in Feminist Interpretation* (Minneapolis, Minnesota, Fortress Press, 2013)

Shiva, Vandana, *Staying Alive: Women, Ecology and Development* (London, Zed Books, 1989)

Sideris, Lisa H., 'Religion, Environmentalism, and the Meaning of Ecology' in OHRE

Smedes, Taede S., *Thuis in de kosmos: Het epos van de evolutie en de vraag naar de zin van ons bestaan* (Amsterdam, Amsterdam University Press, 2018)

Sölle, Dorothee and Louise Schottroff, *Den Himmel erden. Eine ökofeministische Annäherung an die Bibel* (München, DTV, 1996)

Sotitiu, Eleni, 'Eastern Orthodox Monasticism' in ERN, pp. 334–335

Steen, Bart van der et al., *Butler, Negri en Žižek. Een inleiding op de hedendaagse linkse filosofie* (Budel, Damon, 2013)

Sturgeon, Noel, *Ecofeminist Natures: Race, Gender, Feminist Theology and Political Action* (New York/London, Routledge, 2002)

Talstra, Eep, 'Singers and Syntax: On the Balance of Grammar and Poetry in Psalm 8' in J.W. Dyk (ed.), *Give Ear to My Words: Psalms and other Poetry in and around the Hebrew Bible – Essays in Honour of Professor N.A. van Uchelen* (Amsterdam/Kampen, 1996)

Tanner, Kathryn, 'Social Theory Concerning the "New Social Movements" and the Practice of Feminist Theology' in Rebecca S. Chopp and Sheila Greeve Davaney (eds), *Horizons in Feminist Theology: Identity, Tradition and Norms* (Minneapolis, Minnesota, Fortress Press, 1997)

Taylor, Bron (ed.), *Encyclopedia of Religion and Nature* (ERN; London, Continuum, 2005)

Taylor, Sarah McFarland, *Green Sisters* (Cambridge, Massachusetts, Harvard University Press, 2009)

Theokritoff, Elizabeth, '4 Creator and Creation' in CCOT

Theokritoff, Elizabeth, *Living in God's Creation: Orthodox Perspectives on Ecology* (New York, St Vladimir's Seminary Press, 2009)

Theokritoff, Elizabeth, 'Working Salvation in the Midst of the Earth', lecture 2018, see www.youtube.com/watch?v=JNnclcJgC38 (part 1), www.youtube.com/watch?v=BQmRCd0wbW8 (part 2), accessed 12 October 2018

Toorn, Karel van, et al., *Dictionary of Deities and Demons* (DDD; Leiden, Brill, 1995)

Tucker, Mary Evelyn, 'Religion and Ecology: Survey of the Field' in OHRE

Upton, Bridget Gilfillian, 'Feminist Theology as Biblical Hermeneutics' in CCFT

Verstappen, Birgit, *Ekklesia des Lebens im Dialog mit Sallie McFague's Kosmologie und der Befreiungstheologie von Elisabeth Schüssler Fiorenza* (Münster, LIT, 2001; first published as *Ekklesia van leven: Een aanzet tot een discussie tussen theologische kosmologie en bevrijdingstheologie*, 2000)

Vicini, Andrea, 'New Insights in Environmental and Sustainable Ethics', *Asian Horizons* 6:2 (June 2012), pp. 309–328

Voltaire, 'Discours sur la nature de l'homme' in 'Discours en vers sur l'homme' in *Mélanges* (Paris, Gallimart, 1961), pp. 232–233 (first published 1740)

Vonk, Martine, *Sustainability and Quality of Life: A Study on the Religious Worldviews, Values and Environmental Impact of Amish, Hutterite, Franciscan and Benedictine Communities* (Amsterdam, Buijten en Schipperheijn, 2011), https://research.vu.nl/en/publications/sustainability-and-quality-of-life-a-study-on-the-religious-world, accessed 21 January 2021

Waal, Frans de, *Are We Smart Enough to Know How Smart Animals Are?* (New York/London, W.W. Norton & Company, 2016)

Waggoner, P. E. and J. H. Ausubel, 'A Framework for Sustainability Science: A Renovated IPAT Identity', *Proc National Academy of Science* 99.12 (2002), pp. 7860–7865

Walter Kasper, *Einführung in den Glauben* (Mainz, Grünewald, 1973)

Warner, Marina, *Alone of All Her Sex: The Myth and the Cult of the Virgin Mary* (London, Weidenfeld & Nicolson, 1976)

White, Lynn, 'The Historical Roots of our Ecologic Crisis', *Science* 55 (1967), pp. 1203–1207

Williams, Delores S., *Sisters in the Wilderness: The Challenge of Womanist God-Talk* (Maryknoll, New York, Orbis Books, 1993)

Wohlleben, Peter, *The Hidden Life of Trees: What They Feel, How They Communicate – Discoveries from a Secret World* (Vancouver, Greystone Books, 2015; first published as *Das geheime Leben der Bäume*, 2015)

Wolde, Ellen van, *Terug naar het begin*, inaugural lecture, Nijmegen, 2009

Wolde, Ellen van, 'Bijbelse scheppingsverhalen', *Evolutie, cultuur en religie* (Kampen, Klement, 2010)

Wolde, Ellen van, 'God's Covenant with the Living Beings on Earth: An Eco-ethical Reading of Genesis 9:8–17' in Ruben Zimmermann and Stephan Joubert (eds), *Biblical Ethics and Application: Purview, Validity, and Relevance of Biblical Texts in Ethical Discourse*, vol. IX (Tübingen, Mohr Siebeck, 2017)

Wolde, Ellen van, 'Separation and Creation in Genesis 1 and Psalm 104: A Continuation of the Discussion of the Verb רבא', *Vetus Testamentum* 67 (2017), pp. 611–647

Ziel, Tjirk van der, *On the Road to Leisure* (The Netherlands Institute for Social Research, The Hague, 2006)

Zorgdrager, Heleen, 'Reclaiming Theosis: Orthodox Women Theologians on the Mystery of the Union with God', *Internationale Kirchliche Zeitschrift* 104:3 (2014), pp. 220–245

ACKNOWLEDGEMENTS

Although it is impossible to list everyone who supported me one way or another in the process of writing this book, I would like to name some who became directly involved in my research that resulted in the writing of this book. I am grateful to Professor Anne-Marie Korte who taught me a lot about sound researching and scholarly writing and to Professors Jan Boersema, Heleen Zorgdrager and Erik Borgman who assisted me in setting the first stage. Thanks to them I was enriched with very useful comments, corrections and, above all, encouragement.

I am also grateful to all the knowledgeable people who were willing to read parts of the work in progress: Hilda Koster (eco-theologian in the USA), Professor Eep Talstra (Old Testament), Magda Misset-van der Weg (New Testament), Erica Meijers (diaconal studies), Marjolein Tiemens-Hulscher (biologist) and Marc van der Post (liberation theologian in Argentina).

Apart from all the hours that I worked silently at my desk, this research provided me with many interesting contacts in which I could share thoughts and ideas. I am indebted to the people who tipped me, responded to my articles and talks, or sent me a book. I owe many thanks to my reading group of women theologians and to the participants of the OPP (the Dutch branch of the European Society of Women in Theological Research). This book would not have been written without the encouraging response of all the churchgoers who listened to my sermons, and prayed and sang with me. Without the support of Professors Susanne Scholz and, in particular, Nicola Slee there would never have been an English edition.

I mention with love Wim Reedijk, my most important aide, with whom I share the joy in theology and language. He read and translated everything I wrote. I thank Chris Reedijk for correcting the text meticulously. And I thank my children, Bram and Dore van Montfoort, who clearly inherited my writing gene, for lending an ear to my talking about overcoming writing obstacles. They also share in my joy of a theology that is green and full of promise for their lives and the future of our precious planet.

ENDNOTES

1   Richard Bauckham, *Living with Other Creatures: Green Exegesis and Theology* (Waco, Texas, Baylor University Press, 2011), p. 36

2   Lynn White Jr, 'The Historical Roots of Our Ecologic Crisis', *Science* 155:3767 (10 March 1967), pp.1203–1207

3   Paul H. Santmire and John B. Cobb Jr, 'The World of Nature According to the Protestant Tradition' in Roger S. Gottlieb (ed.), *The Oxford Handbook of Religion and Ecology* (OHRE; Oxford, Oxford University Press, 2006), p. 133

4   i.e. normative, descriptive and meta-ethics

5   M. Grooten et al. (eds), *Living Planet Report – 2018: Aiming Higher* (LPR18; Gland, Switzerland, WWF, 2018, www.WWF.org); Andrew Blowers et al. 'Is Sustainable Development Sustainable?', *Journal of Integrative Environmental Sciences* 9:1 (2012), pp. 1–8; Hans Meek, *Ecologica: Waarom verkleining van de menselijke impact op de biosfeer moeilijk maar onvermijdelijk is* (Delft, Eburon, 2017)

6   www.klimaatscenarios.nl/op_weg_naar_knmi21/Zeespiegel_Sybren_Drijfhout_Workshop_KNMI21_28sept2017.pdf, accessed 31 January 2018; see also https://www.ipcc.ch/srocc/, accessed 25 January 2021

7   See http://mpc-vdaf.tropomi.eu/, accessed 26 September 2020

8   https://www.unep.org/resources/report/ipbes-workshop-report-biodiversity-and-pandemics, accessed 23 December 2020

9   Lisa Doeland (ed.), *Onszelf voorbij. Kijken naar wat we liever niet zien* (Amsterdam, De Arbeiderspers, 2018)

10 LPR18, p. 10. The term Anthropocene was co-introduced by the Dutch meteorologist and Nobel Prize winner Paul Crutzen, ibid. in Dirk Sijmons, 'Wakker worden in het antropoceen' in George Brugmans and Jolanda Strien (eds), *IABR – 2014 – Urban by Nature* (Rotterdam, IABR, 2014)

11 LPR18, p. 9

12 LPR20, p. 6, accessed 26 September 2020. See also https://www.un.org/sustainabledevelopment/blog/2019/05/nature-decline-unprecedented-report/, accessed 26 September 2020

13 Jared Diamond, *Guns, Germs, and Steel: The Fates of Human Societies* (London, J. Cape, 1997); Carel van Schaik and Kai Michel, *The Good Book of Human Nature: An Evolutionary Reading of the Bible* (New York, Perseus Books Group, 2016)

14 Friedrich Engels, *The Origin of the Family, Private Property and the State* (1884)
15 Hans Meek, *Ecologica*, pp. 73–77
16 LPR18, p. 22
17 Ibid.; René ten Bos, *Dwalen in het antropoceen* (Amsterdam, Boom, 2017)
18 Thomas Piketty, *Capital in the Twenty-First Century* (Princeton, New Jersey, Harvard University Press, 2014; first published as *Le capital au XXI siècle*, 2013)
19 Jan Juffermans, *Nut & noodzaak van de Mondiale Voetafdruk. Over de mondiale gebruiksruimte, duurzaamheid en mensenrechten* (Rotterdam, Lemniscaat, 2006); Meek, *Ecologica*, p. 111 ff.; https://www.footprintnetwork.org/, accessed 26 September 2020
20 https://data.footprintnetwork.org/#/, accessed 26 September 2020
21 Ibid., accessed 26 September 2020: 'The Ecological Footprint per person is a nation's total Ecological Footprint divided by the total population of the nation. To live within the means of our planet's resources, the world's Ecological Footprint would have to equal the available biocapacity per person on our planet, which is currently 1.7 global hectares. So if a nation's Ecological Footprint per person is 6.8 global hectares, its citizens are demanding four times the resources and wastes that our planet can regenerate and absorb in the atmosphere.'
22 Babette Porcelijn, *Verborgen impact: Alles voor een ecopositief leven* (Amsterdam, Q., 2017)
23 Above all things, one has to take into account that the emission of methane adds considerably to the total amount of greenhouse gases in the atmosphere.
24 See 2.2.4, The creation sings: the Psalms
25 P. E. Waggoner and J. H. Ausubel, 'A Framework for Sustainability Science: A Renovated IPAT Identity', *Proc National Academy of Science*, 99:12 (2002), pp. 7860–7865, https://phe.rockefeller.edu/publication/impact, accessed 26 September 2020; see also sustainablescale.org/ConceptualFramework/UnderstandingScale/MeasuringScale/TheIPATEquation.aspx, accessed 26 September 2020
26 Marco Visscher, 'De nieuwe groene helden', *The Optimist*, 27 September 2014
27 Richard Bauckham, *Living with Other Creatures: Green Exegesis and Theology* (Waco, Texas, Baylor University Press, 2011), p. 230
28 I thank Marjolein Tiemens-Hulscher for adding nuances
29 Bauckham, *Living with Other Creatures*, p. 232; Willem Schoonen, 'Waardeloze natuur, bestaat die?', *Trouw*, 17 March 2018
30 Ed van Hinte in Merel Kamp, 'Niet hergebruiken, maar dóórgebruiken', *Trouw*, 26 October 2017
31 Roel Veraart in Kiki Holman, 'De term duurzame groei spreekt zichzelf tegen', *Trouw*, 10 April 2018; and also René ten Bos in Peter Henk Steenhuis 'Duurzaam is een woord voor managers', *Trouw*, 11 July 2018
32 Meek, *Ecologica*, p. 148
33 I thank Lieve Troch for her advice, January 2015
34 Louise McRae et al. (eds), *WWF Living Planet Report 2016: Risk and Resilience in a New Era*, p. 90, https://www.WWF.nl/globalassets/pdf/lpr/lpr_living_planet_report_2016.pdf, accessed 21 January 2021
35 In a lecture for the American Association for the Advancement of Science, first published in 1967: 'The Historical Roots of our Ecologic Crisis', *Science* 155:3767 (1967), pp. 1203–1207.
36 Bron Taylor (ed.), *Encyclopedia of Religion and Nature* (ERN; London, Continuum, 2005), p. 1736
37 White, 'The Historical Roots', p. 1205. Criticising anthropocentrism does not imply that one may not look at the world from a human perspective or that people don't have a special place or responsibility in the greater whole. It is basically criticising those who either neglect non-human nature or treat it contemptuously.

38   ERN, p. 1736

39   Hendrik-Joost van Soest, *'Welk is het voortreffelijkste schepsel op aarde?' De interpretatie van een omstreden bijbelse voorstelling in het 19ᵉ en 20ᵉ eeuwse Nederland* (Delft, Eburon, 1996)

40   See also 2.2.1 'Subduing the earth' and 'ruling the animals' and 4.4 Elizabeth Theokritoff

41   Henk Manschot, *Blijf de aarde trouw. Pleidooi voor een nietzscheaanse terrasofie* (Nijmegen, Van Tilt 2016), pp. 183–184; English version: Henk Manschot, *Nietzsche and the Earth: Biography, Ecology, Politics* (London, Bloomsbury, 2020). Page references in the following notes are to the Dutch edition

42   I use the term modernity not as a clearly defined historical era, but as a worldview or paradigm that is rooted in antiquity and became dominant in the era that has become known as 'modernity'. The beginning of modernity is mostly situated either in the seventeenth or in the eighteenth century; the era ended with the First World War. One has to reckon always with some form of untimeliness in history in which several worldviews co-exist. Not everyone adopted simultaneously the same modern ideas in this so-called modern era. And although modern thinking is dominant, this is not always shared equally by everyone.

43   White, 'The Historical Roots', p. 1205 f.

44   Timothy Morton, *Dark Ecology: For a Logic of Future Coexistence* (Columbia, University Press, 2016) and *Being Ecological* (London, Penguin, 2018)

45   Birgit Verstappen, *Ekklesia van leven: Een aanzet tot een discussie tussen theologische kosmologie en bevrijdingstheologie* (Zoetermeer, Boekencentrum, 2000). German version: *Ekklesia des Lebens im Dialog mit Sallie McFague's Kosmologie und der Befreiungstheologie von Elisabeth Schüssler Fiorenza* (Münster, LIT, 2001). Birgit Verstappen sketches the development of worldviews since the time of the Bible in relation to God, people and the world. In her PhD thesis she develops a Christian theological perspective in which people as God's creatures collectively find a place to live within the greater whole.

46   See 4.4.2, People as kings and priests

47   Verstappen, *Ekklesia van leven*, p. 24

48   Ibid., p. 27

49   https://www.gereformeerdekerkennederland.nl/belijdenisgeschriften/nederlandse-geloofsbelijdenis and https://www.prca.org/bc_text1.html#a1, accessed 23 January 2021
     Gijsbert van den Brink, *Als een schoon boec: Achtergrond en relevantie van artikel 2 van de Nederlandse Geloofsbelijdenis*, oratie 2007 (https://openaccess.leidenuniv.nl/handle/1887/12625, accessed September 26, 2020) and Gijsbert van den Brink, *En de aarde bracht voort. Christelijk geloof en evolutie* (Utrecht, Boekencentrum, 2017), p. 79 f.; see also Gijsbert van den Brink, *Reformed Theology and Evolutionary Theory* (Grand Rapids, Michigan, Eerdmans, 2020; first published as *En de aarde bracht voort: Christelijk geloof en evolutie*, 2017). Page references in following notes are to the Dutch edition

50   Palmyre Oomen, 'De verzelfstandiging van de natuurwetenschap: Theologische en natuurwetenschappelijke achtergronden', *Geloof en wetenschap: Vijanden-vreemden-tochtgenoten. Tijdschrift voor Geestelijk Leven*, Ann. 72:4 (2016)

51   Oomen, 'De verzelfstandiging', p. 89

52   Michiel Leezenberg and Gerard De Vries, *Wetenschapsfilosofie voor geesteswetenschappen (herziene editie)* (Amsterdam, Amsterdam University Press, 2012), p. 127 ff.

53   Elizabeth A. Johnson, *Quest for the Living God: Mapping Frontiers in the Theology of God* (New York, Continuum, 2007), p. 181 ff. (c. 9 'Creator Spirit in the Evolving World')

54   Palmyre Oomen, 'Theologische perspectieven op de natuurwetenschap', *Geloof en wetenschap*

55 Palmyre Oomen, 'Schepping', *Geloof en wetenschap*

56 Ernst M. Conradie, 'The Earth in God's Economy: Reflections on the Narrative of God's Work', *Scriptura* (2008), pp. 13–36, p. 14

57 Leezenberg and De Vries, *Wetenschapsfilosofie*, p. 166

58 See 4.3.1 Feminism, postmodernity and process

59 Oomen, *Geloof en wetenschap*, p. 91

60 http://w2.vatican.va/content/dam/francesco/pdf/encyclicals/documents/papa-francesco_20150524_enciclica-laudato-si_en.pdf , 52, 129, 134, 146, accessed September 26, 2020

61 Sallie McFague, *Life Abundant: Rethinking Theology and Economy for a Planet in Peril* (Minneapolis, Minnesota, Fortress Press, 2000), p. 77

62 Vandana Shiva, *De armoedige levensvisie van het rijke westen: Milieu- en Derde-Wereldproblemen – het resultaat van geestelijke monocultuur* (Baarn, Ten Have, 1997), p. 49 ff.

63 Naomi Klein, *The Shock Doctrine: The Rise of Disaster Capitalism* (New York, Alfred A. Knopf, 2007), pp. 56–57

64 McFague, *Life Abundant*, p. 82

65 Physicist James Lovelock and biochemist Lynn Margulis coined the term Gaia for the earth including its biosphere. Gaia is the Greek goddess of the earth. In eco-theology and eco-philosophy this term has been adapted in several ways, e.g. by Rosemary Redford Ruether and Bruno Latour.

66 Naomi Klein, *This Changes Everything: Capitalism vs. the Climate* (New York, Simon & Schuster, 2014), chapter 2.

67 McFague, *Life Abundant*, p. 96

68 Ibid., p. 95

69 Quoted in Pamela Philipose, 'Women Act: Women and Environmental Protection in India' in J. Plant (ed.), *Healing the Wounds: The Promise of Ecofeminism* (Toronto, Between the Lines, 1989), pp. 67–75

70 Rosemary Radford Ruether, *Sexism and God-Talk: Toward a Feminist Theology* (Boston, Massachusetts, Beacon Press, 1983); Catharina Halkes, *...en alles zal worden herschapen. Gedachten over de heelwording van de schepping in het spanningsveld tussen natuur en cultuur* (Baarn, Ten Have, 1989); Heather Eaton, *Introducing Eco-feminist Theologies* (London/New York, Bloomsbury, 2005)

71 Eaton, *Introducing Eco-feminist Theologies*, p. 37

72 Halkes, *...en alles zal worden herschapen*, p. 52 ff.

73 See also 3.2.3 Paganism, fertility and the prohibition of images

74 Shiva, *De armoedige levensvisie*, p.47

75 As used by Jean-François Lyotard (1924–1998)

76 E.g. Catherine Keller, see 4.3; see also Conradie, 'The Earth in God's Economy', p. 15

77 Eaton, *Introducing Eco-feminist Theologies*, p. 47

78 Ibid.

79 See 3.2 Protestant resistance

80 Bruno Latour, *Facing Gaia: Eight Lectures on the New Climatic Regime* (Cambridge, Polity Press, 2017; first published as *Face à Gaïa. Huit conférences sur le nouveau régime climatique*, 2015)

81 Elizabeth Theokritoff, *Living in God's Creation: Orthodox Perspectives on Ecology* (New York, St Vladimir's Seminary Press, 2009), see 4.4

82   Christophe Boureux, *Dieu est aussi jardinier: La création, une écologie accomplie* (Paris, Les Éditions du Cerf, 2014), p. 259 ff., see 2.2.2

83   Anne Elvey, 'Matter, Freedom and the Future: Reframing Feminist Theologies through an Ecological Materialist Lens', *Feminist Theology* 23:2 (2015), pp. 186–204

84   The often-cited definition of *The Brundtland Commission Report* of the World Commission on Environment and Development (WCED) in 1987: 'Sustainable development is development that meets the needs of the present without compromising the ability of future generations to meet their own needs.'

85   Meek, *Ecologica*, p. 13

86   Ibid., p. 15

87   *Laudato Si'*, pp. 216–221

88   See 4.2.5 Keller on theology without *theos*

89   Erik Borgman, *Want de plaats waarop je staat is heilige grond. God als onderzoeksprogramma* (Amsterdam, Boom, 2008), p. 11

90   Sarah Coakley, *God, Sexuality and the Self: An Essay 'On the Trinity'* (Cambridge, Cambridge University Press, 2013), p. 100 ff.

91   There are many versions of this speech, delivered somewhere around 1854. The original text has not survived. See Michael McKenzie 'Seattle (Sealth), Chief (ca. 1790-1866)' in ERN

92   Minna Opas, *Different but the Same: Negotiations of Personhoods and Christianities in Western Amazonia* (Turku, Finland, 2008)

93   Sallie McFague, *Super, Natural Christians: How We Should Love Nature* (Minneapolis, Minnesota, Fortress Press, 1997); see also 4.1.1 Neighbourly love for all creatures

94   See 5.3 The fruits of the earth in a church service

95   A term borrowed from Bruno Latour

96   Peter Wohlleben, *The Hidden Life of Trees: What They Feel, How They Communicate – Discoveries from a Secret World* (Vancouver, Greystone Books, 2015; first published as *Das geheime Leben der Bäume*, 2015)

97   Kathryn Tanner, 'Social Theory Concerning the "New Social Movements" and the Practice of Feminist Theology' in Rebecca S. Chopp and Sheila Greeve Davaney (eds), *Horizons in Feminist Theology: Identity, Tradition and Norms* (Minneapolis, Minnesota, Augsburg Fortress, 1997)

98   Ibid., p. 186: 'every cultural element is susceptible to reinterpretation by being placed in new discursive alignments'.

99   Christa Anbeek, *Aan de heidenen overgeleverd. Hoe theologie de 21ᵉ eeuw kan overleven* (Utrecht, Ten Have, 2013); see also 'World-viewing Dialogues on Precarious Life: The Urgency of a New Existential, Spiritual, and Ethical Language in the Search for Meaning in Vulnerable life', *Essays in the Philosophy of Humanism* 25:2 (2017), pp. 171–186 (https://journals.equinoxpub.com/EPH/article/view/33444/pdf, accessed September 26, 2020)

100   Borgman, *Want de plaats waarop*.

101   van den Brink, *Reformed Theology*

102   'pointing out that the extent and recoverable past is wider and more diverse than any particular identification of an authorizing past, makes clear that things could always be different'. Tanner, 'Social Theory', p. 197

103   Kathryn Tanner, *Jesus, Humanity and the Trinity: A Brief Systematic Theology* (Minneapolis, Minnesota, Fortress Press, 2001), p. xviii

104   Akke van der Kooi, 'Kathryn Tanner – De toekomst van de christelijke traditie'. At the monastery of the Dominicans in Zwolle (the Netherlands), 14 April 2018. Unpublished lecture, used with permission of the author.

105 Hilda P. Koster, 'Creation as Gift: Tanner's Theology of God's Ongoing Gift-Giving as an Ecological Theology' in Rosemary P. Carbine and Hilda P. Koster (eds), *The Gift of Theology: The Contribution of Kathryn Tanner* (Minneapolis, Minnesota, Fortress Press, 2015)

106 For the concepts of deconstruction and construction in philosophy and theology see 1.2.7 Postmodernism and 4.3.1 Theology as recycling.

107 1.2.1 Anthropocentrism and exploitation

108 James A. Nash for instance wrote: 'the bulk of the Bible is indifferent, insensitive, or even antagonistic to untamed nature (as opposed to domesticated nature). The Bible is in the main ecologically unconscious.' James A. Nash, 'The Bible vs. Biodiversity: The Case against Moral Argument from Scripture', *Journal for the Study of Religion, Nature and Culture* 3:2 (2009), pp. 213–237

109 I use the term Bible interpretation instead of exegesis because it is broader and includes biblical theology.

110 van den Brink, *Reformed Theology*

111 Marcel Sarot, 'Zo zult Gij het kwaad uit uw midden wegdoen' in Krijn Pansters (ed.), *De volgeling die voorgaat: Leiderschap in het licht van Franciscus van Assisi* (Nijmegen, Valkhof Pers, 2014), pp. 205–206

112 *The Green Bible* (London, HarperCollins, 2008)

113 *Groene Bijbel, Nieuwe Bijbelvertaling* (Heerenveen, Royal Jongbloed, 2016/2017)

114 Ibid., pp. 1903–1914 and preface

115 For the way in which a specific interpretation of Psalm 8:6,7 takes precedence over other creation texts, see 2.2.1 and 2.2.4

116 David G. Horrell, *The Bible and the Environment: Towards a Critical Ecological Biblical Theology* (London, Equinox, 2010), p. 8

117 See 2.3.2 End and new beginning of all living beings

118 Horrell, *The Bible and the Environment*, p. 47

119 Ibid., pp. 11–20

120 Bridget Gilfillian Upton, 'Feminist Theology as Biblical Hermeneutics' in CCFT

121 Horrell differs in this from Laffey, who argues that historical criticism has brought to light the patriarchal character of the culture of Old Israel. For that reason Laffey turned to other exegetical methods that restored the truthfulness of the final version of the texts, and to alternative interpretations. But for eco-theology she finds the historical critical method rather useful. Alice L. Laffey, 'The Priestly Creation Narrative: Goodness and Interdependence' in Carol J. Dempsey and Mary Margaret Pazdan (eds), *Earth, Wind, and Fire* (EWF; Collegeville, Minnesota, Liturgical Press, 2004), p. 24

122 Laffey, 'The Priestly Creation Narrative', p. 24

123 Horrell, *The Bible and the Environment*, pp. 11–20

124 Bauckham, *Living with Other Creatures*, p. 111

125 See 4.3.3 Contra-apocalypse

126 Jacques van Ruiten, *Zwervende teksten van Qumran tot Qur'an*, oratie, Groningen, 11 June 2013

127 For recycling in theology see also 4.3.1 Theology as recycling

128 Rick Benjamins, 'Waar wij ons bevinden: Een lokalisatie op de theologische landkaart' in Rick Benjamins et al. (eds), *Liberaal Christendom: Ervaren, doen, denken* (Vught, Skandalon, 2016), p. 25

129 Ellen van Wolde, 'Bijbelse scheppingsverhalen' in *Evolutie, cultuur en religie* (Kampen, Klement, 2010), p. 91; see also Van Wolde, 'Separation and Creation in Genesis 1 and Psalm 104: A Continuation of the Discussion of the Verb ארב, *Vetus Testamentum* 67 (Leiden,

Brill, 2017), pp. 611–647. The Hebrew word of beginning of Genesis 1:2 lacks the article; thus, it literally reads 'in beginning'.

130 Van Wolde, 'Bijbelse scheppingsverhalen', p. 92

131 https://www.bibelwissenschaft.de/wibilex/das-bibellexikon/lexikon/sachwort/anzeigen/details/tier/ch/4495116a5b09da5d734c45d5062338df/, accessed 9 September, 2017; see also 2.3 God and the animals

132 Richard J. Clifford and Roland E. Murphy, 'Genesis' in Raymond E. Brown et al. (eds), *The New Jerome Biblical Commentary* (NJBC; London, Chapman, 1989)

133 See e.g. 3.4.3, Evolution as meaningful narrative

134 van den Brink, *Reformed Theology*, pp. 114 ff.; more in 3.4.2 God and the earth

135 Jan J. Boersema, *The Torah and the Stoics on Humankind and Nature: A Contribution to the Debate on Sustainability and Quality* (Leiden, Brill, 2001), p. 54; *bara* takes always God as subject (p. 50), but is not the only verb to express the act of creating.

136 Although it doesn't have the parallel structure that is typical for poetic texts in the Hebrew Bible.

137 According to the translation of the Septuagint, Clifford and Murphy, 'Genesis', p. 10.

138 *De Naardense Bijbel: De volledige tekst van de Hebreeuwse Bijbel en het Nieuwe Testament* (Bible translation by Pieter Oussoren; Vught, Skandalon, 2004)

139 See also Clifford and Murphy, 'Genesis', p. 10

140 van Wolde, 'Bijbelse scheppingsverhalen', p. 90

141 The translations of NRSV, Horrel and Van Wolde, respectively

142 E.g. Psalm 104:5, Proverbs 8:29 and Job 38:4. Thus, Van Wolde translates verse 2 'without fundament'; in texts in which the word *tohu* appears in combination with earth, it means without fundament and ground. Ellen van Wolde, *Terug naar het begin* (Oratie, Nijmegen 2009), p. 19

143 Boersema, *The Torah and the Stoics*, p. 75 ff.

144 Horrell, *The Bible and the Environment*, p. 27

145 Boersema, *The Torah and the Stoics*, p. 74

146 Ibid., p. 62

147 Horrell, *The Bible and the Environment*, pp. 26–34

148 In the same way as the sea monsters dominate the water. That is the supposition, although it does not say so literally. In Hebrew it is not the same word, in the LXX it is nearly the same word: *archas* and *archein*.

149 For Genesis 6—9 see 2.3.2; for Psalm 8 see 2.2.4

150 Catherine Keller, *On the Mystery: Discerning Divinity in Process* (Minneapolis, Minnesota, Fortress Press, 2008), p. 63

151 This was also what the founding fathers assumed when North America was conquered. Thomas Berry, *The Great Work: Our Way into the Future* (New York, Three River Press, 1999), pp. 33–47

152 The following is largely based on Alice L. Laffey, 'The Priestly Creation Narrative: Goodness and Interdependence' in Dempsey and Pazdan (eds), *Earth, Wind and Fire*, pp. 24–35. The exact dating of Genesis 1 and 2 is on the whole severely contested.

153 EWF, p. 28

154 Psalm 8 can be understood in the same way; see 2.2.4

155 Bauckham, *Living with Other Creatures*, pp. 227–232

156 Ibid., p. 150

157 Ibid., p. 227

158 In this order respectively: (N)ASV, RSV, NRSV, Van Wolde, *Bibel in gerechter Sprache*, NBV

159 Van Wolde, 'Bijbelse scheppingsverhalen', p. 112 ff.

160 E.g. Psalm 74:13–14, Job 3:8, Isaiah 2:1, but in Job 40—41 God speaks respectfully over these monsters and in Psalm 104 God even plays with them

161 See 1.3

162 Enuma Elish was originally a Sumerian creation myth

163 *Liedboek: Zingen en bidden in huis en kerk* (Zoetermeer, BV Liedboek, 2013). This hymn goes back to a medieval text adapted by Luther on the melody of *Komm, Gott Schöpfer, Heiliger Geist*. The last strophe is in Dutch 'Gij heft de aarde aan het licht [...] eens zal zij bloeien als een roos' ('Thou raises the earth towards the light … and one day she will bloom like a rose').

164 Kirchliche Dogmatik III, 1, 41.2, quoted by Catherine Keller, *Face of the Deep: A Theology of Becoming* (London, Routledge, 2003), p. 84

165 Dorotea Erbele Küster, "'U vergat de God die u gebaard heeft" (Deuteronomium 32,18). Schepping als geboorte en andere voorstellingen van schepping in het Oude Testament' in Anneleen Decoene er al. (eds), *Wanneer de schepping kreunt in barensweeën. Hedendaagse reflecties over schepping.* (Antwerpen, Halewijn, 2008)

166 Keller, *On the Mystery*, p. 64; Keller links the universe as God's body with human beings as an image of God and, thus, the human body with the whole of the cosmos. Thus, she links up with the medieval imagery of a human being as a microcosmos. See 1.2.2 Western worldviews through the ages.

167 Boersema, *The Torah and the Stoics*, p. 52

168 Ibid., pp. 52 and 53

169 Keller *On the Mystery*, p. 56; she makes a connection with mysticism: the dark night of the soul as 'the luminous dark', a darkness that contains light.

170 See 1.2.6 Patriarchy and colonialism

171 Some process theologies make a connection with postmodern scientific insights on chaos and self-organisation. See 4.3.1 Theology as recycling

172 Keller, *On the Mystery*, p. 61

173 Ibid., p. 59

174 Boureux, *Dieu est aussi jardinier*

175 'Enemy of Apathy', Words: John L. Bell (b. 1949) and Graham Maule (1958–2019), Music: John L. Bell, Copyright © 1988 WGRG, Iona Community, Glasgow, Scotland. Reproduced by permission. www.wildgoose.scot

176 See paragraphs 2.2.6 on Proverbs 8 and 2.3.2 on Genesis 6–9

177 Boersema, *The Torah and the Stoics*, pp. 87 and 88

178 Elizabeth A. Johnson, *Ask the Beasts: Darwin and the God of Love* (London, Bloomsbury Publishing, 2015), p. 264

179 To teach children respect for nature, it is important for them to learn to call the animals and plants by their proper names. See Marjolein van Heemstra, 'Bomen', *Trouw*, 4 November 2017. For biologist and author Dick Hellenius, the fact that people of the rainforest even know the names of plants they do not use is an indication of 'an awareness of their surroundings'. *Ademgaten: Denken over dieren* (Amsterdam, Van Oorschot, 2009), p. 124

180 Marjo Korpel and Johannes de Moor, *Adam, Eva en de duivel: Kanaänitische mythen en de Bijbel* (Vught, Skandalon, 2016), pp. 129–130 (original edition: *Adam, Eve, and the Devil: A New Beginning*, 2nd enlarged ed. [Sheffield, Sheffield Phoenix Press, 2015])

181 Brink, *Reformed Theology*, pp. 213–222 distinguishes five fundamental types of interpreting Genesis 2 and 3, ranging from ahistorical/mythical to an as-literal-as-possible interpretation.

182 For an Eastern Orthodox exposition see 4.4.3 Celebrating, fasting and Sophia in our context

183 Horrell, *The Bible and the Environment*, p. 37 ff.

184 This comes back in Genesis 4:11–12.

185 See also 2.4.3 Peace or destruction in the Prophets

186 See 2.3.3 Resting in freedom, the Laws of Sabbath

187 Van Schaik and Michel, *The Good Book of Human Nature*; see also 1.1.2 The growing impact of people on the earth

188 See 1.1.2 The growing impact of people on the earth; Brink, *Reformed Theology*, too, looks for a particular phase in prehistoric times to situate the fall of men; see 3.4.3.

189 The word paradise comes from Latin *paradisus*; the Hebrew *gan* is an enclosed garden

190 Boureux, *Dieu est aussi jardinier*, p. 34ff.

191 In French, the verb être soucieux *de* is used, meaning to be concerned about

192 Boureux, *Dieu est aussi jardinier*, p. 48; Revelation 2:7 and 22:2 speak of one tree, the tree of life; see 2.4.4

193 Ibid., p. 46

194 Ibid., p. 40

195 Ibid., p. 40

196 Ibid., p. 41

197 For a comparison of the visions of paradise and the fall in Eastern Orthodox theology, see 4.4.2

198 Boureux, *Dieu est aussi jardinier*, pp. 88–90

199 Ibid., p. 99; this is also well known in Eastern Orthodox theology. See Theokritoff, 'Working salvation in the midst of the earth', public lecture 2018, https://www.youtube.com/watch?v=JNnclcJgC38 (part 1), accessed September 12, 2018

200 There are many interpretations of 'do not hold to me', better known as *Noli me tangere* in Latin. See R. Bieringer et al. (eds), *'Noli Me Tangere' in Interdisciplinary Perspective: Textual, Iconographic and Contemporary Interpretations* (Leuven, Peeters, 2016)

201 Roland E. Murphy, 'Canticle of Canticles' in NJBC, p. 462ff.

202 Joan E. Cook, 'Everyone Called by My Name: Second Jesaiah's Use of the Creation Theme' in EWF

203 van Wolde, 'Bijbelse scheppingsverhalen', pp. 99–100

204 Or birth of the cosmos

205 Cook, 'Everyone Called by My Name', p. 40

206 The creation that laments is certainly a theme amongst the prophets: Hosea 4:1–3, Jeremiah 12, 11, Joel 1:20 and Romans 8:19–23 – see 2.4.2 The labour pains of creation, Romans 8:19–23

207 Horrell, *The Bible and the Environment*, pp. 49–55

208 See 2.2.1

209 Anne Primavesi, *Cultivating Unity within the Biodiversity of God* (Salem, Oregon, Polebridge Press, 2011), p. 181ff.

210 Also possible is the interpretation that Leviathan is playing. See also 2.2.1, with an exposition of the sea monsters in Genesis 1:2

211 Bauckham, *Living with Other Creatures*, p. 10

212 van den Brink, *Reformed Theology*, p. 145

213 Horrell, *The Bible and the Environment*, p. 51

214 Ibid., p. 51

215 See also 2.2.1

216 Eep Talstra, 'Singers and Syntax: On the Balance of Grammar and Poetry in Psalm 8' in J.W. Dyk (ed.), *Give Ear to My Words: Psalms and other Poetry in and around the Hebrew Bible. Essays in Honour of Professor N.A. van Uchelen* (Amsterdam/Kampen, 1996), pp. 6–8

217 The environment-unfriendly exposition of Psalm 8 is influenced by Hebrews 2:6–9, which quotes Psalm 8: 'you have crowned him with glory and honour, putting everything in subjection under his feet' (ESV) or 'you have crowned them with glory and honour, subjecting all things under their feet' (NRSV). But here the crowning is applied to Christ, not human beings in general. See Talstra, 'Singers and Syntax'

218 See 2.2.2 Paradise Lost? Genesis 2 and 3

219 When the Bible talks of 'heaven and earth', it does not signify the hereafter and this life, or God and us, but everything that exists: the whole universe, the great and the small, the far and the near.

220 In Protestant circles it is well known as a church hymn. It is included in the Dutch hymnbook of 2013 in two versions: 154a and b.

221 *Liedboek*, song 154b

222 Johnson, *Ask the Beasts*, p. 276 ff.

223 Erik Borgman, '"Vlees met de ziel, met het bloed er nog in, mag u niet eten" (Genesis 9,4): Het belang van ritueel slachten als uiting van respect' in Bastiaan Rijpkem and Machteld Zee (eds), *Bij de beesten af! Over dierenrecht en onrecht* (Amsterdam, Prometheus, 2013), pp. 47–61

224 https://en.wikipedia.org/wiki/Canticle_of_the_Sun, accessed 20 January 2020

225 The French *sujet* as a noun means subject or person and as an adjective subjected/submitted to.

226 Frans de Waal, *Are We Smart Enough to Know How Smart Animals Are?* (New York/London, W.W. Norton & Company, 2016)

227 Stefano Mancuso and Allessandra Viola, *Brilliant Green: The Surprising History and Science of Plant Intelligence* (Washington DC, Island Press, 2015; originally published as *Verde brillante: Sensibilità e intelligenza del mondo vegetale*, 2013); neurobiology in plants is, by the way, not a recognised field of study within biology.

228 See also Wohlleben, *The Hidden Life of Trees*

229 Anne Elvey, 'Matter, Freedom and the Future: Reframing Feminist Theologies through an Ecological Materialist Lens', *Feminist Theology* 23:2 (2015), pp. 186–204 and Bruno Latour, *We Have Never Been Modern* (Cambridge, Massachusetts, Harvard University Press, 1993; originally *Nous n'avons jamais été modernes*, 1991) and *Facing Gaia: Eight Lectures on the New Climatic Regime* (Cambridge, Polity Press, 2017; originally *Face à Gaïa: Huit conférences sur le nouveau régime climatique*, 2015)

230 See 1.2.3 Current natural science and 1.3 The task of theology

231 https://decorrespondent.nl/4447/wat-als-een-rivier-rechten-krijgt/53831152903-6457dfb8, accessed 21 September, 2017

232 Wohlleben, *The Hidden Life of Trees*

233 Bauckham, *Living with Other Creatures*, p. 150

234 Bauckham, *Living with Other Creatures*, p. 154, referring to Psalm 148, Daniel 3 and Job 38—39

235 See 2.4.2 The labour pains of creation

236 See 2.2.6 Lady Wisdom: Proverbs 1—9

237 Van Wolde, 'Bijbelse scheppingsverhalen'

238 Habel quoted by Horrell, *The Bible and the Environment*, p. 59ff.

239 The chapters of the NRSV and the Nieuwe Bijbelvertaling are in line with the Hebrew source text as supplied in the most familiar *Biblia Hebraïca Stuttgatensia*, 5th edition, 1997. Some of the other Bible translations have other verse numberings.

240 The Bible in Ordinary Language (*Bijbel in Gewone Taal*) leaves their names untranslated (unlike the other Dutch translation, NBV): 'the monster *Behemoth*' and 'the dragon *Leviathan*'. See Jaap van Dorp, 'Het monster en de draak. Behemot en Leviatan in Job 40–41 in de Bijbel in Gewone Taal', *Met Andere Woorden*, Ann. 33:4 (2014), pp. 10–19. The risk of this translation is that their blending with the beast and the dragon of Revelation comes all too quickly; see 2.4.4 A new earth in the Apocalypse of John.

241 Kathleen M. O'Connor, 'Wild, Raging Creativity: Job in the Whirlwind' in EWF, p. 48

242 Boersema, 'Leerhuis Job', unpublished lecture

243 See 2.2.6 Lady Wisdom: Proverbs 1—9

244 Karel van Toorn et al. (eds), *Dictionary of Deities and Demons* (DDD; Leiden, Brill, 1995), p. 956ff.

245 See also 2.2.4 on Psalm 104:26: 'Leviathan that you formed to sport in it.'

246 DDD, p. 315ff.

247 Horrell, *The Bible and the Environment*, p. 58

248 Ibid., p. 59

249 Ibid., pp. 59 and 60

250 'The fear and dread of you shall rest on every animal of the earth, and on every bird of the air, on everything that creeps on the ground, and on all the fish of the sea; into your hand they are delivered.' Genesis 1 and 9:2 should be seen in the context of the need of people to survive in a hostile environment.

251 Horrell, *The Bible and the Environment*, p. 59

252 Bauckham, *Living with Other Creatures*, p. 220

253 O'Connor, 'Wild, Raging Creativity', p. 54

254 Ibid., p. 54

255 Leonie Breebaart, 'Stilte vond ik op de Zuidpool', *Trouw*, de Verdieping, 2 May 2017

256 Keller, *On the Mystery*, p. 64

257 Boersema, 'Leerhuis Job', unpublished

258 Eep Talstra by email

259 Apocryphal or Deuterocanonical books are biblical books that are not included in the Jewish canon and are likewise not found in most Protestant Bible editions. They are found in Catholic Bible editions. Protestants call these books apocryphal; Catholics call them Deuterocanonical. See Panc Beentjes, *De wijsheid van Jezus Sirach: Een vergeten joods geschrift* (Budel, Damon, 2006), pp. 21–27; see also *Happy the One who Meditates on Wisdom (Sir 14:20): Collected Essays on the Book of Ben Sira* (CBET 43, Leuven, Peeters, 2006)

260 DDD, p. 1694

261 NJBC, p. 455

262 Carole R. Fontaine, 'Proverbs' in Carol A. Newsom and Sharon H. Ringe (eds), *The Women's Bible Commentary*, 3rd ed. (London, SPCK, 2014)

263 DDD, p. 1692

264 According to general theory, the authors or editors of Deuteronomy adjusted the earlier books of Genesis, Exodus, Leviticus and Numbers to accommodate their opinions regarding a central place of worship in Jerusalem and a stern monotheism. See Dr. Th. C. Vriezen and dr. A.S. van der Woude, *De literatuur van Oud-Israël* (Katwijk, Servire, 1976), pp. 196–199

265 DDD, p. 1699

266 As the authors of DDD, p. 1696: 'are we to imagine a male pregnancy?'

267 DDD, p. 1697; the older Dutch translation of 1951 (NBG) is quite faithful in holding on to this imagery. It translates Proverbs 8:24 'Before the oceans were there, I was born / before the springs, rich in water.'

268 Beentjes, *De wijsheid van Jezus Sirach*, p. 120

269 DDD, p. 1696

270 Also in the hymn 'She Sits Like a Bird'; see 2.2.1 The coming into existence of the Cosmos: Genesis 1—2:4

271 DDD, p. 1699

272 NJBC, p. 454

273 See Introduction

274 Horrell, *The Bible and the Environment*, Bauckham, *Living with Other Creatures* and Van den Brink, *Reformed Theology* don't pay attention to Proverbs 8; Boureux does mention the wisdom of Christ and draws parallels with Genesis 1 and 2, but not with Wisdom texts of the Old Testament.

275 Parallels: Matthew 8:18,23–27 and Luke 8:22–25

276 Bauckham, *Living with Other Creatures*, p. 77

277 Parallels: Matthew 14:22–33 and John 6:16–21

278 Elisabeth Schüssler Fiorenza, *Jesus: Miriam's Child, Sophia's Prophet. Critical Issues in Feminist Christology* (New York, Continuum, 1994); see also *Changing Horizons: Explorations in Feminist Interpretation* (Minneapolis, Minnesota, Fortress Press, 2013), chs 17 and 18

279 Probably sometime between 70 and 80, maybe earlier; NJBC, p. 877

280 NJBC, p. 879

281 That doesn't mean that in the Wisdom tradition the notion of human dominion is completely absent; see Wisdom 9:2–3: 'And in your wisdom have established humankind to rule the creatures produced by you, And to govern the world in holiness and righteousness, and to render judgment in integrity of heart.'

282 Celia Deane-Drummond, 'Sophia: The Feminine Face of God as a Metaphor for an Ecotheology', *Feminist Theology*, 6:16 (1995)

283 *Glory to God: The Presbyterian Hymnal* #174, accessed 6 May 2020; text Ruth C. Duck, melody Donna Kasbohm; as hymn 849 included in *Liedboek* as 'Zoek de wegen van de Wijsheid'

284 Ernst Haenchen, *John 1* (Philadelphia, Pennsylvania, Fortress Press, 1984; first published as *Das Johannesevangelium. Ein kommentar*, 1980), p. 101ff.

285 *Bibel in gerechter Sprache* (Gütersloh, Gütersloher Verlagshaus, 2007); NABRE forges a link with the Wisdom tradition in a footnote: 'The Word (Greek *logos*): this term combines God's dynamic, creative word (Genesis), personified pre-existent Wisdom as the instrument of God's creative activity (Proverbs), and the ultimate intelligibility of reality (Hellenistic philosophy).'

286 Matthijs de Jong, 'De proloog van Johannes in de *Bijbel in Gewone Taal*', *Met Andere Woorden* (2012–2014), pp. 27–29

287 Ibid., pp. 27–28

288 Ibid., p. 33

289 Ibid. p.xx

290 Ibid., p. 30

291 'human being' ('mens') is also falling short as the translation of *sarx*. Matter ('Materie'), as the *Bibel in Gerechter Sprache* translates, does emphasise God's incarnation in the creation, but raises new problems.

292 Mary Catherine Hilkert, 'Creation in the Image of God and Wisdom Christology' in EWF, p. 156 in a paraphrase of a text of Elizabeth A. Johnson

293 Horrell, *The Bible and the Environment*, p. 83. Apart from the demiurge, it could well be about revolting angels.

294 Horrell, *The Bible and the Environment*, p. 86

295 Jürgen Moltmann, *Sun of Righteousness, Arise! God's Future for Humanity and the World* (Minneapolis, Minnesota, Fortress Press, 2010; originally *'Sein Nahme ist Gerechtigkeit: Neue Beiträge zur christliche Gotteslehre*, 2008), p. 69

296 I borrow this image from Elizabeth Johnson, who uses it to illustrate the term panentheism, for which she finds support in e.g. Ephesians 4:6; see Johnson, *Quest for the Living God*, p. 188

297 Johan Graafland, *En God schiep: Over dieren en rentmeesterschap* (Heerenveen, Royal Jongbloed, 2015)

298 Bauckham, *Living with Other Creatures*, p. 112

299 See also 2.2.1 and 2.2.4

300 Compare Psalm 49:12,20: 'Mortals cannot abide in their pomp; they are like the animals that perish'

301 Van den Brink, *Reformed Theology*, p. 145 (translation: *Reformed Theology and Evolutionary Theory*, 2020). On the same page, one finds an overview of recent publications on animals in the Bible.

302 Johan Graafland, 'Dierenrechten in bijbels perspectief', *TussenRuimte* 2 (2016)

303 Van den Brink, *Reformed Theology*, p. 144: 'Authoritative interpretations of the creation narrative (especially Genesis 1,28 and 2,19) and Psalm 8 define animals primarily in terms of their subservient use for people's wellbeing.'

304 Genesis 6—9; Psalm 104:20,25; Psalm 148:10

305 See Genesis 1 and Job

306 Genesis 9:2

307 Job 41:25–26

308 This version from the Jahwist codex to which Genesis 2 belongs is combined with that from the Priestly codex of Genesis 1. There are differences. According to the priestly version 'all the fountains of the great deep burst forth, and the windows of the heavens were opened' (Genesis 7.11); thus, the waters that were according to Genesis 1 separated merged again. The Jahwist doesn't mention the primal flood. There the great flood resulted from extreme rainfalls: 'The rain fell on the earth forty days and forty nights' (Genesis 7:12).

309 Freely adopted from NJBC, p. 16

310 The Dutch NBV lays all the blame of earth's injustice on people: 'As God saw that the earth was thoroughly corrupt, that *everyone* had corrupted his ways, he said to Noah, "I have decided to make an end of *all people*, for the earth is filled with violence because of them; now I am going to destroy them along with the earth"' (Genesis 6:12–13; transl. according to NBV). The Dutch translation of 1951 translates this expression with more precision: all living beings ('al wat leeft'): 'And God saw the earth, and see, it was corrupted, because all living beings had corrupted their way on the earth. And God said to Noah: "I decided the end of all living creatures, because of their guilt the earth is filled with violence, and look, I am going to destroy them along with the earth"' (Genesis 6:12–13; transl. according to NBG 1951).

311 See also 2.2.1

312 As in Genesis 1, where the earth brings forth plants without being ordered by God to do so.

313 Mancuso and Viola, *Brilliant Green*, p. 15

314 See also 2.4 Salvation of the earth

315 Horrell, *The Bible and the Environment*, p. 43 ff.

316 The Jahwist version

317 Johan Graafland, 'Mens verantwoordelijk voor lijden van dieren', *Reformatorisch Dagblad* 26 (September 2015)

318 Van den Brink, *Reformed Theology*, p. 146

319 'Repeats' in as much as Genesis 9 follows Genesis 1, not in the sense that the text is of a later date than Genesis 1

320 Horrell, *The Bible and the Environment*, p. 46. Boureux, *Dieu est aussi jardinier*, p. 15, on the other hand, takes eating and being eaten as suffering that is inherently part of creation, because suffering is a result of change or metamorphosis: each form owes its existence to the disappearance of the previous form. Veganism as a form of asceticism is, in his opinion, not an answer to overconsumption, because it is too much on a par with moral thinking, whereas one should also enjoy the good things of the earth.

321 'Jewish Environmentalism in North America' in ERN, pp. 909–913

322 Rabbi Clary Rooda studied in Stockholm and Jerusalem. In 2014 she finished her studies in the Netherlands with a thesis on eco-kashrut: Clary Rooda, *Eco-kashrut and Jewish Tradition: How the Food on our Table can Atone for us*, Levisson Institute, October 2013

323 https://www.levisson.nl/images/stories/artikelen/Scripties/Thesis_Eco-kashrut_and_ Jewish_Tradition_by_Clary_Rooda.pdf, accessed 7 May 2020. The concept of eco-kashrut (eco-kosher) means that food can only be called kosher if during all the phases of its production and sale the ethical prescriptions are warranted. This means that honest taxes must be paid, that workers should be respectfully treated and fairly remunerated, that the environment should be preserved sustainably and that animals should be well treated.

324 Bauckham, *Living with Other Creatures*, p. 96

325 Horrell, *The Bible and the Environment*, p. 47

326 See 2.2.1

327 Barbara E. Reid, 'Sabbath, the Crown of Creation' in EWF, p. 70

328 Only Israelites are mentioned, not all people.

329 This subparagraph is up until this point based on Sharon V. Betcher, 'Sabbath–Jubilee Cycle' in ERN, pp. 1442–1444

330 Wim Brummelman, 'De aarde raakt steeds verder uitgeput', *NRC*, 6 June 2016

331 Betcher, 'Sabbath–Jubilee Cycle'

332 Bauckham, *Living with Other Creatures*, pp. 6, 7

333 Ibid., p. 229

334 Reid, 'Sabbath, the Crown of Creation', p. 68

335 Ibid., p. 75

336 Ibid., p. 74

337 Bauckham, *Living with Other Creatures*, pp. 66, 67. The historical–critical method has been honed in due course by sociological, liberation theological, feminist and postcolonial readings that have provided new insights into the religious, political and socio-economic contexts (additional comment by Magda Misset-van der Weg).

338 Parallel Luke 12:24

339 Van den Brink, *Reformed Theology*, p. 147

340 Bauckham, *Living with Other Creatures*, pp. 11 and 90

341 Parallel Luke 12:6–7

342 According to Van den Brink, *Reformed Theology*, p. 148 this text is 'an example of a more indifferent attitude towards animals'.

343 Michael J. Gilmour, *Eden's Other Residents: The Bible and Animals* (Eugene, Cascade Books, 2014), pp. 86–87 (according to Van den Brink, *Reformed Theology*, p. 147)

344 Bauckham, *Living with Other Creatures*, p. 110

345 See also Hans Schravesande, 'Een dialoog met dieren': 'That is an image of Jesus to which both Jews and Christians can relate', www.kerkenmilieu.nl/een-dialoog-en-met-dieren/ accessed 11 May 2020

346 Bauckham, *Living with Other Creatures*, p. 110

347 E.g. Francis of Assisi and Martin de Porres; see Nancy Pineda-Madrid, '¡Somos Criatures de Dios! – Seeing and Beholding the Garden of God' in PS; for the Eastern Orthodox tradition see 4.4.2 The world as an icon

348 Thus typifies Jan Wolsheimer the attitude of 'de Gereformeerde Gemeente', *Groene Bijbel*, p. 1056

349 Horrell, *The Bible and the Environment*, p. 104 ff.

350 So Catherine Keller; see 4.2.3 The human person

351 'Once when the trumpets sound!', 'Once when the big summer commences', 'Be still, and wait, everything will be fine' are the first lines of (Dutch) songs about this future.

352 Keller, *On the Mystery*, p. 166

353 Catherine Keller, *Political Theology of the Earth: Our Planetary Emergency and the Struggle for a New Public* (New York, Columbia University Press, 2018), p. 58

354 See also 1 Corinthians 15 and Philippians 2

355 The verses 19 and 23 state literally *sons* (*uios*); verse 21 speaks of children (*teknon*). The use of *sons* can be explained because daughters could only inherit if there were no sons and that all believers, both male and female, have been told that they are in that sense considered as sons, and thus, heirs. The imagery of being in labour in relation to salvation (v. 22) also appears in Isaiah 13:8 and 66:7–9 and Mark 13:8. See Sheila E. McGinn, 'All Creation Groans in Labor: Paul's Theology of Creation in Romans 8: 18–23' in EWF, pp. 115–120

356 Horrell, *The Bible and the Environment*, pp. 74-87

357 Brendan Byrne s.j., 'Creation Groaning: An Earth Bible Reading of Romans 8.18-22' in Norman C. Habel (ed.), *Readings from the Perspective of Earth* (*The Earth Bible Volume 1*; Sheffield, Sheffield Academic Press, 2000), p. 198

358 Walter Bauer, *Wörterbuch zum Neuen Testament* (Berlin/New York, Walter de Gruyter, 1971)entry: *ktisis*

359 The last thing is also done by Horrell, *The Bible and the Environment*, p. 75

360 In the Eastern Orthodox theology that idea became dominant; see 4.4.2

361 Bauer, *Wörterbuch zum NT*

362 McGinn, 'All Creation Groans in Labor'

363 Horrell, *The Bible and the Environment*, p. 75

364 See also 2.2.3

365 Johnson, *Ask the Beasts*, p. 279

366 See 2.2.1 The coming into existence of the Cosmos: Genesis 1–2:4

367 Johnson, *Ask the Beasts*, p. 279

368 Boureux, *Dieu est aussi jardinier*, p. 127

369 see 2.2.3 Prophet of creation: Deutero-Isaiah

370 In NABRE Hosea 2:20

371 Isaiah 11:1–9 and 65:25, and 2.3.4

372 e.g. Ezekiel 34:25; Isaiah 35:9 and Leviticus 26:6; see Horrell, *The Bible and the Environment*, p. 92

373 Horrell, *The Bible and the Environment*, pp. 94–95

374 Ibid., p. 96 ff.; Some Bible translations have different chapter and verse numbers, e.g. chapter 3 in NABRE is 2:28—3:21 in NRSV.

375 Ibid., p. 96: Isaiah 24:4 and 33:9; Jeremiah 4:28 and 12:4,11 and 23:10; Amos 1:2; Hosea 4:3

376 Horrell, *The Bible and the Environment*, p. 97

377 Ibid., p. 98

378 In the Hebrew Bible 2:28–29

379 Horrell, *The Bible and the Environment*, p. 105

380 Ibid., p. 106

381 See e.g. Genesis 15:12 and 17; Exodus 14:19–20 and 19:16–18

382 The verdict is God's; God as judge of the earth is also attested in Psalm 82:8 and 96:13.

383 See also Isaiah 66:22; in Isaiah 65:17 we hear, as is the case in Genesis 1:1, the verb '*bara*', create.

384 See 2.2.1, 2.2.4 and 2.2.5

385 Horrell, *The Bible and the Environment*, p. 98

386 Ibid., p. 99

387 Barbara R. Rossing, 'Reimaging Eschatology: Toward Healing and Hope for a World at the Eschatos' in PS, p. 346

388 Horrell, *The Bible and the Environment*, p. 99 ff.

389 Ibid., p. 100 quotes Steven Bouma-Prediger, *For the Beauty of the Earth: A Christian Vision for Creation Care* (Grand Rapids, Michigan, Baker Academic, 2001), p. 114, who quotes M. Eugene Boring, *Revelation* (Louisville, Kentucky, Westminster John Knox, 1989) p. 220

390 See also Van den Brink, *Reformed Theology*, p. 148

391 See 2.2.4 The creation sings: the Psalms

392 Rossing, 'Reimaging Eschatology', p. 330

393 Marina Warner, *Alone of All Her Sex: The Myth and the Cult of the Virgin Mary* (London, Weidenfeld & Nicolson, 1976; Dutch translation: *De enige onder de vrouwen. De maagd Maria: mythe en cultus*, 1990)

394 Rossing, 'Reimaging Eschatology', p. 336

395 Ibid., p. 339

396 Ibid., p. 332

397 Ibid., p. 345

398 Ibid., p. 346 and Theokritoff, *Living in God's Creation*, pp. 171–174

399 Catherine Keller in her lecture on 10 March 2017 in Utrecht; see also 4.2.3 The human person

400 See 2.2.7 Christ the Creator

401 Barbara Bowe, 'Soundings in the New Testament Understanding of Creation' in EWF, pp. 61–63

402 Rossing, 'Reimaging Eschatology', p. 330

403 Ibid., p. 331

404 Haenchen, *John 1*, p. 226

405 Sjef van Tilborg, *Johannes* (Boxtel, KBS, 1988), pp. 45–55

406 I will give a few examples. In hymn 188 of the hymn book it is said that she stands 'thirsty in the sun at midday of her shame'. Joop Smit (*Het verhaal van Johannes. Sleutelfiguren uit zijn evangelie*, [Heeswijk, Berne Media, 2015]) avers: 'That the woman comes unaccompanied to draw water at the middle of the day, is not a reassuring sign, and suggests that there is clearly something wrong with her' (p. 47) and he states: 'The woman had in fact a past with strange men' (p. 48). In the *Evangelische Liedbundel* (Zoetermeer, Boekencentrum, 1999), hymn 70, she is not considered bad but pitiful: 'Failed again! was the refrain that repeated itself in her life. She was a discarded woman, five men had been unfaithful to her.'

407 Van Tilborg, *Johannes*, pp. 45–46

408 Ibid., p. 48

409 Maria de Groot, *De vrouw bij de bron* (Haarlem, Uitgeversmaatschappij Holland, 1980), p. 16 ff.

410 Van Tilborg, *Johannes* , pp. 48–49

411 Van Tilborg, *Johannes*, p. 51

412 See also 4.2 Ivone Gebara: the daily life of poor women

413 https://water.oikoumene.org/en/whatwedo/news-events/water-and-mines-in-southern-africa2019s-zambezi-basin, accessed 24 April 2020

414 See 1.2.7 Postmodernism

415 According to the Bible, the non-human world also includes the angels, and, in some texts, even other deities.

416 Boersema, *The Torah and the Stoics on Humankind and Nature*, p. 74

417 See 1.2.3 Current natural science and 2.2.1 The coming into existence of the Cosmos: Genesis 1—2:4

418 See Introduction

419 Groene Genade (Green Grace) is among others the name of a workgroup of the Dutch reformed Church in Ede; see https://diaconaalsteunpunt.nl/groene-genade/, accessed 3 July 2020

420 See also 2.2 Creation stories

421 See 2.2.1 The coming into existence of the Cosmos: Genesis 1—2:4

422 'Stewardship' in *Encyclopaedia of Religion and Nature*, p. 1598 ff.

423 Boersema, *The Torah and the Stoics on Humankind and Nature*.

424 Gen 43:16,19; Dan 1:11; Isa 22:15; John 2:8

425 Matthew 20:8; Luke 8:3 and 16:1-8

426 Bauckham, *Living with Other Creatures*, pp. 58–62

427 *Encyclopaedia of Religion and Nature*, p. 1598 ff. Moses was seen as the author of the first five books of the Bible.

428 John Calvin, *Commentary on Genesis – Volume 1*, Chapter 2

429 See 4.4

430 Bauckham, *Living with Other Creatures*, p. 36

431 van Soest, '*Welk is het voortreffelijkste schepsel op aarde?*', p. 257

432 Ibid., p. 262

433 Ibid.6, p. 259

434 For the viewpoint of the eco-modernists see 1.1.3 Mainstream solutions

435 Rick Benjamins et al. (eds), *Liberaal christendom. Ervaren, doen, denken*, (Vught, Skandalon, 2016), p. 207

436 Ibid., pp. 209–210

437 Ibid., p. 208; this is a very anthropocentric version of process theology.

438 For seeing people as co-creators but still from within creation see Catherine Keller 4.3.5 Postmodern theology in context

439 As in Henk Vreekamp, *Het jaar van Vivaldi. Hemel en aarde in onze seizoenen* (Utrecht, Kok, 2016)

440 The following historical sketch is founded in Santmire and Cobb, 'The World of Nature',, p. 124 ff.

441 Leezenberg and De Vries, *Wetenschapsfilosofie*, p. 52; see also 1.2 Worldviews

442 There is more about process theology in 4.3.1 Theology as recycling

443 Bauckham, *Living with Other Creatures*, p. 111

444 Cornelis van der Kooi and Gijsbert van den Brink, *Christian Dogmatics: An Introduction* (Grand Rapids, Michigan, Eerdmans, 2017; originally published as *Christelijke Dogmatiek: Een inleiding*, 2012)

445 Typical for liberal anthropocentrism is how Rick Benjamins interprets Catherine Keller's creation theology: 'People have come out of the deep'. Rick Benjamins, *Catherine Keller's constructieve theologie* (Vught, Skandalon 2017), p. 91. Benjamins changes Keller's creatures, without further ado, simply into people. For Keller's theology of creation see 2.2.1 The coming into existence of the Cosmos: Genesis 1—2:4 and 4.3.4 Creation from the deep

446 Most of his works have been translated in German; only a few to English (*When the Gods are Silent*, 1967; *The Roads of Prayer*, 1968). An overview of his ideas can be found in Martin Kessler, *Kornelis Miskotte: A Biblical Theology* (Selinsgrove, Susquehanna University Press, 1997). See Colin Cornell, 'De Engelstalige receptie van K.H. Miskotte', *Ophef* (November 2019).

447 Kune Biezeveld, *Als scherven spreken. Over God in het leven van alledag* (Zoetermeer, Meinema, 2008); this exposition is an expanded version of my article 'Geboeid door Kune Biezeveld. Ook in de natuur is God te vinden', *Soteria* 2 (2017)

448 Biezeveld, *Als scherven spreken*, p. 53

449 Ibid.,, p. 53 ff.

450 Miskotte, *Edda en Thora*, p. 104, quoted in Coen Wessels, 'Zijn wij hier wel voor? Over Miskottes Edda en Thora als hedendaagse bron van wantrouwen tegen de natuur'. Text of a workshop held at a conference dealing with God in everyday life: *Over God in het leven van alledag*, 9 October 2010

451 Wessels, 'Zijn wij hier wel voor?'

452 Biezeveld, *Als scherven spreken*, p. 61

453 Ibid., p. 66

454 Ibid., p. 79

455 Kune Biezeveld, *Spreken over God als Vader. Hoe kan het anders?* (Baarn, Ten Have, 1996)

456 Biezeveld, *Als scherven spreken*, p. 94

457 Biezeveld, *Als scherven spreken*, pp. 85–90

458 The Deuteronomistic redaction is the work of writers or redactors of Deuteronomy and subsequently the books Genesis, Exodus, Leviticus and Numbers rewriting Israel's history by emphasising the dominance of the cult in Jerusalem and its strict monotheism. See Alice L. Laffey, 'Deuteronomistic theology' in Orlando O. Espín and James B. Nickoloff (eds), *An Introductory Dictionary of Theology and Religious Studies* (Collegeville, Minnesota, Liturgical Press, 2007); Martin Noth, 'The Deuteronomistic History', *Journal for the Study of the Old Testament, Supplement series.* 15 (1981)

459 Biezeveld, *Als scherven spreken*, p. 41

460 Ibid.

461 Ibid., p. 42

462 Ibid., p. 74

463 Ibid., pp. 75–76

464 Ibid.,p. 40

465 For the description of the project *Feest van Aarde en Hemel* see also http://www.berthevansoest.nl/Midwinterviering-feest-van-aarde-en-hemel.pdf, accessed 6 July 2020

466 The same: *Feest van Aarde en Hemel*

467 Dr N.G.M. van Doornik, *De kleine triptiek. Handboek van de katholieke leer en het katholieke leven* (Utrecht/Antwerpen, Het Spectrum, 1951), p. 272; more in depth pp. 217–219

468 Hans Boersma, *Nouvelle Théologie and Sacramental Ontology: A Return to Mystery* (Oxford, Oxford University Press, 2009), quoted on https://www.lucepedia.nl/dossieritem/603/nouvelle-theologie-een-sacramentele-benadering-van-de-werkelijkheid, accessed 24 May 2018

469 https://www.lucepedia.nl/dossieritem/603/nouvelle-theologie-een-sacramentele-benadering-van-de-werkelijkheid, accessed 24 May 2018

470 John Hart, 'Catholicism' in OHRE

471 Ibid., pp. 68–70

472 Ibid., pp. 71–72

473 Erik Borgman and Thijs Caspers, 'In dienst van een zoekend geloof. Edward Schillebeeckx en de na-conciliaire periode in Nederland', *Tijdschrift voor Theologie* 54ᵉ jaargang, nr 4 (Winter 2014)

474 Encyclical *Humanae Vitae* (1968)

475 Starting with the appointment of mgr. Gijsen in 1970 in Roermond and mgr. Simonis in 1972 in Rotterdam

476 To name just a few of the most famous among those suffering under Vatican procedures I mention here Edward Schillebeeckx, Hans Küng, Ivone Gebara and Leonardo Boff. Hard measures were also taken against many other lesser-known lecturers at Catholic theological academies and seminars. Common clergy and lay people were likewise either forced to silence or saw their right to lecture suspended. Some lost their job altogether.

477 Pope Paul IV, 'Octogesima adveniens. Apostolic letter to cardinal Maurice Roy', 14 May 1971, http://www.vatican.va/content/paul-vi/en/apost_letters.index.3.html, accessed 7 August 2020

478 http://www.vatican.va/content/john-paul-ii/en/messages/peace/documents/hf_jp-ii_mes_19891208_xxiii-world-day-for-peace.html, accessed 8 July 2020

479 Borgman and Caspers, 'In dienst van een zoekend geloof', pp. 388–389

480 Ibid., pp. 388–389

481 *A New Catechism: Catholic Faith for Adults* (London, Burns & Oates/New York, Herder, 1967; first published as: *De Nieuwe Katechismus. Geloofsverkondiging voor volwassenen. In opdracht van de bisschoppen van Nederland* [Hilversum-Antwerp, 1966]). Its editor was Prof. Piet Schoonenberg, Edward Schillebeeckx' predecessor in Nijmegen.

482 Borgman and Caspers, 'In dienst van een zoekend geloof', p. 392

483 *A New Catechism*, pp. 263, 488–489 and 499–500

484 Ibid., p. 427

485 The speedy acceptance of evolutionary theory is due to the influence of the evolutionary theology of Pierre Teilhard de Chardin, French theologian and palaeontologist (1881–1955). For natural theology see Walter Kasper, *Einführung in den Glauben* (Mainz, Grünewald, 1973), p. 28 ff.

486 *A New Catechism*, p. 6. The English translation deviates here strikingly from the Dutch text. In *De nieuwe katechismus* people exist on a par with other people and 'with things, plants and animals' (p. 7). *A New Catechism* transfers plants and animals to the next paragraph, where they belong to the world of inert matter.

487 *A New Catechism*, p. 10

488 For the loss of the cosmic perspective in philosophy see Henk Manschot, *Blijf de aarde trouw. Pleidooi voor een nietzscheaanse terrasofie* (Nijmegen, Van Til, 2016), pp. 97–99 (English version: Henk Manschot, *Nietzsche and the Earth: Biography, Ecology, Politics* (London, Bloomsbury, 2020)

489 Robert Schreiter, C.PP.S., 'The Relevance of Professor Edward Schillebeeckx, O.P. For the Twenty-First Century', Lecture Tulane University New Orleans, Louisiana October 8, 2009', p. 13, https://schillebeeckx.nl/wp-content/uploads/2008/11/Lecture-on-relevance-Schillebeeckx.pdf, accessed 17 July 2020; Schillebeeckx's books are translated into many languages.

490 Edward Schillebeeckx, *Jesus: An Experiment in Christology* (London, Collins, 1979/New York, Crossroad, 1981), section 3 (first published as *Jezus, het verhaal van een levende* [Bloemendaal, Nelissen, 1975]; third expanded edition, first printed in 1973)

491 Oosterhuis is strongly influenced by the predominantly Protestant 'Amsterdamse school' in exegesis, and his hymns are also, for that matter, frequently sung in Protestant churches. Some of his books and songs are translated in English and German.

492 Hymn 322 in *Liedboek* and hymn 593 in *Gezangen voor Liturgie* (Baarn, Gooi en Sticht, 1996); see also Huub Oosterhuis, *Alles voor allen. Een nieuwe catechismus* (Utrecht, Kok, 2016), pp. 11–13

493 See also Introduction

494 I will just mention a few academic publications in a more or less chronological order, varying from orthodox Protestant to feminist, and interreligious catholic. Most of them are also available in an English or German version. See J.J. Boersema (ed.), *De oogst van Milieu* (Amsterdam, Boom, 2003). Here I will not discuss these publications extensively, though some of these texts will be used further on in this book.

Hendrik-Joost van Soest did research on how the term 'dominion' in Genesis 1 was interpreted during the last two centuries in the Netherlands (van Soest, '*Welk is het voortreffelijkste schepsel op aarde?*', see 1.2.1 and 3.1). Jan Boersema, biologist and environmental scientist, did his doctoral research in theology on an Old Testament study as a contribution to the environmental debate (Boersema, *The Torah and the Stoics*, see chapter 2). Catharina Halkes, professor of feminism and Christianity, analysed how women and nature were imagined in the context of creation theology in order to construct an ecological theology in *...en alles zal worden herschapen. Gedachten over de heelwording van de schepping in het spanningsveld tussen natuur en cultuur* (Baarn, Ten Have, 1989), see 1.2.6. Birgit Verstappen took up the challenge with a PhD on ecological theology in which she tried to unite cosmological and liberation-theological viewpoints: Verstappen, *Ekklesia van leven. Een aanzet tot een discussie tussen theologische kosmologie en bevrijdingstheologie*, 2000; German version *Ekklesia des Lebens im Dialog mit Sallie McFague's Kosmologie und der Befreiungstheologie von Elisabeth Schüssler Fiorenza* (Münster, LIT, 2001), see 1.2.2. Martine Vonk did her PhD with Jan Boersema as her promotor on a research on Christian communities with a small ecological footprint: *Sustainability and Quality of Life: A Study on the Religious Worldviews, Values and Environmental Impact of Amish, Hutterite, Franciscan and Benedictine Communities* (Amsterdam, Buijten en Schipperheijn, 2011), https://research.vu.nl/ws/portalfiles/portal/42209843/complete+dissertation.pdf, accessed 6 August 2020). German Klaus Heinrich Neuhoff earned a doctorate in Tilburg on cosmic Christology from the viewpoint of the eastern Church Fathers in which he also mentioned some twentieth-century eco-theologians: '*Gott alles in allem*' (*1Kor 15,28*). *Theosis, Anakephalaiosis und Apokatastasis nach Maximos dem Bekenner in ihrer Bedeutung für die Kosmische Christologie* (2014), https://research.tilburguniversity.edu/en/publications/gott-alles-in-allem-1kor-1528-theosis-anakephalaiosis-und-apokata, accessed 6 August 2020. Steven Christian van den Heuvel did research on the relevancy of Bonhoeffer's Christology for the current debates on environmental ethics: *Bonhoeffer's Christocentric Theology and Fundamental Debates in Environmental Ethics* (Eugene, Oregon, Pickwick Publications, 2017).

All sorts of specials of theological reviews, on ecology and sustainability, were published, lectures given and congresses organised. An overview of Dutch publications can be found in the Dutch edition of this book, *Groene theologie*, p. 158.

495 Isaiah 32:15 NBG 1951; NRSV: 'Until the wilderness becomes a fruitful field'.

496 Generale Synode van de Nederlandse Hervormde Kerk, *De gaarde een woestijn? De milieucrisis en de verantwoordelijkheid van de kerk. Een verkenning ten behoeve van het gesprek in de gemeenten, aangeboden door de Generale Synode van de Nederlandse Hervormde Kerk* ('s-Gravenhage, Boekencentrum, 1990), p. 92

497 Generale Synode, *De gaarde*, p. 18

498 Ibid., p. 20

499 Ibid., p. 25

500 Ibid., p. 32

501 Ibid., pp. 34–35

502 Ibid., p. 35

503 Ibid., p. 37

504 Ibid., p. 10

505 Jürgen Moltmann, *God in Creation* (London, SCM Press, 1985; first published as *Gott in der Schöpfung. Ökologische Schöpfungslehre*, 1985); on the dangers of a linear model see 1.3.1, 2.1.3, 2.4 and 2.5.1

506 Generale Synode, *De gaarde*, p. 39

507 Ibid., p. 40

508 Ibid., pp. 42–43

509 Ibid., pp. 43–44

510 Ibid., pp. 45–47

511 Ibid., p. 49

512 See 2.2.7 Christ the Creator

513 Generale Synode, *De gaarde*, p. 53

514 Ibid., p. 58. It mentions our responsibility for our neighbours and future generations, the intrinsic value of the whole non-human creation, that all technology should be subservient to the care of creation, how human beings are responsible for the survival of plant and animal species, the relationship between social justice and the preservation of the environment, and that we should preserve the self-restoring potential of nature.

515 Gerrit Manenschijn's book *Geplunderde aarde, getergde hemel. Ontwerp voor een christelijke ethiek* (*Pillaged Earth, Enraged Heaven. An Outline of Christian Ethics*; Baarn, Ten Have, 1988) is explicitly mentioned.

516 Generale Synode, *De gaarde*, p. 58

517 https://www.protestantsekerk.nl/thema/kerk2025/#notakerk2025, accessed 9 July 2020

518 'Van U is de toekomst. Ontvankelijk en waakzaam. Focus voor de Protestantse Kerk in Nederland op weg naar 2025', PKN, 2020.

519 Ibid., pp. 14–15

520 https://www.raadvankerken.nl/product/van-god-is-de-aarde-2/, accessed 9 July 2020

521 Gerard de Korte as acting bishop for church and society keenly promoted the encyclical *Laudato Si'*

522 *Encyclical Letter Laudato Si' of the Holy Father Francis on Care for our Common Home*; see http://www.vatican.va/content/francesco/en/encyclicals/documents/papa-francesco_20150524_enciclica-laudato-si.html, accessed 17 July 2020. This part has been published earlier as a review: '*Laudato Si'* en eco-feminisme', *ZijSpiegel* 5 (2016).

523 LS 2

524 See for instance http://iglesiadescalza.blogspot.nl/2015/08/laudato-si-critique-of-pope-francis.html, accessed 25 June 2018 (on 17 July 2020 this blog was removed); see also chapter 4

525 LS 49 mentions Leonardo Boff, *Ecology: Cry of the Earth, Cry of the Poor* (New York, Orbis, 1995; first published as *Ecologia. Grito da Terra, grito dos pobres* [S. Paulo, 1995])

526 LS 81. The encyclical does not use the term stewardship, but the relationship between humans, creation and nature remains a tricky issue: caring for, being part of, personhood versus matter. For the relationship between person and matter see also 2.2.4 The creation sings: the Psalms

527 LS 98

528 Compare 4.4 Theokritoff

529 LS 101

530 LS 194

531 'Re-Imaging with Laudato Si" in Grace Ji-Sun Kim and Hilda P. Koster (eds), *Planetary Solidarity: Global Women's Voices on Christian Doctrine and Climate Justice* (PS; Minneapolis, Minnesota, Fortress Press, 2017), pp. 47–101

532 Vandana Shiva, *Staying Alive: Women, Ecology and Development* (London, Zed Books, 1989); see also 1.2.6 Patriarchy and colonialism and 4.2 Ivone Gebara: The daily life of poor women

533 See 1.2.6 Patriarchy and colonialism

534 He does quote Proverbs 3:19: 'the Lord by wisdom founded the earth' (paragraph 69)

535 See 2.2.6. Lady Wisdom, 2.2.7 Christ as creator; Deane-Drummond, 'Sophia: The Feminine Face of God as a Metaphor for an Ecotheology', and , Celia Deane-Drummond, *Eco-Theology* (London, Darton, Longman & Todd, 2008), pp. 63–65, 93–95, 110–112, 159–161

536 See 4.1 Sallie McFague: the world as God's body

537 Hildegard von Bingen, *Gott sehen* (München, Piper, 1995). A word that she uses frequently is *viriditas*: 'greenness' or power of life. This refers to God's green fingers with which God creates the world and humans

538 Heather Eaton, *Introducing Eco-feminist Theologies* (London/New York, Bloomsbury, 2005)

539 See 1.1.2 The growing impact of people on the earth

540 Henk Manschot, *Nietzsche and the Earth: Biography, Ecology, Politics* (London, Bloomsbury, 2020; first published as *Blijf de aarde trouw. Pleidooi voor een nietzscheaanse terrasofie* [ijmegen, Van Tilt, 2016])

541 van den Brink, *Reformed Theology*

542 Taede A. Smedes, *Thuis in de kosmos. Het Epos van de Evolutie en de vraag naar de zin van ons bestaan* (Amsterdam, AUP, 2018; not available in English). This author published in English *Chaos, Complexity, and God: Divine Action and Scientism* (Leuven, Peeters, 2004)

543 Manschot refers to Friedrich Nietzsche, *Thus Spoke Zarathustra: A Book for Everyone and Nobody,* also translated as *Thus Spake Zarathustra* (first published in German between 1883 and 1885 as *Also sprach Zarathustra*)

544 Manschot, *Nietzsche and the Earth*, p. 185

545 Ibid., pp. 105–106

546 Ibid., p. 107

547 Ibid., p. 137

548 Ibid., p. 97

549 Ibid., p. 98

550 Ibid., p. 143; Manschot finds his support in Picq, *De Darwin à Levi-Strauss* (Paris, Odile Jacob, 2013) and Philippe Descola *Par-delà nature et culture* (Paris, Galimart, 2005)

551 Ibid., p. 142
552 Ibid., p. 145
553 Ibid., pp. 167–171
554 Ibid., pp. 162–163
555 Ibid., pp. 156–157
556 Ibid., p. 154
557 Ibid., p. 99
558 Ibid., pp. 154–155
559 See Karen Barad, 'Posthumanist Performativity: Toward an Understanding of How Matter Comes to Matter', *Journal of Women in Culture and Society* 28:3 (2003)
560 See Sarah Coakley, *Powers and Submissions: Spirituality, Philosophy and Gender* (Malden/ Oxford/Carlton, Blackwell Publishing, 2002), pp. 90–94
561 Smedes, *Thuis in de kosmos*, p. 86
562 Ibid., pp. 86 and 64
563 Ibid., p. 17
564 Ibid., pp. 56–57
565 Ibid., pp. 61–62
566 Ibid., p. 89
567 Ibid., p. 65
568 Ibid., p. 76
569 Ibid., p. 56
570 Ibid., p. 75
571 Ibid., p. 76–77
572 Ibid., p. 79–80
573 Ibid., p. 85
574 Ibid., p. 68
575 For the term 'grand narrative' see 1.2.7 Postmodernism
576 Van den Brink, *Reformed Theology*, p. 214
577 Ibid., p. 36
578 Ibid., pp. 65 and 288–231
579 Ibid., p. 136
580 Ibid., p. 137
581 Ibid., pp. 27–28
582 Ibid., p. 331
583 Ibid., p. 72; On the Bible and the book of nature see also 1.2.2 Western worldviews through the ages.
584 Van den Brink refers to H. Berkhof, *Christian Faith: An Introduction to the Study of the Faith* (Grand Rapids, Michigan, Eerdmans, 1979; first published as *Christelijk geloof. Een inleiding tot de geloofsleer* [Nijkerk, Callenbach, 1973])
585 Van den Brink, *Reformed Theology*, p. 338
586 Ibid., p. 335
587 Ibid., pp. 339–340
588 Ibid., p. 337
589 Ibid., p. 226
590 See 1.2.7 Postmodernism and 1.3 The task of theology
591 Among others in the working group 'Theologie, Kerk en Duurzaamheid' of the Council of Churches in the Netherlands (see https://www.raadvankerken.nl/organisatie/ projectgroepen/samenlevingsvragen/werkgroep-theologie-kerk-en-duurzaamheid/,

accessed 29 July 2020) and in the Amsterdam Centre for Religion and Sustainable Development (inter-religious) that co-operates with the Free University (VU) (see http://www.godgeleerdheid.vu.nl/en/news-agenda/news-archive/2018/apr-jun/180606-roundtable-religion-and-sustainable-development.aspx, accessed 29 July 2020)

592 See also 1.2.8 Language
593 Bauckham, *Living with Other Creatures*, p. 13
594 See also 1.2.3 Current natural science
595 Serene Jones, *Trauma and Grace: Theology in a Ruptured World* (Louisville, Kentucky, Westminster John Knox Press, 2009), p. 31
596 Conradie, 'The Earth in God's Economy', p. 20
597 Conradie, 'The Earth in God's Economy', p. 25
598 Gender is a term associated with sociocultural constructs of femininity and masculinity; sex refers to biological differences. Opinions differ in what are biological and what cultural components when it comes to being male or female
599 Eaton, *Introducing Eco-feminist Theologies*, p. 37 ff. see also 1.2.6 Patriarchy and colonialism
600 Ibid., p.7; Mary Daly, *Gyn/ecology: A Metaethics of Radical Feminism* (Boston, Beacon Press, 1978) – in this book she turned away from the Christian tradition for good; Rosemary Radford Ruether, *New Women, New Earth: Sexist Ideologies and Human Liberation* (New York, The Seabury Press, 1975); Rosemary Radford Ruether, *Sexism and God-Talk: Toward a Feminist Theology* (Boston, Massachusetts, Beacon Press, 1983); Rosemary Radford Ruether, *Gaia and God: An Ecofeminist Theology of Earth Healing* (London, SCM Press, 1993). Some examples of eco-theology of female religious: Ivone Gebara, *Longing for Running Water: Ecofeminism and Liberation* (Minneapolis, Minnesota, Fortress Press, 1999); Sarah McFarland Taylor, *Green Sister* (Cambridge, Massachusetts, Harvard University Press, 2009); Johnson, *Ask the Beasts*; Marilu Rojas Salazar, *De feministische theologische/thealogische methode van bevrijding vanuit Latijns-Amerikaans ecofeministisch perspectief* (dissertation, Leuven, 2013)
601 Kim and Koster (eds), *Planetary Solidarity* is a collection of essays of twenty eco-feminist theologians from different parts of the world who develop a systematic theological approach. Among those are McFague and Gebara. Keller and Theokritoff do not appear in this collection.
602 McFague, *The Body of God: An Ecological Theology* (London, SCM Press, 1993); Gebara, *Longing for Running Water:* ; Keller, *Face of the Deep*; Theokritoff, *Living in God's Creation*
603 In a certain sense all language is metaphorical, because it never coincides exactly with what it conveys.
604 Sallie McFague, *Models of God: Theology for an Ecological Nuclear Age* (Philadelphia, Pennsylvania Fortress Press, 1987; translated in Dutch as *Modellen voor God. Nieuwe theologie in een bedreigde wereld* [Zoetermeer, De Horstink, 1994]). She developed the image of God's body in *The Body of God: An Ecological Theology* (London, SCM Press, 1993)
605 McFague, *Models of God*, p. 69
606 McFague, *Super, Natural Christians*)
607 Sallie McFague, *Live Abundant: Rethinking Theology and Economy for a Planet in Peril* (Minneapolis, Fortress Press, 2000), p. 10
608 Ibid., p. 12
609 Although the term scientific revolution has been coined during the nineteenth century and does not really do justice to the gradualness and non-synchronicity of the changes in worldview, I nevertheless refer to the term in the way McFague makes use of it.

610 See also 1.2.5 Market economy

611 Sallie McFague, *Life Abundant: Theology and Economy for a Planet in Peril* (Minneapolis, Minnesota, Fortress Press, 2000)

612 Ibid., p. 95; see also 1.2.5 Market economy

613 Mark van Ostaijen, 'De BV Nederland is een misplaatste metafoor', http://www. binnenlandsbestuur.nl/bestuur-en-organisatie/opinie/columns/de-bv-nederland-is-een-misplaatste-metafoor.9558534.lynkx, accessed 30 July 2020

614 McFague, *Life Abundant*, p. 72

615 See e.g. Kate Raworth, *Doughnut Economics: Seven Ways to Think Like a 21st-Century Economist* (London, Random House Business, 2016); she is optimistic about the possibilities and the will to give direction to the global market economy.

616 Sallie McFague, *Blessed are the Consumers: Climate Change and the Practice of Restraint* (Minneapolis, Fortress Press, 2013); Philippians 2:6–8 is the most important source for the doctrine of *kenosis*: 'who, though he was in the form of God, did not regard equality with God as something to be exploited, but emptied himself, taking the form of a slave, being born in human likeness. And being found in human form, he humbled himself and became obedient to the point of death – even death on a cross.' McFague summarises and updates *Blessed are the Consumers* in 'Reimagining the Triune God for a Time of Global Climate Change' in PS.

617 McFague (2017), p. 107–108

618 McFague (2017), p. 111

619 See 3.2 Protestant resistance

620 See 2.2.4 The creation sings: the Psalms

621 McFague (2017), p. 117

622 Gebara *Longing for Running Water*, p. 6

623 Ibid., p. v

624 Lois Ann Lorentzen and Salvador Leavitt-Alcantara, 'Religion and Environmental Struggles in Latin America' in OHRE, pp. 510–534

625 Ivone Gebara, 'Ecofeminismo e Ecoteologia: perspectiva de Ivone Gebara', lecture for a meeting in the Netherlands, 17 October 2006

626 Gebara, *Longing for Running Water*, p. 18

627 Ibid., p. 16

628 Ibid., p. 4

629 For this biography I used the following sources: Arianne van Andel and Anneke Kok, 'Inleiding' in Ivone Gebara, *Omdat de schepper even moest niezen. Postpatriarchale overwegingen in uren van twijfel* (Den Haag, CMC, 2006), pp. 5–10; Elaine Nogueira-Godsey, 'A History of Resistance: Ivone Gebara's Transformative Feminist Liberation Theology', *Journal for the Study of Religion* 26:2 (2013); Lois Ann Lorentzen, 'Gebara. Ivone (1944–)' in ERN; 'Entrevista a Ivone Gebara, brasileña, monja y feminista', http://www.amerindiaenlared.org/contenido/2842/entrevista-a-ivone-gebara-brasilena-monja-y-feminista/, accessed 30 July 2020

630 Nogueira-Godsey, 'A History of Resistance, p. 96

631 Gebara, *Longing for Running Water*, p. vi

632 *Out of the Depth: Women's Experience of Evil and Salvation* (Minneapolis, Fortress Press, 2002; first published as *Le mal au féminin. Reflexions théologiques à partir du féminisme* [Paris/Montréal L'Harmattan, 1999])

633 Gebara, *Longing for Running Water*, p. ix

634 Ibid., p. 8

635 Ibid., p. 21
636 Ibid., pp. 26–27
637 Ibid., p. 32
638 Ibid., p. 34
639 Ibid., p. 38
640 Gebara uses the term dogma for all church promulgations, thus, in a much broader sense than the four ecumenical dogmas or six dogmas of the Roman Catholic Church.
641 Gebara, *Longing for Running Water*, pp. 45–47
642 Ibid., p. 1
643 Ibid., p. 49
644 Ibid., p. 50
645 Ibid., p. 48
646 Marc van der Post, liberation theologian in Buenos Aires, in an email
647 Gebara, *Longing for Running Water*, p. 50
648 Ibid., p. 52
649 Ibid., p. 58
650 Ibid., p. 59
651 Ibid., p. 60
652 Ibid., p. 62
653 Ibid., p. 63
654 Ibid., p. 64
655 Ibid., p. 64
656 Ibid., p. 65
657 Ibid., p. 65
658 Thecla Sloot, *Mensbeeld en bevrijding. Een analyse van de antropologische en theologische ontwikkeling in het werk van Ivone Gebara, exemplarisch gerelateerd aan religiositeit van volksvrouwen in Brazilië* (masterthesis, 1999)
659 Ivone Gebara, 'Women's Suffering, Climate Injustice, Good, and Pope Francis's Theology: Some Insights from Brazil' in PS
660 Gebara, *Longing for Running Water*, p. 68
661 Ibid., p. 71
662 Ibid., pp. 71–72
663 Ibid., pp. 75–76. An illustration of present-day Brazil, with thanks to Marc van der Post via email: President Bolsanaro has added insult to injury when talking about black people, women, homosexuals and other minorities, saying probably aloud what many people think or at least unconsciously harbour.
664 Ibid., p. 79
665 Ibid., p. 81
666 See the next paragraph, 4.2.4 God as relatedness
667 Gebara, *Longing for Running Water*, pp. 81–82
668 Ibid., p. 85
669 Ibid., p. 87
670 Ibid., p. 88
671 See also 2.2.5 Job's suffering in context and 2.2.6 Lady Wisdom: Proverbs 1—9
672 Gebara, *Longing for Running Water*, p. 92. She refers to Brian Swimme and Thomas Berry, *The Universe Story: From the Primordial Flaring Forth to the Ecozoic Era. A Celebration of the Unfolding of the Cosmos* (San Francisco, HarperCollins, 1994), see also Thomas Berry,

The Great Work: Our Way into the Future (New York, Random House, 1999)

673 Gebara, *Longing for Running Water*, p. 93
674 Ibid., p. 94
675 Ibid., pp. 95–96
676 Ibid., p. 95
677 Ibid., p. 96
678 Ibid., p. 97
679 Ibid., p. 98; compare 2.2.4 The creation sings: the Psalms
680 Ibid., p. 99
681 Ibid., p. 101
682 Ibid., p. 102
683 Ibid., pp. 103–104
684 Ibid., p. 105
685 Ibid., p. 108
686 Ibid., p. 110
687 Ibid., pp. 129–131
688 Ibid., p. 123
689 Ibid., p. 124
690 Ibid., p. 124
691 Ibid., pp. 124–127
692 Ibid., p. 114
693 Ibid., p. 110
694 Ibid., pp. 115–116
695 Ibid., p. 120
696 Ibid., p. 109
697 See 4.1.3 The Triune God in times of climate change
698 Gebara, *Longing for Running Water*, pp. 106–107
699 Ibid., p. 107
700 Ibid., p. 164
701 Ibid., p. 166
702 Ibid., p. 13
703 See also 4.1.3 The Triune God in times of climate change
704 Gebara, *Longing for Running Water*, p. 148
705 Ibid., p. 155
706 Ibid., p. 156
707 Ibid., p. 159
708 Ibid., pp. 168–169
709 Ibid., p. 173
710 Ibid., pp. 175–182
711 Ibid., p. 181
712 Ibid., p. 180
713 Ibid., p. 183
714 Ibid., p. 188
715 Ibid., p. 190
716 Ibid., p. 192
717 Ibid., pp. 195–196
718 Ibid., p. 197
719 Ibid., p. 198

720 Marc van der Post, theologian living in Buenos Aires, adds to this from his own experience: 'This is recognizable. Faith becomes more and more marginalised. The parish or chapel provides a very traditional form of worship that is hard for people to share with their children. The communities dwindle and are ageing. The neighbourhood is more anonymous and dangerous to live in. Faith is only challenged among intellectuals.'

721 Gebara, *Longing for Running Water*, p. 202; Pentecostal churches are at the moment an important political force in Brazil

722 'Entrevista a Ivone Gebara, brasileña, monja y feminista', http://www.amerindiaenlared.org/contenido/2842/entrevista-a-ivone-gebara-brasilena-monja-y-feminista/, accessed 3 August 2020

723 Gebara, *Longing for Running Water*, p. 207

724 Rubm Alves, quoted in ibid., p. 208

725 Umberto Eco, quoted in ibid., p. 210

726 Ibid., p. 211

727 Ibid., p. 212

728 Ibid., p. 213

729 Ibid., pp. 214–215

730 Comparing the role of experience and suffering in Gebara's and Schillebeeckx theologies, see Kathleen McManus, 'Reconciling the Cross in the Theologies of Edward Schillebeeckx and Ivone Gebara', *Theological Studies* 66 (2005)

731 This belief has become known as *Ietsism*, something-ism.

732 Keller, *Face of the Deep*, p. 22, referring to Marcella Althaus-Reid, *Indecent Theology: Theological Perversions* in *Sex, Gender and Politics* (London/New York, Routledge, 2001) on the reception of liberation theology in the West.

733 Compare the new paradigm that Henk Manschot suggests and his ecologic critique of science; see 3.4.3 Evolution, ecological crisis and humanity's place in the scheme of things / Earthing peoples

734 See Preface and chapter 1

735 See 4.1.3 The Triune God in times of climate change

736 Michelle A. González, 'Review of *Longing for Running Water: Ecofeminism and Liberation* by Ivone Gebara (Minneapolis, Fortress Press, 1999)', *Journal of Hispanic / Latino Theology* 10:3 (February 2003), pp. 78–80

737 Compare 2.4.5 The woman at the well, John 4

738 See 2.2.7 Christ the Creator

739 Keller, *Face of the Deep*, p. 22

740 Catherine Keller, 'Eschatology, Ecology, and Green Ecumenacy', *Ecotheology* 2 (1997), quoted in Arica Nutt, 'Eine theologische Praxis des Recycling. Ökologie, Gott und Geslecht bei Catherine Keller' in Stefanie Schläfer-Bossert and Elisabeth Hartlieb (eds), *Feministische Theologie Politische Theologie. Entwicklungen und Perspektiven* (Sulzbach, Ulrike Helmer Verlag, 2012), p. 185

741 Santmire and Cobb, 'The World of Nature', pp. 141–142

742 Keller, *Face of the Deep*, p. xv; italics by Keller

743 Judith Butler, *Gender Trouble: Feminism and the Subversion of Identity* (New York, Routledge, 1990)

744 Catherine Keller, 'Dark Vibrations. Ecofeminism and the Democracy of Creation', lecture 6 April 2005, www.users.drew.edu/ckeller/Dark-Vibe.pdf, accessed 20 August 2020

745 See 1.2.7 Postmodernism

746 French postmodernist in particular do so. American postmodernists emphasise the differences between individuals. Keller is rooted in the European tradition.

747 See Jay McDaniel, 'Christianity (7f) – Process Theology' in ERN, pp. 364–366 and Majorie Hewitt Suchocki, 'Process Theology' in *Dictionary of Christian Theology*, pp. 410–412

748 Catherine Keller, *From a Broken Web: Separation, Sexism, and Self* (Boston, Massachusetts, Beacon Press, 1986)

749 See 2.2.1 The coming into existence of the Cosmos: Genesis 1—2:4

750 *Apocalypse Now and Then: A Feminist Guide to the End of the World* (Boston, Beacon Press, 1996) and *God and Power: Counter-Apocalyptic Journeys* (Minneapolis, Minnesota, Fortress Press, 2005)

751 *Apocalypse Now and Then*, p. 14, referred to in Benjamins, *Catherine Keller's constructieve theologie*, p. 43

752 See an explanation of Revelations: 2.4.4 A New earth in the Apocalypse of John

753 In 2.2.1 The coming into existence of the Cosmos, 2.2.5 Job's suffering in context and 2.4.4 A New earth in the Apocalypse of John

754 Nutt, 'Eine theologische Praxis des Recycling', pp. 188–189

755 Keller, *Face of the Deep*, p. 31

756 Ibid., pp. 36–39 and 79

757 Ibid., pp. 81–82

758 Wesley wrote more than 6,000 hymns. For his hymn 'She Sits Like a Bird Brooding on the Waters', about the Spirit brooding on the chaos, see 2.2.1

759 Keller, *Face of the Deep*, p. xviii

760 Van Wolde, *Terug naar het begin*, pp. 20–21

761 Keller, *Face of the Deep*, p. 181

762 Keller, *Face of the Deep*, p. 177 ff.

763 Keller, *Face of the Deep*, p. 172

764 In my opinion this happens when methods used in social sciences become dominant in theology, see 1.3.1. Theology is about the world in relation to God.

765 Plato's story of creation in the *Timaeus* stems from the same period as Genesis 1. Justin, in the second century CE, saw a link between both stories; see Keller, *The Face of the Deep*, p. 46.

766 Especially in Derrida's notion of 'trace' and Deleuze's notion of 'fold', and in the theory of chaos in the interpretation of Progognes, p. 188

767 See 2.2.1 The coming into existence of the Cosmos

768 Keller, *Face of the Deep*, p. 194

769 Ibid., p. 188

770 Ibid.

771 Ibid., pp. 189–190

772 Ibid., p. 190

773 Ibid.

774 Harari, Yuval Noah, *Homo Deus: A Brief History of Tomorrow* (London, Vintage, 2017)

775 Keller, *Face of the Deep*, p. 191

776 Ibid., 198

777 See 2.2.1 The coming into existence of the Cosmos

778 Keller, *Face of the Deep*, p. 198

779 Ibid., p. 196

780 Hadewijch and Columba Hart, *Hadewijch: The Complete Works* (Mahwah, New York, Paulist Press, 1980), p. 245, quoted by Keller, *Face of the Deep*, p. 199

781 Nicholas of Cusa quoted by Keller, *Face of the Deep*, p. 202. In *Cloud of the Impossible: Negative Theology and the Planetary Entanglement* (Columbia University Press, 2014) she goes deeper into Nicholas's mysticism.

782 Keller, *Face of the Deep*, pp. 210–211

783 Ibid., p. 203

784 Ibid., p. 206

785 Ibid., p. 212

786 Ibid., p. xvi

787 Ibid., pp. 65–83

788 The old idea that by becoming human God emptied himself, is based on e.g. Philippians 2:6–8

789 Keller, *Face of the Deep*, pp. 216–217

790 Ibid., pp. 89–90

791 Ibid., p. 214

792 *Natality* is a notion found with philosopher Hannah Arendt

793 Peacock quoted by Keller, *Face of the Deep*, p. 191

794 Ibid., p. 219

795 Ibid.; the world is not simply *capax dei*; it is God who is *capax mundi*. Tehom and Elohim could be seen if not as persons then rather as potentialities of eternal becoming.

796 Ibid., pp. 214–215

797 Ibid., p. 44

798 Ibid., p. 51

799 Ibid., p. 220

800 Ibid., p. 223

801 Ibid., p. 63

802 Ibid., p. 63

803 Ibid., p. 19

804 Catherine Keller, *Intercarnations: Exercises in Theological Possibility* (Minneapolis, Minnesota, Fortress Press, 2017)

805 Benjamins, *Catherine Keller's constructieve theologie*, p. 124

806 I was thus informed by two systematic theologians, the one in a verbal exchange, the other by email

807 Keller, *Face of the Deep*, p. 172

808 Hilda Koster, 'Creation as Gift: Tanner's Theology of God's Ongoing Gift-Giving as an Ecological Theology' in Rosemary P. Carbine and Hilda P. Koster (eds), *The Gift of Theology: The Contribution of Kathryn Tanner* (Minneapolis, Minnesota, Fortress Press, 2015)

809 See 3.4.1 Garden a desert?

810 See also 3.4.3 Evolution, ecological crisis and humanity's place in the scheme of things and 3.5 Issues

811 See also 4.1 McFague and 4.2 Gebara

812 See 4.4 Elizabeth Theokritoff

813 Se e.g. Thomas Berry and Elizabeth A. Johnson

814 Koster, 'Creation as Gift' , p. 268, referring to Cobb and Griffin, *Process Theology*, pp. 52–54

815 Ideological suspicion was coined by the liberation theologian Jon Sobrino

816 Derek Michaud, 'Chaos and "Tehomofobia"', *JCRT* 4:3 (August 2003), p. 117

817 Ibid., p. 115

818 Catherine Keller in her lecture on 10 March 2017 in Utrecht

819 E.g. Kathryn Tanner, Celia Deanne-Drummond, Sarah Coakley

820 https://www.iocs.cam.ac.uk/about/academic-faculty/, accessed 26 August 2020

821 E.g. when she refers to 'The housewife making the sign of the Cross over a loaf before cutting it, or the grandmother censing the livestock of her evening prayers' (4.4.2) and to

mother Theodora (see infra 'Ascesis as the correct use of things')

822 Mary B. Cunningham and Elizabeth Theokritoff (eds), *The Cambridge Companion to Orthodox Christian Theology* (CCOT; Cambridge, Cambridge University Press, 2009); Theokritoff, *Living in God's Creation*

823 E.g. 'Ecology and Christian tradition', https://www.youtube.com/watch?v=JNnclcJgC38 and 'The book of creation: How do you read?' https://www.youtube.com/watch?v=BQmRCd0wbW8, accessed 26 August 2020

824 For writing this paragraph I made use of Mary Cunningham and Elizabeth Theokritoff 'Who are the Orthodox Christians?' in CCOT; 'Orthodox theology' in *The Cambridge Dictionary of Christian Theology* (Cambridge, Cambridge University Press, 2011), pp. 358–360; 'Christianity (6b1) – Christian Orthodoxy' and Christianity (6b2) – Greek Orthodox' in ERN, pp. 333–341; John Chryssavgis, 'The Earth as Sacrament: Insights from Orthodox Christian Theology and Spirituality' in OHRE

825 Missionaries from the Russian church were sent out to e.g. to Siberia, China, Japan, Korea and Alaska

826 Cunningham and Theokritoff (2011), p. 7

827 See also 2.2.6 Lady Wisdom, 2.2.7 Christ the Creator, and Deane-Drummond, 'Sophia'.

828 E.g. Athanasius van Alexandrië, Basilius van Caesarea, Gregorius van Nyssa, Gregorius van Nazianze, Maximus Confessor, Dionysius de Areopagiet, Gregorius Palamas

829 Cunningham and Theokritoff (2011), p. 16

830 Cunningham and Theokritoff (2011), p. 6

831 Gösta Hallonsten, 'Ex oriente lux? Recent Developments in Eastern Orthodox Theology', *Svensk teologisk kvartalskrift* 89:1 (2013), p. 42

832 Heleen Zorgdrager, 'Reclaiming *theosis*: Orthodox Women Theologians on the Mystery of the Union with God', *Internationale Kirchliche Zeitschrift* 104:3 (2014), pp. 220–245

833 Hallonsten, 'Ex oriente lux?', p. 34

834 Ibid., p. 31

835 Ibid., p. 41

836 https://www.patriarchate.org/biography, accessed 28 August 2020

837 ERN, pp. 338–340

838 Ibid., p. 334

839 Ibid., p. 335

840 John Chryssavgis, 'The Earth as Sacrament: Insights from Orthodox Christian Theology and Spirituality' in OHRE, pp. 92–114

841 Ibid., p.97

842 ERN, p. 337

843 Ibid., pp. 335–337

844 Ibid., p. 336

845 Ibid.

846 Theokritoff, *Living in God's Creation*, p. 9, preface by Peter Bouteneff

847 Daniel Munteanu, 'Elizabeth Theokritoff Living in God's Creation. Rezension', *International Journal of Orthodox Theology* 1:2 (2010), p. 192

848 Theokritoff, *Living in God's Creation*, p. 28

849 Ibid., p. 22

850 Ibid., p. 18

851 See 1.2.1 Anthropocentrism and exploitation (White and Morton)

852 Theokritoff, *Living in God's Creation*, p. 27

853 Ibid., p. 29

854 Ibid., p. 30

855 Ibid., p. 32

856 Ibid., p. 26

857 Ibid., p. 33

858 Ibid., p. 35

859 Ibid., p. 42; the Word is the *logos*, see 2.2.7 Christ the Creator/ Incarnation of the Word/ Wisdom, John 1

860 Ibid., p. 50

861 Ibid., p. 46

862 Ibid., p. 54

863 Ibid., p. 51

864 A notion that was common until well into the time of the Reformation, see 1.2.2 Western worldviews through the ages.

865 Theokritoff, *Living in God's Creation*, p. 59

866 Ibid., p. 62

867 Ibid., p. 59

868 See 1.2.2 Western worldviews through the ages

869 Theokritoff, *Living in God's Creation*, p. 90

870 Ibid., p. 66

871 Ibid., p. 67

872 Ibid., p. 70

873 Ibid., pp. 69–70

874 See 2.2.1 The coming into existence of the Cosmos/ 'Subduing the earth' and 'having dominion over the animals'?

875 Theokritoff, *Living in God's Creation*, p. 72

876 Ibid., p. 74

877 As in the Psalms, see 2.2.4

878 Theokritoff, *Living in God's Creation*, p. 79

879 Ibid., p. 80

880 See also 2.2.2 Paradise lost?

881 Theokritoff, *Living in God's Creation*, p. 84

882 Ibid., p. 84

883 Ibid., p. 85

884 Ibid., p. 89

885 Ibid., p. 90

886 Ibid., p. 95

887 Ibid., p. 99

888 Ibid., pp. 102–103

889 Ibid., p. 104

890 Ibid., p. 105

891 Ibid., p. 107

892 Benedictine Rule Chapter 31: The Kind of Man the Cellarer of the Monastery Ought to Be. Quoted by Theokritoff, *Living in God's Creation*, p. 110 (she refers incorrectly to chapter 21)

893 Ibid., p. 113

894 Ibid., p. 119

895 Ibid., p. 120

896 Whether a story is strictly speaking historical is not really essential, says Theokritoff. It expresses the belief of the community that passed it on. See also Helen Waddell, *Beasts and Saints*

897 Theokritoff, *Living in God's Creation*, p. 121

898 Title of honour for a priest's wife, literally it means 'mama'

899 Theokritoff, *Living in God's Creation*, pp. 127–128

900 Ibid., p. 129

901 Ibid., p. 138; the Bible too does not think in terms of animal rights but in people's obligations towards animals; see 2.3 God and the animals

902 Theokritoff, *Living in God's Creation*, p. 145; Mark 9:2–13 on the transfiguration of Jesus in the presence of his disciples. For the creation that praises God see 2.2.4 The creation sings: the Psalms.

903 Ibid., p. 146

904 Ibid.

905 Ibid., p. 149

906 Ibid., p. 150

907 Ibid., p. 153

908 Ibid.

909 Ibid., p. 156

910 Psalm 104 is 103 according to the translation of the Bible that the Greek Orthodox Church uses in its liturgy

911 Theokritoff, *Living in God's Creation*, p. 157; see also 2.2.4 The creation sings: the Psalms

912 Ibid., pp. 159–160

913 Ibid., p. 155

914 Ibid., p. 161

915 Ibid., p. 165; see Matthew 27:45,51

916 Colossians 1:15; see 2.2.7 Christ as Creator

917 Theokritoff, *Living in God's Creation*, p. 181

918 From the Vespers on Tuesday in the first week of Lent, quoted in ibid., p. 171

919 Ibid., p. 173

920 Ibid., p. 178

921 For the land that mourns see 2.4.2 dealing with Hosea 4:3 and 2.4.3 with Joel 1:10

922 Theokritoff, *Living in God's Creation*, p. 180

923 Ibid., p. 184

924 Ibid., p. 187

925 Ibid., p. 189

926 Ibid.

927 Ibid., p. 190

928 Ibid., p. 191

929 Ibid., p. 194

930 Ibid., pp. 195–196

931 Ibid., p. 198

932 Ibid., pp. 198–199

933 Ibid., pp. 200–201

934 Ibid., p. 204

935 Ibid., pp. 205–206

936 Ibid., pp. 206–207

937 Ibid., p. 208

938 Ibid., p. 213

939 Cunningham and Theokritoff (2011), p.11

940 The early Church Fathers, like Maximus Confessor, still associated *Sofia*/Wisdom with the Logos, but after the Council of Ephesus (CE 431) Sofia became more and more identified with Mary; see Deane-Drummond, *Eco-Theology*, p. 63.

941 See 4.1.3 The Triune God in times of climate change

942 The Dutch movement '*nieuwe levensstijl*' (new lifestyle) that succeeded in the 1990s the conciliar process made hardly any impact, possibly because it lacked a liturgical setting.

943 Sarah Coakley, *The New Asceticism: Sexuality, Gender and the Quest for God* (London, Bloomsbury, 2015)

944 Deane-Drummond, *Eco-Theology*, p. 161; pp. 63–65 summarise Bulgakov's theology. His Christian name is either written as Sergii, Sergei or Sergius.

945 In Greek: *o logos sarx egeneto*; the majority of English translations have 'flesh'; *logos* is rendered as 'human' in e.g. the Good News Translation and New Living Translation; see biblehub.com.

946 As *Bijbel in Gewone Taal* (*Bible in Ordinary Language*) does: see 2.2.7 Christ the creator/Incarnation of the Word/Wisdom, John 1

947 See 2.2.7 Christ the creator

948 Keller, *Face of the Deep*, p. 63

949 And/or God and/or the Spirit

950 See 4.3.5 Postmodern theology in context/When Christ's body opens up

951 Deane-Drummond, *Eco-Theology*, p. 100

952 Dealing with the questions concerning non-human suffering, either inherently part of the evolutionary process or not, see ibid., pp. 114–130, 'Ecology and Theodicy', and Van den Brink, *Reformed Theology*.

953 See 4.3.5 Postmodern theology in context/When Christ's body opens up.

954 See 1.3 The task of theology

955 https://cswr.hds.harvard.edu/news/2016/3/1/towards-liturgical-turn-comparative-theology-opportunities-challenges-and-problems, accessed 26 September 2020; see also 'Towards a Liturgical Turn in Comparative Theology?', lecture at Harvard Divinity School by Marianne Moyaert, https://www.youtube.com/watch?v=UNOT3Nlsut0, accessed 26 September 2020

956 See transitionnetwork.org and www.transitieboxtel.nl, accessed 16 September 2020

957 See repaircafe.org

958 Among others Mark 6:30–44

959 See 2.3.2 End and new beginning of all living beings/Life of animals and humans is valuable

960 *Liedboek*, song 718

961 See 3.4.2 Laudato Si'

962 See 2.2.4 The creation sings: the Psalms.

963 See 2.2.1 The coming into existence of the Cosmos: Genesis 1–2:4 and 3.3.2 Rapid modernisation

964 See 1.3 The task of theology and 3.5 Issues

965 *Liedboek*, song 841

966 *Liedboek*, song 978

967 The petition for the preservation of the rainforest was signed by more than 600,000 people in Flanders alone. The campaign during Lent 2002 chose this motto: 'We spend. Who bears the consequences?' See Lieve Herijgers, 'Broederlijk Delen. Kiezen voor duurzaam leven is kiezen voor "het goede leven"', *Tijdschrift voor Geestelijk Leven* jrg. 72:6 (2016) *De aarde die ons draagt en leidt. Oriëntatie op een duurzaam leven.*

968 'Tapestry of Creation' in the Cathedral of Girona, Spain, made in the eleventh or twelfth century probably by Benedictine nuns. See Manuel Castiñeiras, *The Creation Tapestry* (Girona, Catedral de Girona, 2016), p. 40

BIBLICAL INDEX

New Testament

INDEX

363